REIMAGINING PAKISTAN

Praise for the Book

'*Reimagining Pakistan* has a broader focus [than Haqqani's earlier books]. It is an ambitious attempt to lay out an almost forensic analysis of Pakistan's troubles and then to suggest cures. As a diagnostician, Haqqani excels. Building on specialist literature as well as a range of writings, from Barbara Tuchman on historical folly to Irving Janis on the dangers of groupthink, he traces the evolution of the varied myths and obsessions that have confounded Pakistan back to their origins in the country's formative years.'

Max Rodenbeck in *The New York Review of Books*

'Haqqani is far from convinced that Pakistan's present trajectory represents a drift away from some "modernist" vision, whether informed by republican ideals, the separation of religion and politics, or the promotion of a liberal-democratic order. On the contrary, he suggests that Pakistan's founding project was so fraught with ambiguity that its "national purpose" was lost in the confusion and never defined. Only the idea of the country as an "Islamic enterprise" and its implacable hostility to India survived the process. The consequences have been catastrophic and according to Haqqani go far to explain why Pakistan came to see itself as an ideological state in permanent conflict with India. Therein lie also the reasons for Pakistan's thrall to Islamist groups, its near total domination by the army and its disregard for economic reform that has left the country chronically dependent on foreign aid. Haqqani is categorical: nothing short of abandoning its founding discourse will enable Pakistan to embark on a course of self-correction and "evolve as a functional, territorial state".

'Haqqani's blazing honesty—rare among writers from Pakistan—is unlikely to be met with acclaim in his native land.'

Farzana Shaikh in *International Affairs Journal*

'*Reimagining Pakistan* delves further into areas that would be familiar to those who have read Haqqani's earlier writings or indeed other critiques from the country's embattled liberals. Peppering the narrative are descriptions and insights into Pakistan's chronic insecurity syndrome, a mindset of denial and victimhood, a sense of entitlement vis-à-vis the outside world and finally the compulsive need for parity with India. To this cocktail is added the potion of religious nationalism and confrontation with India. From all this have emerged certain quintessentially Pakistani policy approaches—supporting extremists and terrorists to address key ideological obsessions, "securing Kashmir, balancing India and dominating Afghanistan".'

T.C.A. Raghavan, *former high commissioner of India to Pakistan* in *India Today*

'In seven lucid chapters the book provides considerable detail about the manner in which Pakistan has been 'imagined', though the global community perceives it as an 'international migraine' (Madeline Albright). The journalist in Haqqani comes to the fore with gusto and he quotes a range of sources – far and wide – to buttress the many observations and assertions that are made through the book....

'The re-imagining that the book advocates is persuasively conveyed in the last chapter entitled 'Avoiding the March of Folly.' Arguing that Pakistan could adopt a new course as Germany and Japan did after 1945, Haqqani makes a very pertinent observation and suggestion when he outlines the contour of this new national initiative: "It could begin by allowing discussion of alternative imaginings of Pakistan that are not bound by its narrowly defined ideological parameters. Pakistan's military officers might need to do the greatest rethinking."

'Encouraging Pakistan to come out of its carefully constructed cocoon of denial is imperative for any meaningful redress of the many problems that plague that nation. Haqqani is to be commended for illuminating this monumental contradiction.'

C. Uday Bhaskar in *Financial Express*

HUSAIN HAQQANI

REIMAGINING PAKISTAN

TRANSFORMING A DYSFUNCTIONAL NUCLEAR STATE

HarperCollins *Publishers* India

First published in Hardback in India by
HarperCollins *Publishers* in 2018

HarperCollins Publishers India, Cyber City, Building 10-A, Gurugram,
Haryana-122002, India
www.harpercollins.co.in

This edition published in paperback in India in 2020 by
HarperCollins *Publishers*

P-ISBN: 978-93-5357-749-0
E-ISBN: 978-93-5277-770-9

2 4 6 8 10 9 7 5 3 1

Typeset in 10.5/14.5 Sabon LT Std
Manipal Digital Systems, Manipal

Printed and bound at
MicroPrints India, New Delhi

MIX
Paper
FSC FSC® C218906

This product is made of FSC®-certified and other controlled material.

HarperCollins Publishers, Macken House, 39/40 Mayor Street
Upper, Dublin 1, D01 C9W8, Ireland

To my children

Huda, Hammad, Maha and Mira

And all the children of Pakistan

For whom the country needs to be reimagined

Contents

Introduction xi

1. A Resilient 'International Migraine'? 1
2. Faith, Grievance and Special Purpose 33
3. Ideological Dysfunction 63
4. Islamist Rage 96
5. Insecurity and Jihad 121
6. 'The Institution' 160
7. Warriors, Not Traders 199
8. Avoiding the March of Folly 244
9. Afterword 279

Notes 287
Index 331
Acknowledgements 343
About the Author 345

Introduction

FEW FOREIGNERS VISIT PAKISTAN, but those who do often acknowledge the kindness and generosity of most of its 210 million people. Millions of Pakistanis living and working overseas—as unskilled labour in the Middle East, cab drivers and factory workers in Europe and doctors, engineers, bankers or other professionals in North America—have a reputation for hard work and efficiency. But that does not suffice to alter Pakistan's description around the world as 'dangerous',[1] 'unstable',[2] 'terrorist incubator',[3] 'fragile',[4] and 'the land of the intolerant'.[5]

It is not difficult to understand the frustration of Pakistanis, both at home and in the diaspora, over the negative portrayal of their country. They are hurt by adverse comments about anything to do with Pakistan because it reflects poorly on them even though they and their friends and family lead decent, productive lives.

'Pakistanis are a pious, warm and hospitable people,' wrote Richard Leiby, a *Washington Post* reporter who spent a year and a half there, lamenting that the news from Pakistan did not reflect that. He noted, however, that the bad news about Pakistan was not untrue. In his view, 'Just like average Americans', the simple Pakistani people 'pay the price of their leaders' magnificent mistakes'.[6]

The harsh fact remains, however, that scholarly and media discussion of any country focuses on its politics and policies more than on the virtues of its people. Objective analyses cannot ignore the disconcerting highlights of Pakistan's seventy-year history: four full-fledged wars, one alleged genocide, loss of half the country's land area in conflict, secession of the majority population, several proxy or civil wars, four direct military coups, multiple constitutions, long periods without constitutional rule, frequent religious and sectarian discord, repeated economic failures, numerous political assassinations, unremitting terrorism, continued external dependence and chronic social underdevelopment.

Some political scientists and historians described Pakistan, then comprising two wings separated by one thousand miles of enemy territory, as an oddity even in its early years. It was a nation unlike most others. Instead of shared language or even history, Pakistan was founded on the basis of a common religion, under institutions created during British colonial rule. This raised questions about the viability of ignoring ethnic and linguistic diversity; the potential for conflict between sects as well as between modernist and obscurantist definitions of Islam; and the cost of maintaining conflict with India in terms of economic development.

Still, soon after Independence, most journalists and scholars highlighted the hopeful aspirations of Pakistan's leaders and scholars alongside those critical questions. The earliest books on Pakistan were written by Pakistanis, introducing their country to the world, who explained the creation of Pakistan in terms of Hindu–Muslim strife, described Pakistan's potential as a Western ally and defined its strategic salience as well as its capacity to produce large numbers of soldiers.

There were also volumes by British authors, including former civil servants, who advanced the Pakistani account. They explained what they saw as the inevitability of Partition, given the withdrawal of Britain's 'steadying hand' and 'inexorable Hindu–Muslim differences'. The martial virtues of West Pakistan's Muslims as likely anti-communist warriors were extolled in an effort to persuade Western readers, particularly Americans, of the value of Pakistan as an ally in the years to come.

This genre of introductory books included Liaquat Ali Khan's *Pakistan: The Heart of Asia* (Cambridge, MA: Harvard University Press, 1950); Lord Birdwood's *India and Pakistan: A Continent Decides* (New York: Praeger, 1954); Ian Stephens's *Horned Moon* (Bloomington: Indiana University Press, 1955), and *Pakistan* (New York: Praeger, 1963); Ishtiaq Hussain Qureshi's *The Pakistani Way of Life* (New York: Heinemann, 1956) and *The Struggle for Pakistan* (Karachi: University of

Karachi, 1965); and Aslam Siddiqui's *Pakistan Seeks Security* (Karachi: Longman Greens, 1960).

North American academics started studying Pakistan as a political phenomenon in the late 1950s and throughout the 1960s. Their studies were published under neutral-sounding titles such as Keith Callard's *Pakistan, a Political Study* (London: George, Allen and Unwin, 1957), Leonard Binder's *Religion and Politics in Pakistan* (Berkeley: University of California Press, 1961) or Khalid Bin Sayeed's *Pakistan: The Formative Phase* (London: Oxford University Press, 1968).

Scholarship on Pakistan took a decidedly unfavourable turn after the 1965 India–Pakistan war. Pakistan's army was found insufficiently effective in that war and it attempted to save its reputation through media image-building. Its doctrine that 'the defence of East Pakistan lies in West Pakistan' was exposed as hollow. Moreover, violent protests in both wings of the country resulted in the resignation of Field Marshal Ayub Khan, who had ruled for a decade with a semblance of stability, and his replacement in 1969 by General Yahya Khan as the new military dictator.

Civil war and genocide in erstwhile East Pakistan, which resulted in the creation of Bangladesh in 1971, added to uncertainty about both the idea and the prospects of Pakistan. The titles of books on Pakistan from that era reflect the outsider's scepticism. Herbert Feldman published *From Crisis to Crisis* (London: Oxford University Press, 1972) and *The End and the Beginning* (London: Oxford University Press, 1978); and L.F. Rushbrook Williams wrote *Pakistan under Challenge* (London: Stacey International, 1975). Lawrence Ziring's *Pakistan: The Enigma of Political Development* (Boulder, CO: Westview Press, 1980) also painted the picture of a state in disarray.

One needs to look only at the cover of books about Pakistan published since the 1990s to realize that scepticism has since given way to apprehension and foreboding. Journalists and academics alike have extensively documented Pakistan's embrace of extremist ideologies and its sponsorship of terrorist groups in the works published over the last twenty years. The newer studies reflect the concern of analytical minds about most aspects of Pakistan's political orientation, from military intervention in politics to endemic corruption, from questions about nuclear security to its perennial difficulties in relations with its neighbours and the world's major powers.

Books published over the last two decades feature titles like Allen McGrath's *The Destruction of Pakistan's Democracy* (New York: Oxford University Press, 1996), Christophe Jaffrelot's *Pakistan: Nationalism without a Nation?* (London: Zed Books, 2002), Owen Bennett Jones's *Pakistan: Eye of the Storm* (New Haven: Yale University Press, 2003), Mary Ann Weaver's *Pakistan: Deep inside the World's Most Frightening State* (New York: Farrar, Straus & Giroux, 2010), Pamela Constable's *Playing with Fire: Pakistan at War with Itself* (New York: Random House, 2011), Bruce Riedel's *Deadly Embrace: Pakistan, America and the Future of Global Jihad* (Washington, DC: Brookings Institution Press, 2011), James Farwell and Joseph Duffy's *The Pakistan Cauldron: Conspiracy, Assassination and Instability* (Washington, DC: Potomac Books, 2011), Christine Fair's *Fighting to the End: The Pakistan Army's Way of War* (New York: Oxford University Press, 2014), and Tilak Devasher's *Pakistan: Courting the Abyss* (New Delhi: HarperCollins, 2016).

It is not just foreigners who write about Pakistan with dread and dismay; Pakistani authors seem to increasingly share the pessimism. Just browsing through the list of books by Pakistani authors brings us to Roedad Khan's *Pakistan: A Dream Gone Sour* (Karachi: Oxford University Press, 1997), Sherbaz Khan Mazari's *A Journey to Disillusionment* (Karachi: Oxford University Press, 1999), Hassan Abbas's *Pakistan's Drift into Extremism: Allah, the Army, and America's War on Terror* (New York: Routledge, 2004), Ahmed Rashid's, *Descent into Chaos* (New York: Viking, 2008) and *Pakistan on the Brink: The Future of America, Pakistan, and Afghanistan* (New York: Viking, 2012), Imtiaz Gul's *The Most Dangerous Place: Pakistan's Lawless Frontier* (London: Viking, 2010), and Khaled Ahmed's *Sectarian War: Pakistan's Sunni Shia Violence and Its Links to the Middle East* (Karachi: Oxford University Press, 2012).

Even those who try hard not to be seen as too negative about Pakistan cannot avoid acknowledging that there is something wrong that needs setting right. Farzana Shaikh's *Making Sense of Pakistan* (New York: Columbia University Press, 2009) insinuates that Pakistan confuses the average person; Christophe Jaffrelot's *The Pakistan Paradox: Instability and Resilience* (Karachi: Oxford University Press, 2015) speaks of Pakistan being hardy even as it is unstable; and Anatol Lieven's *Pakistan: A Hard Country* (London: Allan Lane, 2011) makes a similar point.

Most Pakistanis would rather gloss over inconvenient truths or be content with blaming different villains for their country's plight when confronted with unpleasant facts. Millions of Pakistanis share the patriotic sentiment 'My country, right or wrong' without knowing the full quote by American statesman Carl Schurz, which goes: 'My country, right or wrong; if right, to be kept right; and if wrong, to be set right.'[7]

Thus, in Pakistan, fingers are pointed at venal politicians, religious leaders and the country's dominant military without too much inquiry into deeper reasons for the country's malaise. Conspiracy theories about external forces and their domestic henchmen harming Pakistan are also part of the staple diet. No wonder that alongside his praise for the piety, warmth and hospitality of Pakistanis, Leiby had also noted their penchant for victimhood.

'A narrative of persecution also runs through the psyche of Pakistan as a whole,' he wrote. 'The public, whipped up by the military and mullahs, is led to believe that the nation's problems are the work of "hidden hands". I noticed how often leaders blamed conspiracies by India, Israel and America—that is to say, Hindus, Jews and Christians—for undermining the country, rather than owning up to social and economic ills of Pakistan's own creation.'[8]

It is also not uncommon to claim that the country would have been different if only the actors on its stage had been different. 'If only Pakistan's founder, Muhammad Ali Jinnah, had not died within a year of its creation' is one of the most popular of such 'if only' contentions. Others include 'If only Pakistan had not become embroiled in the Cold War as America's partner since the 1950s'; 'If only Zulfikar Ali Bhutto's populist politics had not unsettled the established post-colonial order in the 1970s'; and 'If only General Zia-ul-Haq had not adopted Islamisation as the justification for his dictatorship during the 1980s'.

But such assertions are more excuses than explanations for Pakistan's turbulent past and uneasy present. Seventy years after its birth, Pakistan is a volatile semi-authoritarian, national security state, which has failed to run itself consistently under constitutional order or rule of law. Examining the causes of Pakistan's persistent dysfunction, including an inquiry into its foundational idea, is more important than building a 'positive image' through half-truths.

Martha Brill-Olcott and Marina Ottaway defined a semi-authoritarian regime as one where effective power continues to be wielded by individuals or institutions who determine the state's interest and block effective transfer of power. 'Semi-authoritarian countries may have a reasonably free press, for example,' they write, adding, '...the regime may leave space for autonomous organizations of civil society to operate, for private business to grow, and thus for new economic elites to rise.'[9] That Pakistan fulfils that definition almost to a T is evident.

Pakistan also manifests the defining characteristics of a 'national security state' as identified by David R. Mares: '...the military institution itself is intimately involved in leading the political system and its goals are to transform the country's political and economic institutions.'[10] The real question, however, is why Pakistan became a semi-authoritarian, national security state and how it might evolve differently. The answer might lie in understanding Pakistani nationalism and the sentiment it has generated and sustained.

Pakistan was born out of the demand in 1940 for a separate state or group of states comprising the Muslim majority provinces of British India. It was presented to the subcontinent's Muslims variously as an idea for their protection as a community after the departure of the British or the springboard for Islam's revival in the modern world. Either way, it was more an emotion—a response to fears stoked about the future of Islam and Muslims in a Hindu-majority democratic state—than an idea that had been fleshed out in detail.

Pakistan has meant different things to different people since its birth. Much of the country's dysfunction is the result of its inability to answer questions bred by conflicting expectations. How Islamic is Pakistan meant to be? What does it mean to be an Islamic state in modern times? What should be the balance of power between a central Pakistani government and the various provinces representing various nationalities and ethnic groups? Must Pakistan forever be at war with India to justify its existence as a separate state? If so, how can it avoid dominance by the military and militants?

Although ideological questions have preoccupied Pakistanis, theirs is not the only contemporary nation state that started out as an idea. It differs from others, however, in not evolving an identity beyond the grievances that fuelled the demand for a separate Muslim state in the subcontinent. The combustible mix of religion and politics, the pursuit of nuclear weapons, the acceptance and encouragement of terrorism, and the angry tone in its relations with the rest of the world are all by-products of the indignation that helped create Pakistan and has since been nurtured by the Pakistani state.

Other countries, on the other hand, focus on changing in light of altered circumstances. The United States, for example, started out as a union of thirteen states and a republic wherein franchise was limited to white men. Its founding principles included individual freedom, rule of law and democracy, but their practice today differs significantly from how it was conceived in 1776. Americans have constantly reviewed the ideas that make them a nation and have worked consistently to adapt to varying realities.

Today's US comprises fifty states and allows citizenship and voting rights to men and women of all races. Its economy and social mores are very different now than they were at the time of its founding. Americans admire their founding fathers but do not hesitate to acknowledge their failings. Those founding fathers tolerated slavery, and some even practised it themselves, even as they laid out a charter for the fundamental rights of man. Over time, the US went on to abolish slavery only to replace it with racial segregation, which was substituted by the notion of racial equality.

There is robust debate in American society over the extent to which the US lives up to its goals, but no one considers such debate a threat to America's current existence. The evolution of America from a slave-owning society that limited franchise only to white men of European origin to a diverse, multi-ethnic nation is a result of argument and deliberation. There is widespread recognition of imperfections. Discussions about what might be the best course for the new nation began at the time of writing the US Constitution and continue until now.

One cannot change something without acknowledging or recognizing it. Pakistan has tended to deny deficiencies as a means of scuttling debate about alternative policies. According to Fakir Syed Aijazuddin, a writer belonging to an elite Punjabi family of Lahore, 'Pakistan is close to Julian Barnes's alternative definition of a net as "a collection of holes tied together with string". It is less a country than a mesh of voids, bound by coils of self-interest.' But few others are that candid.

Writing in November 2017, Aijazuddin went on to describe Pakistan's reality without seeking refuge in its 'noble ideology'. He noted that the 'vacuum in leadership within each political party' was 'ringed by the loyalty of its electorate'. Pakistan's economy, he wrote, 'is a mosaic of potholes, of gaping deficits: budget deficits, fiscal deficits, trade deficits, recurring deficits in the railways and PIA'. There was also 'a trust deficit between the legislature, the judiciary and the armed forces'.[11]

The situation demands more than ever that Pakistanis apply their mind to figuring out how to set their country right instead of insisting there can be nothing wrong with it. This book is my effort at compiling historical facts, political realities, and economic veracities that are often denied as part of Pakistan's 'positive' narrative. It is an invitation to change the way Pakistanis imagine their nation and state so that its reality changes, which might work a lot better than living in denial.

1

A Resilient 'International Migraine'?

PAKISTAN HAS COME A long way since it emerged as a new country on the world stage seventy years ago. When Pakistan's first prime minister, Liaquat Ali Khan, visited the United States in 1950, he encountered several reminders of Americans' ignorance about Pakistan. Vice-President Alben S. Barkley introduced him to the US Senate as the prime minister of Pakistan, 'which originally was a part of India'. According to the account of a British diplomat, Liaquat had to respond seriously to a California businessman who asked him at a luncheon 'whether the blank space between the two parts of Pakistan as shown on the menu card was Africa'.[1]

No one around the world's major capitals is that oblivious to Pakistan any more. If anything, Pakistan has become a country of concern to Americans and the rest of the world, after being a Western ally for several decades. Although Pakistan lost its eastern wing, East Pakistan (now Bangladesh), in 1971, it has managed to survive and, in the view of its elite, thrive as an independent state. Pakistan's civil servants and official economists point out that its people are living longer than at the time of Pakistan's birth and the country's literacy rate and per capita income have also gone up significantly.

Pakistanis take pride in their nuclear-armed military, which is the world's sixth largest fighting force, as well as in the achievements of many individual Pakistanis who have excelled in global business, world sports, or gone on to win international recognition including two Nobel prizes. But that has not prevented the rest of the world from seeing or describing Pakistan in negative terms. Pakistan ranks behind other comparable nations in several key indicators, especially those relating to human development and is unable to shed the image of a militarist and militant-infested country.

In the global imagination, Pakistan is the country chosen by terrorist mastermind Osama bin Laden as his home for the last several years of his life. Pakistan is identified in the West as a country prone to military coups. It is known for its strict blasphemy laws targeting religious minorities, as well as for imprisonment, murder and lynching of individuals for religious reasons. International media coverage highlights Pakistan's sponsorship of terrorist groups such as Lashkar-e-Taiba (which conducted the Mumbai attacks in 2008), the Afghan Taliban and the Haqqani Network that attacks NATO troops and Western civilians in Afghanistan.

Other stories on Pakistan relate to restrictions on the role of women or the substantial number of economic migrants moving into Europe pretending to be refugees. Western diplomats publicly voice worries about Pakistan's lackadaisical approach to nuclear weapons and its tendency to seek aid with promises that are not kept. In the Arab world, Pakistanis are often referred to contemptuously as 'muflis', meaning destitute or bankrupt, while Indians and Afghans consider the Pakistani state an implacable foe.

The Pew Global Attitudes Surveys for multiple years have shown that a very small percentage of Americans holds a favourable view of Pakistan while even among the Chinese, generally considered Pakistan's all-weather friend, only 30 per cent say they like Pakistan, the same number as those voicing approval for rival India.[2] A BBC World Service poll found that Pakistan is one of the most unpopular countries in the world, only a rank above the least popular Iran, with only 15 per cent looking upon Pakistan favourably and 55 per cent respondents across the world viewing the country in 'mainly negative' terms.[3]

That disapproval manifested in US president Donald Trump's address at Fort Myer, a military base just outside Washington, DC on 21 August 2017. 'We can no longer be silent about Pakistan's safe havens for terrorist organizations, the Taliban, and other groups that pose a threat to the region and beyond', Trump declared in the harshest public criticism of Pakistan by any Western leader. 'Pakistan has much to gain from partnering with our effort in Afghanistan. It has much to lose by continuing to harbor criminals and terrorists,' he added.

According to Trump, 'The Pakistani people have suffered greatly from terrorism and extremism. We recognize those contributions and those sacrifices. But Pakistan has also sheltered the same organizations that try every single day to kill our people. We have been paying Pakistan billions and billions of dollars at the same time they are housing the very terrorists that we are fighting. But that will have to change, and that will change immediately. No partnership can survive a country's harboring of militants and terrorists who target US service members and officials. It is time for Pakistan to demonstrate its commitment to civilization, order and to peace.'[4]

Trump's comments were immediately condemned widely in Pakistan. Pakistan's National Security Council issued a strongly worded statement saying it 'rejected the specific allegations and insinuations made against Pakistan', insisting that Trump's statement was meant to 'scapegoat Pakistan'. The statement defended Pakistan's role in the war in Afghanistan and said it had worked to promote peace in Afghanistan. 'The Committee observed that Pakistan has consistently supported all international efforts for a stable and peaceful Afghanistan,' the council's statement said. 'On its own part, Pakistan has taken indiscriminate actions against all terrorist networks and sacrificed tens of thousands of troops and civilians in this fight.'[5] The official statement was accompanied by street protests in many Pakistani cities.

Although Trump's comments were only a more straightforward articulation of concerns that several world leaders had expressed for many years, the attitude in Pakistan was to deny that it had done anything wrong. Pakistani media promoted the perspective that has become something of a hallmark for Pakistan's response to policy criticism. It was seen as an attack on the country that only required national unity and bold-faced denial, and would be foiled with Allah's blessings.

Moreover, in the view of many Pakistanis, especially its privileged classes, Pakistan is simply too important in geostrategic terms to be ignored. According to this belief, if the United States turns against Pakistan, it will only become more attractive as a partner to other global powers, China and Russia; Pakistan has not only attained its place under the sun, it is foreordained, and how it views itself matters more than how others see it.

Sense of Self

There is always a gulf between how a nation views itself and how others view it, but Pakistan is unique in terms of the breadth of that gap. While Pakistanis often do not see much of the criticism of their country as valid, outsiders describe it as an 'incubator of terrorism', a 'crisis state' or even as 'a state perpetually on the brink of failure'. Perhaps it is the frequency and vehemence of outside criticism that makes Pakistanis defensively deny any fundamental defect either in the origins or the trajectory of their country. They point to Pakistan's resilience, its ability to recover from disasters and its seventy-year history of outlasting predictions of imminent demise to reject critical comments as 'Pakistan bashing'.

Almost all nations have an embellished or modified narrative, which overlooks or explains deficiencies that others tend to highlight. Thus, Americans might want to speak less of slavery or atrocities against Native Americans and the British might play down the carnage of colonialism. But few nations resort to absolute denial of any transgression and project themselves as victims of others' wrongdoing as has become associated with Pakistanis. In Pakistan, a perception has been officially cultivated that anyone who offers facts, statistics or opinions that do not coincide with the national narrative does so at the behest of Pakistan's many external enemies.

The machinery of state is able to, by and large, control discussion of the country's achievements and challenges within Pakistan but that does not stop critical debate around the world. In case of Pakistani scholars and commentators, nationalist sentiment also colours their assessment of the country's balance sheet. The result is the widening gulf between an overly optimistic Pakistani view, supported by a few non-Pakistani sympathizers, and the generally pessimistic mainstream international discourse on Pakistan.

A few weeks after the November 2008 terrorist attacks in Mumbai, former US Secretary of State Madeline Albright said that 'Pakistan has everything that gives you an international migraine. It has nuclear weapons, it has terrorism, extremists, corruption, it's very poor and it's in a location that's really, really important.'[6] Characterizing Pakistan as 'a very difficult place', Secretary Albright seemed to echo the view of those who argue that Pakistan's weaknesses are the result of inherent difficulties because, as Anatol Lieven titled his book, Pakistan is 'a hard country'.

If Pakistan was destined to be problematic, critics might ask, why was it created in the first place? Perhaps it is questions like this that irk Pakistanis most. Since Pakistan already exists and the rest of the world would rather see stability in a nuclear-armed country, questions about history must be seen as an intellectual exercise. Instead, they are seen in Pakistan as part of plots that are consistently being hatched against it. Bengali leader, Huseyn Shaheed Suhrawardy (who served as Pakistan's prime minister in 1956) had noted as early as March 1948 that Pakistan's elite was predisposed to 'raising the cry of "Pakistan in danger" for the purpose of arousing Muslim sentiments and binding them together' to maintain its power.[7] Seventy years later, Pakistan's nationalism has become intertwined with apprehensions of a permanent stage of siege.

Pakistan is now a territorial state, secured by a large military and the possession of nuclear weapons. More than 95 per cent of its citizens are Pakistanis by birth and have known no other nationality. Contemporary Pakistan need not seek national identity in the idea of a separate homeland for Muslims of the Indian subcontinent, which was always vehemently debated ever since it was first mooted. But insecurity remains the hallmark of Pakistan's political and intellectual conversation. Even a comment about, say, Pakistan's relatively low ranking among nations for book readership, is portrayed as an attack on the idea of Pakistan.

Most Pakistanis cling emotionally to the two-nation theory that led to the partition of British India and the creation of Pakistan instead of viewing themselves as citizens of a modern territorial state. For them, it is important still to win the argument over Pakistan's conception. Any discussion of poor performance in the economic or social sphere, or about differences among Pakistan's ethnic groups is often described as questioning the country's very right to exist, which it is not.

The world has long recognized and respected Pakistan as a significant country notwithstanding scholarly reservations about the two-nation theory. Even Indians, most of whom see Pakistan's emergence with a sense of historic loss, no longer question Pakistan's existence even if they dispute the reasoning behind its creation. But that has done little to transform Pakistan's nationalism away from the ideological debates preceding its foundation.

For Pakistanis born after 1947, being Pakistani by birth should be a matter of fact, not one that requires rationalization by a state ideology. Still, a self-justifying attitude over the two-nation theory underlies almost all discussions in the country. It is almost as if Pakistanis still need to convince themselves and the world that their decision to create a new country was the right one.

The reason for this defensiveness might lie in the unique circumstances of Pakistan's emergence as a nation and a state. Unlike nation states that evolved over time, Pakistan was the product of a conscious political demand. Even the name of the new country where none existed before was deliberately crafted as an acronym of its component provinces as well as a word with a meaning: 'the land of the pure'. Pakistan's founder, Muhammad Ali Jinnah, was a brilliant politician who pulled together diverse groups and rallied them to the cause of protecting undivided India's Muslims by grouping Muslim-majority provinces.

Jinnah saw the demand for Pakistan as a means of ensuring that India's Muslim majority was not ignored while writing India's post-Independence constitution. According to historian Ayesha Jalal, he was prepared to negotiate whether Pakistan 'would seek a confederation with the non-Muslim provinces, namely Hindustan, on the basis of equality at the all-India level, or whether, as a sovereign state, it would make treaty arrangements with the rest of India'.[8]

Ironically, support for the idea of Pakistan was strongest in regions where Muslims were a minority and Jinnah, as well as most of his principal lieutenants, belonged to areas that would not fall in Pakistan. To emerge as chief negotiator on behalf of Muslims, Jinnah and the All-India Muslim League had to prove their support in the Muslim-majority provinces. 'Such support', Jalal points out, 'could not have been won by too precise a political programme since the interests of Muslims in one part of India did not suit Muslims in others.' Jinnah invoked religion as 'a way of giving a semblance of unity and solidity to his divided Muslim constituents'.[9]

Jinnah 'could not afford to state precisely what the demand for "Pakistan" was intended to accomplish'. The demand for Pakistan, therefore, had to be 'specifically ambiguous and imprecise to command general support, something specifically Muslim though unspecific in every other respect'.[10]

The ambiguities that characterized the demand for Pakistan could not persist once the demand was fulfilled with the creation of an independent country. Just as invoking religion enabled Jinnah to rally Muslims to the demand for Pakistan, his successors chose to run the country by summoning Islamic sentiment in varying degrees. Many of Pakistan's problems—from falling behind in secular education to the rise of Islamist extremism—can be traced to the country's founding on the basis of religious nationalism.

Some of the difficulties awaiting Pakistan—forging a nation out of disparate ethnic groups connected to each other mainly by religion, costly competition with a much larger neighbour, mobilizing resources for a new country from a geographic region that did not yield much revenue before Independence, being caught between competing global powers—had been predicted by critics throughout the 1940s.

American journalist, Tom Treanor, described the idea of Pakistan as similar to the notion of the southern states' secession that led to the US civil war. 'Every instinct will persuade you that there shouldn't be a Pakistan,' he wrote in *Los Angeles Times* after interviewing Jinnah in

March 1943.[11] British author, Beverly Nichols, warned that Pakistan would be an empire founded on hate. K.L. Gauba, an author and politician from Punjab who was born a Hindu and converted to Islam, wrote a book titled *The Consequences of Pakistan* in 1946, posing tough questions about Pakistan's defence and economy. In his view, Pakistan would not be able to pay for its defence and would have financial difficulties from its inception.[12] Abul Kalam Azad, a Muslim leader of the Indian National Congress questioned the viability of maintaining East and West Pakistan as a single state and expressed concerns about inter-ethnic relations in the new country.

Dr Syed Abdul Latif, a Muslim scholar who initially supported the Muslim League, wrote to Jinnah in May 1941: 'Pakistan in its latest form will neither establish Muslim States properly so-called; nor get rid of the Hindu-Muslim-Sikh problem; nor afford any security to the Muslim minorities in the proposed independent Hindu India, unless a wholesale exchange of population is effected, which no one favours.'[13] In the foreword to the 1943 book *The Pakistan Issue*, Latif further elaborated his concerns. He feared that Muslims left in India after Partition would become weaker by virtue of being a smaller minority than before while the Muslims of Pakistan would become susceptible to religious fanaticism.

'You cannot, as is your dream and hope, establish therein the Rule of God,' he wrote, anticipating debates about sharia and treatment of 'non-Muslims as Zimmis or protected subjects'. Latif also warned against Pakistan comprising 'two poverty-stricken patches' that would be 'torn from each other by vast spaces of land and sea and incapable of evolving between them any unified life or federal administration'. He questioned the tenability of Jinnah's demand for a land 'corridor running through a territory populated predominantly by non-Muslims' to connect Pakistan's two wings. Would Pakistan be able to 'develop a powerful navy to preserve that linkage, especially in times of stress and war'? Would it be able to 'run a modern state' with 'economic resources so limited and undeveloped?' Latif wondered.[14]

Critics foresaw the likely rise of an Islamic fundamentalist tide as well as the threat to democratic governance by an army disproportionately larger than the country's revenue base. But supporters of Pakistan's creation had ignored all warnings, choosing sentiment over arguments. They rejected reasonable critique of political choices, portraying it as manifestations of hostility towards Islam and Muslims, an attitude that has been reflected consistently in Pakistan's national conversation.

When, on 15 August 1947, the new country actually came into existence, the pride of Pakistanis was palpable to the world. They had paid no heed to treatises with elaborate arguments and had created an entirely new country while following their hearts. It might be argued that the march to Pakistan would have been abandoned had Jinnah's followers taken the negative projections about its prospects seriously. A corollary to that is the view of some ultra-nationalists that Pakistan must turn a deaf ear to what the rest of the world thinks, knows or believes. They believe Pakistan should continue to create a narrative of history, as well as the future, all its own; Pakistan would survive solely on the strength of the commitment of its resilient people to the idea of Pakistani nationhood.

The truth often lies between the extremes. In Pakistan's case, predictions of state failure or collapse have certainly proved wrong (except for the separation of erstwhile East Pakistan, which became Bangladesh in 1971). But equally unfulfilled is the promise of a young Muslim nation rising to greatness on the crossroads of the Middle East and South and Central Asia. One can sympathize with the sentiment of Pakistanis who must constantly defend their country against criticism ranging from questioning of its very creation to its current policies. But it is equally important to understand that mere survival does not equate success and that progress often requires uninhibited introspection.

The idea of Pakistan faced criticism during and after Partition, and several policies of the Pakistani state have often been viewed negatively by others since then. The Pakistani response to criticism has consistently been aggressive. For example, when Jinnah's death in September 1948 led to speculation about the future of the country, the Pakistani response was not to merely answer the questions being raised but to attack those positing the questions. Given that Jinnah was a towering personality and his death was indeed a huge loss, concern about its impact on the future of Pakistan was not entirely unfounded.

A wire service report from Reuters stated that US diplomatic sources were wondering whether 'Mr Jinnah's disappearance from the political scene would weaken Muslim determination to maintain the partition of India'. This anonymous report stirred an emotional reaction and *Dawn*, then the quasi-official newspaper of Pakistan, responded with an indignant editorial. Titled, 'To the Americans', the editorial questioned the American diplomat's 'pitifully inadequate' understanding of the 'conception of Pakistan' and wondered whether the comments in the Reuters report could have come from a friend of Pakistan. Instead of responding to the quoted remark as commentary, *Dawn* reacted as though it were an insidious conspiracy. 'Far from weakening the Muslim determination to maintain the partition of the Indo-Pakistan subcontinent', the editorial fired back, 'the demise of the Quaid-i-Azam will strengthen it a thousandfold. That's our last word to the world.'[15]

This tendency to react strongly to negative comments by outsiders has often been accompanied with virtual censorship. Since the 1950s, foreign academics and journalists have been categorized as 'pro-Pakistan' and 'anti-Pakistan', based on their writings. Such categorization has often affected their ability to obtain visas to travel to Pakistan, making it obligatory for those who wish to continue visiting the country to temper their observations. Foreigners residing in Pakistan also feel compelled sometimes to advance the Pakistani narrative, either because they start believing it or because it ingratiates them to their host government. The experience of Jacques Nevard, who served as the *New York Times* correspondent based in Karachi during the early 1960s, illustrates this phenomenon and differs little from that of foreign journalists stationed in Pakistan in subsequent years.

Nevard arrived in Pakistan in 1963 and found that he was being prevented from doing his job as a reporter through a complex web of bureaucratic red tape. Pakistani officials were anxious over US military assistance to India in the aftermath of the 1962 Sino-Indian war, which led to pressure on Nevard to write only positive things about Pakistan for his American readers. Anything that showed Pakistan in poor light could jeopardize support for aid to Pakistan among the US public or policymakers. When Nevard wrote an article that described Karachi as 'probably the most unloved big city in the world', it resulted in strong reaction. Some of those protesting to the *New York Times* over the article were ostensibly Americans sympathetic to Pakistan.

One letter to the *Times*' editor admonished him that 'Pakistan needs the help of the rest of the world and inaccurate reporting cannot help, particularly when the debate on Foreign Aid is at such a critical stage in the United States Congress.'[16] Another 'scathing critique of Nevard's piece' made an argument that has been said or written hundreds of times since then. 'Your esteemed representative appears only to see the worst side of the country and none of the bright things, or the generous hospitality of the people among Karachi's 2.5 million souls,' it said, without refuting a word of what Nevard had written. It was as if the reporter had failed in his duty of showing the sunny side even if he was not inaccurate in his description of what he saw.[17]

The newspaper's editor responded by pointing out that 'it was a reporter's obligation to write about those things he considers important even if they do not shed particular glory on the country in which he is stationed'. But the episode only affirmed Nevard's 'skepticism about the quality of news' that foreigners got from Pakistan. He noted that local journalists reporting for foreign media were 'being subjected to constantly increasing pressure from the Pakistani government'. He also observed that 'it was not only the journalists who experienced pressure from the government authorities'. The country was not a typical tourist destination for Americans and consequently many of the Americans who visited Pakistan were US government employees. Nevard noted that even those who visited Pakistan under the aegis of the US government 'provide a field day for all kinds of local civil servants'.[18]

The desire to control the narrative has persisted throughout Pakistan's history though methods and tactics of managing the flow of information have varied over time. During the 1960s, Nevard had only to deal with angry letters to his editor, Americans influenced by Pakistani civil servants, and stringers modifying their stories under official guidance. By 2006, the *Times*' Carlotta Gall discovered that Pakistan's security apparatus had become far more pugnacious. 'After five days of reporting in and around Quetta, Pakistan, I had somehow irritated the secretive but powerful Directorate for Inter Service Intelligence, the ISI,' she wrote in her book *The Wrong Enemy,* describing the day Pakistani agents raided her hotel room.[19]

According to Gall, 'They went through my clothes and seized my computer, notebooks and a cellphone. When one of the muscle men grabbed my handbag from me, I protested. He punched me twice, hard, in the face and temple, knocking me over. I fell back onto the coffee table, smashing the cups there, grabbing at the officer's fleece to break my fall and nearly pulling him down on top of me.' An English-speaking officer 'who appeared to be in charge' informed Gall that she was 'not permitted to visit' a neighbourhood she had visited and that 'it was forbidden to interview members of the Taliban' as she had tried to.

'He refused to show me any ID or say who they were,' Gall went on, 'but he said we could apply to the Special Branch of the police for our belongings the next day. As they were leaving, I told them that the photographer should stay with me. The officer refused. "He is Pakistani, we can do with him whatever we want." That was chilling. I knew they were capable of torture and murder, especially in Quetta, where the security services were a law unto themselves. They drove off in a white jeep. I took down the license number and later found it belonged to the Special Branch police service. The car was just a cover. In fact, the men were military intelligence. They drove to the Military Intelligence building in Quetta.'[20]

In addition to harassing journalists in an effort to 'manage' how Pakistan is presented to the world, Pakistani politicians also target critical foreign leaders with rhetoric aimed at ridiculing or dismissing their denunciations of Pakistani policy. When a group of US Congressmen condemned Pakistan's well-documented support of jihadi terrorist groups in 2016, the chairman of Pakistan's Senate, Raza Rabbani, said the people of Pakistan were 'appalled' by their views. He spoke of 'a marked lack of respect and recognition of the tremendous contribution made by the Pakistani people and the armed forces' in the fight against terrorism, without addressing the US Congressmen's concerns about Pakistan's support for the Afghan Taliban.

'The people of Pakistan are now forced to ask the question whether they are dealing with friends or foes' among Americans, Rabbani said in language similar to that used in the *Dawn* editorial sixty-nine years earlier. His statement also contained the now familiar Pakistani argument about others' 'double standards'. Rabbani seemed to suggest that 'their conspicuous silence on the killings of unarmed civilians in Kashmir, the treatment being meted out to African-Americans in their own country and the effort to impose India on the NSG [Nuclear Suppliers Group] in violation of all norms of nuclear non-proliferation'[21] somehow disqualified the Congressmen in question from raising reasonable questions about Pakistan's conduct in relation to Afghanistan.

Rabbani had once also reacted to statements by British and American governments about enforced disappearances and human rights violations in Pakistan by describing them as manifesting 'the Brahman, Jewish and white racial mindset'.[22] There appears to be continuity in Pakistan's response to anything that does not project Pakistan positively. The language in *Dawn*'s denunciation of Reuters' speculation about Pakistan's future following Jinnah's death in 1948 is very similar to Rabbani's criticism of the Congressmen and his comments about Western human rights observers. No one who is a friend of Pakistan must say anything that harms its reputation; anyone who dares to ask tough questions or make adverse remarks must be prepared to be categorized as Pakistan's enemy.

On the few occasions when diplomacy requires that critics be not rejected as anti-Pakistan or having a 'Brahman, Jewish, and white racial mindset', the standard Pakistani response is to highlight the insensitivity of others to its sufferings. After President Trump's criticism of Pakistan, army chief Gen. Qamar Javed Bajwa publicly told the US military that 'Pakistan doesn't need aid'. Ignoring Trump's comment about billions of dollars in aid already given to Pakistan, Bajwa said, 'More than financial or material assistance, we seek acknowledgement of our decades-long contributions towards regional peace and stability, understanding of our challenges and most importantly the sacrifices Pakistani nation and its security forces have rendered in [the] fight against terrorism and militancy.'[23]

The combination of aggressive rejection of reproach and insistence on victimhood insulates the Pakistani public from recognizing that anything in Pakistan needs fundamental revision. Any foreigner offering an unflattering portrayal of the country—from reporting honour killings to citing unfavourable economic statistics—is invariably described by Pakistani officialdom as 'ignorant' or 'beholden to anti-Pakistan lobbies'. Pakistanis voicing reservations about the country's direction are treated even worse. They are characterized as 'traitors' or 'enemy agents' acting at others' behest. It is almost as if no one who is knowledgeable, wise, objective or honourable can find anything about Pakistan worth disapproving.

From the Pakistani hyper-nationalist standpoint, there is always something sinister about asking questions when the answers should be obvious and there is no need to dig into historical records when the one true version of history has already been written down in Pakistani textbooks. As for global rankings and hard statistics, these should only be deemed relevant when they show Pakistan in a positive light and must be ignored when they do not. In any case, one can always fall back on the contention that whatever is being pointed out is not limited to Pakistan. It is not unusual to hear Pakistanis argue that 'Fanaticism (or poverty or poor governance or lack of attention to social sectors, depending on the topic under debate) can be found everywhere'; 'We are a young country and seventy years is not long in a nation's life'; 'Things are not as bad as they are being portrayed'; or 'That happens everywhere'.

Image and reality

Policy debates in most countries involve acknowledgement of threats and challenges alongside discussion of strengths and opportunities. In Pakistan, however, there seems to be an obsession with the country's 'image' at the expense of ignoring unpleasant realities that might need changing. Pakistan's glass must always be presented to the world as half-full and the positive indicators must be highlighted without the context of the negative ones.

Since 2002, when Pakistan's stock market was listed as one of the best performing stock markets in the world, Pakistani commentary often cite this factoid to rebut critical assessments of the country's economy. Pakistan's businessmen have often cited 'Pakistan's image' as the only problem in attracting investment. 'After a turbulent decade in which Islamist militants staged frequent gun and bomb attacks on cities, some investors still refuse to visit Pakistan,' a foreign correspondent reported, quoting the founder of a Pakistani private equity firm. 'When people visit Pakistan, they see it's actually opposite of what they expect,' the businessman told the reporter.[24]

Ignored in the self-laudatory commentary about the stock market's performance were other less positive facts. The Karachi Stock Exchange's market capitalization in 2016 stood at a meagre $89 billion, which compares unfavourably with the $320 billion capitalization of the Dhaka Stock Exchange in Bangladesh. Pakistan's image is only part of the problem; the real problem still is the set of economic and security policies that have hampered the expansion of listings, volume and capitalization of Pakistan's stock market. Discussing that, however, would be described by many Pakistanis as negativity towards the country. Why look at other indicators when the market performance figure taken on its own looks good for Pakistan?

Instead of the binary debate over whether Pakistan is a success story or a failure about to materialize, it is important to assess both the achievements and disappointments of the last seventy years. It is equally important to acknowledge historic mistakes or structural flaws, especially if things have to be set right for the future. Comparisons with other countries and states offer an opportunity to understand how others avoided pitfalls similar to the ones facing Pakistan as well as a chance to recognize the worst possible consequences of persistently bad policies.

Dismissing unflattering analysis as 'anti-state' or 'foreign-inspired' shuts the door for course correction.

That Pakistan has made progress since its inception is not in dispute. Life expectancy in 1951 stood at forty in Pakistan;[25] it rose to sixty-six by 2014.[26] There are also fewer Pakistanis living in poverty and the literacy rate has quintupled since Independence. The literacy rate for Pakistan in 1947 was 11 per cent,[27] rising to 56.44 per cent[28] by 2015. But these figures cannot be discussed in isolation and without reference to achievements of other countries. For example, India's literacy rate rose from 12 per cent to 74.4 per cent over the same period and for a much larger population.[29] National pride should not deter Pakistanis from confronting the fact that education has not been their national priority the same way as, say, acquiring nuclear weapons.

For almost fifteen years after Independence, Pakistan made no allocation for literacy in its national budget.[30] Between 1947 and 1957, Pakistan's literacy rate remained unchanged or declined, albeit marginally. The failure was attributed in official reports to 'unstable administrative and organizational arrangements'.[31] Even now, 40 per cent of Pakistan's population cannot read or write.[32] Fifty-seven per cent of Pakistan's adult population above the age of fifteen, 31 per cent of Pakistani men and 45 per cent of Pakistani women remain illiterate, according to 2015 estimates.[33] As of 2014, Pakistan is home to the third largest illiterate population globally and there are only fifteen countries in the world with a lower literacy rate than Pakistan.[34]

In May 2017, it was reported that the national literacy figures had shrunk by 2 per cent in the preceding year. 'The literacy rate in Balochistan has fallen to 41 per cent' in 2016 compared to 44 per cent a year earlier, the report stated, citing figures from Pakistan's official annual economic survey. Apparently, the figure for Sindh's literate population declined by 5 per cent and even the generally privileged Punjab province suffered a 1 per cent reduction in its literate population. There is also a huge urban–rural gulf in literacy rates, which stand at 74 per cent in urban areas and 49 per cent in rural areas.[35]

The Education Development Index of the United Nations Development Programme (UNDP) ranked Pakistan at 146 out of 195 countries for its performance in education in 2016.[36] Pakistan has the

GDP ratios in the world of around 9.98 per cent,[64] a GDP growth rate of 4.7 per cent[65] and a population growth rate of 2.075 per cent,[66] Pakistan needs foreign as well as domestic investment in addition to drastic changes in local laws—all of which need broad political consensus and stability, both of which are lacking.

Pakistan's Achilles heel is its consistent failure to invest in developing talent across the life cycle—through education and employment—to enhance human capital. Absence of skills and talent commensurate with the size of the population acts as a major impediment to economic success. The WEF's *Global Human Capital Index for 2017* ranked 130 countries on how well they are developing their human capital and Pakistan was ranked at 125. The Index found South Asia and sub-Saharan Africa lagging in 'ensuring that people's skills grow and appreciate in value over time', but even among South Asian countries, Pakistan came in last, behind top regional performer Sri Lanka (ranked 70), Nepal (ranked 98), India (ranked 103), and Bangladesh (ranked 111). According to the WEF, 'With the exception of Sri Lanka, the rest have yet to reach the 60 per cent threshold with regard to developing their human capital.'[67]

Despite its poor performance in most non-military indices, Pakistan has managed to evade crises and failure status over the decades primarily because the international community has bailed out Pakistan through aid and loans on account of its geostrategic relevance.

Instead of considering the external assistance as a temporary bonus that gives them time to lay the foundations of self-sustaining success, Pakistanis have tended to act as if the world owes Pakistan. Because of that hubris, Pakistan ranks 147 out of 188 countries in the world on the Human Development Index (HDI), which measures health, standards of living and education.[68] DHL's Global Connectedness Index, which measures cross-border flows of trade, capital, information and people, places Pakistan at ninety-nine out of 140 countries,[69] indicating that Pakistan is less connected globally than several countries poorer than it. Also, Pakistan ranked 158th on the UN Global E-government Survey which placed it in the bottom thirty countries according to a report published by the UNDP.[70]

The Quality of Nationality Index (QNI), which measures factors 'that make one nationality better than another in terms of legal status in which to develop your talents and business' ranks Pakistan at 153 out of 161 countries. The index explores the scale of the economy, human development and peace and stability as well as the ability to travel visa-free and to settle and work abroad without cumbersome formalities. Pakistan's low ranking on this index means that Pakistan's passport is less likely to enable an individual to travel and settle across states than the citizenship of at least 152 other countries in the world.[71]

While it ranks low on measures of accomplishment, Pakistan ranks alarmingly high on the Fragile States Index (formerly Failed States Index), an annual ranking of 178 nations on the basis 'of their levels of stability and the pressures they face'. Pakistan falls under the 'High Alert' countries and ranks number fourteen.[72] After a ten-year analysis of trends in Pakistan, scholars who worked on the index for 2016 reached the conclusion that 'there has been a marginal improvement in demographic pressures, refugees and IDPs [internally displaced persons], human flight and brain drain, uneven economic development and human rights and rule of law'. They noted, however, 'a worsening of all other indicators like poverty and economic decline, state legitimacy, public services, security apparatus, factionalized elites and external intervention and especially the issue of group grievance'.[73]

More than 70 per cent of Pakistan's population does not have access to safe drinking water and the United Nations Children's Fund (UNICEF) estimates that more than 70,000 children die every year due to diarrhoea and other diseases related to unsafe water and poor sanitation facilities. After a study conducted by the Pakistan Council of Research in Water Resources (PCRWR), Minister for Science and Technology Rana Tanvir Hussain informed parliament in March 2017 that only 72 per cent of Pakistan's water supply schemes were functional and 84 per cent of those had supplied water that was not fit for consumption.[74] Another study by the same institution found that fifty million Pakistanis were at risk of arsenic poisoning from contaminated groundwater, far more than previously thought, because of 'indiscriminate ground water exploitation'.[75]

The ultra-patriotic Pakistani response to this somewhat dismal picture of their country is to describe every negative mention of Pakistan in global academia and media as reflecting hostility instigated by Zionists or Hindus. More serious Pakistanis try to explain away the country's shortcomings, often attributing them to the bad hand that Pakistan was dealt by the circumstances of its birth, its hostile relationship with India, its being a victim of wars and terrorism initiated by external great powers and its misfortune in lacking leadership. Neither attempts to examine structural and systemic flaws, or is willing to acknowledge collective errors and misplaced priorities that do not go away merely by changing leaders.

That Pakistanis must have a more optimistic view of their country than others do is understandable. But the overly defensive approach to poor global rankings or outsiders' disapproving impressions and the aggressive rejection of Pakistanis who highlight the threats and challenges, makes it harder to reorder mistaken national priorities. The collective wisdom in Pakistan seems to be that nothing in Pakistan's predicament is the result of wrong policy choices made by its leaders and that the only thing Pakistanis need to do is to fend off discussion of the negatives, rather than attend to the negatives themselves.

Survival against the odds

Pakistan has indeed defied all predictions about its imminent collapse but the result is not greater self-confidence as a nation. Instead, a dismissiveness towards what others think about their country has crept into the collective Pakistani psyche. This works well against assaults on the idea of Pakistan that have become irrelevant with time but also blinds Pakistanis to harsh facts and tough comparisons they should not ignore. Comparisons with India and Bangladesh are often pertinent, given the shared history of Pakistan with both countries.

It is not enough to recount Pakistan's ability to survive against the odds. Pakistanis must figure out why India, which inherited similar institutions from the British Raj, maintained democracy consistently after Independence while Pakistan could not. They should also examine how Bangladesh has been able to expand its economy while reducing its population after breaking off from Pakistan.

Pakistan 'was not, like Poland, a nation which had been deliberately suppressed and the idea of which had haunted politics for hundreds of years'.[76] It was an entirely new and contrived entity. Even after beginning its life 'with a separate army, a separate flag and a self-contained political and economic system',[77] it had to find its place in the world. As British commentator Guy Wint pointed out, the first years of a new nation 'are spent searching for its identity' and Pakistan decided to base itself as an independent state on the same grounds that it had sought its creation. Islamic nationalism, pan-Islamism and competing with 'Hindu India' superseded the prospect of Pakistan deciding, coolly and calculatedly, its material interests while also embracing the ethnic, linguistic and cultural differences of its peoples.

The Pakistani state sought to create a composite Pakistani nation by enforcing a national language, a contorted narrative of history and a set of political views described subsequently as 'the ideology of Pakistan'. American political scientist Lawrence Ziring points out that 'a fictitious air of individuality' is not unique to Pakistan and that all states try to create the assumption that because they exist 'they were meant to be and will always be'. But history demonstrates that 'States that once were, are no more and it is beyond question that currently recognized states will in no time join those that have gone before them.'[78]

According to Ziring, 'Pakistan must be classified with the weaker political entities. It was a premature, feeble offspring at birth and although it survived a critical infancy, it never gained the strength necessary to combat its inborn ailments.'[79] In his view, 'Pakistan's frontiers are for most part crisis prone, its neighbors largely bellicose, and the fear persists that foreign machinations aim at exploiting the country's inherent weakness.'[80] But it is Pakistanis who have proven to be their worst enemies. Their 'inability to coalesce as a nation is mirrored in the failure of the country's leadership to transcend personal rivalry, internecine conflict or professional pride'.[81]

At the time of its inception, Pakistanis found that international opinion was far more sympathetic to India than to their new country. Arab nationalist leaders admired Mohandas Karamchand Gandhi, a Hindu, for confronting the British more than they supported Jinnah. A few months before Partition, Jinnah had shared with the American consul general in India, John J. Macdonald, his disappointment and frustration with the lack of international support for the Indian Muslims' demand for a separate homeland. He had spoken of a reception for him in Cairo in December 1946, where 'a group of prominent Egyptians' told Jinnah that, their warmth for a brother Muslim notwithstanding, they 'found his policy annoying'. The Egyptians had accused Jinnah of being 'in league with the British instead of working for Indian independence'.[82]

The Western attitude was no better. It was symbolized by *Time* magazine's reporting on the Independence of India and Pakistan. The article about Pakistan was titled 'Better off in a Home' while that referring to India bore the headline 'Oh Lovely Dawn'.[83] *Time*'s description of the celebrations marking Independence in Pakistan's capital, Karachi, reflected scepticism about the new country's prospects.

'A crimson carpet spilled down the steps of the yellow sandstone Sind Provincial Legislative Assembly Building in Karachi. A turbaned, barefoot Moslem carefully dusted it off, pressed it with an enormous flatiron,' the *Time* report said before turning to sarcasm about Pakistan's founder, Jinnah. 'All was now ready for the Pooh-Bah of Pakistan, in whose austere person are combined the offices of Governor-General, President of the Constituent Assembly and President of the Moslem League.'

There was also an observation about the contradiction between the religion-based demand for Pakistan and its leadership comprising westernized, secular Muslims. 'Although Pakistan is frankly a Moslem state (the most populous in the world), and set up to satisfy Moslem demands,' *Time* reported, 'there was none of the atmosphere of religious dedication that marked Delhi ceremonies.' In the reporter's view, 'Karachians, however, did not welcome Pakistan with the wild enthusiasm that swept the new dominion of India' largely because 'After all, Pakistan was the creation of one clever man, Jinnah; the difference between a slick political trick and a mass movement was apparent in the contrast between Karachi and New Delhi.'[84]

The Western journalist's fascination with India's diversity contrasted with the uncertainty about Pakistan right from the beginning. 'As the great day approached, Indians thanked their varied gods and rejoiced with special prayers, poems and songs,' the *Time* report stated. 'Poetess Sarojini Naidu set the theme in a radio message: "Oh lovely dawn of freedom that breaks in gold and purple over the ancient capital",' it said, followed by a colourful description.

'Delhi's thousands rejoiced,' the report said. 'The town was gay, with orange, white and green. Bullocks' horns and horses' legs were painted in the new national colours, and silk merchants sold tri-coloured saris. Triumphant light blazed everywhere. Even in the humble Bhangi (untouchable) quarters, candles and oil lamps flickered brightly in houses that had never before seen artificial light. The government wanted no one to be unhappy on India's Independence Day. Political prisoners, including Communists, were freed. All death sentences were commuted to life imprisonment. The Government, closing all slaughterhouses, ordered that no animals be killed. The people made it their day. After dawn, half a million thronged the green expanse of the Grand Vista and parkways near the Government buildings of New Delhi.'[85]

From the perspective of Pakistanis, British prime minister Clement Atlee's declaration that he expected India's partition to be tentative was also ominous. Attlee said in a debate in the House of Commons on 10 July 1947, 'For myself, I earnestly hope that this severance may not endure and that the two new Dominions which we now propose to set up may, in course of time, come together again to form one great member state of the British Commonwealth of Nations.'[86] That view was reinforced by the last British Secretary of State for India, Lord Listowel, who said, 'It is greatly to be hoped that when the disadvantages of separation have become apparent in the light of experience, the two Dominions will freely decide to reunite in a single Indian Dominion, which might achieve that position among the nations of the world to which its territories and resources would entitle it.'[87]

The misgivings about Pakistan did not end after it survived its initial years. In 1956, American scholar Hans J. Morgenthau, a major figure in the study of international politics in the twentieth century, wrote: 'Pakistan is not a nation and hardly a state. It has no justification in history, ethnic origin, language, civilization, or the consciousness of those who make up its population. They have no interest in common, save one: fear of Hindu domination. It is to that fear, and to nothing else, that Pakistan owes its existence, and thus far its survival, as an independent state.'[88]

Morgenthau poked fun at the Pakistani state, which comprised two geographically separated regions, East and West Pakistan. 'It is as if after the Civil War Louisiana and Maryland had decided to form a state of their own with the capital in Baton Rouge. In fact, it is worse than that,' he asserted. According to Morgenthau, 'The two parts of Pakistan are separated not only by 1200 miles of Indian territory, but even more by language, ethnic composition, civilization and outlook. West Pakistan belongs essentially to the Middle East and has more in common with Iran or Iraq than with East Bengal. East Bengal, in turn, with a population which is one-third Hindu, is hardly distinguishable from West Bengal which belongs to India and gravitates toward the latter's capital, Calcutta.'[89]

In Morgenthau's view, 'Even Jinnah, the creator of this strange state, did originally not believe in its viability' and there were 'few politicians in Karachi' at the time who really believed in it. 'If there are solutions which could assure the future of Pakistan, only extraordinary wisdom and political skill will find them and put them into effect,' he observed, adding prophetically that it was 'hard to see how anything but a miracle, or else a revival of religious fanaticism, will assure Pakistan's future.'[90]

Such doubts about Pakistan's viability reflected analysis and opinion, not plans to eliminate Pakistan but they left a mark on the psyche of Pakistanis. Pakistan's early leaders eagerly sought support for the new state from the doubters, such as Attlee, as well as the sceptical Arab politicians. For the British, as well as the Americans, Pakistan burnished its anti-communist credentials while appeals to the unity of the Muslim world, the ummah, have also been a crucial part of Pakistan's international outreach. Pakistanis take rightful pride in overcoming the opposition and becoming central to Anglo-American strategy as well as finding friends and backers among the Arabs.

The British and Americans were extremely supportive in helping Pakistan's government stand on its feet. The British left behind senior military officers and civil servants at Jinnah's request. The governors of three out of four Pakistani provinces and the chief commissioner of Balochistan for the first two years after Independence were British as were civil service heads of several departments. Sir Terence Creagh-Cohen, an Irishman from the erstwhile Indian Civil Service, helped organize Pakistan's Foreign Service. Some British civil servants remained on their jobs even after retirement as consultants well into the late 1950s. The Pakistan Army was commanded by a British officer until January 1951, the Pakistan Navy until January 1953 and the Pakistan Air Force until July 1957, a full decade after Independence.

Pakistan was also the beneficiary of generous training programmes for its fledgling bureaucracy and military, with young officials receiving training in Britain, Australia and Canada under the Commonwealth rubric. The country's civil and military leaders were quick to take advantage of the cold war between the US–led Western and the Soviet–led communist blocs, offering to join American military alliances soon after Pakistan's creation. This ensured the flow of US food, economic and military assistance, which protected Pakistan against the fulfilment of some of the worst predictions about its prospects.

None of this has dissuaded Pakistanis from building a narrative of victimhood that dismisses the role of any factor other than the grace of God and the endurance of Pakistan's people in shaping the country's history. It is important to examine this version to understand why Pakistanis are bothered less by the tribulations that worry the rest of the world even when the world's fears are rooted in hard facts and cold numbers. The Pakistani narrative tends to assume that critical analysis and dire predictions reflect animus and ill will towards Pakistan instead of reading them simply as evaluations.

Pakistan's former foreign minister Abdus Sattar is one of many prominent Pakistanis who have laid out the story of Pakistan as believed by the majority of Pakistanis. According to him, 'Pakistan emerged onto the world stage on 14 August 1947 after a two-pronged struggle: first, for independence from colonial rule and secondly, freedom for the people of Muslim majority areas from the looming threat of economic, social and political domination by another people manifestly dismissive of their urge to preserve their separate identity.'[91]

The country found itself beset with problems from the moment of its birth. 'The partition plan of 3 June 1947 gave only seventy-two days for transition to independence', Sattar writes, adding, 'Within this brief period, three provinces had to be divided, referendums organized, civil and armed services bifurcated, and assets apportioned. The telescoped timetable created seemingly impossible problems for Pakistan, which, unlike India, inherited neither a capital nor government nor the financial resources to establish and equip the administrative, economic and military institutions of the new state. Even more daunting problems arose in the wake of the partition. Communal rioting led to the killing of hundreds of thousands of innocent people. A tidal wave of millions of refugees entered Pakistan, confronting the new state with an awesome burden of rehabilitation.'[92]

This account makes no mention of the general air of cooperation between advocates of Pakistan and the British rulers of India, nor does it answer the question as to why, after asking for Pakistan, the Muslim League leaders had not prepared for India's division. It only emphasizes that Pakistan was able to overcome these odds and survive, through sheer determination and national will.

Even the loss of Pakistan's eastern half—which accounted for 54 per cent of the population and one-fifth of the land area of the original country—barely twenty-four years after Independence is seen only as a blip, not as a great misfortune, in Pakistan's nationalist accounts. In the words of former finance minister Shahid Javed Burki, after 1971 Pakistan 'is much smaller in size, its population is more homogeneous, and its international borders are virtually settled. Its geopolitical situation is also very different from the one in which it found itself at the time of its birth. And nobody today questions the economic viability of the state of Pakistan.'[93] Thus, while it was dismissed at its inception as an anomaly both as a state and a nation, 'Pakistan is no longer a geographical, cultural, religious or economic absurdity. In fact, if anything—and for historical reasons—it has become a viable entity.'[94]

'Resilience has been part of Pakistan's story from the country's inception', wrote Maleeha Lodhi, former ambassador to the United States and former high commissioner to the United Kingdom, more recently, dismissing 'the single-issue lens through which outsiders have lately viewed the nation'. According to her, 'The prism of terror and extremism has deflected attention away from the strength and stability of [Pakistan's] underlying social structures which have enabled the country to weather national and regional storms and rebound from disasters—natural and manmade.'[95]

Lodhi asserts that Pakistan 'has always been more than an entity that lurches from crisis to crisis.' She cites its 'promising potential' while listing 'an able pool of professionals and technically trained people, a hardworking labor force, a growing middle class, an enterprising business community, an energetic free media, and a lively arts, literature and music scene' as Pakistan's strengths.[96]

'Pakistan is located at the intersection between the Middle East, South Asia and Central Asia, three critical regions in the world,' Lodhi once reportedly told an American audience, repeating a common talking point, adding, 'The country is also important because it is a nuclear state, it has a Muslim identity, it plays an active, diplomatic role in the world and it has an economic vision for itself.'[97]

According to her, Pakistan has the ability to link the three regions it straddles and provide economic prosperity for both itself and the countries around it but its ability to do so is impeded by 'unresolved issues between Pakistan and India' and the baggage of history relating to Afghanistan. 'Pakistan, therefore, has been really at the center of many regional storms,' Lodhi said. 'There were wars in our region that we did not initiate.'[98]

Pakistan, in this narrative, has faced what Lodhi calls a 'triple blowback'. According to her, the first blowback was from the war against the Soviet occupation in Afghanistan; the second was after 11 September from the US intervention in Afghanistan and the impact of that war; and the third was Pakistan's limited capacity to handle the consequences of those wars. Lodhi sees location as one of Pakistan's challenges, forcing the country to spend time, effort and resources to deter 'aggression'. She blames circumstances, not policy choices, for Pakistan's insecurity-driven decisions. 'We built up our forces, we acquired nuclear capability,' Lodhi said, 'but that also meant we were not able to meet our people's need in education, in health and in public services.'[99]

The 'there-is-nothing-fundamentally-wrong-with-Pakistan' and 'Pakistan-has-survived-against-all-odds' description leads to claims such as 'Pakistan's cultural plurality and open society are sinews of its strength' even as global freedom watchdogs list extrajudicial killings, laws targeting religious minorities and restrictions on expression among Pakistan's poor human rights record. Lodhi insisted in the preface to an edited volume defensively titled '*Pakistan: Beyond the Crisis State*' that Pakistan 'has a significant industrial base, an elaborate infrastructure of roads and communication links, a modern banking system, a large domestic market and a thriving informal economy', which have helped it avert a national breakdown even in the throes of severe financial crisis.

'Pakistan', says Ishrat Husain, former governor of the State Bank of Pakistan, 'is one of the few developing countries that have achieved an average annual growth rate of over 5 per cent over a period of six decades.' According to him, per capita incomes in constant terms have multiplied four to fivefold in seventy years while the incidence of poverty has halved from 40 per cent to less than 20 per cent. Listing 'other remarkable achievements that the country can proudly boast of', Husain writes, 'A country with 30 million people in 1947 couldn't feed itself and had to import all its food from abroad. In 2012, the farmers of Pakistan are not only able to fulfill the domestic needs of wheat, rice, sugar, milk for 190 million people at much higher per capita consumption level but also export wheat and rice to the rest of the world.'[100]

Pakistan has emerged as the world's third largest exporter of rice, Husain points out. 'An average Pakistani earns about $1,200 in 2012 compared to less than $100 in 1947', he continues. 'Agriculture production has risen more than five times with cotton attaining a level of more than 14 million bales compared to 1 million bales in 1947. Pakistan has emerged as one of the leading world exporters of textiles. The manufacturing production index is well over 13,000 with a base of 100 in 1947. Steel, cement, automobiles, sugar, fertilizer, cloth and vegetable ghee, industrial chemicals, refined petroleum, and a variety of other products that did not exist at the time are now manufactured for the domestic market and, in many cases, for the world markets too.'[101]

It is interesting that more recent comments about Pakistan's resilience and accomplishments bear a striking resemblance to similar observations made by Pakistanis repeatedly over the years. Notwithstanding the changes in Pakistan's geography and circumstances, the narrative of survival against the odds has been remarkably consistent. In a 1967 book marking the twentieth anniversary of Pakistan's creation, Ghulam Ali Allana wrote how predictions about the country's failure had been proved wrong. 'When Pakistan was first demanded as a separate homeland for the Muslims of this sub-continent, its enemies branded it as a "political monstrosity",' he wrote. 'As the will of the Muslims, under the leadership of Quaid-i-Azam, began to be more and more determined, Pakistan's opponents began to predict that the new country would on its very inception face an economic collapse, and that, "Economically speaking, Pakistan is a bankrupt proposition".'[102]

According to Allana, the Hindus 'tried their best to strangulate the economic life of Pakistan' once 'Pakistan had become inevitable'. He attributed the large-scale flight of capital from territories that constituted Pakistan, not to the communal violence that threatened Hindus and Sikhs in Pakistan or Muslims in India, but to a Hindu economic strategy. 'Hindu big business began to shift their headquarters from Lahore to Delhi', Allana lamented, quoting the decision of the Punjab National Bank in May 1947 to transfer its registered offices from Lahore to Delhi 'for carrying on the business of the company more economically, more efficiently and more conveniently'. In Allana's view, the banks and public companies that left Lahore for Delhi did so to make Pakistan 'an economic desert'.[103]

'Pakistan started under most trying and difficult conditions,' Allana asserted fifty years ago, making an argument one sees reflected in the work of contemporary writers. According to him, 'There were hardly any big private enterprises in the hands of Muslim businessmen, and with the migration of Hindu big business, a gloomy prospect stared us in the face. But the story of Pakistan's growing soundness in the field of national economy is a glorious chapter in our history. Our economy has been going from strength to strength, and we have completely confounded our critics and ill-wishers.' He then proceeded to make comparisons of public and private sector production 'to illustrate the point that we have done an excellent job during the last twenty years'.[104]

The question that remains unaddressed in this line of reasoning is whether the rise in agricultural and industrial production and even the increases in per capita income, would not have occurred if the provinces now comprising Pakistan had been part of some other political entity. After all, if Pakistan's success as a state is to be measured in increases in agricultural and industrial production, should strides in productivity in Bangladesh since breaking away from Pakistan be considered an argument for Pakistan's malfunction?

Alongside the data on Pakistan's economic achievements since 1947, Pakistan's quasi-official history acknowledges the country's persistent need to borrow and seek aid. But these economic problems are, in Lodhi's words, 'rooted in poor state management, not Pakistan's economic fundamentals'.[105] In fact, this last point has been an essential part of the Pakistani national narrative over the years: Pakistan has just not found a great leader since Jinnah, the Quaid-i-Azam (literally, the great leader) 'to unlock Pakistan's potential'. Its problem is only 'poor governance, rule without law, and short-sighted leadership', which have 'mired the country in layers of crises that have gravely retarded Pakistan's progress and development'.[106]

The two-pronged approach of many Pakistani writers painting a sunny picture of their country is to insist that Pakistan's accomplishments serve as both its justification and its potential while laying its problems at the door of historic injustices or current international malfeasance. Responsibility for collective failure or miscalculation can be avoided by lamenting the absence of good leaders. There appears little willingness to consider that Pakistan might need to review some of the fundamental assumptions in its national belief system—militarism, radical Islamist ideology, perennial conflict with India, dependence on external support, and refusal to recognize ethnic identities and religious pluralism—to break out of permanent crisis mode to a more stable future.

That attitude was on full display when in May 2017, the Lahore Literary Festival organized several public panel discussions in London, as part of the effort to project a positive image of Pakistan. According to a report in *Dawn*, one panel was titled 'Against All Odds: The Price of Prosperity in Pakistan Today' and its speakers comprised a 'group of heavyweights' including Lodhi, Ishrat Husain and Shuja Nawaz (author of *Crossed Swords*, a comprehensive book on the Pakistan Army). The reporter noted that 'all the speakers—with the exception of Nawaz—patted Pakistan on the back for continuing to function when many around the world had written it off as a failed state' but 'they didn't get to grips with what had pushed it to the brink in the first place'.[107]

2

Faith, Grievance and Special Purpose

CHOOSING A COHERENT NARRATIVE that appeals to supporters, while ignoring the scrutiny of others, has been part of Pakistan's DNA since the demand for its creation was first made. So is the conception of an embattled nation constantly under attack, striving for survival, and moving forward through ad hoc measures with God's grace.

The 1940 resolution asking for separate states for Muslims in India did not use the term 'Pakistan' to describe the demand. The name was adopted later and even then, details of what the Pakistan scheme meant remained sketchy. Jinnah preferred ambiguity over specificity in his complex negotiating strategies in dealing with the British and the Indian National Congress. The Muslim League was projected as the sole voice of Muslims well before it could qualify as fully representative of the community. By the time a majority of Muslims had rallied to Jinnah's cause, the terms Muslim League, Muslim and Pakistan had become intermingled.

The Muslim League's initial demand in 1940 sought independent status for 'areas in which Muslims are numerically in a majority, as in the north-western and eastern zones of India'. Of the five provinces of British India that had Muslim majorities, only three (Sindh, Balochistan and Khyber Pakhtunkhwa, then known as North-West Frontier Province, NWFP) were overwhelmingly Muslim. Even though their proportion of Muslims was high (Sindh was 71 per cent Muslim, Balochistan 87 per cent and NWFP 92 per cent), their total population, including that of princely states and tribal agencies adjoining them, was only 10.8 million according to the 1941 census. The bulk of Pakistan's population was to be provided by Punjab with 28.4 million people and Bengal with 55.02 million. But Muslims in Punjab were only 57.1 per cent of the total and in Bengal 54.7 per cent.[1] If the original demand for Pakistan comprising Muslim-majority provinces of British India had been accepted, Pakistan's population would have been 40 per cent non-Muslim.

The logic of partitioning India on the basis of Muslim and non-Muslim majorities had to be extended by partitioning the provinces of Punjab and Bengal on a similar basis. But that was not considered by the supporters of the demand for Pakistan until the very end. Even after the British and the Indian National Congress reluctantly agreed to the partition of India, Jinnah continued to negotiate with princely states with non-Muslim majorities and even accepted the accession of one (Junagadh) to Pakistan. The emotional appeal for Pakistan was based on the notion of incompatibility of Hindus and Muslims but that incompatibility could be ignored, for example, if the Hindu raja of Travancore or the maharaja of Jodhpur were willing to merge their Hindu-majority fiefdoms into Pakistan!

Gandhi, who had fought for India's independence from the British, was deemed by Jinnah his primary rival. It was Gandhi's personal religious devotion that had driven Jinnah, a secular politician, out of the Congress and on to demanding Pakistan. Gandhi believed that the religious divisions that were being invoked to demand India's partition had been fuelled by British officials 'who could not bear to see the British leave India, and who had clung all along to the theory that if they could only support the Muslim League actively, to the point at which it could be held that the British could not leave India to civil war, then the British would be compelled to stay'.[2] He saw British support for the Muslim League and for the 'chieftains' that the British had installed as rulers of 562 princely states, as a stratagem to undermine India's freedom struggle. But for most Muslims across the subcontinent, Jinnah was able to paint Gandhi as a Hindu chauvinist who would eliminate Muslim identity once the British quit India without dividing it.

None of the Muslim League stalwarts, including Jinnah, wrote a book detailing their idea of Pakistan. The few books advocating Pakistan that appeared between 1940 and 1947 were often exhortatory in nature rather than explanatory. Their purpose was solely to rally Muslims behind Jinnah in support of Pakistan, not to explain what a future Pakistani state might look like or how it would be run. Like all political propaganda, the urgings for support to Pakistan did not require consistency of reasoning. The Muslims of provinces where they were a minority had to be scared of what awaited them if power devolved to Hindus after independence. Sikhs and Hindus in Punjab and Bengal, however, had to be persuaded not to fear Muslim dominance.

One of the earliest books in the genre of advocacy for Pakistan was titled *Pakistan, A Nation* and published by the Lahore-based publisher Sheikh Muhammad Ashraf in 1941, with two further editions following, the last of them in 1946. Its author was listed as 'El Hamza', which has an Arab ring to it. Another short book, *Pakistan Explained*, was released by Northern India Publishers in Lahore in 1945, ostensibly written by Alp Arsalan, meaning 'heroic lion'. Alp Arsalan was the second ruler in the Turkic Seljuk dynasty and is identified with the Muslim history of conquest. A third book in 1946, titled *Pakistan and Muslim India*, published by Home Study Circle, Bombay, listed its author as 'M.R.T.' These books could possibly have been written by civil servants or government functionaries in search of anonymity; otherwise there was no need for authors to adopt nom de plumes.

El Hamza's book is an early representative of the type of polemic that aroused Muslims in favour of Pakistan and that has been continually used after the country's creation to stir nationalist sentiment. The book dwells at length on the 'Hindu–Muslim Problem', talks of 'Bania Imperialism' and dismisses the Indian nationalist movement as 'the Aryo-Dravidian Hindu Imperialist Doctrine'.[3] It warns of 'protracted civil war' if India is maintained as one political entity and offers no economic plan or development strategy for the nation whose cause it advocated. According to El Hamza, division would not only avert civil war, it would pave the way for better relations between two communities (Muslims and Hindus) which would otherwise be at war.

'If Pakistan and Hindustan are recognized as distinct political units,' the author argued, 'the bonds of sympathy between the two countries will grow in numbers and strength with the passage of time; but if the separation is made after an appeal to force, the two nations will thenceforth regard each other as "natural" enemies.'[4] The history of India–Pakistan relations over the last seventy years disproves that vacuous argument. The passions generated in the process of British India's partition continue to consume the subcontinent. These are kept alive on both sides by fresh invective of the type offered by El Hamza and there is no sign of the bonds of sympathy that division was supposed to have created.

While building the case for Hindus and Muslims being two different nations by virtue of their different faiths and historic experiences, El Hamza also attempted to reconcile the existence of large numbers of non-Muslims in Pakistan as it was then envisaged. Here he resorted to mental gymnastics that have resurfaced in recent years in the notion of the Indus Valley and the Ganges Valley forming two distinct 'racial, religious, climatic, economic' entities throughout history, and Pakistan and India being separate long before the 1947 partition.

According to this account, unsubstantiated by archaeological or historic evidence, 'Aryan tribes of the first invasion, including men, women and children, settled on the Pakistan side of Jumna. They drove out the original inhabitants and preserved their purity of race. The river was later crossed and the country to the east penetrated by the hordes of Aryan men who married the native Dravidian women. The resultant Aryo-Dravidian race has since inhabited the Ganges Valley.'[5] Thus, while 'Hinduism is of the monsoon as Islam is of the desert',[6] religion need not be the only reason for Pakistan being separate from India. 'The Pakistani Hindus are true children of the soil and are of the same race as their Muslim fellow-countrymen,' El Hamza explains. 'They have a fine and liberal religion, and practise very little of the caste exclusionism and untouchability of the orthodox Aryo-Dravidian Hindu.'[7]

Interestingly, there was no room for the Bengalis of what was to be East Pakistan in this envisioning of a new state. After all, Bengali Muslims were as much of the monsoon as Sindhi Hindus were of the desert. If Pakistani Hindus were to be sons of the soil because of their racial and ethnic connection to the Indus Valley, how would a Pakistan including Bengal reconcile to Muslim children of the Ganges?

In the end, the violence attending the birth of Pakistan drastically reduced the country's Hindu, Sikh and other non-Muslim population to the point where it is less than 3 per cent today. Notwithstanding the 'fine and liberal' religion of the Hindus of the Indus Valley, as described by El Hamza, they were eventually pushed out of Pakistan to join their 'Brahmin Bania imperialist' co-religionists in India. A large number of Muslims from amongst the 'Aryo-Dravidian' people of the Ganges Valley—locally referred to as 'Muhajirs'—moved to Pakistan and were prominent in its administrative and academic life until being sidelined by ethnic prejudice beginning in the 1970s and culminating in the 1990s.

Although the more numerous East Bengalis remained part of Pakistan for twenty-four years, the prejudice of the type mustered by El Hamza and others never accepted them as true Pakistanis. Field Marshal Ayub Khan, who became Pakistan's first indigenous army commander and first military ruler, complained in his 1967 autobiography that Muslim Bengalis 'have been and still are under considerable Hindu cultural and linguistic influence' and had 'all the inhibitions of downtrodden races and have not yet found it possible to adjust psychologically to the requirements of the new-born freedom'.[8]

Clearly for Pakistani leaders like Ayub, opposition to 'Hindu influence' was the greater definer of Pakistani identity than the 'racial, religious, climatic, economic' reasons that were invoked before Independence to justify the need for Pakistan.

A more Islamist version of Pakistani nationalism was espoused by Fazal Karim Khan Durrani in his 1944 book *The Meaning of Pakistan* (Lahore: Islamic Book Service). 'We cannot be true Muslims, we cannot lead a truly Muslim life, we cannot carry out the duties that Islam lays upon us,' he wrote, without the creation of Pakistan. According to him,

'The Muslims of India, as indeed of the whole world since the days of the Umayyads, have for centuries lived a life of purposelessness,' which 'must now be replaced by a fierce fanatical passion for service of our people. "Islam and the Muslim nation first and everything else afterwards." This must now be the attitude of every single Muslim in this country.'[9]

Durrani dismissed the emphasis on the geographical unity of India. 'This emphasis is in a large measure an irrelevancy,' he insisted, adding, 'Maps are made and remade as political forces change and it is the creative mind of man rather than mountains and rivers that determines the fate of nations.' At the same time, the 'Muslims must never forget' that 'there is not an inch of the soil of India which our fathers did not once purchase with their blood'. In grandiloquence that has surfaced several times in Pakistan's history since Independence, he declared, 'We cannot be false to the blood of our fathers. India, the whole of it, is therefore our heritage and it must be re-conquered for Islam.' Beginning with a strong and stable Pakistan, the goal of Muslims must be 'to build up in time a larger Islamistan'.[10]

As such bombast reflects, Pakistan's creation involved mobilizing the sentiment of British India's Muslims against the fear of Hindu domination in a unified, independent India and holding out the prospect of global Islamic revival. The campaign for Pakistan comprised statements, fiery speeches and written propaganda material, none of which addressed critical issues and practical plans for running a country. The theme was that without Pakistan, the Muslims would live under the threat of 'the Hindu enemy' and their faith and way of life would be in danger. Muslims were destined to regain the glory of their earlier empires and Pakistan would be the stepping stone to restoration of Islam's glorious past.

A general election with limited franchise in 1945–46 had enabled the Muslim League to claim that it was the sole representative of the Muslims. The right to vote in the 1945–46 election was reserved for college graduates, landowners, income tax payers (which meant the very well-to-do at the time) and those who served in the military or government services. These groups, comprising about 15 per cent of British India's population at that time, continue to be the core that defines Pakistan to this day. For Jinnah, the vote served as the mandate for him to negotiate on behalf of Muslims, a position the British argued they had no choice but to accept.

The poll campaign generated religious fervour and its result seemed to indicate that Muslims were unhappy at the prospect of being dominated by Hindus. But the election results did not settle the question of what India's Muslims really wanted. As historian Ayesha Jalal points out, even the limited Muslim vote 'had not ratified a specific programme because no programme had actually been specified. No one was clear about the real meaning of "Pakistan" let alone its precise geographical boundaries.'[11]

In Punjab, where the Muslim elite had been reluctant followers of Jinnah, the tide was turned with the help of conservative religious elements. Afzal Iqbal notes that 'The spectacular victory of the Muslim League in the Punjab elections in 1946 (79 of the 86 Muslim seats as against only two out of 86 Muslim seats in 1937) cannot be understood only in terms of Quaid-i-Azam's charisma. One cannot ignore the use that was made of the religious emotions by the ulema [Islamic scholars], the sajjada nashins [hereditary heads of Sufi shrines] and their supporters.'[12] According to several accounts of this campaign, including Iqbal's, the message of the religious propagandists was simple. 'Those who vote for the Muslim League are Muslims, they will go to Heaven for this good act. Those who vote against the Muslim League are kafirs [non-believers], they will go to hell after their death. They were to be refused burial in a Muslim cemetery.'[13]

The clerics helping to get out the vote for Jinnah and the Muslim League reduced the argument in favour of creating Pakistan to a simple question of survival of Islam in the South Asian subcontinent. The sort of 'logic' these religious leaders used was best summarized in one of the speeches of Muslim League stalwart, Maulana Abdul Sattar Niazi. 'We have got two alternatives before us, whether to join or rather accept the slavery of Bania Brahman Raj in Hindustan or join the Muslim fraternity, the federation of Muslim provinces,' he thundered. 'Every

Pathan takes it as an insult for him to prostrate before Hindu Raj and will gladly sit with his brethren in Islam in the Pakistan Constituent Assembly. A Pathan is a Muslim first and a Muslim last.'[14] As Iqbal notes, 'It is a fact that the people of Pakistan talked in the only idiom they knew. Pakistan was to be the laboratory of Islam, the citadel of Islam.'[15]

Since Independence, the state of Pakistan has persisted with maintaining the threat perception about Hindus, now represented by India, wanting to eliminate or subjugate the Muslims. The aspiration for Islamic unity and revival has also been an integral part of Pakistan's global outlook, beginning with hosting the Grand Mufti of Palestine and leaders of Egypt's Muslim Brotherhood in 1949 to the 2017 announcement of an 'Islamic NATO' commanded by former army chief Gen. Raheel Sharif. Jinnah had earlier exchanged correspondence with the Muslim Brotherhood's founder, Hasan al-Banna, who offered support for 'the sacred Pakistan movement'.[16] Over the years, the fortunes of the Muslim League as the embodiment of the ideology of Pakistan waned and the army stepped in as the organization defining the interests of Islam and Pakistan in the subcontinent. Thus, ideology and grievance rather than the pragmatic interests of a territorial state and its citizens have often determined Pakistan's direction over the years.

Absence of Plans

US president Franklin Roosevelt's personal representative for India, William Philips, noted after meeting Jinnah on 7 April 1943 that the founder of Pakistan could 'hold masses of people spellbound for hours at a time' with 'his concept of an independent Moslem nation' but avoided specifics. 'When I tried to pin him down to further particulars with regard to the economic life of a future Pakistan and to the problem of minorities, for he had not only Hindus and Sikhs to deal with, he was vague and non-committal, waving them aside as "matters of detail",' Philips noted.[17]

Five years later, when US diplomat Raymond Hare met Jinnah in May 1947, the absence of a plan beyond independence was still an issue. Hare found Jinnah's style of conversation 'restrained but forceful, with emphasis on argument of the close-knit legal type', avoiding questions that might veer away from the case for Pakistan. Jinnah 'made his usual points about the need to maintain the geographic integrity of Bengal and the Punjab within an independent Pakistan, and he argued that communal differences would subside once decisions were taken and people knew where they stood'. Hare observed that this was a dangerous argument since it could be applied 'equally well to a united India'. He found Jinnah's presentation 'too fine spun and legalistic' and lacking the elements that help in formulating practical policies.

In his conversation with Hare, Jinnah outlined what has since become Pakistan's strategic vision. Jinnah contended that without the existence of Pakistan, a 'Hindu controlled India with all of its manpower, resources and imperialist tendencies', would attempt to fill the vacuum created by the British departure. Pakistan could block this development vis-à-vis the Indians, he argued, 'but the Pakistan–Middle East bloc would need assistance from Britain and the United States if it were to stand up to Soviet aggression'.[18]

When Hare met him again in July 1947, Jinnah 'appeared quite relaxed about the prospect of a divided India and all that it implied'. He told Hare that in his view 'the work of the Boundary Commission was relatively uncomplicated and that the Partition Council should function smoothly since it had the safety valve of an arbitral commission to resolve any outstanding differences'. Jinnah joked that he 'surely didn't want to resort to war yet' with India and seemed reconciled to 'the partitioning of the Punjab and Bengal which would lead to what he had derisively described as a "moth-eaten" Pakistan.'[19]

The visiting Americans were not the only ones who noticed that the founding leadership of Pakistan had no detailed plans for their future state beyond arguments about why it must be created. Soon after arriving as the last British viceroy in India, Lord Louis Mountbatten started a series of meetings with the subcontinent's political leaders. After meeting one of Jinnah's lieutenants in the Muslim League, he noted that his interlocutor told him 'the usual tale of woe about Congress perfidy against the Muslim League' and insisted that Pakistan was the solution to India's problems. 'I pointed out that the Pakistan principle could be applied also to the extent of partitioning the Punjab and Bengal,' Mountbatten recorded, adding that the Muslim League leader agreed 'with the logic' of the argument but 'appealed to me to "temper logic with mercy!"'[20]

To force Jinnah and his associates into putting flesh on the skeleton of their idea for Pakistan, Mountbatten asked his staff to draw up a list of 'awkward questions' that he could put to Jinnah. The questions related to Pakistan's geography as well as its prospects in the spheres of defence and finance. These included: Would Pakistan 'be strong enough to face Russia and Hindustan at one and the same time?' How would Pakistan 'maintain a separate Army and Air Force' and build 'munition factories and other industries necessary to support such forces?' 'What are the resources in finance, minerals and expert manpower to justify such a course?' 'Would not the financial position in Pakistan be such that it would be difficult to maintain its social services and impossible to make adequate provision for defence?'[21] Ironically, the answers to these questions, which eventually impacted Pakistan's future once it was born, were never adequately given before Independence.

British officials in the subcontinent maintained meticulous records and these included notes of all their conversations and exchanges with local leaders. The British started discussing the eventual independence of India in 1942 and the process culminated in 1947. Official records of British discussions with Indian leaders, along with other documents pertaining to the sunset of British rule in India from 1942 to 1947, have been edited by Commonwealth historian Nicholas Mansergh and published in twelve volumes. In the 13,295 pages comprising thousands of official documents, one thing stands out. While the Congress leaders often discussed with the British their plans for what India would need after

Independence, the Muslim League offered no plans for how it would run Pakistan and did not discuss what arrangements might be needed before Independence to enable the smooth functioning of a new country.

Between April and August of 1947 the one issue that received relatively serious attention of the Muslim League leaders was the division of the British Indian armed forces. Liaquat Ali Khan, who would become Pakistan's first prime minister, as well as Jinnah, discussed detailed proposals for the division of the armed forces[22] but not for other matters. Jinnah told the British he would like to see the armed forces divided before June 1948—the original date set for British withdrawal—and if that was impossible, he wanted the British to lay down the principles of division.[23] On subjects such as maintaining continuity in civilian administration, Mountbatten complained at the end of June 1947—less than two months before Independence—that 'for the last three weeks we have been trying to get an answer out of Jinnah and he has always put off an answer'.[24]

Pakistan, unlike India, would not start out with a functioning capital, central government or financial resources, which necessitated greater homework on the part of the Muslim League leaders. Unfortunately, they did little by way of preparation for running the country they had demanded. Many of Pakistan's teething problems were the result of this ill-preparedness but Pakistani accounts of the country's early days paint them as hardships inflicted on Muslim Pakistan by its non-Muslim enemies.

Amid the emotive appeals for division of India, there was considerable lack of clarity even about basic matters such as the citizenship of Pakistan. On 1 August 1947, just days before Pakistan's birth, Jinnah was reported as saying, 'I am going to Pakistan as a citizen of Hindustan,' implying that the citizenship between the two entities might overlap or even be transferable. 'I am going because people of Pakistan have given me the opportunity to serve them,' he said, adding, 'But this does not mean I cease to be a citizen of Hindustan. Just as Lord Mountbatten who is a foreign citizen has accepted the Governor-Generalship of Hindustan in response to the wishes of its people, similarly I have accepted the Governor-Generalship of Pakistan. But I shall always be ready to serve the Muslims of Hindustan.'[25]

The vagueness about the venture was accompanied also by unrealistic sanguinity. Jinnah told Mountbatten in April 1947 that Pakistan would be able to work out its own constitution within six months and arrangements could also be made within that period to divide between Pakistan and Hindustan 'all subjects except Defence'.[26] This was an overly optimistic assessment. Pakistan remained without a constitution for almost nine years after Independence and the first Constituent Assembly, which Jinnah presided over, did not agree on even the basic principles of the constitution in his lifetime, which lasted just one year and one month after Independence.

Fourteen days after the announcement of Partition, on 17 June, Liaquat informed the British that the Muslim League had decided to locate the headquarters of the Pakistan government temporarily in Karachi. He wrote to Mountbatten that 'Accommodation, office and residential, will, therefore, be required at Karachi by the 15th of August 1947, for the Ministers, officers and staff of the Government and the Members of the Constituent Assembly' and asked for 'readjustment in regard to the accommodation occupied by military units and formations in Karachi'.

Liaquat suggested that it would 'be best if the military authorities who have considerable experience in these matters, could be requested to undertake the provision of the accommodation, together with the necessary furniture, telephones, etc., required by the Pakistani government'. He asked that the commander-in-chief 'issue necessary instructions to the appropriate Military authorities regarding the provision of accommodation and transportation facilities' and said, 'It would be desirable to appoint a senior Military officer to be in charge of the whole operation.'[27]

It is noteworthy that the Muslim League had campaigned for Pakistan for seven years without deciding what its capital might be. The Bengalis proposed Dhaka while others suggested Lahore and even Multan, a historic city in the south of Punjab. But the subject was never seriously discussed while rallying Muslims to the cause of Pakistan. After belatedly deciding on Karachi as the capital, Muslim League leaders expected the

British Indian Army to resolve the problems they might encounter in accommodating the government of their new country. This was one of the earliest manifestations of Pakistan's tendency to rely on the military as the solution to problems normally falling in the civilian domain.

The Muslim League leaders could have anticipated both the need of a capital and the difficulties they might face in their choice of Karachi but their decisions were guided by passion, not practical considerations. Otherwise they would have realized that Karachi, a smallish port city, had served as the capital of the relatively smaller province of Sindh only since 1937 and lacked the infrastructure for what would be a large federal government. Muslim League leaders had decided on Karachi as interim capital partly for emotional reasons as it was Jinnah's birthplace. In doing so they ignored British suggestions that Lahore might be more functional as interim capital.

Lahore had been the capital of undivided Punjab since the coronation of Maharaja Ranjit Singh in 1801 and had been developed by the British since 1849 as an administrative headquarters. The division of Punjab meant that several government officials and their offices would be moving out of Lahore, making room for the new Pakistan government. There was ample government accommodation in Lahore and part of the Pakistan government's work was moved there after Independence. Eventually Pakistan built an entirely new capital, Islamabad, in the 1960s but until then the country's government was constantly constrained by having an improvised capital.

In addition to the administrative problems posed by an ill-equipped capital, the choice of Karachi also had political consequences. Chaudhri Muhammad Ali narrates how the Muslim League ministry of Sindh resented the province's capital being taken over by the new central government. As head of the civil service, Ali felt 'It was essential that the central government should be in full control of the seat of its administration.' In May 1948, a 567-square mile 'Karachi Capital Area' was designated and put under the federal government's authority. Sindhi leaders, including Muslim Leaguers, opposed separation of Karachi from

Sindh and had to be pacified by Jinnah himself.[28] After maintaining its headquarters in Karachi for a while, the Sindh government later shifted to Hyderabad and the metropolis did not return to Sindh's administration until 1970.

Pakistanis often recount how civil servants in Pakistan's early days worked out of makeshift offices, lived in tents and ran the government with limited stationery supplies. While the account is generally accurate, and the sacrifice of the officials admirable, it is equally important to understand that the difficulty was the result of a poor choice. Pakistan's founder had selected the country's capital to be located in a city lacking adequate facilities, preferring it over another provincial capital with a better establishment.

At least some of the anguish that is now retold as one of Pakistan's starting handicaps could have been mitigated by some anticipatory planning. But recognizing that would amount to accepting responsibility; it would diminish the narrative of victimhood that animates conversations and passes off for analysis through much of Pakistan's history.

Lack of forethought at the time of Independence was not limited to the choice of capital. It also cost Pakistan its share of India's assets, both financial and military. Pakistan was allocated a 17.5 per cent share in the assets and liabilities of British India. Cash balances were held by the Reserve Bank of India (RBI), which held back the transfer of Rs 750 million for months.[29] Fighting in Kashmir, which the Muslim League initiated with the help of Pashtun tribal raiders immediately after Partition, jeopardized Pakistan's share of 165,000 tonnes of arms, ammunition and other military material.[30] By 31 March 1948 India had transferred only 4,730 tonnes and another 18,000 tonnes by 10 September 1948.[31] To this day, Pakistanis assert that India denied 142,000 tonnes of defence stores that should have come to Pakistan.[32] It is undeniable that India did not hand over all the assets that were due to Pakistan as part of the partition process. But the expectation of Pakistani leaders that they would get military equipment and money from an enemy against whom they had initiated military conflict was wholly unrealistic.

'Jazba' and 'Special Purpose'

That Pakistan endured the ill-preparedness of its own founders is commendable but there is little deliberation in Pakistani accounts about that lack of readiness. Take the matter of the loss of assets. Mountbatten, among others, had considered how a bitter separation might result in India's Congress leaders withholding Pakistan's assets. The British solution to the problem was the creation of a Partition Council headed by a joint British Governor-General. The Muslim League, however, decided that Jinnah would be Pakistan's Governor-General from day one and that there was no need for an ostensibly neutral British head of state even for a short while to ensure equitable division of assets.

Pakistanis might learn how to make better choices in future by recognizing that their leaders at the time made a policy choice that had adverse consequences. Instead, the nation only remembers angrily that it was deprived of something that should have rightfully been theirs.

Pakistanis often use the Urdu word 'jazba', variously meaning 'passion, spirit, and strong feeling or emotion' as the guarantor of Pakistan's success in all fields, from the sport of cricket to the economy and warfare. When things go wrong, it is not poor planning, technique or execution that is blamed; it is 'the lack of sincerity and jazba' of someone or other. Passionate nationalism is not unique to Pakistanis but they are among possibly a handful of nations that tend to completely ignore the details that nations normally consider in charting their course. This tendency also has its roots in the formative phase of Pakistan.

For instance, Mountbatten had discussed with Jinnah 'the importance of having a common Governor-General with a British team to see partition through till 31 March 1948' soon after the announcement of the partition plan on 3 June 1947. According to British records, Jinnah said that he 'realized all the disadvantages of giving up the common Governor-General' but he was 'unable to accept any position other than that of Governor-General of Pakistan on the 15th August'. This view was presumably based, not on the business-like needs of dividing a subcontinent, but the excitement of Muslim League supporters who wished to see their Quaid-i-Azam as Pakistan's first head of state.

The minutes of the subsequent conversation between Jinnah and Mountbatten are quite telling. Mountbatten asked Jinnah, 'Do you realize what this will cost you?' Jinnah responded, 'It may cost me several crores of rupees in assets.' Mountbatten 'replied somewhat acidly, "It may well cost you the whole of your assets and the future of Pakistan".'[33] Jinnah explained to Mountbatten that 'he wished to have British Governors in every province of Pakistan except Sind, which, since it would be under his personal observation in Karachi, could have a Muslim governor'. As the three heads of the Pakistan Defence Services would also be British, Jinnah said that 'the only way in which he could sell the idea of all these British high officials to the inhabitants of Pakistan would be if he himself became the Governor-General'.[34]

Ironically, to this day the State Bank of Pakistan's annual balance sheet reflects Pakistan's assets held at the Reserve Bank of India. Withholding of assets features on the list of Pakistan's grievances against India but the circumstances that led to Pakistan losing those assets, and how an option might have existed for a more equitable transfer, is almost never discussed. Outrage against foreigners and enemies serves a far more useful political purpose than critical examination of national leaders' decisions.

Choosing to risk financial assets was not the only gamble of Pakistan's founding fathers. The Muslim League's lack of a concrete plan to deal with negotiating the accession of princely states was another. It has mired Pakistan in a long-lasting conflict that has led the country to fight several wars, with little gain. Jammu and Kashmir was one of 562 princely states that were required by the terms of Partition to accede either to India or to Pakistan based on contiguity and the wishes of the majority of their population.

Because Pakistan had not negotiated with the states beforehand, and Jinnah had continued until the last minute to try and persuade several princes ruling Hindu-majority states to join Pakistan, the accession of Jammu and Kashmir (which had a Hindu maharaja and a predominantly Muslim populace) became an extraordinary bone of contention between the two states born out of British India.

Fourteen of the 562 princely states had Muslim majority populations and were contiguous to or located within the territory of Pakistan. The Muslim League's lack of preparation meant that on the day of Pakistan's independence, only one of these states—Swat—had joined the new Muslim dominion. This contrasted with India's ability to integrate by Independence Day all but six of the 548 princely states that became part of the Indian Union. Thus, Pakistan's territory remained undefined for several months after Independence. The princely states in Pakistan eventually fell in line, while one—Kalat in Balochistan—was coerced through military action in March 1948.[35]

Jammu and Kashmir posed a problem because it adjoined both India and Pakistan. Its maharaja, Hari Singh, initially flirted with remaining independent while its popular Muslim political leader, Sheikh Abdullah, was closer to the Congress than to the Muslim League.

Pakistan tried to strengthen its hand in Jammu and Kashmir with the help of armed volunteers, recruited from amongst Pashtun tribesmen. Muslim League leaders from Punjab sought the help of Muslim army officers, who in turn ran a military operation that was kept secret from their British commanders.[36] On the one hand, this approach politicized Pakistan's army in its earliest days. On the other, it paved the way for India's direct military involvement. The Muslim League had missed the boat on winning Sheikh Abdullah over, but Pakistan could have built on a Standstill Agreement it signed with Maharaja Hari Singh and sought his accession to Pakistan.

By launching an ill-planned tribal invasion, Pakistan drove the maharaja into India's arms. The invasion was aimed at incorporating the entire territory of Jammu and Kashmir into Pakistan, but the mujahideen, as the invaders were called, failed in capturing the state capital, Srinagar. India retained most of Kashmir's population. Although its own rule over the state's Muslim population has been characterized by periodic local discontent repressed by brute force, Pakistan has not been able to change the territorial status quo since 1948.

Initiating a war and not winning it is not the optimal way of starting life as a new country. The use of force eroded Pakistan's moral argument about Kashmir belonging to Pakistan because of its Muslim majority. Unable to take Kashmir militarily, Pakistan hoped to get it through a United Nations–sponsored plebiscite. It has, however, failed to maintain international support over the issue and has ended up supporting militants and terrorists since the late 1980s to force India's hand. Kashmir has become another one of Pakistan's national causes without an endgame or pragmatic strategy for success in sight. Kashmir is considered part of Pakistan by destiny and Pakistan is deemed by Pakistanis to be destined to endure because of its people's martial Muslim spirit, their national jazba and their patriotic passion. This attitude has been consistent since Pakistan's inception and has only grown over the years.

Pakistanis do not like acknowledging their failure to plan as their weakness. Nor are most of them willing to examine the downside of their own actions. Pakistan had risked its financial assets to prove a political point and its leaders also made no preparations to negotiate accession with the princely states. The tribal invasion of Jammu and Kashmir paved the way for India's invasion of the state, sowing the seeds of a permanent casus belli. But Pakistani accounts of history gloss over these colossal misjudgements, insisting, instead, only on wrongs done to Pakistan.

The phenomenon of Pakistani lack of introspection is explained by British civil servant and historian, L.F. Rushbrook Williams. 'To most Pakistanis the creation of their country seems a miracle, the direct gift of God, the crown of an effort which, without His help, must have been doomed to failure.' After serving in Pakistan's early administration and visiting it frequently in subsequent years, Williams identified the 'deeply held conviction' among Pakistanis about its divine purpose and wrote: 'This firm faith in Divine guidance is fundamental to the Pakistani outlook.'[37] From Jinnah and Liaquat to contemporary Pakistani leaders, the belief persists that policymaking is secondary to maintaining national pride and morale, as God is somehow looking out for Pakistan.

The twin concepts—that God protects Pakistan and that pride and morale are more important than making plans—also explain Pakistani attitudes towards bad news. For example, on 16 December 1971—the day Pakistan's armed forces in erstwhile East Pakistan surrendered to the joint forces of India and Bangladesh—Pakistani newspapers led with headlines proclaiming impending victory. In the days preceding the surrender, there was little discussion either in the media or among policymakers about the military prospects in the country's eastern wing. The commander of the eastern garrison issued statements to the effect that Indian forces would enter Dhaka only over his dead body. Once news of surrender reached West Pakistan, people crowded into mosques to pray, thinking that the military debacle was punishment for their sins.

Zulfikar Ali Bhutto, who picked up the pieces as Pakistan's president (and later as prime minister) after the 1971 break-up of the country, reflected the national psyche when he spoke to the US ambassador soon after taking office. Although Pakistan had just lost its eastern half and lost a war, Bhutto told Ambassador Joseph Farland that 'Pakistan had a real reason for coming into being' and that 'this very reason justified its survival'.[38] Loss of half the country did not merit reflection, only reassertion of its Divine purpose was needed.

Rushbrook Williams, the civil servant and scholar, had pointed out five years earlier an 'obsessive preoccupation' of Pakistan's elite with political and ideological matters 'to the exclusion of matters at least equally and probably more important for the welfare of the country.' He observed: 'What counted for far more with my [Pakistani] friends was how power was to be divided between the Centre and the Provinces and between East and West Pakistan; how far the shape of a modern State could be squared with the principles of Islam; and how the different competing interests—landlords, religious leaders, business men, industrialists—could receive recognition of their claim to power and influence.' Williams regretted that Pakistan's leaders 'came to live in a kind of artificial gold fish bowl of their own creating, which distorted their sense of values and fixed their attention not upon the needs of the country but on competition for power, influence and spoils of office'.[39] Ideological nationalism seems to be the instrument of the country's elite to retain control without addressing substantive social and economic issues.

Given their lack of administrative experience, Muslim League politicians depended on British and British-trained administrators and military men in running Pakistan during its formative years. To their credit, these officials kept the country going and disproved the direst predictions about Pakistan's imminent breakdown and disintegration. But the cost of survival, as pointed out by Ayesha Jalal, was the weakening of the democratic processes, 'intrinsic to maintaining a fragile federal equation'.[40] Pakistan fell under bureaucratic control and military dominance soon after its creation. Disputes with neighbours as well as between East and West Pakistan bred 'a massive insecurity complex that more often than not erased the distinction between perceptions of external and internal threats to the country's existence'.[41]

Jalal may be right in pointing out that 'For all its litany of woes, Pakistan is not going to disappear from the map of the world in a hurry.'[42] But it is important to examine why the strategy that has ensured Pakistan's survival thus far might not prove to be the best recipe for its further political and economic evolution. State failure does not always follow each time a warning of failure is put forward. But federations can, and do, splinter and economic collapse or social disintegration is not unknown. The Soviet Union crumbled under the burden of an inefficient economy failing to bear the costs of a huge military establishment and Yugoslavia split into its various parts after surviving seventy-four years.

There is, therefore, no reason to dismiss out of hand any analysis that suggests that Pakistan's frailty could lead to worse consequences than those desired by its citizens and well-wishers. Pakistan must recognize and overcome its challenges, if it wants to change its image as a fragile nation. Dismissing Pakistan as a bad idea, as many authors do, and defending Pakistan as it is on grounds that other countries are worse off, as some Pakistanis and Pakistan apologists do, should not be the only options in discussing an important country.

Beyond Survival

One of Pakistan's greatest challenges since its creation has been what historian Mubarak Ali calls 'the monumental task of formulating a national identity distinct from India'. In Ali's words, 'Born out of a schism of the old civilization of India, Pakistan has debated over the construction of a culture of its own, a culture which will not only be different from that of India but one that the rest of the world can understand.'[43] This desire to disown any similarity with India and to insist that Pakistan was not the outcome of political divisions in British India but the culmination of a deeper schism spread over centuries has led to the creation of what is described in Pakistani textbooks as 'the ideology of Pakistan'.

Jinnah had not spoken of Pakistan before Partition as an ideological state even though he framed the demand for Pakistan on the basis of the two-nation theory. The core argument of the two-nation theory was similar to the 'two nations theory' adopted by Ulster Unionists in Ireland in 1913. The Unionists in Ireland argued that the island's Protestants were a different nation from its Catholics because of their different religion, historic experience and even racial origin. Jinnah's 'two-nation theory' applied a similar argument to the Muslims of the South Asian subcontinent. Contrary to what Pakistani children are taught in schools, the Islamic ideology currently in vogue in Pakistan did not give birth to the country; it was born after Pakistan's creation in its present form.

The new country did not have a history or identity as Pakistan beyond what had been created amid the political struggle of the last few years of British Raj. It was home to several distinct ethnic groups, speaking different languages, some of whom (like Sindhis, Baloch and Pashtuns) had known self-rule before the advent of the British. Pakistan could have recognized its diversity and evolved as a multi-ethnic, multi-language federation with political and cultural autonomy for its constituting units. Instead, its leaders chose to base Pakistani identity on a national ideology.

Liaquat spoke of the 'Islamic way of life'[44] as being Pakistan's goal and laid the foundation for the future development of an ideological state. An important consideration in doing so was to deal with the question, as defined by Ayub Khan, 'Considering that the people of Pakistan are a collection of so many races with different backgrounds, how can they be welded into a unified whole whilst keeping intact their local pride, culture and traditions?'[45] Beginning with Liaquat, moving forward with Ayub Khan and culminating with Zia-ul-Haq, Pakistan's leaders proceeded to delineate a 'noble and eternal' ideology that would give Pakistan 'a tremendous power of cohesion and resistance',[46] insisting that it was on the basis of Islam 'that we fought for and got Pakistan'.[47] Islam, hostility to India, and the Urdu language were identified as the cornerstones of this new national ideology.

Pakistan's leaders have always feared ethnic nationalism as a threat to the country's integrity in addition to worrying that India might use ethnic differences among Pakistanis to divide and devour the new country.[48] They have also discouraged use of languages other than the designated national language, Urdu, as part of 'the politics of making a nation against a backdrop in which that nation has been assumed to exist already'.[49] Very soon after Independence, 'Islamic Pakistan' had started defining itself through the prism of resistance to 'Hindu India', while at the same time describing Islam as the delineator of national identity against disparate ethnicities.

'If we let go the ideology of Islam, we cannot hold together as a nation by any other means', explained a Pakistani academic a few years after East Pakistan broke away to become Bangladesh. 'If the Arabs, the Turks, the Iranians, God forbid, give up Islam, the Arabs yet remain Arabs, the Turks remain Turks, the Iranians remain Iranians, but what do we remain if we give up Islam?' he wondered.[50] Interestingly, few people recognized the potential downside of invoking religion as a national unifier. Islam could as easily divide Muslims along sectarian lines as it helped to unite them against a shared enemy. Moreover, religious demagogues, theologians and clerics could hardly be kept away from politics when politics revolved around religion. The westernized politicians, administrators and generals who made Islam the cornerstone of Pakistan's existence did not anticipate either future sectarian divisions or the empowerment of religious activists as their rivals.

Once Pakistan was declared an Islamic state, clerics and Islamists began asserting their right to make it conform fully to their interpretations of Islam. The 'ideology of Pakistan' has created a nexus between the 'custodians of Islam' and the country's military, civil bureaucracy and intelligence apparatus, which collectively sees itself as the guardian of the Pakistani state. Inflexibility in relations with India, and the belief that India represents an existential threat to Pakistan, has led to maintaining the large military the country inherited from the British Raj, which, in turn, helped the military assert its pre-eminence in the country's life. As Pakistan could not pay for its defence and economic growth, it always sought foreign allies who might make its financial burdens lighter. This resulted first in Pakistan's alliance with the West, especially the United States, for most of Pakistan's life as a nation and has recently resulted in reliance on China.

I have described the emergence of this policy tripod—religious nationalism, confrontation with India and external dependence—in my book *Pakistan Between Mosque and Military*.[51] Each element of the tripod has influenced the other, sometimes in imperceptible ways. Sometimes one factor required distortions and convoluted explanations to manage the other. Thus, India had to be painted in the Pakistani view as an enemy of Islam to bolster Pakistan's self-image as a bastion of Islam. The US had to be persuaded of Pakistan's anti-communist credentials to be able to secure weapons, which were needed to confront the Indians, notwithstanding the relatively minuscule influence of communists within Pakistan.

The greatest threats to Pakistan's central authority, however, have come from groups seeking regional autonomy, ethnic rights or political inclusion. Islamist terrorists have also become a threat to the country's security in recent years. Successive Pakistani governments have linked these threats also to foreign-backed plans to weaken Pakistan. During the cold war, ethnic parties were linked to India and 'the communists', even when there was no threat to Pakistan from communists.

Pakistanis saw no contradiction in seeking alliance with the West against communism while courting communist China as Pakistan's 'all-weather friend' because of a shared interest in containing India. More recently, jihadi terrorists have attacked Pakistan's security forces as part of their effort to further Islamize Pakistan. But the national security establishment still insists that these groups are backed by foreign powers (especially India) even though Pakistan's own support of these groups is well documented.

Furthermore, invoking Islam as the binding force for Pakistanis has not always worked out as planned. Political and doctrinal disagreements amongst Islamist groups have resulted in endless debates about who is or is not a Muslim and what interpretation of Islam should form the basis of law in the process of Pakistan's Islamization. Between 1989 and 2017, there were 3,063 incidents of sectarian violence in Pakistan, resulting in the death of 5,686 people and leaving 11,181 injured.[52]

Jinnah, a Shia Muslim himself, would be appalled to find that a large group of clerics wants the Shias to be declared non-Muslims for legal purposes just as the Ahmadis, another group active in supporting Pakistan's creation, were cast out through a constitutional amendment in 1974. Violent attacks on Shias spiked between 2001 and 2017, with 464 reported incidents in which 2,679 Shias were killed and 4,840 injured.[53] In the fourteen years since 2003, 21,912 civilians and 6,825 security force personnel have been killed by Islamist terrorists. Although Pakistan remains a haven for several jihadi groups, its security forces have also battled some of these groups and official records claim the killing of 33,755 terrorists or insurgents.[54]

The sectarian and religious battles appear to have been foretold by British historian Arnold Toynbee, who had generally been very sympathetic to Pakistan in his writings. In 1955, Toynbee wrote that 'it would be a calamity if Pakistan were ever to become a Muslim state in an exclusive and intolerant way'. He noted that Pakistan's leaders saw 'a common adherence to Islam' as 'manifestly a force that binds a majority of the people of Pakistan together' but warned that 'Islam might become a far more disruptive force than the racial and linguistic differences which Islam at present overrides'.[55]

Toynbee pointed out something that had been ignored by those trying to forge national unity through religion. 'Pakistani Islam is not unitary,' he reminded, adding that several sects of Islam 'the Shia and the Ahmadiyya, as well as the Sunnah' are part of the Pakistani mosaic. According to Toynbee, 'Pakistan could never be identified, as some Islamic countries can be, with some particular Islamic sect.' He also stressed that 'Pakistan cannot live without good relations, not only between her own citizens, but between herself and her neighbours' and emphasized the need for minorities in India and Pakistan to be considered 'not hostages, but ambassadors and interpreters, helping Pakistan and the Indian Union to live as good neighbours'.[56]

The warning, however, did not prevent Pakistan from going down the road of religious nationalism and a state of permanent antagonism with India. In his speech to Pakistan's Constituent Assembly barely seven months after Independence, Bengali leader Suhrawardy had warned that Pakistan was on a perilous course. As the prime minister of undivided Bengal, he had witnessed the horrors of communal violence and had aided the Muslim League in creating the Hindu–Muslim polarization that helped it win Muslim votes for Pakistan. But that was a different time requiring different politics. Suhrawardy now feared that the newly founded state might destroy itself by adopting a version of Islam that is not based 'on toleration, equality, brotherhood' and by 'establishing in effect a communal state within Pakistan'.[57]

Suhrawardy regretted the effort to ethnically cleanse Pakistan of its Hindus and Sikhs and to 'blame the authorities of the Indian Union that they sent their missionaries here amongst the masses and are asking them to leave'. Pakistan was created by 'raising the cry' that 'the rights of Muslims were in danger', he observed, adding that the rulers of Pakistan were now 'raising the cry of Pakistan in danger for the purpose of arousing Muslim sentiments and binding them together in order to maintain' power. According to Suhrawardy, 'a state which will be founded on sentiments, namely that of Islam in danger or of Pakistan in danger, a state which will be held together by raising the bogey of attacks' and which is kept together 'by keeping up a constant friction' with India would be 'full of alarms and excursions'. In that state 'there will be no commerce, no business and no trade. There will be lawlessness.'[58]

Seventy years and the loss of erstwhile East Pakistan later, Suhrawardy's words seem prophetic. Ideological polarization and the fear of Indian hegemony, coupled with generous assistance from foreign allies, have helped Pakistan survive but the country remains a land of alarm, insecurity and instability. Instead of taking pride in having defied all predictions of collapse, Pakistanis must now start figuring out why such forecasts have persisted for so long. Unless Pakistanis adopt a course that makes discussion of Pakistan's perilousness redundant, there will remain few people outside Pakistan who will be impressed by its intelligentsia's self-congratulation for survival and resilience.

Almost every discussion of Pakistan, especially in India, inevitably tends to be about the logic and raison d'être of the country's creation. The process of partitioning a subcontinent along religious lines did not prove as neat as Jinnah had anticipated. Jinnah was a lawyer who saw Partition as a solution to potential constitutional problems in an independent India. In his first address to Pakistan's Constituent Assembly on 11 August 1947 he had said that he saw it as 'the only solution of India's constitutional problem', which in his view related to 'the feeling that exists between the two communities wherever one community is in majority and the other is in minority'.[59]

For Jinnah, Partition was a constitutional way out of a political stalemate, as he saw it, and not the beginning of a permanent state of hostility between two countries or two nations. This explains his expectation that India and Pakistan would live side by side 'like the United States and Canada',[60] obviously with open borders, free flow of ideas and free trade. It is also the reason why Pakistan's Quaid-i-Azam insisted that his Malabar Hill house in Bombay be kept as it was so that he could return to the city where he lived most of his life after retiring as Governor-General of Pakistan.[61]

For several years after Independence, better educated migrants from India—Muhajirs, as opposed to sons of the soil—secured better jobs and higher positions in the new state of Pakistan. Over the years, Pakistan has evolved into an Islamist ideological state, a short cut to resolving the complex inter-ethnic, social and economic dynamics among its peoples.

After the loss of its eastern wing, which became Bangladesh in 1971, Pakistan has been completely dominated by one ethnic group, the Punjabis, who tend to favour the ideological model for Pakistan and are heavily represented in the military, the media and the bureaucracy.

Political scientist Benedict Anderson, in his book *Imagined Communities*, defined a nation as 'an imagined political community, imagined as both inherently limited and sovereign'.[62] According to Anderson, a nation is a socially constructed community, joined by the imagination of people who perceive themselves as part of that group. Many writers, including Salman Rushdie, have argued that Pakistan was 'insufficiently imagined', given the ambiguities inherent in the demand for Pakistan.

Pakistanis born after Partition have known no other homeland and millions now know only Pakistan as their country. They would likely be willing to discuss its history objectively and chart a different future for Pakistan if they are not constantly conditioned to believe in a state ideology. Pakistan's young median age today means that an overwhelming majority of its current inhabitants were born in a country called Pakistan and, therefore, do not need an explanation other than their birth to be its citizens. In any case, the emphasis on Islam to unite the various Pakistani ethnicities and communities has had a consequence quite different from building a strong Pakistani personality.

A 2009 British Council survey of Pakistanis between the ages of eighteen and twenty-nine revealed that because of the emphasis on Islam, 72 per cent of young Pakistanis defined themselves as Muslims first and

Pakistanis second.[63] The ethnic identities this ideology was supposed to mitigate remain intact, except in Punjab where being Pakistani and Punjabi Muslim are considered synonymous.

For the sake of young Pakistanis, who want to be citizens of a functioning state, a reimagining of Pakistan is needed, going beyond the bitterness of the 1947 Partition and the subsequent disasters inflicted upon Pakistanis by their own rulers and leaders. Pakistan, like any other nation, is not a monolith. Its people have energy, talent and aspirations for a good life like anyone else.

One can disagree over or even be agnostic about whether the creation of the state of Pakistan in August 1947 was a tragedy or not. But there is no doubt that the failure of Pakistanis to create a more tolerant and democratic state and the difficult reconciliation between India and Pakistan have proved catastrophic. Ever since their nation's creation, Pakistanis have felt compelled to defend their nationhood and to constantly define and redefine their identity.

Pakistan's unfortunate history may justify the description of Pakistan as being 'insufficiently imagined', but imagination is by definition not a finite process. An entity that is insufficiently imagined can be reimagined.

Pakistan's economy is stagnant, its population is increasing rapidly and its institutions of state are too tied to a national ideology rooted in Islamist discourse to be able to address its multidimensional challenges. With terrorists trained in Pakistan showing up all over Europe and in places as far from one another as Mali and Indonesia, Pakistan's change of direction is now a global concern. International assistance, especially from the United States and some from China and Saudi Arabia, has brought Pakistan back from the brink in the past. But rising xenophobia and Islamo-nationalism—exhibited prominently after the discovery of Osama bin Laden in a Pakistani garrison town—coupled with Pakistan's policies in Afghanistan make continued US support for Pakistan difficult.

Although China remains supportive, it is likely to develop reservations about Pakistan's ideological direction because of concerns over the support for Uyghur jihadists by Pakistani ones. It is no longer easy for

Pakistan's military or civilian elite to create a semblance of stability with covert arrangements with the United States or with China.

If the influence of Islamists in Pakistan continues to rise, it would most likely be increasingly adversarial towards the US and the West. Islamist enthusiasm for creating an Islamic East Turkestan would not sit well with China. This would only increase Pakistan's isolation. In any case, Pakistan's direction as a nation cannot and should not be determined by the US, China and other outsiders; the principal actors in this process would have to be Pakistanis.

Dismissing the possibility of Pakistan ever falling under the rule of extremist Islamists—as some Pakistani scholars and leaders do—is also erroneous. Such 'it-can-never-happen' prognostication has proved wrong in the past and could prove wrong again. Writing in 1963, Ian Stephens had rejected 'any practical possibility' of Pakistan 'falling under the sway of the mullahs, influential and active though some of them such as Maulana Maududi are'. In his opinion, the power of theocrats had 'proven perceptibly less than in that other ideological state of the 1940s, which most progressives regard so much more amiably, Israel'.[64] We all know how wrong that assumption has turned out to be in subsequent years.

It is more realistic to acknowledge that the currently defined 'ideology of Pakistan' nurtures extremist Islamism and obstructs Pakistan's evolution as a normally functioning state. Pakistan's pursuit of strategic objectives disproportionate to its capacity has been inadvertently encouraged by its alliance with the United States and China. The first step in reimagining Pakistan would be to abandon the narrow ideological paradigm of Pakistani nationalism. If Pakistan is here to stay, its leaders must free its people of the burden of believing that it is constantly besieged and under threat.

Armed with nuclear weapons, Pakistan does not need to live in fear or insecurity. The state of insecurity fostered in Pakistan is psychological and should now be replaced with a logical self-confidence. Once pluralism and secularism are no longer dirty words, and all national discussions need not be framed within the confines of an Islamist ideology, it will become easier for Pakistan to tackle the jihadi menace. The state would have to end support for any militant jihadi group based on false strategic premises. Jihadi terrorism is now a threat to Pakistan and must be eliminated for Pakistan's sake.

The shift away from ideological nationalism to functional nationalism— 'We are Pakistanis because we were born in Pakistan' as opposed to 'We are Pakistanis because our forebears resolved to create an Islamic state'—will help change the milieu in which various Islamist extremist and jihadi groups recruit and operate in Pakistan. Once the state has resolved to end support to all jihadis and is reconciled to a pluralist Pakistan open to multiple visions for the country's future, extremists would have to contend for Pakistani hearts and minds rather than having a captive following generated by a national narrative taught in schools and promoted by the national media.

Pakistan must also overcome archaic notions of national security. Instead of viewing itself as a 'warrior nation' it could be a 'trading nation' that can take advantage of its location for economic purposes. Pakistan could easily be the trans-shipment route for goods and services between India, the Middle East and Central Asia. It could have oil and gas pipelines running through it, with attending benefits. India and Afghanistan would be major trading partners instead of being viewed as permanent enemies or strategic threats. High literacy, global connectivity, increased agricultural and industrial productivity and a prosperous citizenry would be the goals of the state in a reimagined Pakistan.

These objectives would replace Pan-Islamism, jihadism and pursuit of parity with India and strategic depth which have been Pakistan's unattained ambitions of its first seven decades. Only by reimagining itself can Pakistan find peace with itself and its neighbours and stop being viewed by the rest of the world as a troubled state, a failing state or a crisis state. Then, Pakistanis could take pride in a range of accomplishments instead of merely repeating how their resilience helped their country survive, while being seen by others as an 'international migraine'.

3

Ideological Dysfunction

IN APRIL 2017, A twenty-three-year-old journalism student was lynched by a mob at his university in Mardan, north-western Pakistan. 'Mashal Khan', said a report in the British newspaper *Guardian*, 'was known for questioning his peers and speaking out against injustice and corruption.' After a heated discussion one day, he 'was seized from his dorm room by a mob that stripped and beat him, then shot him dead'. Khan was accused of making offensive comments about Islam— 'a dangerous charge in a society where perceived disrespect for the religion can ignite violent anger'.[1]

Instead of focusing on the murder, the administration of the university chose first to launch an investigation into Khan's alleged blasphemy. The local cleric in Khan's hometown refused to lead his funeral prayers, saying he could not pray for a blasphemer.

Uproar by Pakistan's diminishing liberal and secular activists, coupled with fear of negative international attention, forced the university's provost to change course and attribute the blasphemy investigation to 'a clerical error'. Protests around the country and on social media resulted in arrests of some of those involved in the lynching. But once the protests died down, the dead young man's family faced threats to back off from seeking justice. Within two months of the lynching, Khan's father filed a petition in Pakistan's Supreme Court seeking the government's help in relocating his daughters and himself to the federal capital, Islamabad, due to security threats in the Khyber Pakhtunkhwa province and the family's hometown, Swabi.[2]

The case was just one of many instances of growing religious intolerance and violence in 'a country where blasphemy laws are often misused for revenge or personal gain'. It was the first blasphemy killing at a Pakistani university and the fact that Khan was 'by all accounts a respectful Muslim' helped garner sympathy for him. 'A lot of people can identify with him,' novelist Mohammed Hanif was quoted as saying at the time. 'He was an average college student. And the landscape of the university was familiar to many.'[3]

No one spoke out for a mentally unstable man beaten to death by thousands of people who burned his corpse after killing him in 2012, accusing him of desecrating the Quran. The mob in Ahmedpur East town of Punjab's Bahawalpur district had 'stormed a police station where the man was being interrogated' and ignored the police assessment about the victim's mental state. The victim had been arrested after residents said he threw pages of the Quran into the street, according to a media report at the time.[4]

'While the man was being questioned, some people started making announcements over mosque loudspeakers, urging residents to go to the police station and punish him,' said the report, adding that within hours, thousands gathered outside the police station and demanded that the man be handed over to them. They burned several police vehicles and wounded seven officers before grabbing the man and dragging him into the street, where he was beaten to death and his body set on fire.[5] No one was punished for orchestrating or participating in the lynching.

Since 1990, at least sixty-five people have been murdered in Pakistan over blasphemy allegations. Most have not received even the minimal compassion that Khan attracted because of his youth and the brutality of his killers that was witnessed by millions on videotape posted on the Internet. But the fact that those who did not participate in his murder recorded it on video with their cellphones instead of trying to save Khan's life was itself telling. Pakistan's view of itself as a 'citadel of Islam' has created an environment in which violence is normal provided it is committed in the name of Islam.

In high-profile killings of people accused of blasphemy, victims have been publicly demonized while the killers have been hailed as heroes. In 2011, Salmaan Taseer, the governor of Punjab criticized Pakistan's draconian blasphemy laws, describing them as 'man-made' and subject to change. He was assassinated by one of his own bodyguards after he voiced sympathy for Asia Bibi, a Christian mother of five sentenced to death for allegedly insulting Prophet Muhammad. Taseer's killer, Mumtaz Qadri, was described as a 'defender of the Prophet's honour' by clerics, and lawyers showered rose petals on him when he was brought to court for the first time for trial as a murderer.[6]

Public opinion was deemed heavily against Taseer and Bibi (who is still in prison) and such was the fear of vigilante violence that even President Asif Ali Zardari, a friend and ally of Taseer, did not attend Taseer's funeral 'out of concern for his own security'.[7] In a rare display of the writ of the state against an individual murdering a senior official for religious reasons, Qadri was convicted of murder. He was executed in 2016 after the Supreme Court upheld his conviction, and received a hero's burial.[8] Qadri's burial site, near Islamabad, has been converted into a shrine, built with millions of rupees in donations and receiving thousands of visitors coming to pay homage to a martyr.[9]

Instead of trying to calm down the religious fervour generated by extremist clerics, Pakistan's government and state institutions have tended through most of its history to exacerbate religious sentiment. Just before the Khan murder, officials had announced a clampdown on blasphemous material on social media, asking Facebook and Twitter to help it identify users so they could be prosecuted. By keeping blasphemy centre stage, the government stokes the fire that leads to actions by vigilantes, who are not always pious individuals acting on religious sentiment.

'Laboratory of Islam'

None of Pakistan's founding fathers probably desired or even anticipated the widespread violence in the name of religion that has now become associated with their country. But the current state of Pakistan is, in some ways, the culmination of the process of defining Pakistan through Islam that began soon after the country's creation. Some academics attribute Pakistan's troubles to its inception and the ambiguity about what it means to be a Pakistani. According to Chatham House scholar Farzana Shaikh, 'It is the country's problematic and contested relationship with Islam that has most decisively frustrated its quest for a coherent national identity and for stability as a nation state capable of absorbing the challenges of its rich and diverse society.'[10]

Pakistanis, including those with a modern outlook, do not like the country's history being discussed in the context of what psychologist Erik Erikson described as 'identity crisis'.[11] They often argue that 'liberals both in Britain and the US tend to be unsympathetic towards Pakistan because of their liberal bias against the idea of a religion being used as an ideology to create a state'.[12] Even if one rejects the notion of an identity crisis, extreme and violent manifestations of religious sentiment in Pakistan stem from the fear that Islam is under threat. Angry Islamists reject tolerance of others because they suspect such tolerance would dilute their religion. The fear of erosion of the Islamic way of life had rallied the subcontinent's Muslims to the cause of Pakistan; it shaped Pakistan's state ideology and now manifests itself in sectarian strife and fundamentalist demands.

The intimate relationship between Islam and Pakistani identity means that men of faith are portrayed as defenders of the country's ideology, making it difficult for the Pakistan government to act against those who act aggressively to protect the faith that defines the Pakistani state and nation. The extremists are seen, at worst, as misguided patriots and true believers whose enthusiasm must be harnessed for the greater good instead of being punished.

In their effort to create a new nation and state, Pakistan's founders had simultaneously offered two visions of Pakistani nationalism. The first was what one historian, Faisal Devji, defines as 'Muslim Zion'—a land where the Muslim minority dispersed across a vast subcontinent could escape the majority's persecution, which they rightly or wrongly feared.[13] The other vision for Pakistan is described by another historian, Venkat Dhulipala, as a 'New Medina'—'the harbinger of Islam's renewal and rise in the twentieth century, the new leader and protector of the global community of Muslims, and a worthy successor to the defunct Turkish Caliphate'.[14] The speeches and interviews of Jinnah and his lieutenants in the run up to Partition suggest that both visions were put forth, depending on the audience.

For instance, the Muslim League leader in the United Provinces (UP), Nawab Ismail Khan, had convened a conference of ulema and prominent

Muslim intellectuals to 'draft a blueprint for an Islamic Constitution' soon after the League's demand for separate Muslim states was first made in 1940. The politicians and scholars convened at the Nadwatul Ulema, a madrasa in Lucknow, and delegated the task of drafting a document on an Islamic constitution to Muhammad Ishaq Sandelvi, who produced a 300-page manuscript. That document was used by the ulema as their primary source for recommendations for Pakistan's Constituent Assembly after Independence.[15]

The Muslim League had enrolled the support of a faction of the traditional ulema for the 1945–46 election under the banner of Jamiat Ulema Islam or Society of Islamic Scholars. Maulana Shabbir Ahmad Usmani, a stalwart of the conservative Deoband madrasa, led this effort and gathered 5,000 clerics at a conference.[16] During the election campaign on behalf of the Muslim League, 'Usmani glorified Pakistan as the first Islamic state in history that would attempt to reconstruct the Islamic utopia created by the Prophet in Medina.' He used the names of Pakistan and Medina interchangeably 'to solidify their identification in the public mind' and often invoked 'powerful metaphors from early Islamic history'. Usmani asserted that Pakistan would be a place 'where Muslims could practise their religion with complete freedom, for it was only in such a land that the Muslim community could develop to its fullest potentiality'.[17]

In his book *The Punjab Bloodied, Partitioned and Cleansed,* Ishtiaq Ahmed details how Jinnah gave a free hand to Sunni clerics and mashaikh (heads of Sufi shrines) in Punjab to mobilize Muslim voters. The religious leaders promised that Pakistan would reflect 'Islam's idealized Islamic past'.[18] Punjab governor, Sir Bertrand Glancy, reported to the viceroy in September 1945: 'Muslim Leaguers are doing what they can in the way of propaganda conducted on fanatical lines; religious leaders and religious buildings are being used freely in several places for advocating Pakistan and vilifying any who hold opposite views.'[19]

In another report in December, he observed that 'Among Muslims, the Leaguers are increasing their efforts to appeal to the bigotry of the electors. Pirs and Maulvis have been enlisted in large numbers to tour the Province and denounce all who oppose the League as infidels. Copies of the Holy Quran are carried around as an emblem peculiar to the Muslim League. Firoz[20] [Sir Firoz Khan Noon] and others openly preach that every vote given to the League is a vote cast in favour of the Holy Prophet.'[21]

By February 1946, Glancy's complaints about the Muslim League's fanatical oratory in Punjab had become more strident. 'Maulvis and Pirs and students travel all around the Province and preach that those who fail to vote for the League candidates will cease to be Muslims; their marriages will no longer be valid and they will be entirely excommunicated.'[22]

Meanwhile, just as the ulema and mashaikh spoke of Pakistan in religious terms, Jinnah and Liaquat tried to play down the religious factor when necessary. Speaking in Quetta in October 1945, Jinnah mocked those who said they did not understand the idea of Pakistan. 'If you do not understand it, then what is it that you are opposing?' Then he went on to define Pakistan in terms that can best be described as Muslim nationalism, not a promise to create an Islamic theocracy. 'Pakistan means partition,' he said. 'Pakistan means division. It means you must take Hindu provinces of yours and leave out Muslim provinces where we want to establish our own government.'[23]

In a speech at the Aligarh Muslim University around the same time, Liaquat stressed that Pakistan meant 'the establishment of free, independent, democratic and sovereign states in those areas and zones in which the Muslims are in a majority'. He hoped that the boundaries of Pakistan would be 'the present provincial boundaries of the Punjab, NWFP, Balochistan and Sindh in the north-west and Bengal and Assam in the north-east'. Then he proceeded to respond to questions about Pakistan's future constitution. 'Pakistan will be a democratic state and its constitution will be framed by the people of those areas through a constituent assembly elected by them,' he declared, making no mention of Islam as the foundation of the new state.[24]

The contradictory assertions were later welcomed or criticized by the Muslim League's supporters depending on where they stood. The League's treasurer, the raja of Mahmudabad, appreciated Jinnah's 'statement that the government of Pakistan will be on democratic lines with state control over the key industries'. He expressed the 'hope that the constitution of Pakistan will be modelled on the latest, up to date experiences of the practical working of democracy rather than vague and indefinite slogans such as Hakumat-i-Ilahiyya [God's Rule], etc'.[25] But the lack of specificity about how Pakistan would be run, which helped garner support for the demand for Pakistan, also created confusion that has lasted throughout Pakistan's history.

After Independence, Jinnah attempted to set Pakistan's direction away from a theocracy by telling Pakistan's Constituent Assembly that he envisaged a Pakistan where, over time, 'these angularities of the majority and minority communities, the Hindu community and the Muslim community' would vanish. Ideally, 'In course of time Hindus would cease to be Hindus, and Muslims would cease to be Muslims, not in the religious sense, because that is the personal faith of each individual, but in the political sense as citizens of the State.'[26]

In this speech, Jinnah made a declaration that pointed in the direction of a secular envisioning of Pakistan. 'You are free,' he said, 'you are free to go to your temples, you are free to go to your mosques or to any other place of worship in this State of Pakistan. You may belong to any religion or caste or creed—that has nothing to do with the business of the State.'[27] But one speech was not enough to clarify the deliberate ambiguity that had characterized the campaign for Pakistan's creation in the preceding seven years. A few months after stating that religion has nothing to do with the business of state, Jinnah went on to describe Pakistan as 'this mighty land' that had 'been brought under a rule which is Islamic'.[28]

Conventional wisdom in Pakistan is that if Jinnah had lived on, he would have been able to define Pakistan's direction away from the confusion that followed. Jinnah's death in September 1948, less than thirteen months after Independence, left the country in the hands of politicians and British-era civil servants, none of whom had anywhere near Jinnah's stature. Instead of adopting the secular nationalism proposed in Jinnah's address to the Constituent Assembly, contending factions invoked religious arguments to advance political agendas. These arguments kept alive the pre-Partition passions and helped the ruling oligarchy in postponing the making of the constitution. Civilian leaders bargained for power behind the scenes, refusing to hold general elections. Once a Muslim officer took command of Pakistan's army in 1951, the army too became part of the elite that chose to define Pakistani nationalism in religious terms.

A major problem in Pakistan's early years related to the power equation between East and West Pakistan. The majority of the country's population resided in its eastern wing and democracy would have favoured Bengali politicians' ascent to power. Partition riots had reduced the population of non-Muslims in West Pakistan from 20 per cent to a nominal 3 per cent but Hindus still constituted 22 per cent of East Pakistan's population.

Prominent East Pakistani politicians, notably Suhrawardy, advocated secularism and demanded elections, confident of winning a majority of votes with the Hindu minority serving as a dependable vote bank. It was, therefore, in the interest of West Pakistani politicians to play the religion card. They postponed elections as long as they could, hoping to limit the influence of the Hindu vote in East Pakistan by insisting that Pakistan retain separate electorates and implement Islamic law.

Canadian academic Khalid Bin Sayeed conducted a survey during the early 1960s and found that West Pakistanis who thought Islam was an effective bond of unity for the new country constituted a far greater proportion of the total than East Pakistanis who held the same view. According to Sayeed, 87 per cent of West Pakistan's populace deemed Islam to be the glue that would keep Pakistan together while only 66.7 per cent of East Pakistanis thought the same. An overwhelming majority of East Pakistanis 'including students, teachers, civil servants, other professionals and housewives' told Sayeed that 'the Quran does not exercise much influence on their day-to-day activities but they have deep reverence for the Quran as a sacred book'.[29]

Thus, the exigencies of maintaining the West Pakistani political, bureaucratic and military elite in power were the major reason why, after Jinnah's death, the secular Muslim nationalist path was hurriedly abandoned. The first formal step towards transforming Pakistan into an Islamic ideological state was taken in March 1949 when Liaquat, as prime minister, presented the 'Objectives Resolution' in the Constituent

Assembly. The resolution laid out the main principles of a future Pakistani constitution. It provided for democracy, freedom, equality and social justice 'as enunciated by Islam', opening the door for future controversies about what Islam required of a state.

Objectives of State

The 'Objectives Resolution' was a curious mix of theology and political science. It insisted that 'sovereignty over the entire universe belongs to Allah Almighty alone' and asserted the view that the state of Pakistan had been delegated authority by God, which could only be 'exercised within the limits prescribed by Him' as a sacred trust. The state 'shall exercise its powers and authority through the chosen representatives of the people'; it would observe 'the principles of democracy, freedom, equality, tolerance and social justice, as enunciated by Islam'; and its objective would be to enable Muslims 'to order their lives in the individual and collective spheres in accordance with the teachings and requirements of Islam as set out in the Holy Quran and the Sunna.'[30]

Non-Muslim opposition members and a solitary Muslim parliamentarian, expressed serious qualms about committing the new state to 'ordering their lives in accordance with the teachings and requirements of Islam'. But Liaquat described it as 'the most important occasion in the life of this country, next in importance only to the achievement of independence'.[31] In one way, it was. After the 'Objectives Resolution' there was no turning back from Pakistan's status as an Islamic ideological state.

Soon the Constituent Assembly was discussing proposals for official collection of Zakat—the Islamic obligation of alms giving. Some members argued that Zakat was a substitute for income tax and once Zakat collection begins, income tax should cease to be collected. Islamic arguments were invoked both for and against land reforms. Demands for Islamic education followed. Ishtiaq Hussain Qureshi, an academic who served as a deputy minister in Liaquat's cabinet, assured the members of the Constituent Assembly that the country would have 'some kind of organization for the purpose of collection of zakat, which as all of us know is incumbent upon every Muslim to pay'.

Qureshi also agreed with the need for an 'organization to conduct research into Islamic learning' and 'institutions which may tell Muslims what exactly they should understand by Islam'.[32] Browsing through the record of the Constituent Assembly debates, one finds gems like one member suggesting, 'Nonpayment of Zakat is a sin according to religion but I think steps should be taken henceforth to make nonpayment of Zakat as an offence too.'[33] Another called for arrangements by the state to facilitate 'the five times' prayers and fasting' and warned that 'non-Muslims always take advantage of our goodness' and asked that the state 'be very cautious of them'.[34]

Outside the Assembly, the education minister was busy supporting an educational system based on Islamic ideology. The Punjab University set up a Department of Islamiat (Islamic Studies) and undertook the preparation of an Encyclopedia of Islam. The Peshawar University set up a Department of Islamic Theology, following the Dhaka University, which already had a Department of Islamic Studies. Unable to promise new universities due to paucity of resources, the education ministry could only publicize its keenness in improving 'facilities for the teaching of Islamic subjects' and adding Islamiat to the curriculum at the university stage. The government reported with pride that Radio Pakistan was regularly broadcasting a large number of talks on Islam.[35]

Liaquat had described Pakistan as a test centre for Islamic principles in the contemporary world. The Objectives Resolution, he said, would provide Muslims 'the opportunity that they have been seeking, throughout these long decades of decadence and subjection, of finding freedom to set up a polity, which may prove to be a laboratory for the purpose of demonstrating to the world that Islam is not only a progressive force in the world, but it also provides remedies for many of the ills from which humanity has been suffering.'[36]

Over the years, several experiments have been attempted in the laboratory, some abandoned soon after being started. One such experiment related to promotion of the Arabic language as a means of reorienting the country away from its Indian connection and towards the

Middle East. It was a response to the demand of East Pakistan's Bengalis that their language, Bangla, be designated a national language alongside Urdu. The suggestion to adopt Arabic—the language of the Quran—as the national language, was officially encouraged without regard to the fact that only a handful of Pakistanis knew the language and virtually no one spoke it at home as their mother tongue. Another proposal was to change the script of the Bengali language from its Sanskrit base to an Arabic-Persian one.[37]

The semi-official newspaper, *Dawn,* reported on a reception in Karachi in April 1948, where Sheikh Saleh Ashmawy, personal envoy of the Grand Mufti of Palestine, called upon Pakistanis to 'Rally round Islam, rally round the Quran, rally round Mecca, and rally round Arabic'. He and other speakers called for 'establishment of Islamic States under the Quranic construction' and warned against the Muslim world being 'ground to atoms by surrounding alien forces'. Sheikh Ashmawy advised Pakistanis to give up the English language, make Urdu the state language and adopt Arabic as the second language.[38]

The president of the Muslim League, Chaudhry Khaliq-uz-Zaman announced in 1949 that Pakistan would bring all Muslim countries together into Islamistan—a pan-Islamic entity.[39] The Pakistani government also convened a World Muslim Conference in Karachi the same year, to promote Pan-Islamism.[40] This conference led to the formation of the Motamar al-Alam al-Islami (Muslim World Congress), which played a crucial role in encouraging the sense of Muslim victimhood that has been at the heart of the global Islamist movement. Towards the end of 1949, the Pakistani government reached out to the governments of other Muslim countries about forming an Islamic conference. Only Egypt, then still a monarchy with close ties to Britain, and Saudi Arabia showed any interest.[41] Other early experiments also included attempts to create 'a system of collective bargaining and collective security' for Muslim nations.

The state's pan-Islamist orientation attracted Islamists from across the world to Pakistan. Controversial figures, such as the pro-Nazi former Grand Mufti of Palestine, Al-Haj Amin al-Husseini, and leaders of Islamist political movements like the Arab Muslim Brotherhood became frequent visitors to Karachi. Prominent convert to Islam,

Muhammad Asad, who was born in Austria-Hungary as Leopold Weiss was appointed as head of a 'Department for Islamic Reconstruction' and subsequently sent to the United Nations as deputy permanent representative without being naturalized as a Pakistani citizen. Asad had written and spoken about the revival of an Islamic state and that was his principal qualification for being seen as an ideologue for Pakistan despite his European origins.

Asad played an important part in describing Islam as Pakistan's 'raison d'être'—a French term that was not part of the lexicon of the subcontinent's Muslim politicians. In October 1947, Asad had said in a lecture on Radio Pakistan that the purpose of Pakistan was 'to help the community to coordinate its spiritual and intellectual resources' and to 're-create the Islamic atmosphere so necessary for a revival of Islamic life in its practical aspects'. After joining the Foreign Service, he wrote a policy memorandum that said: 'Pakistan had been established on a purely ideological basis—non-nationalist, non-racial groupment [sic] of peoples bound together solely by their adherence to a common religious and cultural ideal.' Asad advocated 'a dynamic policy with a view to the Muslim world as a whole' and warned that not doing so would cause Pakistan to 'lose its ideological coherence and thus, in time, its raison d'être'.[42]

Asad further argued that ignoring the Islamic ideology 'placed us at so great a disadvantage vis-à-vis our main adversary, India, and had brought about, among other things, the loss of Kashmir'. He proposed a two-pronged foreign policy. On the one hand Pakistan 'should immediately set about to work, in cooperation with the Arab states, for the creation of something like a League of Muslim Nations'; on the other hand, it should aim 'with all our strength at expanding our influence over all of the Persian Gulf, which was politically as well as economically our pre-destined life-line.'

Ironically, the ideas of Asad, the scholarly European convert to Islam, had greater influence on Pakistan's orientation than many public figures belonging to the geographic region that constituted Pakistan. But he was not the only exponent of how to run an Islamic state. Various scholars and clerics vied with one another to outline Pakistan's future on the basis of Islam's past. Different heads of state and government adopted different scholars as their religious guides at different times. Some, like Syed Abul Ala Maududi, founder of the Jamaat-e-Islami (Islamic Party) presented their case for an Islamic state to the public and wielded great intellectual influence without joining the government.

The Jamaat-e-Islami (JI) was the South Asian analogue of the Arab Muslim Brotherhood. Established in 1941, it had stayed out of the political fray before Partition. Maududi had criticized the Muslim League and its goal of Pakistan, saying a westernized elite could not be trusted to create an Islamic state. After Independence, however, the Jamaat changed its approach, embraced the idea of Pakistan and called the Muslim League's bluff by demanding that it create the Islamic state it promised while seeking votes in 1945-46. As Leonard Binder points out, 'Maududi now described the Islamic state and told the politicians how to bring it into being.'[43]

Maududi reminded Pakistan's leaders that Islam was not just a faith but an ideology and that Islam was a way of life and about political power. He saw Islam as the only alternative to materialist ideologies, like capitalism and communism. He sought to establish sovereignty of God and believed that the 'Country belongs to God, rule by God's law and rule by pious people.' Maududi also put forth the concept of 'theo-democracy', which meant a theologically circumscribed democracy where the law of God was implemented by the people's representatives—something akin to what Ayatollah Khomeini established through 'Vilayat-e-Faqih' (Governance of the Jurist).

By the time of his death in 1979, Maududi had become a major ideological influence in Pakistan and the Jamaat-e-Islami was embedded in Pakistan's ideological establishment with support from military rulers Gen. Yahya Khan (1969–71) and Gen. Zia-ul-Haq (1977–88).

Although Liaquat, the mover of the Objectives Resolution, was assassinated in 1951 and Asad, the European-origin ideologue of the Islamic state, left the Government of Pakistan a year later, the concept of Pakistan as a laboratory for Islam's political revival was firmly entrenched by the time of their leaving the scene. In the decades since then, Pakistan has gone on to try and define by law who is or is not a Muslim, adopted (and abandoned) interest-free banking, considered segregation of the sexes in public, and endeavoured to implement sharia. The quality of education in Pakistan has declined as a result of attempts to comply with clerical demands.

The number of clerics has also increased exponentially. At Independence in 1947, there were only 137 madrasas (Islamic seminaries) in Pakistan. Nine years later, a 1956 survey reported that the number of madrasas had increased to 244 in West Pakistan.[44] By 1995, the ministry of education estimated the figure at 3,906, which increased to 7,000 in 2000 and 35,000 by 2016.

'Around 26,000 madrasas are registered in Pakistan with a religious umbrella organization called Ittehad-e-Tanzeemat-e-Madaris,' reported the *Washington Times*. 'Experts believe around 9,000 unregistered madrassas operate in the South Asian country too.'[45] Under Gen. Zia-ul-Haq's Islamizing dictatorship, madrasas became 'supply lines for jihad' in the anti-Soviet war in Afghanistan.[46]

Since those educated in madrasas are unsuited for occupations other than as mullahs, they have an incentive to build more mosques with attached madrasas to provide them a living. Madrasa education 'creates barriers to modern knowledge, stifling creativity and breeding bigotry', asserts one analysis of the phenomenon. 'It is this foundation on which fundamentalism—militant or otherwise—is built.'[47]

Pakistan's founding generation were primarily Western-educated, and even the religious ulema of the time were known for erudition. That has changed over the years with each major sect spawning a religio-political party, recruiting new members from madrasas, and generating sectarian strife to increase their political clout. Clerical leaders sometimes create controversies that seem ludicrous in this day and age but for their followers these become the most important and urgent question. Modern educated individuals with a religious bent also join the polemic.

Among the many instances of the absurdity of some of the experimentation with Islamization was the recommendation in 1980 by a leading nuclear scientist that 'djinns [or genies], being fiery creatures, ought to be tapped as a free source of energy'. He expected Pakistan's energy problems to be finally solved by this means. Dr Bashiruddin Mahmood noted that King Solomon—a Biblical figure also mentioned in the Quran—had harnessed energy from djinns. 'I think that if we develop our souls we can develop communications with them,' he explained.[48]

No one has, of course, been able to build djinn engines. But the emphasis on Islam in Pakistani life has created a situation where influential figures such as Mahmood continue to be viewed as serious scientists after embracing an alternative reality not upheld by science.

Islamic Enterprise, Secular Management

For its first twenty-five years, Pakistan was an Islamic enterprise run by secular management. Most Muslim League leaders were western-educated individuals with a secular outlook on life as were Pakistan's first batch of civil servants and generals. But they chose, for political reasons, not to support the strict separation between religion and politics. Pakistan's establishment hoped 'to relegate Islam to the sphere of policy rather than law' while rhetorically describing the country as an 'Islamic State'.[49]

Liaquat was the first and 'most indefatigable exponent' of this approach. He explained to the nation even before the Objectives Resolution that an Islamic society was one with 'no inner conflicts, where a man gets just reward for his toil and where there are no parasites'. According to him, 'The foremost duty of a government based upon Islamic principles was to end all "exploitation".'[50] After the resolution was passed he dispelled 'the notion that Pakistan would be a theocratic state wherein the "ulema" would reign supreme'. Liaquat stressed the equality of all citizens—Muslims and non-Muslims alike—and spoke of Islamic socialism.[51]

'What he meant by this is not quite clear, for it was used more or less as a slogan', Binder notes, adding, 'At times it seemed to mean something a bit different from the usual notions of either Islam or socialism, as when he asserted that he believed in "no other 'ism' except Islamic Socialism".'[52] The government's economic policy was simply outlined in religious terms. 'A distinctive economic system was found to be the product of the Islamic laws on alms-giving, inheritance, the denial of usury and the protection of the rights of private property. That the Islamic state was responsible for the material welfare of all its citizens was derived from the pension scheme of Umar I in seventh-century Arabia. The resultant which Liaquat called Islamic socialism was no more than capitalism plus social security plus God.'[53]

'Unctuous references to Islam became the order of the day in discussions of industrial development,' Binder states, while describing Pakistan's earliest years in his 1961 book. It was almost as if Pakistan's leaders were hoping 'that the general aim of the material welfare of the "common man" would overshadow the religious injunction against the giving or taking of interest'. Thus, to Pakistan's founding generation, Islamic economics was a buzzword, and they did not intend to introduce 'anything like forced saving and state capitalism, or even the abolition of banks'.[54]

The Islamic grandiloquence of Pakistan's founders, however, could not remain just that. Liaquat and his successors tended to see no contradiction between British parliamentary democracy and Islam but others started a debate on what a true Islamic political system might be. The ulema insisted that sharia law as handed down over time must be the only law in an Islamic state. Some modernists proffered the theory that the Islamic concept of 'Ijma' (consensus) could be extended in modern times to legislation through parliament, expecting that this would avoid disrupting administrative and political institutions inherited from the British Raj.

Professor Ishtiaq Hussain Qureshi, a deputy minister, told a political science conference at Lahore in March 1950 that the important task before those making the constitution was to adjust the eternal principles of Islam to the needs of the modern age.[55] He explained that Islam was not a system of rigid laws; it 'requires a new interpretation at every stage of our development'.[56] But that led to the question, 'How far can we go in discarding precedents without injuring principles?'[57]

At the same conference, Tamizuddin Khan, the president of the Constituent Assembly, spoke against closing 'the gate of Ijtihad'—the ninth-century Sunni consensus that major religious questions had been answered and there was no further need to exercise personal reasoning in religious matters. He relied on the poet-philosopher Muhammad Iqbal as his authority. Justice S.A. Rahman of the Federal Court insisted that Islam's eternal principles left 'a very wide field for evolutionary progress in the political and social spheres. The time has now arrived when the power of Ijtihad should be removed from the representatives of the schools to a Muslim Legislative Assembly.' [58]

Meanwhile, the clerics and Islamists also remained active in continuing to push for a version of Islamic law that put them centre stage in its implementation. In addition to Maududi and the Jamaat-e-Islami, clerics of the Sunni Deobandi school also sought a role in making Pakistan an Islamic state. Most Deobandi clerics had opposed Jinnah and the Muslim League, fearing that the partition of India would only weaken and divide its widely dispersed Muslim population. But the Jamiat Ulema Islam had supported the Muslim League, and its leader Maulana Usmani had been elected to Pakistan's Constituent Assembly. He arrived in Karachi in December 1947 with the intention of holding Pakistan's leaders to their promise of making Pakistan an Islamic state.

According to a report published in *Dawn* on 1 January 1948, Usmani had set up an office in the home of Maulana Ehtisham-ul-Haq Thanvi and, within days, that house 'became a centre for the continuous comings and goings of the Karachi "ulema", and their supporters.' The Jamiat Ulema Islam passed a resolution 'demanding that the government appoint a leading alim [religious scholar] to the office of Shaikh al-Islam, with appropriate ministerial and executive powers over the qazis [Islamic judges] throughout the country'. Plans were also announced 'to organize public opinion throughout the country in "favour of a purely Islamic Constitution for Pakistan"'. The ulema also worked out 'a complete table of organization of a ministry of ecclesiastical affairs' with suggested names for every position. They proposed that 'this ministry be immune to ordinary changes of government'.[59]

Liaquat and others at the helm of affairs in Pakistan's earliest years were not religious men. The country's secular elite had decided to declare

Pakistan an Islamic state because it realized that Pakistanis had multiple identities and religion might be an easier tool in creating a Pakistani identity. The experience of language riots on behalf of Bengali in East Pakistan had pointed out the difficulty of subsuming ethnic identities into a new Pakistani identity. If being Pakistani could be made synonymous with being Muslim, a Pakistani Muslim nation might be forged with less difficulty.

Creating an ideological state was not as easy as it seemed. Islam meant different things to different people and Pakistan's ideological evolution could not be left to clerics or even to the will of the people. Institutions of state had to control the process of building the new nation; ensuring the supremacy of these state institutions required greater centralization of authority. The secular elite, beginning with Liaquat, assumed that they would continue to lead the country while rallying the people on the basis of Islamic ideology. Thus, theologians and Islamist activists were to be used as allies but not empowered so much that they would start writing laws or running government departments.

If the Objectives Resolution was the secular elite's attempt at paying lip service to Islam without a push back from the Islamists for a greater share in power, they did not fully succeed. Moreover, if the Muslim League and its various leaders could invoke religious arguments for political ends, so could the Islamists. There was also the potential for secular competitors for power to enrol the help of clerics and religious agitators to put opponents on the defensive. Politicians and even civil servants and generals could now plot against each other by orchestrating attacks on a rival for being 'un-Islamic' and, therefore, unsuited to serve in whatever position the plotter coveted for himself or his allies.

A major manifestation of the pitfalls of religion-based politics came in January 1953, when clerics of various Muslim denominations demanded that the Ahmadi sect be declared non-Muslim for legal purposes. Widespread riots soon followed, resulting in dozens of deaths and considerable loss to property. Reflecting what has been a consistent pattern in Pakistan's history, the religious demand also had a worldly purpose. Punjabi politicians had instigated the clerics in the hope of dislodging the government of Bengali prime minister, Khawaja Nazimuddin, who had taken office after Liaquat's assassination two years earlier.[60]

Nazimuddin turned down an ultimatum from the ulema to declare members of the Ahmadi sect as a non-Muslim minority and to dismiss Foreign Minister Chaudhri Zafrullah Khan, who was an Ahmadi. The ulema also demanded that other Ahmadis occupying key posts in the state must also be removed from their offices. Punjab chief minister Mumtaz Daulatana had activated the protestors in the hope of bringing down the federal government and becoming prime minister. But once the riots began in March, the violence could not be calibrated. By April, the military had to be called in to restore order and martial law was enforced in Lahore, lasting for over a month.[61]

The argument against the Ahmadis, who follow the nineteenth century religious leader Mirza Ghulam Ahmad as 'messiah' or 'prophet' and consider themselves Muslims, was that the sect's core beliefs are not in accordance with the fundamentals of Islam. In effect, the anti-Ahmadi riots represented the demand that the state define who is a Muslim for legal purposes because the Islamic state must distinguish between its Muslim and non-Muslim subjects.

Nazimuddin was an orthodox Sunni and was one of the few Muslim League leaders at the time known for their religious piety. But he felt he could not arrogate to himself, or anyone else in the machinery of government, the right to pronounce judgement on the faith of anyone who considered himself a Muslim. Various Islamic sects oppose each other because of differences over fine points of theology and if the state got involved in declaring one sect non-Muslim for legal purposes, the process would not stop with the Ahmadis but could go on until only one official sect was lawful.

Nazimuddin's decision to refuse the ulema's demands had wide support at the time across the government and Pakistani society. The Ahmadi issue was limited to Punjab as that is where the sect had its principal following. Non-Punjabi politicians did not associate themselves with the clerics or the Punjabi politicians supporting them. Pakistan's secular leadership succeeded in pushing back a religious demand and the army enforced order, putting the Islamists and their rioting followers in their place.

Still, the events of that year highlighted three inter-linked problems that have dogged Pakistan's internal politics since Independence: part of the state apparatus used religion and religious groups for a political purpose; the extent of the religious groups' influence and the sentiment unleashed by them could not be fully controlled; and the military stepped in to deal with the symptoms of the chaos generated by religious-political agitation, without any effort to deal with its causes.

At the time, the government set up a commission of inquiry, headed by the chief justice of the Lahore High Court, Muhammad Munir (who went on to become Chief Justice of Pakistan), to look into the causes of the anti-Ahmadi disturbances. In 117 sittings, the commission examined 3,600 pages of written statements and 2,700 pages of evidence. It went through 399 documents; 'a large number of books, pamphlets, journals and newspapers'; and 'a large number of letters, each extending to several pages and a few to even more than a hundred pages, were received, each of which has been carefully perused by us'.[62]

Its conclusion was that heeding the demands of the theologians in matters of state was a slippery slope and that Pakistan would do well to avoid it.

The 387-page report of the Munir Commission reflects the thinking of Pakistan's ruling elite in the country's early years. The report scrutinized 'with the assistance of the ulema' their 'conception of an Islamic State and its implications' and declared, 'No one who has given serious thought to the introduction of a religious State in Pakistan has failed to notice the tremendous difficulties with which any such scheme must be confronted.'[63]

'The Quaid-i-Azam said that the new State would be a modern democratic State,' it continued, adding that Jinnah's concept of Pakistan required that sovereignty must be vested in the people and 'the members of the new nation' should have 'equal rights of citizenship regardless of their religion, caste or creed'. The Munir Commission cited Jinnah's speech of 11 August 1947 to the Constituent Assembly of Pakistan to argue that Pakistan's founder clearly wanted religion 'to have nothing to do with the business of the State' and serve only as 'a matter of personal faith for the individual'.

The most important statement of the Commission, however, related to the differences among the clerics, which would divide Pakistanis more than religion could unite them. 'The ulema were divided in their opinions when they were asked to cite some precedent of an Islamic State in Muslim history,' Justice Munir reported, pointing out that 'no two learned divines are agreed' even on the fundamental definition of who is a Muslim.

'If we attempt our own definition as each learned divine has done and that definition differs from that given by all others, we unanimously go out of the fold of Islam,' Munir noted. 'And if we adopt the definition given by any one of the ulema, we remain Muslims according to the view of that alim but kafirs according to the definition of everyone else.'[64]

The Munir Commission said in its report that it 'dwelt at some length on the subject of Islamic State' to point out 'the numerous possibilities' of 'ideological confusion' that had 'contributed to the spread and intensity of the disturbances' of 1953. According to the Commission's report, 'That such confusion did exist is obvious because otherwise Muslim Leaguers, whose own Government was in office, would not have risen against it; sense of loyalty and public duty would not have departed from public officials who went about like maniacs howling against their own Government and officers; respect for property and human life would not have disappeared in the common man who with no scruple or compunction began freely to indulge in loot, arson and murder; politicians would not have shirked facing the men who had installed them in their offices; and administrators would not have felt hesitant or diffident in performing what was their obvious duty.'

In Justice Munir's words, the anti-Ahmadi riots demonstrated that if 'you can persuade the masses to believe that something they are asked to do is religiously right or enjoined by religion, you can set them to any course of action, regardless of all considerations of discipline, loyalty, decency, morality or civic sense'. Munir warned that Pakistan was 'being taken by the common man' as an Islamic State. In his view, this belief had been encouraged 'by the ceaseless clamour for Islam and Islamic State that is being heard from all quarters since the establishment of

Pakistan'. In words that were not heeded, the chief justice cautioned against letting the 'phantom of an Islamic State' haunt the new country.[65]

Regimented Islamic Nationalism

Notwithstanding Munir's warnings against the 'ceaseless clamour for Islam and Islamic State', religious exhortations continued to consume the nation's energies. But religious arguments were only one reason why Pakistan's leaders could not agree on a constitution until 1956. The West Pakistani elite did not want to cede much power to the East Pakistanis and, avoiding elections, stuck to behind-the-scenes deal making and palace intrigues.

After the failed 1953 onslaught over the Ahmadi issue, political Islamists and traditional clerics did not mount a major challenge to the westernized politicians and administrators for a few years. Pakistan functioned without major changes to the British administrative framework, and Pakistan's alliance with the United States ensured flow of aid and investment. By 1957, army chief, Gen. Ayub Khan, had become a significant actor in political machinations and in October 1958, a few months before the country's first scheduled national elections, he decided to assume absolute power through a military coup.

Ayub Khan saw himself as Pakistan's saviour. In addition to maintaining a strong defence and developing the economy, he also wanted to forge a nation above 'smaller provincial loyalties'. He wanted to clarify Pakistani nationalism, which he recognized 'was based more on an idea than on any territorial definition'.[66] As a soldier, Ayub was trained for regimentation and discipline. Being an army man, he considered the army, not the politicians or religious scholars, as best suited to fashion Pakistan's future. After all, the army was the most organized and uncorrupted institution in the country and Ayub's strategy of close alignment with the West would ensure the flow of resources for the country's industrialization and economic growth.

Ayub's close companion and his secretary for information, Altaf Gauhar, revealed several years after his death that soon after taking power, Ayub had written a paper in 1959 on the 'Islamic Ideology in Pakistan', which was circulated to army officers among others.[67]

Ayub explained his views about ideology in his autobiography, *Friends, Not Masters*. In his view, man's 'greatest yearning is for an ideology for which he should be able to lay down his life'. An ideology made lives 'much richer, more creative' and provided 'tremendous power of cohesion and resistance'. According to Ayub, a society organized on the basis of ideology 'can conceivably be bent but never broken'. Pakistan's obvious ideology was Islam but after Independence, 'we failed to define that ideology in a simple and understandable form'. Considering 'Islamic ideology as synonymous with bigotry and theocracy' reflected ignorance. 'The time has now come', Ayub wrote, to 'define this ideology in simple but modern terms and put it to the people, so that they can use it as a code of guidance'.[68]

Being a straightforward soldier who had spent more time in the British Indian Army than the Pakistani one, Ayub did not have time for elaborate theories of the Islamic state. He simply wanted to do what he perceived was good for the state he now led and declare it as Islamic. Ayub also did not think highly of the ulema and spoke of their conflict with 'the educated classes'. He wanted to rise above the intricate and mutually contradictory versions of religion offered by theologians and clearly opposed their role in governance.

Ayub proceeded to define and outline the issues of a simplified 'Islamic ideology' and created the institutional structure for drilling it into the minds of Pakistanis at all levels. After Jinnah and Liaquat, Ayub had the most national visibility of any leader in Pakistan in his time. He had served as army chief since 1951 and ran the country as president and absolute dictator from October 1958 to March 1969. Even after he was forced to relinquish power amid widespread protests in East and West Pakistan, Ayub's version of Islamo-nationalism remains the dominant creed within Pakistan's armed forces.

Ayub wondered how he might be able to 'weld' the people of Pakistan, 'a collection of so many races with different backgrounds', into 'a unified whole whilst keeping intact their local pride, culture, and traditions'.[69] In his view it was true that 'national territorialism' had no place in an Islamic society. But he reconciled Pan-Islamism with nationalism by arguing that 'those living in an area are responsible for its defence and security and development. Attachment to the country we live in and get our sustenance from is therefore paramount.'[70] Thus, it was okay for Pakistan's various ethnic groups to retain their culture but they could not consider themselves separate nationalities as Pakistan was now the country that should have their loyalty.

Ayub wanted the state to exercise the function of religious interpretation and wanted an Islamic ideology that would help him in the 'defence and security and development' of Pakistan. He saw Islam as a nation-building tool, controlled by an enlightened military leader rather than by clerics. His vision was shared by most of his fellow military officers even though the younger officers had started reading Maududi and other theoreticians of the Islamic state and even started developing close relations with religious scholars.

Ayub's prescription for national consolidation was to combine Islamic ideology and economic development. He thought his charisma, sincerity and absolute power would suffice to overcome the deficiencies that had characterized the politicians' efforts in building an ideological state during Pakistan's first decade. For all his pragmatism and modernist orientation, Ayub was not willing to embrace Suhrawardy's challenge to the concept of Pakistan as an ideological state.

The emphasis on ideology, Suhrawardy had argued, 'would keep alive within Pakistan the divisive communal emotions by which the subcontinent was riven before the achievement of independence'.[71] Suhrawardy argued in favour of seeing 'Pakistan in terms of a nation state' wherein a 'durable identity between government and people derived from the operation of consent'.[72] Suhrawardy supported a pro-Western foreign policy and saw little gain for Pakistan in impractical visions of pan-Islamism.[73] He felt, however, that the government should explain the rationale of Pakistan's external relations to the people and secure their support for its alliances abroad instead of operating secretly.

When Ayub introduced the 1962 Constitution that provided for a presidential system with indirect elections for president, its initial version deleted 'Islamic' from Pakistan's official name and used the term 'Republic of Pakistan'. He later restored the original designation 'Islamic Republic of Pakistan' and attempted to reconcile his modernizing vision with a firm commitment to Islamic ideology. Under Ayub's command, the Pakistan Army put its weight behind the notion of an ideological state.

The success of Ayub's policy of close ties with the United States and Pakistan's economic development under his rule impressed many observers at the time. Ayub was praised as a reformer and a visionary, a genuinely enlightened dictator. Pakistan's economy grew significantly during his decade in power and the country also survived an ill-conceived war with India in 1965.

Ayub tried to take the monopoly over interpreting Islam away from the traditional clerics by creating the Central Institute for Islamic Research headed by modernist scholar Fazlur Rahman. Instead of limiting his knowledge of Islam to the limited curriculum of a traditional madrasa, Rahman had gone on to study Islam at Oxford University. He taught Islamic Studies at Canada's McGill University before returning to Pakistan at Ayub's invitation and his scholarship focused on explaining Islam as a dynamic religion, which could adjust its injunctions to different times. The ulema and Maududi's Jamaat-e-Islami, however, opposed Rahman's views, such as his suggestion that Islam forbade extreme usury but not reasonable interest as charged by modern banks.

Rahman was eventually forced to resign once street protests grew in Ayub's last year in power. The ulema were also able to frustrate Ayub's effort to let the government's meteorological department determine the appearance of the new moon marking the beginning of an Islamic month. Clerics liked the privilege of sitting on a Ruet-e-Hilal (Sighting of the Moon) Committee and cherished the attention they received while announcing sighting of the moon on occasion of major Islamic festivals. On more than one occasion, separate days for beginning or end of Ramadan were announced by the government and the ulema. Although the government officials had better 'astronomical knowledge and instruments for precise observation',[74] the ulema insisted that Islam required observation of the moon by pious Muslims and only the clerics fulfilled that criterion.

Islamists also pushed back on Ayub's efforts at controlling what he saw as the 'menace of over-population' through a comprehensive family planning programme. 'I cannot believe that any religion can object to population control', Ayub declared, adding that 'no good religion can object to anything aimed at the betterment of human lot, because all religions, after all, come for the good of the human race and human beings do not come into the world for the religions.'[75] But once Ayub's hold over power was weakened, mullahs railed against family planning and birth control as conspiracies of unbelievers aimed at keeping down the number of Muslims.

After Ayub, no Pakistani ruler pursued population control as a major national imperative though less publicized family planning projects have remained operational. The Islamic state could not officially promote birth control, though it could look the other way if individual believers sought to practise it. Ayub's changes to the Muslim family law, regulating the practice of polygamy and unilateral divorce by men, were also watered down by the ulema, who insisted on retaining traditional norms of marriage and divorce.

While his endeavours to disseminate modernist interpretations of Islam generally failed, Ayub succeeded in popularizing Islamic ideology as the country's binding force. He succeeded in this realm through consolidation of state control over education and the media, which were a significant part of Ayub's reforms. The study of Islam or 'Islamiat', which had been talked about since Pakistan's earliest days, began receiving considerable emphasis.[76] The study of history, geography and civics at primary and secondary school levels was collapsed into a single subject called 'Social Studies'. Curricula and textbooks were standardized, presenting a version of history that linked Pakistan's emergence to Islam's arrival in the subcontinent instead of it being the outcome of a dispute over the constitution of post-colonial India.

The history of Islam was presented, not as the history of a religion or civilization, but as a prelude to Pakistan's creation.

The textbooks in Ayub's era glorified Muslim conquerors, painted Hindu–Muslim relations as intrinsically hostile and questioned the ability of Pakistanis to manage democratic rule. Ayub also created a Ministry of Information and a Bureau of National Reconstruction, which ensured that a message similar to the one taught at schools was available to everyone else through radio, television, films, magazines, books and newspapers.

Ayub may not have liked clerics and religious–political leaders but he agreed with their characterization of India as a Hindu state and that of Hindus as irreconcilable enemies of Islam and Muslims. 'It was Brahmin chauvinism and arrogance that had forced us to seek a homeland of our own where we could order our life according to our own thinking and faith,' he wrote.[77] He saw India, not as a neighbour with whom Pakistan had some disputes, but as an eternal enemy with 'expansionist designs'. He spoke of a 'fundamental opposition between the ideologies of India and Pakistan'[78] and claimed that 'India particularly has a deep pathological hatred for Muslims and her hostility to Pakistan stems from her refusal to see a Muslim power developing next door.'[79]

Dismemberment

By the time Ayub stepped down and transferred power to the army chief, Gen. Yahya Khan, estrangement between East and West Pakistan had heightened. Bengalis felt that Ayub had built up the western wing's economy at the expense of East Pakistan's prosperity. There was resentment against West Pakistani dominance and a desire to alter the power equation within Pakistan. Yahya's regime lasted only two years, from March 1969 to December 1971, but its impact is felt to this day.

Pakistan lost its eastern wing after a series of events that began with Pakistan's first general election on the basis of universal adult franchise, which was held in December 1970. Yahya expected that a free and fair election would yield a hung parliament, with several political parties vying for power. Several of his ministers and officials divided their support among three factions of the Muslim League and three Islamist parties in a campaign that was painted in the media as a battle between supporters of godless ideologies and the defenders of Islamic values. In the end, however, the election results defied the military regime's expectations.

The avowedly secular Awami League, founded by Suhrawardy and now led by the popular Bengali leader Shaikh Mujibur Rahman, won a majority by sweeping the polls in East Pakistan. It won more than 72 per cent of East Pakistan's popular vote and ended up with 160 seats out of 300 contested seats; its uncontested success on seven seats reserved for women gave it a total of 167 seats in the 313-member National Assembly, an absolute majority at the national level.[80] In West Pakistan, the Pakistan Peoples Party (PPP) led by Zulfikar Ali Bhutto won eighty-one out of 138 seats for the National Assembly, mainly from Sindh and Punjab. The addition of four seats reserved for women would take its tally up to eighty-five. Its share of the popular vote, however, was only 38.89 per cent.[81]

Balochistan and the North-West Frontier Province gave a plurality to the Pashtun nationalist National Awami Party (NAP) and the orthodox Jamiat Ulema Islam (JUI), which had aligned itself with the left-wing parties instead of other Islamists. The parties that described themselves as 'Islam Loving' fared poorly. The three factions of the Muslim League, between them, won eighteen seats. The Jamiat Ulema Pakistan (JUP) ended up with seven seats while the Jamaat-e-Islami managed only four seats. The Islamic parties' share of the popular vote was around 10 per cent nationwide.

Both major parties ignored the ideological concept of Pakistan in their campaigns. The Awami League sought a loose confederation between Pakistan's two wings rather than a centralized state, easing of tensions with India and a reduction in military spending. Bhutto spoke of 'Islamic Socialism' and demanded closer alignment with China against India. Ironically, his espousal of 'Islamic Socialism' was considered a challenge to Pakistan's Islamic moorings even though Liaquat had used the same term to describe his visualization of an Islamic Pakistan.

Thus, the election results were a huge disappointment for Yahya, who had started defining the army as 'the guardian of Pakistan's ideological frontier', not only the defender of its borders. Pakistan-based British author, Herbert Feldman, had noted the development of 'a distinctly obscurantist tendency' and 'an unconstructive harping on Islam' following Yahya's rise to power. This was ironic because Yahya was known for a distinctly irreligious lifestyle. That did not stop him issuing martial law decrees mandating strict punishments for publishing or possessing 'any book, pamphlet, etc., which was offensive to the religion of Islam'.[82]

Yahya also banned the import of all printed material originating in India. The twin bans, on material against Islam and materials from India, reflected the two major elements of the military's thinking. For this mindset, being seen as protecting Islam was synonymous with defending Pakistan; ideas originating in India, including those from India's large Muslim population, had to be blocked in case they subvert Pakistani national identity that was just beginning to take shape.

With that frame of mind, the military was not enamoured of either Mujib or Bhutto. One (Mujib) was too close to India and vowed to declare Pakistan a secular state. The other (Bhutto) espoused a socialist ideology, had fallen out with Ayub towards the end of his regime and was not liked by Yahya and his generals. But Bhutto was relatively more reconcilable. He was from West Pakistan, had been part of the ruling elite, shared the military's disdain of India and, while opposed to clerics, had acknowledged Islam's role in public life.

Instead of accepting Mujib's overall majority, Yahya accepted Bhutto's argument that East and West Pakistan had given separate mandates and that the two must be reconciled before the elected Constituent Assembly could meet.

Considerable evidence has now surfaced that Yahya and other generals planned military action in East Pakistan even as they organized separate parleys involving Yahya, Bhutto and Mujib. Major Gen. Khadim Hussain Raja, who served as general officer commanding in East Pakistan acknowledged such plans in his posthumously published memoir. According to him, 'General Yahya had visualized the possibility of a military crackdown accompanied by the suspension of all political activity', leading to the preparation of 'a plan called Operation Blitz' in January–February 1971. The plan involved 'the armed forces of the country' moving 'against defiant political leaders'.[83] It did not mean much to the 'guardians of Pakistan's ideological frontiers' that the political leaders in question had just won an overwhelming popular mandate.

Official Pakistani accounts insist that the military onslaught against the Awami League and its supporters started after talks broke down in March and Awami League supporters openly defied Pakistani authority. The result was widespread rebellion by the Bengalis, with Bengali units of the Pakistan Army joining the rebels, and West Pakistani forces were accused of attempting genocide of the Bengalis.

US national security adviser Henry Kissinger, who fashioned America's 'tilt towards Pakistan' in the ensuing crisis, noted that 'the Indians who one normally would expect to favour a break-up of Pakistan aren't so eager for this one'.[84] Admiral Syed Muhammad Ahsan, who served as governor of East Pakistan from September 1969 to March 1971, agreed with that assessment. He told US officials later that he did not believe in the theory that India engineered Mujib's electoral victory and subsequent stance on autonomy. 'Prior to March at least, separation was not Mujib's intention', Ahsan observed. He also said that 'India's position has, despite public outcry, been relatively moderate and its hands before the events in March were relatively clean.'[85]

But soon after starting military operations, Pakistan blamed India for the events in East Pakistan. Faced with Pakistan's military might, a large number of Awami League activists and East Bengali Hindus crossed the border into the Indian states of Tripura, Assam and West Bengal. Defecting Bengali soldiers and officers from the Pakistan Army soon joined them. These trained military men had pre-empted a Pakistani order to disarm and detain all ethnic Bengalis in the army.

Mujib was arrested and taken to West Pakistan but other Awami League leaders announced the formation of a Bangladesh government in exile based in the Indian port city of Calcutta. India then asserted that millions of refugees had poured in, creating a refugee emergency. The Indian external intelligence service—Research and Analysis Wing (RAW)—recruited and trained a guerilla army from the refugee camps.

Soon the Bangladesh Mukti Bahini (Liberation Army) was methodically attacking the Pakistani forces throughout the country's eastern wing.

Pakistani soldiers were trained to fight in the continental climate of West Pakistan's border with India. Most of them had never set foot in East Pakistan and did not speak the Bengali language. In the tropical climate and heavily vegetated terrain of Bengal, they felt lost. Moreover, the Mukti Bahini not only had the support of the people, but its soldiers also knew their territory better. Pakistan alleged that regular Indian forces operated alongside the guerillas, pretending to be part of the hastily raised liberation army.

The brutality of the Pakistan Army shocked Western diplomats and journalists on ground in Dhaka. 'Here in Dhaka we are mute and horrified witnesses to a reign of terror by the Pakistan military,' began a telegram to the State Department, signed by Archer Blood, US consul general in East Pakistan. 'Evidence continues to mount that the Martial Law authorities have a list of Awami League supporters whom they are systematically eliminating by seeking them out in their homes and shooting them down.' Blood, who was a career foreign service officer and had been stationed in Dhaka since 1970, had titled his cable, 'Selective Genocide'. He gave vivid details of massacres conducted by Pakistani troops and informed Washington that the army was supporting non-Bengali Muslims in 'systematically attacking poor people's quarters and murdering Bengalis and Hindus'.[86]

Several reporters were expelled for describing the Pakistan Army's carnage in their dispatches, including Sydney Schanberg of the *New York Times*. His final story from Dhaka, published in the paper on 4 July, ran under the headline: 'An Alien Army Imposes Its Will: East Pakistan'.

'Doesn't the world realize that they're nothing but butchers?' Schanberg's story began, quoting a foreigner, 'who has lived in East Pakistan for years', speaking of the Pakistan Army. 'That they killed—are still killing—Bengalis to intimidate them, to make slaves out of them? That they wiped out whole villages, opening fire at first light and stopping only when they got tired?' Schanberg questioned the army's design of 'Islamic integrity' for Pakistan. He cited a westerner as saying, 'It's a medieval army operation as if against serfs', adding that the West Pakistanis 'will use any method just to own East Pakistan'.[87]

Unmoved by international criticism, Yahya asked the nation, in an address to the nation in June, to express 'gratitude to Almighty Allah' for the army's success in East Pakistan. After blaming external forces for the challenges Pakistan faced, Yahya had declared that 'Every one of us is a mujahid'—a holy warrior.[88] Although Pakistan had lost to India in previous wars, its military believed it could beat India if it tried to fight on behalf of the Bengalis. To add to its strength, the Pakistan Army had recruited thousands of volunteers from Islamist groups in East Pakistan. These razakars (volunteers) and mujahideen terrorized critics of the Pakistani state.

In the end, however, none of Pakistan's efforts to hang on to its eastern wing worked.[89] The Indian Army began military incursions into East Bengal on 21 November in support of the Mukti Bahini. On 3 December 1971, Pakistan attacked India from the west in the hope of forestalling the fall of East Pakistan. India recognized Bangladesh as a sovereign country three days later and marched into East Pakistan in aid of the Bangladesh government in exile.

Independent observers believe that the Pakistan Army killed between one hundred thousand and two hundred thousand Bengalis in a nine-month period, whereas Bangladesh puts the figure at three million. Pakistani forces suffered only thirteen hundred fatalities in combat operations in the eastern wing and another fourteen hundred during war along the West Pakistan border.[90]

Pakistani forces in the eastern wing surrendered to the Indian military and Mukti Bahini on 16 December 1971. Although India declared that it had no territorial ambitions and saw further conflict 'pointless',[91] Yahya vowed to continue the war with India. 'We shall fight alone if we must,' he said in an address to the nation. The headline of *Dawn*, Pakistan's major English newspaper, on the day of Pakistan's surrender read, 'Victory on All Fronts'. The West Pakistanis were fed ideological hype, without immediately being told of their military's ignominious defeat.

'No sacrifice will be too great to preserve this Islamic homeland of the 120 million people of Pakistan,' Yahya declared while announcing a new constitution that would provide greater autonomy to East Pakistan. He described the army's conduct as 'reminiscent of the highest traditions of the soldiers of Islam'[92] and failed to concede that Pakistan had lost more than half its population and a significant part of its territory. It was as if dismemberment was only a temporary setback in Pakistan's march towards its Islamic destiny. Four days after the surrender, on 20 December 1971, Yahya was removed from power by his own commanders.

Bhutto, leader of the majority political party in West Pakistan, was installed as president and chief martial law administrator to effect a transition to civilian rule in what was left of Pakistan. Bhutto then freed Mujib from prison and Mujib returned to Dhaka in triumph to become prime minister of Bangladesh.

For West Pakistanis, fed on rhetoric of imminent victory in jihad, the loss of East Pakistan represented a colossal anticlimax. The war—and East Pakistan—had been lost and there was no way of turning the tables. Amid nationwide depression, reported the *New York Times*, 'People went to mosques to pray and weep.' Editorials in Pakistani newspapers demanded why Yahya had not told the people that defeat was so near and why he had not ordered the army to fight the Indians to death.[93]

4

Islamist Rage

THE TRANSFORMATION OF EAST Pakistan into Bangladesh should have been an opportunity to revise the two-nation theory and the 'ideology of Pakistan'. The Bengalis had proved that ethnicity and demands for a rightful share of the country's resources was a stronger factor in determining their nationalism than Islam. West Pakistani soldiers, on the other hand, had demonstrated how a shared faith did not prevent them from committing atrocities against fellow citizens whom they considered lesser Muslims or lesser Pakistanis. But instead of lessening reliance of religion as a factor in politics, the loss of East Pakistan only moved Pakistan towards a closer embrace of ideological nation building.

With East Pakistan gone, Pakistan lost the moderating influence of secular Bengali politicians. Punjab that had been the heartland of religious politics now constituted the majority in a new Pakistan. Pakistan was now geographically compact, with a dominant ethnic group (the Punjabis) and a military that sought to avenge its humiliation in Bangladesh. Ethnic Baloch and Pashtun politicians were the last remaining secularists but they could not hope to have any national influence. Bhutto, the consummate politician, decided that he would implement his plan for a socialist economy with a stronger dose of religious fervour. He believed that this was what the people wanted and he was the man to give it to them.[1]

Pakistan after 1971 was demographically almost 97 per cent Muslim. Moreover, the British-era judges, civil servants, politicians and military officers, who peddled Islamic rhetoric without necessarily believing it, were gradually fading from the scene. The newer generation had grown up with the post-Partition Islamic sloganeering and ideological regimentation. Under Bhutto, Pakistan still juggled between the needs of a modern state and pressure from clerics to recreate a bygone era. But the balance had shifted in a way that some action to 'enforce Islam' had to follow the promises, unlike Pakistan's initial years when assurances of Islamization sufficed.

Bhutto portrayed himself, in the words of political scientist Anwar Syed, as 'a Socialist Servant of Islam'. To rebut the argument of his Islamist opponents that socialism was 'antithetical to God and religion', Bhutto 'advertised his personal dedication to Islam' and 'insisted that he was a good Muslim'. He said, 'he was proud of being a Muslim; indeed, he was first a Muslim and then a Pakistani'.[2]

Bhutto liked to narrate how, as foreign minister during the 1965 war, he 'had resisted India and chased its foreign minister out of the Security Council', which could only be possible because he was 'a servant of Islam'. He also insisted that Islam 'is the basis of Pakistan' and if a political party did 'not make Islam the main pillar of its ideology, then that party would not be a Pakistani party. It would be an alien party.'[3]

By 1974, Bhutto had gradually phased out the more secular left-wing members of his PPP from power. Socialist intellectuals with middle-class backgrounds made way for traditional landowners who had now joined the party. The PPP's then secretary general, Mubashir Hasan, wrote later that he observed 'Bhutto's tilt towards an obscurantist interpretation of Islam'.[4] The first major manifestation of that inclination in constitutional and legal terms occurred when Islamist groups rioted against the Ahmadi sect. The riots began after a clash in May between Islamist and Ahmadi students at the railway station of Rabwah, the town where the Ahmadi sect has its headquarters.

Islamist demands against the Ahmadis were no different this time around than they had been almost two decades earlier. But in 1953, Prime Minister Nazimuddin had been willing to call in the army to stop the rioters and Justice Munir had written his report pointing out the problem with the state accepting demands to define which sect was or was not Islamic. Now, Bhutto was unwilling to follow in Nazimuddin's footsteps and there was no one of Munir's stature to remind the government that it should not allow clerics to dictate legislation.

Even though the Ahmadis had, as a community, backed Bhutto in the 1970 election, Bhutto decided to join the religious parties he had defeated at the polls in amending Pakistan's constitution (framed only a year earlier) to define 'Muslim' in a way that specifically excluded Ahmadis from the fold of Islam. The Islamists got their biggest legislative victory since the Objectives Resolution and that too after losing a general election.

Pakistan went to polls for a second time in 1977, with consequences almost as monumental as the last time. Nine opposition parties, including a unified Muslim League and three religious parties, came together in the Pakistan National Alliance (PNA) to challenge Bhutto's PPP. The alliance's rallies drew large crowds, especially in large cities upset with Bhutto's authoritarian streak. Although at least one liberal and one major left-wing party were part of the PNA, its campaign was driven by the Islamists. Bhutto countered that by emphasizing religious issues himself.

The PPP manifesto promised to 'ensure that Friday is observed as the weekly holiday instead of Sunday, make the teaching of the Holy Quran an integral part of eminence as a centre of community life, establish a federal Ulema academy and other institutions' and a variety of other concessions to Islamic sentiment. 'The closing weeks of the spring campaign found each side asserting its past service to Islam and its promise to bring about an Islamic system of government more quickly or more effectively,' observed Leonard Binder. A Pakistani newspaper, 'in a rare case of dissent from this trend' wrote in an editorial, 'For God's sake leave Islam alone'.[5]

According to the editorial, 'What is simply disgusting is an attempt by the contestant parties to drag the name of Islam into the electioneering with each striving to prove that he alone is a bigger Muslim than the others.' But the same newspaper still accepted election advertisements exhorting its readers to cast their votes 'for the promotion of Islamic values and establishment of Islamic order'.[6]

The religiously charged election resulted in a PPP victory, which was immediately contested by the PNA with violent street protests.

Most independent observers pointed out that the PPP had padded its victory, not stolen the election. The PNA allegations of election rigging were exaggerated as was the extent of the PPP's electoral victory. But as Marvin Weinbaum noted, 'whatever the extent or origins of the election irregularities, in just a matter of days the legitimacy of the entire electoral exercise had been irretrievably lost'.[7]

The dispute over election results might have been resolved through a political settlement but instead, the PNA's protests ended up demanding Bhutto's resignation and the full enforcement of Nizam-e-Mustafa (The system of the Prophet). Bhutto was accused of being the antithesis of an Islamic leader and protestors demanded a more pious leadership for a more Islamic Pakistan.

A month into the protests, Bhutto announced that 'Sharia law would be enforced in six months' and declared 'immediate total prohibition on the use of alcohol, complete ban on gambling in all forms and [on] night clubs'.[8] His expectation that this would subside the passion of the protestors was not fulfilled. Eventually, the army stepped in and Gen. Zia-ul-Haq seized power in yet another military coup. Although he initially promised free and fair elections within ninety days, Zia went on to rule for eleven years, declaring 'Islamization' as his principal objective. His dictatorship marked the pinnacle of Pakistan's embrace of Islam as the national ideology.

Zia had started Islamizing the army even before he toppled Bhutto and secured absolute power. One of his lieutenants, Lt Gen. Jahan Dad Khan, wrote that Zia was 'a devout Muslim' for whom 'it was a matter of faith' to 'propagate Islam wherever he could'. He changed the Pakistan Army's motto to Iman (Faith), Taqwa (abstinence), Jihad Fi Sabeelillah (war in the way of God). According to Khan, Zia 'urged all ranks of the army during his visits to troops as well as in written instructions, to offer their prayers, preferably led by the commanders themselves at various levels. Religious education was included in the training programme and mosques and prayer halls were organized in all army units.'[9]

If Liaquat, Ayub, Yahya and Bhutto were non-practising Muslims using Islamic symbolism to bind the nation together, Zia was more overtly observant and visibly zealous in making Pakistan an Islamic state. Like all dictators invoking religion in statecraft, power was his goal and there was much hypocrisy in his religiosity. But he wrote laws and created institutions to empower Pakistan's clerics in a way that had not been done before. Zia's US-backed decision to launch jihad against the Soviet Union in Afghanistan also bred religious militancy, which Pakistan is dealing with to this day.

The most prominent legislation under Zia was perhaps the Hudood Ordinance in 1979,[10] which introduced punishments such as stoning, flogging and amputation for crimes such as adultery (zina), theft and consuming alcohol.[11] Although stoning and amputation were not actually carried out, there were several public floggings in Zia's initial years. But keeping draconian laws on the books, even when punishments they specified were not fully carried out, had its own downside. The laws became an instrument of blackmail in a corrupt law enforcement system, adding to the burden of an already underfunded judiciary, which now had to deal with a plethora of cases relating to alleged un-Islamic behaviour.

The adultery or Zina laws became contentious because they gave a man's testimony double the weight of a woman's evidence.[12] This weakened the position of women when they filed charges of rape. Several rape victims ended up being imprisoned for adultery under the law, raising the number of women prisoners nine years after the implementation of the Hudood Ordinance to around 6,000. The numbers dropped somewhat after Zia's exit from power.[13] But the stories of individuals wrongfully accused of adultery after being raped continue to fracture the positive image Pakistanis seek for their country abroad.[14]

Other examples of Zia's Islamization include the blasphemy laws, creation of shariat courts with powers to strike down and challenge laws that were deemed not Islamic, ordinances forbidding Ahmadis from engaging in any practice that might make them seem Muslims, and introduction of Zakat and Ushr religious taxes. Zia also ordered heads of government departments to organize prayers for their staff every day,[15] creating an excuse for government officials to take time off from work ostensibly for prayer.

'The ideology of Pakistan is Islam and only Islam,' Zia once thundered, declaring secularism to be a threat to the country. 'There should be no misunderstanding on this score. We should in all sincerity accept Islam as Pakistan's basic ideology,' he said, adding that if that was not done Pakistan would 'be exposed to secular ideologies'.[16]

Zia's definition of Pakistan's Islamic ideology precluded efforts to reconcile Islam with modern ideas, opposed anything remotely secular and unleashed the debates about 'who is a Muslim' and 'what does it mean to enforce Islam in the twentieth century' that Justice Munir and others had warned about in Pakistan's first decade.

The ideology of Pakistan now had a more unambiguously theocratic orientation. It was also more specifically tied to defining Pakistan as a nation distinct from India. 'We are going back to Islam not by choice but by the force of circumstances,' Zia declared, arguing that the raison d'être of Pakistan stemmed from 'our cultural and moral awareness' about Islam being 'our only salvation'.

For Zia, explanations of Pakistan's genesis in terms of protecting the subcontinent's Muslim minority against Hindu domination and enforcement of Islamic laws were interconnected. If Islam was not central to the idea of Pakistan 'we might as well have stayed with India', he said. Islam was 'the fundamental factor' in the creation of Pakistan. 'It comes before wheat and rice and everything else. I can grow more wheat; I can import wheat but I cannot import the correct moral values,' Zia explained.[17]

Under Zia, Pakistan's judiciary and administration were infused with individuals with a decidedly Islamist outlook. The military, and especially the much enlarged Inter-Services Intelligence (ISI) agency, also assimilated the harder-line definition of Pakistan's ideology. Unilateral amendments to the Constitution made it impossible for politicians and political parties to describe themselves as 'secular' and still participate in the political process. Universities and the media were largely purged of individuals advocating a non-religious world view.

The scope of national debate was narrowed to a choice between various interpretations of Islam instead of being open to the more fundamental question of whether Islam should have such a central role in state policy or not.

Although Zia was killed in a plane crash in 1988, Pakistan has not recovered from his Islamization. Since then, several civilian governments have been elected and, in between, another military dictatorship, this time led by Gen. Pervez Musharraf, ruled for almost nine years from 1999 to 2008. All of them, with some exceptions, have publicly acknowledged the need for rolling back Islamic militancy and rationalizing Islamic laws such as those relating to blasphemy. But no one has been able to systematically reopen debate on how Pakistan might make policy decisions based on economic and social necessities rather than on the basis of religious affectation.

Meanwhile, demands for further Islamization have not subsided. In 1989, the shariat court and the Supreme Court requested the Qisas and Diyat (Retribution and Compensation) Ordinance, which provided for those convicted of murder or assault to pay 'blood money' to the victim's family instead of going to prison.[18] This amounted to putting the choice of prosecuting a murderer's fate in the hands of the victim's heirs, making it easier for the rich to buy freedom after a violent crime. It also led to a massive increase in 'honour killings'—where a male family member kills a woman or her lover for bringing 'dishonour' to the family.

In case of 'honour killings', perpetrators could now act with impunity as they would face no legal consequences. After all, they perpetrate the crime and are also in a position to forgive themselves as the family of the victim. Over the last several years, a thousand or so honour killings are now reported in Pakistan each year.[19] A well-known case is that of Samia Sarwar, whose family hired an assassin to kill her and later forgave the assassin and decided not to pursue any charges under Islamic law.[20]

Even after such legislation, Pakistan is still not Islamic enough for some. During the early 1990s, Prime Minister Nawaz Sharif's government 'ordered TV actresses to wear veils over their heads', made the death penalty mandatory for individuals convicted of blasphemy or 'defiling' Prophet Muhammad's name and debated 'whether banks should be allowed to charge interest in violation of religious doctrine'. A *Washington Post* report told of how the directors of a television play 'wrestled with a scene in which a woman's head had to be covered with a scarf while her hair was being shampooed'. The government also refused during the 1992 Olympics 'to allow women's swimming events to be shown on television because the swimsuits were considered too immodest for Islamic sensibilities'.[21]

More recently, in 2016, the official Council of Islamic Ideology (CII) announced that it was deliberating a '"model" women's protection bill, which allows a husband to "lightly" beat his wife "if needed" and prohibits mixing of the genders in schools, hospitals and offices'. The CII claimed that its proposed bill would give women 'all the rights given to them under Sharia', while prohibiting interaction between men and women (except those specifically permitted to meet by Islamic law) 'at recreational spots and offices'. The law also sought to ban 'dance, music, and sculptures created in the name of art'.[22]

CII's proposed 163-point bill was in response to a provincial assembly discussing legislation to protect the rights of women. It covered 'property, marriage, motherhood, crimes and violence against women, apostasy', as well as 'the instruments of state "acceptable" for a woman to be involved in'. A woman human rights activist and academic pointed out that it was unconstitutional to allow a husband to beat his wife, in addition to being a violation of 'international laws and treaties that Pakistan has signed and is bound by'.[23] Such arguments have little effect on Pakistan's Islamists. The country remains mired in 'Islamic' issues, more than forty years after it started Islamization in earnest in response to the loss of its eastern wing.

Sunni extremism in Pakistan has generally been associated with Wahabis represented in terrorist organizations such as Lashkar-e-Taiba (LeT), which was responsible for the 2008 Mumbai attacks, or Deobandi Sunnis organized as the Taliban and their many offshoots. Now, however, even the syncretic Barelvis, often deemed less orthodox and more tolerant than the Wahabis or Deobandis due to their reverence for Sufis, have embraced violence. Mumtaz Qadri, the bodyguard who killed Punjab governor Salmaan Taseer in 2011, was a Barelvi. In November 2017, some 3,000 supporters of a firebrand Barelvi cleric, 'many armed with sticks and iron rods', blocked the main entrance to Islamabad for twenty days.

Led by Khadim Hussain Rizvi, the colourful leader of Tehrik-e-Labaik-Ya-Rasoolullah (TLYR), the protestors demanded strict adherence to Pakistan's blasphemy laws and stricter laws against other religious sects. Rizvi, known for lacing his speeches with four-letter words and choicest Punjabi abuses, projected himself as the guardian of the 'Prophet's honour'. He also railed against Hindu and Jewish agents in addition to speaking about fighting alongside the Pakistan Army for Islam and Pakistan. Pakistan's military-intelligence complex supported Rizvi, along with other Barelvi leaders, during and after the Musharraf years as potentially moderate alternatives to Deobandi and Wahabi clerics who had gained strength from state patronage since the era of Gen. Zia.

A sit-in by 3,000 people in a country with a population of 210 million should not have been a serious threat either to law and order or to the stability of the government but it became one. Rizvi had called the protests over changes to electoral laws, which he claimed unacceptably altered the language of the oath for lawmakers declaring Prophet Muhammad as God's final prophet. The change in the oath's wording was minor; it had substituted the words 'solemnly swear' with 'affirm' but the insignificance of the change did not mean much to the enraged Islamists. The original language was restored and the government said it was a clerical error any way but that was not enough to calm Rizvi's bloodthirsty followers from threatening violence.

The timing of Rizvi's relatively small sit-in with larger consequences was also interesting. It came after the disqualification of former prime minister Nawaz Sharif, his re-election as leader of the ruling Pakistan

Muslim League-N, and the rejection by parliament of a bill that would have made it unlawful for political parties to be headed by someone disqualified to be a member of parliament. Between Punjabi swear words, Rizvi declared like other religious demagogues before him, 'We will lay our lives, but we will not step down from our demands.' His followers chanted 'Labaik Ya Rasool Allah, Labaik' (I am here, Prophet of God, I am here), not noticing the irony of declaring honourable intent in response to a cleric's vulgar language.

The 3,000 protesters got more airtime on Pakistan's military-backed TV channels than a crowd this size deserved. The fear of violent riots and vigilante justice over blasphemy allegations caused the already embattled government to act slowly and cautiously. The Islamabad High Court ordered the protestors to clear the streets. When the government acted finally, with the high court order in hand after almost twenty days of patience, it only generated widespread violence.[24]

The army's spokesman tweeted to appear neutral between protestors and the government, as if the army was above the government and not its part. 'COAS telephoned PM. Suggested to handle Islamabad Dharna peacefully avoiding violence from both sides as it is not in national interest and cohesion,' declared Maj. Gen. Asif Ghafoor, head of Inter-Services Public Relations. Rizvi reassured his supporters that 'The military will not act against us because we are doing its work.' The crisis ended with a truce brokered by the army chief, resulting in the resignation of the law minister and a commitment from the government that it would accept the protestors' views on blasphemy. The TLYR was given representation on the textbook board of the education ministry to ensure that the material in school textbooks conformed to the Barelvi mullahs' concept of respect for Islam and its prophet.

'In one brief page and six gut-wrenching points,' *Dawn* wrote in an editorial about the agreement between Rizvi and the government, 'the state of Pakistan has surrendered its authority to a mob that threatened to engulf the country in flames. The federal law minister has been sacked—in return for a promise by the protesters to not issue a fatwa against him.' It wondered whether the decision had been 'made out of desperation or fear' and pointed out that it amounted to accepting 'that mobs and zealots have a right to issue religious edicts that can endanger lives and upend public order'.

According to *Dawn*, 'Zealots had already demonstrated the power of mob violence and the strength of the politics of intolerance and hate. Now, a blueprint has been created for holding state and society hostage.'[25] The newspaper's resentment stemmed from the fact that a relatively small group of protestors has been allowed to twist the arm of an elected civilian government with the help of the powerful military. It was, however, just the latest of many occasions in Pakistan's history when religious fanaticism intersected with political expediency to erode personal freedoms and the writ of the state. It can be argued that Khadim Rizvi's success in forcing the government's hand is a direct outcome of the Pakistani elite's reliance on Islam as the definer of Pakistan's nationalism.

Manufactured Outrage

According to British sociologist, Anthony D. Smith, nationalism often involves 'Rediscovering in the depths of the communal past a pristine state of true collective individuality', and nationalists strive to identify 'the spirit and values of' some 'distant Golden Age'.[26] The challenge of Pakistani nationalism has always been to determine the country's relationship with history. If Pakistan represents the revival of the 'Golden Age' of Islam, it must come to terms with the fact that none of the major Islamic empires—from the Umayyads and Abbasids to the Ottomans and Safavids—were centred in today's Pakistan; If Pakistan represents the resurgence of Muslim sultans who ruled the subcontinent, they too ruled from Delhi, not Karachi or Islamabad.

Pakistan could always acknowledge the history of the territory that it incorporates as the history of Pakistan's various peoples. This would involve recognizing the history of the Sindhis and the Baloch, of the Pashtuns and the Punjabis, as well as the various tribes and communities that inhabit today's Pakistan. The country would then be seen as a federation of diverse communities that became part of Pakistan at the end of British rule as a result of complex politics during the Indian independence struggle. But Pakistan's leaders have always dreaded that this might lead to assertion of ethnic nationalism and irredentism, a concern accentuated by the separation of Bangladesh. For them, it is imperative that the creation of Pakistan be attributed, not to the political dynamic that started with the introduction of representative institutions under the Raj, but to an inherent incompatibility between the subcontinent's Muslims and non-Muslims.

The Pakistani version of history denies that a vast majority of Muslims in the subcontinent, including the parts that are now Pakistan, are members of local communities that converted to Islam at some point in time. Thus, Pakistanis view themselves as, simultaneously, the descendants of Arabs and Persians, as well as being related to the Turks and the Mongols. This creates such incongruities as a Punjabi belonging to the Jat tribe (that includes Hindus and Sikhs) lecturing Baloch or Sindhi students about his (and Pakistan's) heritage being linked to the Muslims who ruled Cordoba and Granada in Spain. It is almost as if the creation of Pakistan has magically bridged differences of DNA, broken off ties to India and Hindus and linked people from the land of the Indus to wherever Muslims might have achieved greatness at any point of time in the last fifteen centuries.

Accepting that Pakistan is a newly conceived nation state that would create history as it goes forward, rather than historic appropriation or distorting the past, was a realistic alternative that was never given a chance. Pakistan could acknowledge its Indian heritage as well as the Muslim-ness of a majority of its population. It could recognize its diversity and admit that its lands have been ruled by different people at different times. It could even concede that some of its people, notably Punjabis, were later converts to Islam than others and some did not have a track record of self-rule while others did. Instead, successive Pakistani leaders and most of the country's intelligentsia preferred to build the 'ideology of Pakistan' on the twin pillars of Islam and antagonism towards India.

In recent years, the rise of 'Hindutva' in India has helped Pakistan's ideologues advance their case but even before that the fear of 'the other' served as an important element in composing Pakistan's nationalism. Envisioning India as a 'permanent enemy' has led to militarism and militancy—a subject we will examine in detail in a subsequent chapter. But the adoption of Islam as the basis of nationhood, instead of as a system of beliefs designed for individual and collective spirituality or piety, has also contributed to social anarchy, political conflict and sectarian strife.

Defining Pakistan's nationalism through Islam exposed the country to the paradox of setting a national boundary upon a universalist faith. There were, as some scholars have pointed out, a 'range of civilizational levels as well as the range of Islamic pasts'[27] for Pakistanis to choose from, making the unifying faith a source of great contention. As a consequence, Pakistan's Islamists, and often the state apparatus, have sought to manipulate religious sentiment to bolster nationalist feeling without intending to establish the Islamic state they constantly talk about.

Islamic ideology not only sets Pakistan apart from India, notwithstanding many commonalities of history, culture and social mores; it also musters a diverse nation's energies in pushing back on policy pressures from major international powers. In some ways, it is a weapon amid weakness even if it is a gun held to one's own head. Constant indignation at real or perceived indignities against Islam are a useful device for Pakistan's politicians and Islamists. They distract from substantive economic and social issues. Quite often, religious rage is generated through falsehoods and rumours, which are systematically deployed as vehicles of policy.

The periodic outbreaks of protest over insults to Prophet Muhammad and Islam are hardly spontaneous. In each case, the protesters do not react to something they see or become aware of in the ordinary course of life. Most of the objects of complaint—a remark made in private, a book published in the West or a movie that has not been released in Pakistan—are not widely accessible and yet the public is whipped into a fury. The Islamists first introduce the objectionable material to their audience and then instigate outrage by characterizing it as part of a supposed worldwide conspiracy to denigrate Islam.

The emergence of social media and the swiftness of international communications have made it easier to choreograph global campaigns and, in Muslim-majority countries, Islamists tend to be among those who are most effectively organized to take advantage of technology for political ends. But Pakistan has been a centre of campaigns to protect Islam and the Prophet's honour, each starting with frenzy and fizzling out without attaining its stated objective.

An early prototype of a Muslim mass-mobilization campaign in the subcontinent was the controversy over the book *Rangeela Rasool* (Colorful Prophet), a salacious version of Prophet Muhammad's life. Published in British India in 1927, the controversial book was hardly a best-seller. In fact, it went mostly unnoticed until Muslim politicians encountered it two years later and complained. The British authorities arrested and tried the book's publisher, Rajpal, only to acquit him. Agitation by Muslim groups encouraged a young illiterate carpenter by the single name Ilmuddin to stab the publisher to death in Lahore. Ilmuddin was given the title of ghazi (warrior for the faith) by Islamist political groups and was defended in court, albeit on technical grounds (and unsuccessfully), by Jinnah. The British amended the Indian Penal Code to add punishment for blasphemy and incitement of religious hatred.

The *Rangeela Rasool* controversy helped polarize Hindus and Muslims, particularly in Punjab. Pakistani leaders sometimes cite the book's publication as an example of how the Islamic faith would have been threatened under non-Muslim rule had the British left the subcontinent undivided. 'Defending the honour of the Prophet' is easy to project as a worthy cause, not to be opposed or criticized even by secular Muslims. If a secular public figure dares to point out that the faith of 1.6 billion people can scarcely be threatened by a book with a print run of only 1,000 copies, he can easily be targeted as a defender of blasphemers.

Like all modern political tactics, religious protests tend to be timed for best effect. A well-timed protest keeps religious tumult alive at a time when it is most needed. Take the example of the protests in 1971, during the Bangladesh war, against *The Turkish Art of Love*, a sex manual containing derogatory references to Prophet Muhammad that was published in 1933. The protests were organized by Jamaat-e-Islami, which had lost badly in the 1970 election and was collaborating with Yahya's military regime against Bengalis. During the ensuing riots, Christian churches were attacked, and liquor shops (which were legal at the time) were looted. The British Council building in Lahore was also attacked. The riots helped put the British on notice for sympathizing with the Bangladesh cause.

On 21 November 1979, students affiliated to the Jamaat-e-Islami's student wing burned down the US embassy in Islamabad on the basis of rumours that the US had a hand in the seizure of Islam's holiest shrine, the Grand Mosque in Mecca. Several embassy officials were trapped in the burning building and it took the Pakistan military four hours to arrive at the site and several more to restore order even though Zia's residence as military chief and the Pakistan Army's headquarters in Rawalpindi were less than half an hour's drive from the location of the US embassy in Islamabad. Two Americans and two Pakistani employees of the embassy died in the incident.[28]

A decade later, on 12 February 1989, a protest in Islamabad against British author Salman Rushdie's book *Satanic Verses* turned violent, causing great embarrassment to the newly elected civilian government led by Benazir Bhutto. The book parodied the prophet of Islam and was deemed offensive by most Muslims once their attention was drawn to some of its passages. But the book had been published a year earlier, in 1988, and no one in the Muslim world had taken notice of it until Pakistani cleric-politician Maulana Kausar Niazi, then known for close ties with Pakistani intelligence, wrote a series of articles about it in the Pakistani press.

After the publication of Kausar Niazi's articles in the Urdu press, another veteran of similar campaigns, Maulana Abdul Sattar Niazi called a conference of ulema to demand action against Rushdie. As a young man, Sattar Niazi had been part of the campaign for Pakistan's creation. After Independence, he had been part of almost every religious–political campaign starting with the anti-Ahmadi protests of 1953. The government had already banned *Satanic Verses* and officials in Bhutto's administration did not know what else to do in response to the ulema's fresh campaign.[29]

For their part, the Islamist organizers of the anti-Rushdie protests took the position that the publication of the book was an American–Zionist conspiracy against Islam. When a major demonstration led by the two Niazis against *Satanic Verses* was organized in Islamabad on 12 February 1989, the protesters attacked the US Information Service building. They were carrying signs that read, 'America and Israel: Enemies of Islam'.[30] Police had to shoot at the mob to disperse demonstrators and protect the lives of Pakistanis and Americans inside the building. Five demonstrators were killed.[31]

More recently, in September 2012, thousands of cellphone subscribers in Pakistan received an anonymous text message announcing a miracle: an earthquake on Tuesday, 18 September, had destroyed the Washington, DC movie theatre that was exhibiting *Innocence of Muslims*, the controversial film that triggered violent protests in several Muslim countries. An email version of the text message even included a picture of a mangled structure. Allah, the texter claimed, had shown His anger against the movie's insult to Islam and Prophet Muhammad, and with Him on their side the faithful should not be afraid to vent their anger against the West, which belittles Islam and abuses Islam's prophet.[32]

There was, of course, no earthquake in Washington and no movie theatre had been destroyed. In fact, the movie never made its way beyond YouTube. But for several days, the fabricated text message and email made the rounds, forwarded and re-forwarded around Pakistan and in some cases to the Pakistani diaspora. It was part of a campaign to arouse Muslim passions by what author Salman Rushdie has termed 'the outrage industry'.[33]

Similar false mass messaging convinced millions after 9/11 that Jews had been warned to stay away from the Twin Towers, implying a conspiracy that many still believe without a shred of evidence. In 2011, after US Special Forces killed Osama bin Laden, anonymous messages suggested that the raid in Abbottabad was a staged event and bin Laden had been killed months earlier.

In case of the *Innocence of Muslims* protests, the Pakistani government tried to align itself with the protesters' cause by declaring a public holiday and calling it 'Love of the Prophet Day'.[34] Although 95 per cent of Pakistan's 190 million people are Muslim, only an estimated 45,000 took part in demonstrations around the country against the film. The protests mattered largely because of their violence: as many as seventeen people were killed and scores injured.[35]

The outrage industry ensures that Pakistanis continue to blame others for their condition, raging over their impotence instead of focusing on economic, political and social issues. At the same time, successive civilian and military governments in Pakistan have chosen to appease the dial-a-riot Islamist hardliners rather than confront them. A multitude of Islamist groups has sprouted, including jihadi militants battle-hardened in Afghanistan and Kashmir and a competition of sorts now takes place among them over who is the greater champion of the honour of Islam and its Prophet.

In the process of moulding a nation on the basis of Islam, Pakistan has ended up earning for itself the reputation for being home to the world's angriest Muslims.

Restoring Balance

Nations, like individuals, can sometimes be swayed by emotion in defining their self-interest. In Pakistan's case, constructing national identity by means of a national ideology has severely constricted policy options. In its initial years, Pakistan's leaders were able to juggle between ideological demands and the practical needs of running a modern nation. Now, however, Pakistan has gone too far down the ideological rabbit hole to be able to embrace pragmatic policies in any number of fields including economics, education and relations with the rest of the world.

Pakistan's leaders cite public opinion and religious sentiment as the justification for tolerating intolerance and bigotry while they do little to shape public opinion differently. In fact, Pakistan's steady drift towards religious extremism is a result of state policies and the tendency of individuals and institutions to gain advantage by arousing emotion. On many occasions, when Pakistani leaders have made rational choices for worldly reasons, they have avoided explaining their reasoning to the general populace. Instead, religious reasons have been evoked constantly to keep Islamic passions alive even while making decisions such as joining Western alliances.

Soon after Independence, Pakistan's leaders determined that the country's military and economic needs would be better served with a cold-war alliance with the West. But the Pakistani people were still encouraged to pursue the dream of pan-Islamism. Prime Minister Suhrawardy came under fire for suggesting that an alliance of Islamic countries would not enhance Pakistan's security needs because 'zero plus zero is equal to zero'. Suhrawardy's rivals argued that Pakistan was aligning, not with the West, but with brotherly Islamic countries such as Iraq, Iran and Turkey when Pakistan joined the Baghdad Pact and the Central Treaty Organization (CENTO). Instead of letting the Pakistani people discuss the advantages, or otherwise, of partnering with the United States, Pakistani officials chose to foster anti-Americanism and pan-Islamism in the hope of using it to their advantage in negotiations with the Americans.

Similarly, several national leaders, beginning with Suhrawardy, have also been castigated for advising Pakistanis against confrontation with India. It has proved easy throughout Pakistan's post-Independence history to reject ideas, however reasonable, on grounds that they do not conform to Pakistan's Islamic ideology or because they would detract from the country's raison d'être. This allows influential groups to exploit popular emotions to maintain policies that favour their vested interests. Militarism and militancy have dominated Pakistan's choices even as they brought no advantage in enhancing national security or prosperity.

A major consequence of the preoccupation with ideology has been to create the dichotomy of increased dependence on the very donors whom

Pakistanis love to hate but whose assistance is crucial in maintaining an expansive national security state. Pakistan is, of course, not the only nation where rhetoric trumps cold calculation of national interest. In 2015, Greece elected a government which reflected the nation's anger against European demands for austerity and restraint. Prime Minister Alexis Tsipras made defiant statements against Germany at a time when his country most needed German support in getting out of a debt crisis.

Tsipras's poll ratings rose as a result of the grandstanding even though bank deposits in Greece fell, further aggravating the country's economic crisis. Defiant statements won Tsipras applause from his fellow countrymen but the net impact of these statements on the national economy was negative.

Compare such emotion-based decision making with the conduct of East Asian nations including China and South Korea. After years of describing the United States as the centre of global imperialism, the Communist Party of China had no qualms about partnering with the Americans to modernize and expand China's economy. The South Koreans built a self-sustaining economy with a cumulative aid input from the US of only $15 billion since 1950 by avoiding confrontation with America and by cooperating with erstwhile enemy Japan.

Pakistan received $40 billion in bilateral US aid over the same period. Instead of utilizing aid as a catalyst for indigenous growth, Pakistan has ended up becoming dependent on aid. Donor funding serves as a substitute for revenue generation while wars and terrorism have deterred investment.

On the one hand, Pakistanis are motivated by the notion of national honour in refusing to trade with India until the Kashmir dispute is resolved; on the other, they remain dependent on others to pay Pakistan's bills. Government officials celebrate whenever one of Pakistan's foreign benefactors approves a loan instead of regretting the fact of having to borrow so much so often.

Securing Kashmir, balancing India, and dominating Afghanistan are Pakistan's ideological obsessions even though pragmatic considerations necessitate a course correction. For instance, Pakistan could adopt an approach to Kashmir similar to that of China over Taiwan. It doesn't need to give up its claim, but it could move on other issues with India first. Chinese president Jiang Zemin suggested as much in his address to Pakistan's Senate in December 1996.

In any case, realism demands recognition of the fact that Pakistan no longer enjoys the support of the international community on the Kashmir issue. When Prime Minister Sharif raised the Kashmir issue in the United Nations General Assembly in 2014, he was the only head of government to mention Kashmir out of 193 speakers. Yet, Pakistani leaders refuse to budge from their stance that Kashmir is the core issue in India–Pakistan relations. Ideology and pride come in the way of charting a sensible course.

Similarly, Pakistan could befriend the government in Kabul to ensure that Afghan territory is not used to support ethnic insurgents against Pakistan instead of insisting on demanding a say in who rules Afghanistan. But Pakistani officials remained suspicious of former president Hamid Karzai and refuse to shut down the Afghan Taliban even after bonhomie with President Ashraf Ghani.

Terrorism has cast a long shadow on India–Pakistan relations since 1989 and also jeopardizes Pakistan's relations with the West. But Pakistan's establishment refuses to completely give up the option of sub-conventional warfare, which it sees as a force multiplier and influence enhancer. To give up jihad is anathema to the noisy Islamists who can be counted on to launch fatwas against anyone who suggests that the national interest requires focusing on economic growth rather than settling disputes with neighbours by force.

It seems that changing Pakistan's discourse is a prerequisite for changing its course. Pakistan views itself as an Islamic ideological state in a state of permanent conflict with India—a vision that enhances the military's dominance, keeps Islamists politically assertive and enables certain economic interests to prevail.

Admittedly, seventy years of ideological orientation cannot be reversed overnight. Any attempt to phase out the invoking of religion as ideology would have to be gradual. Civilian and military leaders would have to work together to ensure over time that Pakistanis realize the pitfalls of their contrived national narrative. The first step in that direction would be to open debate over alternative paths for the country, something that has almost been shut down since the Zia era.

Pakistanis need to hear rational arguments, say, about the cost of economic experiments in the name of Islam or the devaluation of higher education resulting from ideological indoctrination. They would then learn that only 25 per cent of women are part of Pakistan's labour force, which limits the country's productivity; its pursuit of 'interest-free' banking has hardly been successful; its reputation for 'honour killings' and its restrictions on personal freedoms discourage international tourism and investment; and the notion of permanent hostility with Hindus, Jews or Christians reduces flexibility in choosing trading partners.

In the realm of education, even Pakistanis with degrees in medicine and engineering still lack the scientific outlook that comes from empiricism. Instead of enabling Pakistan to succeed as a nation, the ideology of Pakistan has created barriers to its success. Ideological debates consume the nation's time and energy, and vested interests can easily be couched in ideological terms to prevent reforms.

Every authoritarian ruler in Pakistan, including its four military dictators, has invoked the national ideology to justify authoritarianism, while the landowning class thwarted much-needed land reform for years by citing medieval Islamic jurists. On many an occasion, individuals in business or industry have attempted to push their rivals out of business with the help of hired religious leaders. Others have refused to pay interest on bank loans while seeking court decisions against the very notion of interest on religious grounds. Pakistan's court system is often clogged with suits, petitions and appeals seeking to overturn one aspect or another of the law for Islamic reasons delaying the legal process in both criminal and civil matters.

The most egregious example of a futile, ostensibly religious, debate in Pakistan's history relates to Zia's decision to ban urinals in public bathrooms at airports and train stations on grounds that urinating while standing was a violation of Islamic norms.[36] Under Zia, clerics also argued over whether Islam allowed a bowler in the game of cricket to try and restore the sheen of the ball by rubbing it against their pants;[37] whether women could play for Pakistan in international sports competitions;[38] and whether doctors of one gender could see patients of the opposite gender.[39] While in recent years some of these arguments have declined in significance, others continue to surface.

A national ideology based on a major world religion continues to provide grounds for endless argumentation, given Islam's long history and the diversity among its adherents.

The other part of the ideology of Pakistan—permanent enmity with India—also impedes business-like decisions. It makes sense that, like all countries, Pakistan must maintain security along its borders and preparedness for defence of the country against military adventurism by all neighbours and potential enemies. What does not make sense, however, is the ideologically motivated decision to forego potential economic advantages and useful exchange or interaction. Pakistan could benefit from trade and tourism as well as from accessing India's institutions of higher education and medical facilities.

Chronic power shortages in Pakistan could be mitigated by purchasing electricity from Indian states bordering Pakistan. But Pakistanis have become ideologically predisposed to viewing relations with India as a zero-sum game. There is little room for discussing cooperation with India, and Pakistanis proposing a different approach towards India run the risk of being dubbed as 'traitors'.

Some Pakistanis would argue that the state ideology has helped Pakistan survive against the threat of disintegration, especially after the loss of Bangladesh. But that suggests that Pakistan, as a nation and as a state, cannot sustain itself except through ideological rhetoric, which, in turn, must be sustained through issues that mean little for most people in the twenty-first century. If that is the case, Pakistan has no choice but to stay mired in conceptual argumentation as Islamization has proved to be a recipe for unceasing internal conflict.

The alternative is for Pakistan to evolve as a functional, territorial nation state and a working federation of its various component ethnicities and nationalities. For that to happen, its leaders must take a stand against the unidimensional preoccupation with ideology. Balance must be restored in the priorities of Pakistani society by focusing on day-to-day, real-world issues. Pakistan's parliament, media and courts currently spend a disproportionately large amount of time and resources on discussing philosophical questions and imaginary threats.

It is important to note that on at least three occasions in Pakistan's history, the determination of its leaders to push back prevailed against the demands of religious activists and clerics. On all three occasions, political and military leaders as well as judges of superior courts came together to prevent illiberal interpretations of religion from becoming the law of the land.

The first of these was the refusal in 1953 of Prime Minister Khawaja Nazimuddin to remove his foreign minister for being an Ahmadi and to declare the Ahmadi community a non-Muslim minority. Although the government was forced to impose martial law in Lahore to quell riots, it successfully made its case to the public that giving in to religious rioters would only lead to further sectarian divisions. The Pakistani military helped the civilian government put down the riots while the judiciary helped in the form of the Munir Commission report, which showed the obscurantism and contradictions of the clerics' views.

Twenty-one years later, in 1974, the political leadership sought political advantage by appeasing clerics making anti-Ahmadi demands. Prime Minister Zulfikar Ali Bhutto declared it an 'achievement' that he secured support of all major political parties in amending the constitution to declare Ahmadis non-Muslim under law. A few years later, military ruler Zia legislated restrictions on Ahmadi professions of faith, making it a punishable offence for an Ahmadi to act in a manner that made him or her seem to be a Muslim. The judiciary upheld Zia's laws on grounds that by acting like a Muslim or using nomenclature used by Muslims, an Ahmadi offended Muslims and, therefore, deserved the punishment prescribed by Zia. Had Bhutto, Zia and the judges acted like Pakistan's leaders did in 1953, Pakistan could have avoided being saddled with a constitutional amendment and laws that are deemed by the rest of the world to be violative of the Universal Declaration of Human Rights.

Prime Minister Nawaz Sharif's decision in 1997 to restore Sunday as the weekly holiday instead of Friday was the second occasion on which the clerics' opinion was rejected without much reaction. Pakistan had adopted Friday as the weekly holiday in 1977, in the last days of the elder Bhutto's rule, and had persisted with it for almost two decades. Exporters and traders argued that they lost at least three days a week in their business because while Friday was off in Pakistan, businesses were shut on Saturday and Sunday in countries that were Pakistan's major trading partners.

Sharif, a businessman himself, accepted the business community's argument, legislated the change of weekly holiday and reminded the clerics that there was no specific command in the Quran or Hadith mandating a Friday shutdown. The judiciary rejected pleas calling for reinstatement of the weekly holiday on Friday, settling the matter, which has not been brought up seriously by anyone ever since.

More recently, in 2016, the third instance of the Pakistani state's defiance of clerical pressure manifested in the execution of Mumtaz Qadri, the police bodyguard who had killed Salmaan Taseer, governor of Punjab. Taseer was accused by Sunni clerics of supporting blasphemers when he supported amendments to Pakistan's blasphemy laws and Qadri killed him 'to avenge the Prophet's honour'. Although Qadri admitted the crime, clerics described him as a man of faith acting in defence of Islam and demanded that he not be executed. Pakistan's Supreme Court upheld a lower court's verdict against Qadri. Prime Minister Sharif enrolled the support of the army chief, General Raheel Sharif, to carry out the sentence in an effort to convince an otherwise sceptical world that Pakistan was turning away from Islamist extremism.

Predictions that the decision to execute Qadri would plunge Pakistan into religious disturbances were proved wrong. Pakistan's elite supported the execution so that other bodyguards would not, in future, threaten their protectees. Although some fanatics declared Qadri a saint and built a huge mausoleum over his grave, the general public accepted the view that individuals could not be allowed to act as judge, jury and executioner over blasphemy allegations.

These three instances show the potential for rational decision making if Pakistan's politicians and the permanent state machinery resolve to ignore or marginalize Islamists. Turning away from the ideological model of state requires willingness to at least question Pakistan's self-characterization as a 'citadel of Islam', and a global centre for Islamic revival. Beginning with Jinnah's 11 August 1947 address to the Constituent Assembly, there is sufficient ground to argue that Pakistan could as easily be envisaged as a modern territorial state as it has been visualized as an Islamic, ideological one.

A reimagined Pakistan would not necessarily embrace Jacobin secularism wherein the state attempts to restrict or limit the practice of religion. It would simply recognize that the individual can be pious, the society can be religious but the state should be non-confessional if it is to be different from what Pakistan has become. The constant refrain of Islamizing a Muslim-majority country, coupled with the belief that this nation must always be in conflict with its largest neighbour because of religious differences, is in many ways at the heart of most of Pakistan's current problems.

5

Insecurity and Jihad

AS GEN. ZIA-UL-HAQ UNDERTOOK what he described as 'Islamization' of Pakistan, the *New York Times* noted that its advocates saw it 'as essential therapy to resolve a longstanding national crisis of identity'. The newspaper interviewed a 'liberal and worldly Pakistani official', who sympathized with the overall aims of Islamization even though he worried about parts of it 'like many intellectuals'. The official summed up his views in a question, 'If we are not Muslims, what are we? Second-rate Indians?'[1]

Thus, while the clerics might be interested in following the letter of tenth-century Islamic jurisprudence to, say, allow husbands 'lightly' beat their wives, Pakistan's worldly politicians, civil servants and military officers seem to consider Islam the organizing principle in confronting India, whom they deem Pakistan's 'permanent enemy'. Since Zia, only one prime minister (Nawaz Sharif) and one army chief (General Aslam Beg) have espoused Islamist ideas bearing similarity to Zia's views. But even the most modern and westernized leaders, ranging from Harvard-educated Benazir Bhutto to self-professed Ataturk fan Pervez Musharraf, have failed to stop Pakistan from descending farther into an Islamist quagmire.

At least part of the explanation for why personally secular, civil and military leaders find it difficult to reverse even the most egregious obscurantism lies in their unwillingness to change Pakistan's collective view of its largest neighbour. An army officer, for instance, might understand that the clerics' demands for segregation of the sexes or an interest-free economy are incompatible with the needs of a modern society. But he cannot overcome the inculcated prejudice about 'Muslim Pakistan' being threatened by 'Hindu India' and by ethnic identities within the country.

Pakistani officers consider the most regressive clerics patriotic because, after all, they would never make common cause with Pakistan's external enemies—the Indians and whoever else Pakistani intelligence might know or imagine as conspiring against the country at any given moment. Liberal and secular thinkers, on the other hand, are permanently suspect. If they speak up for any ethnic group, they must want Pakistan's disintegration; if they ask for a secular state, they could be asking for eliminating Pakistan's identity and a virtual reincorporation into India; and if they question the army's political role or its budget, they must be in league with 'the enemy'.

While India is Pakistan's permanent enemy in this widely held view among Pakistan's elite, other enemies also feature in the calculus that leads to accepting Islamist disorder over pluralist clarity: Israel is as much Pakistan's enemy as India; the United States is a 'fair-weather friend' that does not understand Pakistan's regional compulsions and tries to bully Pakistan into compliance with policies that would weaken Pakistan; most Western nations are too beholden to the Americans to independently understand Pakistan's point of view; Saudi Arabia and other Gulf Arab countries, who helped radicalize Islam in Pakistan, do not respect Pakistan despite what Pakistan has done for them; and Iran's Shia clerical regime is always trying to use Pakistan's Shias to force Pakistan's hand in breaking up a close relationship with Sunni Arab countries.

Like every country, Pakistan must, of course, maintain a strong military capability to defend itself. Fear of a much larger and more resourceful neighbour is also not exclusive to Pakistan, nor is the existence of specific disputes. What sets Pakistan apart is the belief that India has not accepted Pakistan's existence as a nation or state and is constantly conspiring to invalidate its creation. This insecurity has been nourished throughout Pakistan's history, beginning with the country's founders, making it the cornerstone of Pakistani nationalism. Any other foreign individual or country that is seen as speaking or acting against Pakistan is also often seen as deliberately or naively adopting India's anti-Pakistan agenda.

'Pakistan was born under inauspicious circumstances,' wrote Aslam Siddiqui, a senior government official and propagandist in the 1960s, laying out the argument. According to him, 'Powerful forces were at work to cripple and thwart its very establishment as a viable state. These pressures created many complications and complexes. Strategically, Pakistan occupied a critical position in the region as well as in the world. It constitutes the borderland of the free world; it cannot therefore escape the strains of global rivalries. Pakistan also has an ideology which entails certain preferences. This is not liked by its major neighbours.' Siddiqui concluded that these factors 'combined to create many problems for the young State of Pakistan' and Pakistan's policies since Independence have only been a response to adverse conditions.[2] Echoes of this succinct description of the context of Pakistan's orientation can be found in virtually all explanations for Pakistan's sense of insecurity.

The alternative view, that Pakistani leaders cultivated the fear of an existential threat as a means of bringing their diverse peoples together, has been suppressed within Pakistan. The concept of an 'existential threat' helps in bypassing the complex issues of national identity and formulating a distinct culture.

Soon after Pakistan's birth, its founders had insisted that the Pakistani nation would unite around one faith (Islam) and one language (Urdu). This conceptualization was immediately challenged in East Pakistan by Bengalis demanding equal status for their Bengali language. Although Bengali was eventually given the status of national language, 'unity through diversity' was never accepted as the Pakistani ideal. In fact, under successive authoritarian and semi-democratic regimes, Pakistan has endeavoured to forge national unity through conformity, including conformity with a specific narrative of history and acceptance of shared threats as the basis of Pakistani nationhood.

Jinnah himself had complained soon after Independence of 'vigorous propaganda' about Pakistan being 'a temporary madness', which was aimed at forcing Pakistan 'to come into the [Indian] Union as a penitent, repentant, erring son'. He saw a 'well-planned, well-organized, and well-directed' effort 'to paralyse the new-born dominion of Pakistan'.[3] Jinnah's successors also encouraged the belief that India's real intention was to reverse Partition. Aided by textbooks and constant repetition in the mass media, this anxiety has now become an article of faith for many Pakistanis.

In less than two decades, India and Pakistan went to war in 1965 as a result of Pakistan's attempts to infiltrate guerillas into Kashmir. Pakistanis were told that India had attacked their country and that the United States stabbed Pakistan in the back by suspending delivery of weapons and spare parts. This accentuated the belief in Pakistan being the object of conspiracies by enemies of an Islamic revival. Morale boosting stories about angels and saints directing Indian bombs away from Pakistani targets reinforced the conviction that Allah had a special design for Pakistan's protection.[4]

At the United Nations Security Council, Foreign Minister Zulfikar Ali Bhutto laid out Pakistan's view of itself as David facing Goliath in its neighbourhood. 'Pakistan is a small country,' he said, adding, 'You have only to look at a map of the world and see our size to be aware of our resources and our ability. We are facing a great monster, a great aggressor always given to aggression.'[5] He elaborated Pakistan's vision of its security that has been tweaked but not changed in the years since. 'During the eighteen years of our independence we have seen India commit aggression time and again,' Bhutto said.[6]

According to Bhutto, 'Ever since 1947, India has followed the road of aggression. It has committed aggression against Junagadh, against Manavadar, against Mangrol, against Hyderabad and against Goa. It brought about a situation which has caused the Sino-Indian conflict. It has committed aggression against Pakistan. And Pakistan, according to Indian leaders, is its enemy number one. Pakistan is supposed to be the country which is the fulcrum of India's fundamental policies.' Bhutto also said, 'We have always known that India is determined to annihilate Pakistan,' echoing the sentiment that has become a defining element of Pakistani nationalism.[7]

'Pakistan's basic principle,' according to Bhutto, 'was the bringing about of a permanent settlement between the two major communities,' a reference to Hindus and Muslims of the subcontinent. Then he invoked the Pakistani version of history of conflict between the two communities running for centuries. 'For seven hundred years,' Bhutto insisted, 'we sought to achieve an equilibrium between the people of the two major communities, and we believed eventually that the only way to live in lasting peace with India was to establish our homeland, to establish a country smaller in area.' Pakistan was created so that it would be 'capable of having a relationship, a modus vivendi, with a great and powerful neighbour'.[8]

The creation of Pakistan, in Bhutto's account, was inspired by the example of European countries that 'had to separate in order to get closer together'. He cited the example of Sweden and Norway and said, 'We believed that with the creation of Pakistan we would be able to establish a permanent peace, a permanent understanding, between the people of India and the people of Pakistan.'[9] According to Bhutto, it was India's inherent aggressiveness that made peace impossible. It did not matter that most accounts of history do not support the notion of a seven-hundred-year conflict between Hindus and Muslims nor was it relevant that the contemporary state of Pakistan could not speak for all of the subcontinent's Muslims, one-third of whom were citizens of the contemporary state of India.

Less than six years later, in December 1971, Bhutto was back in the United Nations to speak for Pakistan on the eve of the surrender of Pakistani forces in Bangladesh after yet another war. He cited the example of the rivalry between Rome and Carthage and quoted the Roman historian, Cato the elder, who had told his countrymen, 'Carthage must be destroyed.' Instead of speaking of Pakistan as 'a small country' as he had done in 1965, Bhutto now bombastically compared Pakistan with the Roman Empire. 'If India thinks that it is going to subjugate Pakistan, Eastern Pakistan as well as Western Pakistan—because we are one people, we are one state,' he declared, 'then we shall say, "Carthage must be destroyed." We shall tell our children and they will tell their children that Carthage must be destroyed.'[10]

Bhutto's grandiloquence about Pakistan destroying India in a conflict that would last for generations unless Pakistan's terms were fulfilled came one day before the surrender of the large contingent of Pakistan Army in Bangladesh. Such poetic licence with historic facts or current reality has been an integral part of Pakistan's view of self. 'The Pakistani nation is a brave nation,' Bhutto had said in the same speech, adding 'One of the greatest British generals said that the best infantry fighters in the world are the Pakistanis.' He promised that 'We will fight. We will fight for a thousand years, if it comes to that,' advising the world to 'not go by momentary military victories'. After all, 'Stalingrad was overwhelmed. Leningrad was besieged for a thousand days' but that did not result in the defeat of the Soviet Union in the Second World War. Pakistanis were 'people who want to be free and who want to maintain their personality'. They would fight and 'will continue to fight for principles'.[11]

Of course, the promise of fighting for one thousand years did not prevent Bhutto from seeking compromise or making concessions when he met Indian prime minister Indira Gandhi at Simla in 1972. Pakistan wanted repatriation of its 90,000 prisoners of war (POWs) and a little humility was needed in the aftermath of a massive military defeat. India and Pakistan signed the Simla Accord, agreeing to resolve all issues including the dispute over Jammu and Kashmir bilaterally. This meant that Pakistan could no longer raise the Kashmir dispute in the United Nations. The ceasefire line in Kashmir was redefined as the Line of Control, signifying greater permanence. The POWs were repatriated and diplomatic relations restored. But this only deferred the commitment to fighting forever instead of bringing it to an enduring end. Within a few years, Pakistanis started arguing that the Simla Accord was signed under duress and that it was open to interpretation other than restricting Pakistan from internationalizing the dispute.

Considering that India had not invaded West Pakistan even after decisively defeating Pakistani forces in Bangladesh, the argument that India wanted to eliminate Pakistan sounded less convincing to others. If India's goal had been to remove Pakistan from the map, it would have behaved differently. East Pakistan had been lost, a large number of Pakistani troops were prisoners of war, and the morale in West Pakistan was low. Pakistan did not have a nuclear deterrent and its allies, the United States and China, had not intervened militarily on its behalf. Still,

India made no attempt to undo Pakistan beyond helping the creation of Bangladesh but that did not change Pakistani perceptions.

'What India wants is a subservient Pakistan, which should remain constantly under Indian influence,' General Zia, the dictator who succeeded Bhutto in power, told a foreign journalist in 1981, reflecting a twist in the explanation for Pakistan's sense of insecurity. The threat was not just that Pakistan would be destroyed but that it would be treated, in Zia's words, 'like some of the smaller states'. Pakistan could not 'accept that position' and 'India should know that very well'.[12] Little has changed in Pakistan's view of the need to fight constantly for survival or respect even after the acquisition of nuclear weapons, which for other nuclear states has served as an ultimate guarantee of security.

Nothing illustrates the psychological nature of Pakistan's insecurity than the burning down of a yoga centre in Islamabad by armed men a few years ago after the anchor of a television show described it as 'a potential threat to national security'. The Geneva-based Art of Living Foundation, which ran the centre, was duly registered in Pakistan. The TV anchor suggested that its connection to Indian wellness guru Sri Sri Ravi Shankar made it dangerous.[13] That a yoga facility managed and run by Pakistanis as part of a European non-governmental organization should be deemed a national security threat by a nuclear power, leading to action by armed men, is indicative of the irrationality of Pakistan's national security dialogue.

Among the many unfounded arguments about Pakistan being in constant danger is the oft-repeated assertion that India was planning to turn Pakistan into a desert by withholding its water or to cause floods by dumping more water into rivers. Most of Pakistan's rivers flow through the Indian state of Jammu and Kashmir but the Indus Waters Treaty between the two countries precludes the possibility of India diverting or withholding the supply of water downstream. Many countries in the world share rivers and it is rare for a lower riparian to express alarm at regular intervals about the upper riparian's intentions to deprive it of water. After all, dams cannot be built overnight and rivers are not like water on tap that can be turned off without warning.

The Indus Waters Treaty gives Pakistan exclusive rights to the water of three rivers and places strict conditions on India's use of the Indus tributaries. Disagreements are subject to arbitration by the World Bank. Pakistan has fallen behind in plans to construct reservoirs for its own use and its track record in water management is widely considered very poor.[14] But these facts do not prevent Pakistani hardliners, such as Lashkar-e-Taiba chief Hafiz Saeed from claiming that 'India irrigates its deserts and dumps extra water on Pakistan without any warning' or Kashmiri terrorist leader, Syed Salahuddin declaring that 'India wants to turn Pakistan into an arid desert'. The proposed response to the potential water problem is often a military one. 'If this continues, a new jihad will begin. Our fighters and all of Pakistan's fighters are ready to avenge Indian brutality in whatever form,' Salahuddin was reported as saying.[15]

Because of bluster like that, Saeed and Salahuddin remain heroes in Pakistan even after being identified as terrorists internationally. The US announced a reward of $10 million for information on Saeed's whereabouts in 2012[16] while Salahuddin was designated as a global terrorist in 2017.[17] From the Pakistani point of view, the world does not understand India or Pakistan's concerns about it and that allows Pakistan to act in the interest of its security the way Pakistanis deem fit. Whenever Pakistani authorities have detained Saeed or others of his ilk in response to international pressure, Pakistan's courts have set them free. On one occasion, the chief justice of Lahore High Court, Khawaja Sharif, remarked in court that Saeed could not be called a terrorist for killing Hindus because Hindus were responsible for terrorism by occupying Kashmir.[18]

In recent years, the rise of 'Hindu nationalism' in India is cited in Pakistan as evidence of implacable hostility between Muslim Pakistan and Hindu India. But it is important to note that the notions in Pakistan of Hindu–Muslim relations being eternally strained and Pakistan being under a permanent threat from India predate the political rise of Hindutva during the 1990s. Pakistan's leaders were speaking of Pakistan and Islam being in danger even during the decades immediately after Partition when leaders of the Hindutva movement saw India's government appeasing the country's Muslim minority. Statements and assertions by post-Independence Indian leaders, such as Jawaharlal Nehru, that India had accepted Pakistan in 'good faith' had little impact.

'Pakistan has come into being, rather unnaturally I think,' Nehru had told students at the Aligarh Muslim University in January 1948, less than five months after Pakistan's creation. 'Nevertheless, it represents the urges of a large number of persons. I believe that this development has been a throw-back, but we accepted it in good faith,' he said, denying the desire 'to strangle and crush Pakistan and to force it in to a reunion with India'. According to Nehru, that allegation was 'based on fear and complete misunderstanding of our attitude'. He said he believed in 'a closer union' with Pakistan as he did with 'many other neighbouring countries'. But this was not meant 'to strangle or compel Pakistan' because 'an attempt to disrupt Pakistan would recoil to India's disadvantage'.

'If we had wanted to break Pakistan, why did we agree to Partition?' Nehru asked, adding that it would have been easier to prevent Pakistan's creation 'than to try to do so now after all that has happened'. He recognized that there was 'no going back in history' and it was 'to India's advantage that Pakistan should be a secure and prosperous State with which we can develop close and friendly relations'. Nehru declared unequivocally, 'If today, by any chance I were offered the reunion of India and Pakistan, I would decline it for obvious reasons. I do not want to carry the burden of Pakistan's great problems. I have enough of my own. Any closer association must come out of a normal process and in a friendly way which does not end Pakistan as a State, but makes it an equal part of a larger union in which several countries might be associated.'[19]

Nehru's affirmation so soon after Independence did not prevent Pakistan's embrace of fear and insecurity as critical elements of its national identity. Now, when those advocating Hindutva are actually in power in India, and some extremists talk about breaking up Pakistan to end its constant support of terrorism in India, there is even less willingness in Pakistan to give up a jingoist approach to national defence.

Significantly, Pakistan's attitude towards the perceived Indian threat has changed little in seventy years. Pakistani officials' avowed fear of a decidedly more Hindu sentiment espoused by Prime Minister Narendra Modi in 2017 differs little from the vehement derision that characterized Nehru's overtures in 1948. In 2016, army chief General Raheel Sharif echoed the sentiment expressed by Bhutto in 1971. He declared, as many have done throughout Pakistan's history, that Pakistanis 'understood the conspiracies' against their country and would fight them for as long as it takes. 'We are aware of our enemies, know their tactics and to spoil their designs we would go beyond even the last limit,' General Sharif said, reminding everyone that 'Pakistan's army was second to none and a battle-hardened force'.[20]

National Security Theology

It is not unusual for rulers and states to seek legitimacy as defenders of a particular faith and many armies in history have been motivated to fight in the name of religion. In Pakistan's case, however, an entire theology has been evolved about the state and its army that means little to the over one billion followers of Islam around the world that are not Pakistani. This includes claims about the significance of the country's birth on a holy night in Ramadan—the Muslim month of fasting—and purported mention of an army of believers that will fight Hindus before Judgement Day.

In its early years, Pakistani leaders referred to the country as 'Mamlakat-e-Khudadad', (the kingdom bestowed by God), which was not different from similar assertions by other kingdoms and states. The country's largely secular elite bolstered the spirits of beleaguered Muslim refugees from India by pointing out that God had a special plan for the new country, which is why it was born on the auspicious Lailatul Qadr (the Night of Power or Night of Destiny) which occurs every year on the night between 26 and 27 Ramadan. The Act of British Parliament that granted independence to the two dominions, India and Pakistan, determined that independence would begin at midnight on 15 August 1947, which was a Friday. This too was portrayed as having religious significance.

Lailatul Qadr in 1947 was on the night between 14 and 15 August but after celebrating Independence Day on 15 August in 1948, Pakistan's cabinet decided to move its observance to 14 August to avoid sharing celebrations with India. Most Pakistanis are not even aware that Pakistan's first postage stamps bore the 15 August date as the date of the country's Independence. It is not uncommon for public speakers and television anchors to insist that Pakistan was born through God's special dispensation on the holy night of Lailatul Qadr and on the holy day of Friday even as Pakistan now celebrates its Independence a day earlier. The 'auspicious date of creation' story serves the purpose of connecting religious observance with the creation of Pakistan and is a useful preface for the idea of a country with a special religious purpose.

In recent years, the notion of God's special dispensation for Pakistan has no longer been limited to benign actions such as the adjustment of the country's Independence Day. Several clerics have started claiming that the Quran and the Hadith (statements attributed to Prophet Muhammad) predicted the creation of Pakistan. According to this nationalist theology, which does not fit into Islam's universalism, Pakistan's jihad against Hindu India is part of the prophecies about the days preceding the end of the world and the Second Coming of Jesus. Since the righteous must stand against Dajjal (the anti-Christ) and with Mahdi and Jesus (Isa ibn Maryam), this version of faith makes support of the Pakistani state an integral part of Islam.

An undated Urdu language booklet titled, '*Pakistan aur afvaaj-e-Pakistan ka tazkira Quran aur Ahadith mein*' (Mention of Pakistan and Pakistan Army in the Quran and the Hadith) summarizes this unusual theological definition of Pakistan's national purpose. Written by Mufti Ghulam Farid Haqqani of Peshawar, the book cites a Hadith attributed to Prophet Muhammad, which says, 'Among my followers, two groups have been granted absolute protection from hellfire. The first is the army that will wage jihad against Hindus in Hindustan and the other is the Muslim army that fights alongside Jesus (whom Muslims consider one of Islam's Prophets) after his second advent.' Mufti Haqqani insists that this Hadith speaks of the virtue of Pakistan's army, which is dedicated to fighting Hindus forever.[21] Similar arguments are also offered by evangelists and self-identified 'security analysts', many of whom receive official patronage and are covered on national television.

One of the most prominent exponents of ultra-nationalist theology is Syed Zaid Hamid, a demagogue who presents a programme on national security issues on a private television channel and claims to have fought in Afghanistan in the 1980s with the Afghan mujahideen. According to British author Anatol Lieven, 'there can be no doubt' that Hamid is close to the ISI 'though he told me that he had never been an ISI officer'.[22] Hamid's lectures about Pakistan's eternal conflict with India and God's plan for Pakistan include repeated references to the Hadith about Ghazwa-e-Hind (Battle of India) that prophesize a great battle in India between true believers and unbelievers before the end of time.

Hamid once reminded his audience that Muslim military generals launched numerous attacks on Constantinople for 900 years just to prove a Hadith predicting the Muslim conquest of that city. Constantinople eventually fell to a Muslim army in 1453. In Hamid's view, it is just a matter of time before the Ghazwa-e-Hind Hadith comes true. 'The people of Pakistan are destined for victory in Ghazwa-e-Hind, as prophesied by Prophet Muhammad himself,' he insists, vowing that Pakistanis 'would conquer India' and 'then march onward to fight against Israel in Palestine'.[23]

In Hamid's world view, ostensibly shared by Pakistani military and intelligence officers, civilian governments seeking accommodation with Pakistan's neighbours worry too much about material losses, and even the fear that the country might break up is immaterial. 'Bearing losses is one thing and the breaking of a country is another,' he thunders. 'Losing religion, faith and honor is different. Allah willing, nothing would happen of this sort.' Hamid encourages Pakistanis to defy all material calculations and confront even the Americans if they enter Pakistan from Afghanistan. If the US and India try to act in concert to undo Pakistan, God would be on Pakistan's side.

'Our rulers are certainly unholy; people are, certainly, sold out in the media,' Hamid says in what has become a refrain of some Pakistani Islamists. 'We are not doing any diplomacy at all; we are weak economically too. But by the Grace of Allah, we are not a dead nation.' Hamid's nationalist exhortations continue with preparing Pakistanis for a long war. 'Even if we get a beating initially, beating means they might bomb our cities, and we'll have to leave some territories in the border areas,' he says, discussing possible scenarios of an imaginary US–India collusion. 'It is not a big deal,' he says, 'to take the territory back by regrouping, reorganizing, and launching counter-attacks.' What matters is the 'morale of a nation' and 'the nation which is alive, whose morale is high, who has the confidence of victory and who has faith in his Allah, will win in the end.' In his opinion, if the Prophet's prophesy about Constantinople's conquest came true 900 years ago, surely the prophecy about the conquest of India will also be fulfilled one day. Pakistanis need only have faith and stay their course.[24]

Hamid and others of his ilk reject outright any practical effort to mend fences with India and also create a fictional conflict between the United States and Pakistan. Israel, which until recently had little to do with South Asia, is also portrayed as a major enemy of Pakistan. Such religion-based nationalism does not help Pakistan operate in the real world and drags Pakistani policymakers into a world of make-believe. One of its major recent consequences has been that global terrorist groups, al-Qaeda and the Islamic State of Iraq and al-Sham (ISIS), are now competing for recruitment in Pakistan, aided by competing claims of divine support.

The South Asian region has a long history with jihadi movements, dating back to the eighteenth century and now Pakistan has become the region's jihad capital. During the 1980s, it became the staging ground for global jihad as part of the internationally backed guerilla war against the Soviet Union in Afghanistan. At the time, radical Islamists poured into Afghanistan through Pakistan and received advanced military training to fight the Soviets. Later, many returned to their home countries to conduct terrorist attacks. The rise of the Taliban in Afghanistan and the Pakistan-backed insurgency in Kashmir against India also stoked jihadism in the region.

The first generation of al-Qaeda commanders and ideologues were veterans of the anti-Soviet Afghan war. ISIS too has been influenced greatly by the so-called Arab-Afghans and their disciples. During the war against the Soviets and the ensuing Taliban rule, ancient prophecies of Khurasan—which includes modern Afghanistan—resurfaced to inspire jihadists and promise great heavenly rewards. These prophecies foreshadowed the appearance of the Mahdi or Messiah and the ultimate battle between good (pure Islam) and evil before Judgement Day. According to one Hadith, an army with black flags would emerge from Khurasan to help the Mahdi establish his caliphate at Mecca.

This was not the first time that the Khurasan Hadith had been cited to mobilize Muslim soldiers. Sayings attributed to Prophet Muhammad were often transmitted orally; formal written compilations did not emerge until more than a century after his death in AD 632. This made it possible for rulers and commanders to conveniently cite the Hadith to justify political decisions or advance battle plans. The Hadith describing an army from the east wielding a black flag was used by the Abbasids to orchestrate their revolt against the ruling Umayyad dynasty in AD 747. At the time, Abbasid partisan Abu Muslim organized an army with black flags in Khurasan to march east on Damascus.

Like most medieval prophecies, the Islamic ones also comprise metaphorical statements open to interpretation. One Hadith instructs true believers to join the nation from the east with black flags 'even if you have to crawl over ice'.[25] Another says, 'Armies carrying black flags will come from Khurasan, no power will be able to stop them and they will finally reach Eela (the al-Aqsa Mosque in Jerusalem) where they will erect their flags.'[26] This prediction of final victory was a convenient recruitment tool for al-Qaeda when it was firmly established in Khurasan (i.e., Afghanistan) during the Taliban era.

ISIS shares the stated desire of all Islamist groups to replicate the social order of Islam's pristine era, the time of Prophet Muhammad and of the four 'Rightly Guided Caliphs' that followed him. Soon after declaring himself the modern-day caliph, ISIS leader Abu Bakr al-Baghdadi named the provinces of his caliphate after the provinces of the early caliphate. These provinces, or wilayats, consist of Algeria (wilayat al-Jazair), Libya (wilayat al-Barqah, wilayat al-Tarabulus and wilayat al-Fizan), Sinai (wilayat Sinai), Saudi Arabia (wilayat al-Haramayn), Yemen (wilayat al-Yaman) and Afghanistan-Pakistan (wilayat Khurasan). ISIS propaganda often speaks of defeating the West while referring to it as Rum, the historic Arab name for the Roman Empire.

Reverting to historic names for Muslim countries summons Muslim pride for Islam's early conquests, when inspired Arabs went forth from the cities of Mecca and Medina in the Arabian Peninsula to create a vast caliphate incorporating parts of the erstwhile Persian and Roman empires. Invoking the Hadith and pronouncements from Islam's earliest period foreshadow the resurrection of Islam's lost glory; in addition to seeking reward in the hereafter, young Muslims are motivated to fight battles and seek victories that were ostensibly foretold fourteen centuries earlier by the Prophet.

While much of the contemporary Middle East fell under Muslim rule during the period of the 'Rightly Guided Caliphs', Muslims had to wait for several centuries before expanding their conquest to the Indian subcontinent. The Hadith predicting the great battle for India is often referred to as the Ghazwa-e-Hind Hadith, various versions of which have been recycled each time a Muslim leader or would-be conqueror attempted to raise an army to invade India.[27]

In one version of the Hadith, attributed to Thawban, a freed slave of Prophet Muhammad, '[t]he Messenger of Allah said: "There are two groups of my Ummah whom Allah will free from the Fire: The group that invades India, and the group that will be with Isa bin Maryam, peace be upon him."'[28] Isa bin Maryam is the Quranic name of Jesus, whose return to earth alongside the Mahdi is held in Islamic tradition to be a seminal event of the end of time.

In another version, narrated by Abu Hurairah, one of the companions of Prophet Muhammed, '[t]he Messenger of Allah promised us that we would invade India. If I live to see that, I will sacrifice myself and my wealth. If I am killed, I will be one of the best of the martyrs, and if I come back, I will be Abu Hurairah Al-Muharrar.'[29] Al-Muharrar translates as 'the one freed from the fire of hell'. In another version from Abu Hurairah, warriors 'headed towards Sindh and Hind' were promised the reward of worldly success and freedom from hell.[30] Abu Hurairah quoted Prophet Muhammad as saying, '[d]efinitely, one of your troops would do a war with Hindustan. Allah would grant success to those warriors, as far as they would bring their kings by dragging them in chains. And Allah would forgive those warriors (by the Blessing of this Great War). And when those Muslims would return, they would find Isa Ibn Maryam [Jesus] in Syria.'

Just as the prophecies of Khurasan became popular during the wars in Afghanistan, the Ghazwa-e-Hind divinations became a staple of the Islamist discourse after the launch of jihad in Indian-controlled parts of Kashmir in 1989. Throughout the 1990s, Pakistani official media also encouraged discussion of the Ghazwa-e-Hind Hadith to motivate jihadists. In fact, every major Pakistan-based jihadi group that launched terrorist attacks across the border claimed that their operations were part of the battle for India promised by the Prophet. For these Pakistani groups, supported by Pakistan's Inter-Services Intelligence, the target of jihad should be the modern state of India and its 'occupation' of Kashmir.

For example, Lashkar-e-Taiba has often spoken of Ghazwa-e-Hind as a means of liberating Kashmir from Indian control. The group's founder, Hafiz Muhammad Saeed, has declared repeatedly that '[i]f freedom is not given to the Kashmiris, then we will occupy the whole of India including Kashmir. We will launch Ghazwa-e-Hind. Our homework is complete to get Kashmir.'[31] Pakistani propagandist Zaid Hamid has also repeatedly invoked Ghazwa-e-Hind as a battle against Hindu India led from Muslim Pakistan. According to Hamid, 'Allah has destined the people of Pakistan' with victory and 'Allah is the aid and helper of Pakistan'.[32]

Several Islamic scholars, especially from India, have questioned the veracity of the Ghazwa-e-Hind Hadith and reject its repeated contemporary citation as 'Pakistani terrorists' anti-India propaganda'. According to Maulana Waris Mazhari of the Darul Uloom Deoband seminary in Uttar Pradesh, India, the conflict between India and Pakistan over Kashmir was not jihad; and the dream of establishing 'Muslim hegemony throughout the entire world' was fanciful. 'The term ghalba-e-Islam, the establishment of the supremacy of Islam, used in the context of the Quran and the sayings of the Prophet (Hadith), refers not to any political project of Muslim domination,' Mazhari wrote, 'but, rather, to the establishment of the superiority of Islam's ideological and spiritual message.'[33]

Mazhari pointed out that 'the statement attributed to the Prophet regarding the Ghazwa-e-Hind is found in only one of the Sihah Sitta, the six collections of Hadith reports of the Sunni Muslims—in the collection by al-Nasai'. He rejected its current interpretations as 'rhetoric of the self-styled jihadists' that is 'based less on proper scholarly analysis of the Islamic textual tradition than on strident, heated emotionalism and a deep-rooted hatred and feeling of revenge'.[34] It reflected a 'distorted understanding of Jihad', which started 'in the very first century of Islam itself, when intra-Muslim wars were sought to be christened by competing groups as Jihads'.[35]

In fact, Mazhari argued that the Hadith about Ghazwa-e-Hind would have been narrated by many more companions of Prophet Muhammad and cited in multiple collections of the Hadith 'considering the merits or rewards of the Ghazwa-e-Hind that it talks about'.[36] Given that only one companion of the Prophet reported it, Mazhari suggests that 'it is possible that this Hadith report is not genuine and that it might have been manufactured in the period of the Umayyad Caliphs to suit and justify their own political purposes and expansionist designs'.[37]

Even if the Hadith were true, Mazhari argues, '[t]he battle against India that it predicted was fulfilled in the early Islamic period itself, and is not something that will happen in the future. This, in fact, is the opinion of the majority of the Ulema, qualified Islamic scholars.'[38] Mazhari saw the Ghazwa-e-Hind Hadith as an instrument of propaganda in 'the proxy war engaged in Kashmir by powerful forces in Pakistan in the guise of a so-called Jihad', which he and other ulema consider 'nothing but deceit'. He also noted that there was no historic record of the Hadith being cited by the many Muslim conquerors of the subcontinent and the ulema that accompanied them.[39]

Other Indian clerics have offered alternative explanations of the Hadith. Maulana Abdul Hameed Nomani of the Jamiat Ulema-i-Hind (Society of Indian Islamic Scholars) says that this Hadith was fulfilled at the time of the Four Righteous Caliphs, when several companions of the Prophet came to India in order to spread Islam. Mufti Sajid Qasmi, professor at Darul Uloom Deoband, believes that the Hadith might also refer to the invasion of Sindh by Arabs under Muhammad bin Qasim in the eighth century. On the other hand, Maulana Mufti Mushtaq Tijarvi of Jamaat-e-Islami India has suggested that the Hadith is not genuine at all and perhaps a fabrication intended to justify Qasim's invasion.[40]

Although the idea of Ghazwa-e-Hind as a war against the contemporary Indian state has not been universally accepted, it continues to feature in the Pakistani discourse. Jihadists have differed on interpreting the Hadith, especially in the aftermath of the 11 September 2001 attacks, when al-Qaeda was uprooted from Afghanistan and the Pakistani government led by Gen. Pervez Musharraf chose to side, albeit only partially, with the United States. Divisions among jihadists about attitudes towards the Pakistani state and government are reflected in their interpretation of Ghazwa-e-Hind as directed solely against modern-day India or encompassing also Pakistan.

The defeat of the Taliban and the arrival of NATO forces in Afghanistan in 2001 shifted al-Qaeda's major operations to Iraq and Yemen even though Osama bin Laden continued to hide in Pakistan.

For some time, discussion of the epic battle for India diminished in the jihadi discourse while grand strategies for the expulsion of Western influence from the Middle East took centre stage. The death of Osama bin Laden and the rise of ISIS, however, have revived global jihadist interest in Ghazwa-e-Hind.

The Pakistani offshoot of the Taliban, Tehrik-e-Taliban Pakistan (TTP), which has declared war on the Pakistani state, maintains that their war is the Ghazwa-e-Hind forecast by Prophet Muhammad. In their interpretation, the reference to India is said to cover Afghanistan, Pakistan and India. In one May 2013 TTP video, entitled 'Ghazwa-e-Hind 3', footage of militants loyal to Mullah Fazlullah are supplemented with a critique of ISIS for limiting its jihad to Kashmir. According to Fazlullah, 'the India jihad begins from Attock [in Pakistan]; the India jihad is in the land of Pakistan; the area of Lahore is in the India jihad; Multan is in India; all the towns of Punjab are in the India jihad that we are waging. Therefore, the Ulema should rise up and explain the borders of the India jihad, explain these sayings of Prophet Muhammad, explain to the public the boundaries of India, which areas were in India 50 years ago, what were their boundaries...'[41]

The militant Islamist group Jamaat-ul-Ahrar, itself a member of TTP's coalition, has argued that Hind at the time of Prophet Muhammad referred to 'a very large area which today includes Pakistan, Kashmir, India, Bangladesh, Bhutan, Nepal, Maldives, Sri Lanka and Burma'. The group invited Muslims to 'aid the Mujahideen in Khurasan' and 'to work for an Islamic state in Pakistan'. Jamaat-ul-Ahrar promised that '[o]ur jihad will not stop till Pakistan is conquered but we will keep fighting until entire Hind is under the Sharia of Allah. We shall keep going and conquer every country in our path [with Allah's will] until we reach Filisteen [Palestine] and there we shall erect the black flags in al-Quds [Jerusalem].'[42]

The Islamic Movement of Uzbekistan (IMU), an affiliate of al-Qaeda, has also adopted the broader definition of battle for the Indian subcontinent by naming its Urdu-language magazine 'Ghazwa-e-Hind'.

The first issue of the magazine was posted on the Jamia Hafsa Urdu Forum (JHUF)—named after a seminary in Islamabad—on 15 November 2011. The magazine featured articles on jihad in Pakistan, including summaries of past speeches by Osama bin Laden and IMU scholar Abuzar Azzam.

One such article argued that the jihad in Pakistan did not depend upon the American presence in Afghanistan, as the jihadists were fighting for the implementation of sharia in Pakistan and to avenge the deaths of prominent jihadists at the hands of the duplicitous Pakistani regime. 'Undoubtedly, we will continue to wage jihad in Pakistan till we avenge the killings of Taher Jan, Abu Muhammad al-Turkistani, Baitullah Mehsud, Abdul Rahman al-Kanadi, Sheikh Osama bin Laden and many more,' argued IMU. 'We will continue to fight till Islam arrives in Islamabad. It does not matter even if the Americans leave Afghanistan.'[43]

In May 2014, IMU released a video of its Mufti Abuzar Azzam discussing Ghazwa-e-Hind. He argued that 'Hind' includes not just India but also Pakistan, Sri Lanka, the Maldives, Kashmir, Burma and Bangladesh; and explained that the jihad in Pakistan—a part of Ghazwa-e-Hind—is necessary for the success of the jihad in Afghanistan—the jihad in Khurasan.[44]

The recent revival of interest in the Ghazwa-e-Hind prophecy reflects rivalry between competing jihadi groups. Al-Qaeda, now led by Ayman al-Zawahiri, faces the prospect of extinction as its Arab cadres defect to ISIS, founded by Abu Bakr al-Baghdadi. Zawahiri has worked to build alliances with Pakistani jihadi groups and make inroads into India's Muslim population because it helps him remain relevant in the face of ISIS.

Al-Qaeda has apparently sought support from Kashmiri and Uyghur groups for its expanded battle on the Indian subcontinent. In December 2013, Kashmir-based Dukhtaran-e-Millat (Daughters of the Nation) leader Asiya Andarabi revealed in an interview that a member of al-Qaeda had approached her to seek 'the group's support in the jihad in Pakistan for enforcement of sharia and to start Ghazwa-e-Hind from Pakistan'.[45] Moreover, the Pakistan-based Uyghur jihadi group Turkestan Islamic Party (TIP) released a video in April 2014 proclaiming jihad against China as necessary for the fulfilment of the Prophet's purported Ghazwa-e-Hind prophecy.[46]

In September 2014, Zawahiri announced the formation of al-Qaeda in the Indian Subcontinent (AQIS), which his ally Maulana Asim Umar reinforced with a call for global jihad by Indian Muslims. That same month, AQIS took responsibility for an attempt to hijack the Pakistan frigate PNS *Zulfiqar* in the Karachi naval yard. The operation was most likely undertaken by terrorists who had already been operating with one of several regional groups active on behalf of al-Qaeda. But in the event, al-Qaeda sought credit for the parent group, almost as if it sought to assert its brand against the appeal of ISIS. Zawahiri may be banking on the Pakistani state's entrenched policy of tolerating and supporting any group that targets India to ensure al-Qaeda's survival in the post–Osama bin Laden phase.

An AQIS spokesman explained on 8 September 2014 that AQIS seeks to raise the 'flag of jihad' in the whole region and that while they seek to 'liberate' Indian Muslims from Hindus, Pakistan is its 'doorstep' for jihad. The spokesman insisted that the Karachi 'operation gives a clear message to India that Ghazwa-e-Hind has only just begun. We shall never forget your oppression of our brothers in Kashmir, Gujarat and Assam; and you shall reap what you have sowed.'[47]

The formation of AQIS was announced only after ISIS leader Baghdadi proclaimed the revival of the caliphate during the Muslim holy month of Ramadan in June 2014. In his call for global jihad, Baghdadi listed the countries and regions where mosques were being desecrated and Islamic sanctities violated. He argued in his video message that 'Muslims' rights are forcibly seized in China, India, Palestine, Somalia, the Arabian Peninsula, the Caucasus, Sham (the Levant), Egypt, Iraq, Indonesia, Afghanistan, the Philippines, Ahvaz, Iran (by the rafidah, or Shia), Pakistan, Tunisia, Libya, Algeria and Morocco, in the East and in the West.' Baghdadi exhorted, 'So, raise your ambitions, O soldiers of the

Islamic State! For your brothers all over the world are waiting for your rescue, and are anticipating your brigades. It is enough for you to just look at the scenes that have reached you from Central Africa, and from Burma before that. What is hidden from us is far worse. So, by Allah, we will take revenge.'[48]

The newly proclaimed caliph's speech contained several references to India, Kashmir and Pakistan, in addition to Afghanistan, Burma and China. In the past, al-Qaeda had successfully recruited fighters from each of these countries and regions. Other than accepting Baghdadi's caliphate, Zawahiri's only option now seemed to be to protect his turf, to take advantage of Pakistan's rivalry with India and to rally groups that have pursued jihad in South Asia based on the Ghazwa-e-Hind prophecies.

Al-Qaeda's efforts to consolidate itself in the Khurasan–Hind battleground were complicated by some groups in the region announcing their support for ISIS. In October 2014, Ansar al-Tawhid al-Hind (supporters of monotheism in India) pledged allegiance to ISIS. The pledge came in an Urdu audio speech from the group's leader, Maulvi Abdul Rehman al-Hindi, and was made public by its media arm, al-Isabah.

Abdul Rehman al-Hindi had surfaced a year earlier with calls for Indian Muslims to join the group and wage jihad. Moreover, al-Isabah had released videos with titles such as 'From Kandahar to Delhi'. In pledging allegiance, Abdul Rehman al-Hindi spoke at length about the historical caliphates, describing the religious necessity of re-establishing such an entity. He expressed support for the 'sincere and lionhearted mujahideen' of ISIS and called upon all Muslims, and those in India in particular, to pledge allegiance to the group. As he concluded, '[a]fter the establishment of the Islamic State we do not consider allegiances to organizations and groups to be legitimate.'[49]

'I take this opportunity,' al-Hindi intoned, 'to call all Muslims, especially of India, to rise, aspire to be part of one Ummah, one army, under one leader, and break the shackles of humiliation and disgrace.

This disgraceful pacifism will not benefit you, so why do you wait until your women are raped and blood of your sons spilled? And beware of the nationalistic democratic attitudes of some of our misguided Islamic organizations.'[50] Subsequently al-Isabah released a video eulogizing an Indian fighter killed in a suicide raid in Afghanistan, confirming that the group had turned operational.[51]

In January 2015, ISIS announced the formation of the Khorasan Group, with former Taliban leader Hafiz Saeed Khan—also known as Mullah Saeed Orakzai—as its commander. The new ISIS offshoot covers Pakistan, Afghanistan, India and Bangladesh, as well as some parts of Central Asia—areas deemed by jihadists to be part of the historic Khurasan and Hind mentioned in the Islamic prophecies.

One year earlier, Saeed had lost out in a power struggle within Tehrik-e-Taliban Pakistan (TTP) and so joined the ISIS bandwagon in an effort to reassert himself. His allies include several key members of the TTP now influential within the Khorasan Group: former spokesman Shahidullah Shahid, Khyber tribal region leader Gul Zaman, Peshawar chief Mufti Hassan, Kurram chief Hafiz Quran Daulat and Hangu leader Khalid Mansoor.[52]

Pakistani officials, including Interior Minister Chaudhry Nisar Ali Khan, dismissed ISIS's claims of having a significant presence in the country, arguing that such claims are in fact manifestations of leadership conflicts within the TTP. According to these Pakistanis, the TTP remains the potent force in Pakistan's north-west tribal region. However, in June 2014, a group calling itself al-Wafa Foundation for Media Production released a video entitled, 'We are your Army in Pakistan'. In the video, one fighter named Habibullah Habib expressed brotherhood with ISIS and offered it money and men.[53]

Another Pakistani jihadi group, Caliphate and Jihad Movement, similarly pledged allegiance to ISIS and Baghdadi in July 2014. The group praised ISIS and offered itself as an 'arrow of the arrows' to Baghdadi in Pakistan, and congratulated the declaration of the caliphate, praying that it will extend to Afghanistan, India and Pakistan. The group then claimed responsibility for the four attacks in Pakistan's Sindh province, which included the strikes on policemen in Karachi and the Latifabad area of Hyderabad between 25 May and 6 July 2014.[54]

Jundallah (Soldiers of Allah), also based in Pakistan, followed the Caliphate and Jihad Movement in pledging allegiance to Baghdadi. It promised to unify the ranks of fighters in the Afghanistan–Pakistan region and India. In November 2014, a message posted on a jihadi online forum reported that Jundallah chief Ahmed Ghardan Abu Yahya had announced his pledge during a visit from a delegation led by ISIS's Zubeir al-Kuwaiti. The message added: 'Praise be to Allah, many from the jihadi organizations, groups, and brigades in Khorasan and India agreed to meet with the delegation of the Islamic State. With permission from Allah, the Lord of the Worlds, you will hear another glad tiding.'[55]

While ISIS boasted of success in expanding into Afghanistan, Pakistan and India, AQIS has been active in producing recruitment and propaganda material in Bengali. The Bengali section of AQIS has released videos encouraging Bangladeshi Muslims to enter the jihadi battlefield.[56] There have also been credible reports of al-Qaeda affiliates being active in the Muslim-majority Maldives, as several Maldivian nationals are believed to have travelled to Pakistan's north-west tribal region for training alongside other jihadists.[57]

In his speech announcing the formation of AQIS, al-Zawahiri had argued, 'Bangladesh, which they claimed to have won from Pakistan so that it may get its freedom, is being turned into a subjugated surrogate of India. These anti-Islamic policies that assail Islamic beliefs, symbols and the noble Prophet of Islam are only a manifestation of complete subjugation to India. The events in Bangladesh enjoy the blessings of both India and America, since their interests in fighting Islam overlap, and this is why their bilateral relations are becoming stronger day by day.'[58]

In what was clearly an effort to appeal to the anti-Indian sentiment among Pakistan's jihadists in particular, Zawahiri railed against India.

'It is democratic India that killed thousands of Muslims in Kashmir, Gujarat, Ahmadabad, and Assam...The events in Bangladesh and Burma are not too distant from the oppression and killings of Muslims in Kashmir or the racial cleansing in Assam, Gujarat and Ahmadabad either.' He spoke of the need to 'make a serious effort to bring an end to these oppressions on Muslims in Bangladesh, India, Burma and Sri Lanka' and reassured 'our brothers and our people in Kashmir, Assam, Gujarat, and Ahmadabad who are living under the dark shade of Hindu occupation'.[59]

Al-Qaeda appears to be attempting to maintain support among radical Islamists in the subcontinent by directing its ire at India. Its leaders have been active in Afghanistan and Pakistan since the anti-Soviet jihad of the 1980s and maintain close ties to the Pakistan-supported Afghan Taliban and Kashmiri jihadi groups. By focusing on India, al-Qaeda hopes to retain the support of Pakistan-backed groups, which interpret the Ghazwa-e-Hind Hadith to mean reconquest of Hindu India without hitting Muslim Pakistan. Even in Zawahiri's statement about AQIS, Pakistan was mentioned only as a country that needed to be brought under full shariat rule while Hindu India was portrayed as the enemy of Islam.

ISIS, on the other hand, has accepted the allegiance of groups that are violently opposed to both the Republic of India and the Islamic Republic of Pakistan. ISIS affiliates appear to have opted for the alternative interpretation of Ghazwa-e-Hind, offered by groups such as the TTP, to pursue jihad in all parts of historic Hind. Indeed, in an ominous declaration, one South Asian ISIS member proclaimed, '[o]ur struggle is ongoing and Insha'Allah after defeating Pakistan Army, we won't just stop in Pakistan; rather we shall continue our advance into Kashmir and India until the laws of Allah are implemented globally and the whole world comes under the rule of one Muslim Khalifah.'[60]

Pakistan's efforts to consolidate itself by popularizing theology as national or even national-security policy have unleashed violent forces that Pakistan is now contending with. Instead of strengthening the country and raising the morale of its people in permanently confronting India, the 'Ghazwa-e-Hind' type of thinking has resulted in terrorist attacks within Pakistan and set the stage for divisions among jihadis that are hurting Pakistan's security instead of enhancing it. The theologically rooted view of what threatens Pakistan—as opposed to what might really threaten Pakistan—undermines the prospect of a realistic foreign policy. Conspiracy theories and contending interpretations of religious prophecies cast Don Quixotes tilting at windmills as 'national security experts' rather than producing hard-thinking analysts anticipating actual policies of other governments.

Conspiracism

In 1991, *Washington Post* reporter Steve Coll wrote from Islamabad about Pakistan's 'political culture of shadow games'. Almost twenty years later, in 2010, *New York Times* reporter Sabrina Tavernise observed that 'Conspiracy is a national sport in Pakistan.'[61] According to Coll, 'Here, the acronyms of intelligence agencies, such as MI (Military Intelligence), ISI (Inter-Services Intelligence) and IB (Intelligence Bureau, are part of everyday vocabulary.' He cited 'unproven reports' about 'secret wiretappings, videotapings and sexual blackmail schemes' and expressed surprise that 'nearly everyone of prominence believes his or her telephone is bugged'.[62]

Coll quoted Pakistani newspaper reports about the then prime minister Nawaz Sharif 'crooning love songs to a girlfriend in Bombay who may be an Indian spy' based on the intelligence agencies' wiretaps of the prime minister's phone. A separate newspaper report, attributed to a different intelligence service, accused the then opposition leader Benazir Bhutto of 'using her Karachi home as the secret headquarters of a terrorist organization backed by India'.[63]

Conspiracism has been a permanent staple in Pakistan's political life. It is defined in the *Oxford English Dictionary* as 'the belief that major historical and political events are brought about as the result of a conspiracy between interested parties, or are manipulated by or on behalf of an unknown group of influential people; belief in or advocacy of conspiracy theories'. Scholars describe 'conspiracy theory' as 'a proposed plot by powerful people or organizations working together in secret to accomplish some (usually sinister) goal'.[64] Both definitions can be seen at work in Pakistan as the dominant mode for explaining the country's state of affairs.

Pakistanis have consistently been fed the idea that the country is surrounded by enemies and that someone or other is trying to subvert its very existence. They are told that only the country's military is capable of protecting Pakistan against internal and external enemies. Civilians do not always understand the threats to Pakistan while some actively collude with enemies after being bought off. When the invulnerable military fails, as it did for example in Bangladesh in 1971 or against domestic terrorists more recently, it can only be because of schemes hatched by enemies in secret.

It is not unusual for fabricated news, forged documents and fictitious videos to be circulated through Pakistan's mainstream media. Many Pakistanis believe the United States ordered the murder of Pakistan's first prime minister Liaquat Ali Khan because a widely circulated document, purportedly a declassified American diplomatic cable, says so. It does not matter that the document was fake. Audio tapes claiming to be recordings of American, Israeli and Indian intelligence operatives plotting to divide Pakistan abound in social media. When Ralph Peters proposed in an article that the greater Middle East (including Pakistan) would find greater peace by altering its map to reflect ethnic coherence, his opinion was projected as some secret, devious plan.[65] Hardly anyone paused to think that individual flights of fancy about reshaping the world are not unusual.

When many US classified documents were unofficially released on the Internet as 'WikiLeaks', major Pakistani newspapers 'carried stories that purported to detail eye-popping American assessments of India's military and civilian leaders', quoting Americans who described 'senior Indian generals as vain, egotistical and genocidal'. American diplomats were reported as saying that India's government was 'secretly allied with Hindu fundamentalists' and that Indian spies were 'covertly supporting Islamist militants in Pakistan's tribal belt and Balochistan'. The unsympathetic remarks about Indian generals like 'one is said to be "rather a geek", another to be responsible for "genocide" and compared to Slobodan Milosevic' were accompanied by 'accounts of gushing American praise for Pakistan's top generals'.[66]

Although the disclosures amounted to a confirmation of 'the worst fears of Pakistani nationalist hawks' and could threaten relations between Washington and New Delhi if true, they were based on a fake document that did not come from WikiLeaks. British newspaper the *Guardian* conducted an 'extensive search of the WikiLeaks database' and 'failed to locate any of the incendiary allegations' in an actual leaked American cable. "Enough evidence of Indian involvement in Waziristan, Balochistan," read the front-page story in the *News*,' the *Guardian* reported, pointing out that similar headlines and stories appeared in the Urdu-language *Jang*, Pakistan's best-selling daily and several other newspapers. According to the British paper, 'The controversial claims, published in four Pakistani national papers, were credited to the Online Agency, an Islamabad-based news service that has frequently run pro-army stories in the past.' It was a case of 'WikiLeaks being exploited for propaganda purposes', the *Guardian* concluded, blaming Pakistan's military for circulating the fake cable.[67]

Such officially sanctioned deception, including projection of embellished Pakistani accomplishments and tailoring of history to conceal failings and failures, has altered the psyche of Pakistani citizens, making them see conspiracy in every corner. Conspiracism has bred an aversion to dispassionate examination of facts and precluded realism in policymaking. That, in turn, makes it difficult to reduce or manage the country's myriad problems with alternative prescriptions that might not conform to conspiracist assumptions.

Social scientists point out that, for believers, the fact that 'one massive, sinister conspiracy could be successfully executed in near-perfect secrecy suggests that many such plots are possible'.[68] If foreign powers or secretive elites pulled the strings in depriving Pakistan of Kashmir or taking East Pakistan away, they must be the reason for widespread corruption, domestic terrorist attacks, falling exports, water or electricity shortages and even the failure of a Pakistani team in an international sports competition.

Scholars who have studied the reasons for a society's propensity to conspiracism point out that they are often rooted in a desire to explain away hardship. According to Cass Sunstein and Adrian Vermeule of Harvard University, 'Terrible events produce outrage, and when people are outraged, they are all the more likely to seek causes that justify their emotional states, and also to attribute those events to intentional action.'[69] The desire to find an easy scapegoat for problems that are often complex, involve randomness and would otherwise require difficult choices is a hallmark of conspiracy theories. In Pakistan's case, conspiracies offer simple explanations and relief to an otherwise hapless populace, confirming their existing biases.

Having endured repression under military dictators or authoritarian elected civilians for most of its existence, Pakistan is not a completely open society. 'In a closed society, secrets are far easier to keep, and distrust of official accounts makes a great deal of sense,' Sunstein and Vermeule point out. 'In such societies, conspiracy theories are both more likely to be true and harder to show to be false in light of available information. But when the press is free, and when checks and balances are in force, it is harder for government to keep nefarious conspiracies hidden for long.'[70]

Experts also maintain that isolation and 'group think' are important parts of convincing people that they are victims of a conspiracy. Those who mistrust other groups, rely exclusively on sources from their own group for their acquisition of knowledge.[71] In this sense, willingness to believe conspiracy theories is the result of a structural information disadvantage. People insulated from other sources of information or brought up on tendentious information not only believe conspiracies about others but are also willing to generate or believe conspiracies about the *other* in a polarized environment.[72]

When a state deploys conspiracism, it engages in disinformation campaigns aimed at a political objective. This may include rallying nationalism, undermining a foreign adversary, or creating a consensus on an important issue. Disinformation and propaganda campaigns have a long history of scapegoating enemies and furthering the interests of the domestic elite. The USSR convinced its people that the West was failing and immoral while the Kim regime in North Korea has brainwashed a generation of people to hate their neighbours.[73]

In Pakistan's case, insularity from outside views—the idea that unbelievers cannot be trusted—and state-sponsored disinformation aimed at defining nationalism for a new country have both contributed to a predisposition towards generating and believing conspiracy theories. Vast numbers of Pakistanis remain ready to believe conspiracy theories involving 'enemies of Islam and Pakistan', taking the cue from their leaders and inspired by the large number of 'security analysts' dominating the media landscape.

The tendency to portray all challenges, or even tough questions, as a conspiracy date back to political strategy of the All-India Muslim League prior to Pakistan's creation. The Muslim League labelled all its Muslim critics as 'Hindu agents' and all foreign journalists or writers who questioned Pakistan's viability as part of conspiracies against Islam and Pakistan. Thus, Pakistan started out with the notion that there could be no honest disagreement with its founders and leaders and that all those who disagreed needed to be seen as enemies.

These imagined (or real) machinations have been used to justify unconventional actions by both civilians and military in the political arena. It is virtually impossible to hold a serving or retired military officer accountable for a crime without the spectre of 'conspiracy against the army'. Politicians have also tried often to get away with allegations of conspiracy when faced with charges of wrongdoing or corruption. It is not rare or unusual for a businessman to try and discredit rivals with rumours of ties to foreign interests, the wrong religion, or association with perennial conspiracy targets such as the Freemasons. Even two army chiefs have been subject to rumours spread by their domestic foes of being closet Ahmadis—a religious sect often accused of conspiring against Pakistan's purity.[74]

The preoccupation with conspiracies is an outgrowth of the mentality that Pakistan is constantly under threat and is permanently endangered. In the post-Zia era, the military has become the principal fount of that idea, coupled with the belief that soldiers know what is best for the country more than civilians and that greed and corruption make Pakistani scholars and politicians vulnerable to the influence of 'the enemy'.

The views of Lt Gen. Hamid Gul illustrate this thinking better than others. Gul was, in the words of journalist Khaled Ahmed, 'a star soldier who got to command two of Pakistan's top strike formations besides heading the Military Intelligence (MI) and the Inter-Services Intelligence (ISI)'. He publicly declared that he could not abide 'a state not based on Islam,' and 'was unbothered by conscience when he reached out to the Haqqani Network [in Afghanistan] and worked for a Taliban utopia in Pakistan'. Gul also 'bravely confessed having rigged the 1990 election as ISI chief to oust the Pakistan People's Party (PPP) from government'.[75] In all his actions, he insisted that he was acting to protect Pakistan from external and internal enemies even when he acted outside the chain of command or in violation of the country's constitution.

Gul is not the only senior military officer espousing views that combine conspiracy theories, Islamist ideology and the concept of Pakistan being permanently under threat. Maj. Gen. Zaheerul Islam Abbasi was arrested while trying to orchestrate 'an Islamic coup' in 1995 to create a regime 'based on Quran and Sunnah'. Officers like Gul and Abbasi collaborated with conservative clerics, 'who in turn agreed with al Qaeda chief Ayman al-Zawahiri's treatise proving how Pakistan was not an Islamic state despite the constitution and a supra-constitutional shariat court'.[76]

Lt. Gen. Shahid Aziz, who served in senior positions under Gen. Musharraf, revealed his preference for an Islamist Pakistan in his 2013 book, *Yeh Khamoshi Kahan Tak: Ek Sipahi ki Dastan-e-Ishq-o-Junoon* (How Long This Silence: A Soldier's Story of Passion and Madness). Aziz was 'no mean soldier; he saw action in Kashmir and was trained at the

National Defence University before being appointed director, military operations. As major general, he headed the analysis wing of the ISI. He was director-general, military operations (DGMO) and in 1999 planned the overthrow of Nawaz Sharif's elected government. In 2001, after 9/11, he was chief of the general staff, a post from where most officers ascend to the top job of army chief.'[77]

In his book Aziz, the professionally trained military officer, speaks of the 'eye of Dajjal' (Antichrist) on the US dollar bill, which to him symbolizes 'the grand conspiracy set in motion by the Freemasons and many powerful families in league with the American Neocons'. In his world view, all major events in the world were 'in line with the Jewish conspiracy outlined in The Protocols of the Elders of Zion', notwithstanding the fact that the protocols have been proved to be a European anti-Semitic forgery. For him, 'only the Quran stands in the way' of the modern world's 'Satanic way of life'.

Aziz sees the world 'being run according to a secret plan by a powerful secret organization that has first conquered global banking, followed by the media and entertainment. This plan is being worked out with the help of the United Kingdom, the IMF and the World Bank, the funded think tanks and their intellectuals, big corporations and reputable universities.'[78]

One could dismiss generals Gul, Abbasi and Aziz as occasional cranks, the likes of whom can be found in the ranks of any government or military. But in Pakistan's case, successive governments have methodically fostered the belief that 'Islamic Pakistan' is constantly besieged and is a target of anti-Islamic, satanic and godless global conspiracies. Since Independence, Pakistanis have been consistently told that India and Hindus are at the heart of all 'evil designs' against Pakistan but the country is equally threatened by others, including westernized, modernist reformers and not-so-religiously-observant politicians.

The paranoia about the conspiratorial enemy leads to surrealistic discussions about real-life problems. 'Here in Pakistan, we love our conspiracy theories', wrote the magazine *Herald* in a 2015 article listing the wildest conspiracy theories prevalent in the country, often spread by mainstream media. According to the conspiracy theorists, 'Most of the country's troubles and travails are, in fact, not homegrown, but the result of an omnipotent Jewish lobby—also known as a *yahoodi saazish*. And if it's not the Jews stirring up trouble, it *must* be the Indians.'[79] One of the most outrageous imagined plot suggested that Pakistan's worst flood in a century, which affected twenty million people in 2010, had been engineered by the US Central Intelligence Agency (CIA) with the help of the High Frequency Active Auroral Research Program (HAARP).[80]

Other patently absurd conspiracy claims include allegations against Malala Yusafzai, who shared the 2014 Nobel Peace Prize with an Indian. Malala was seventeen years old when she became a Nobel laureate, the youngest ever, and had been shot by the Taliban as a teenager for refusing to accept their opposition to female education. A majority of conservatives alleged that she was working against Islam and Pakistan's sovereignty and many Pakistanis insisted 'that local and international media are unnecessarily creating hype around the young activist'. Some politicians claimed that the 'campaign' to promote Malala proved the existence of an 'international lobby' behind the whole issue.[81]

Believing this account meant that a foreign intelligence service had managed to recruit Malala at age eleven or twelve, which is when she started writing a blog about her right to an education being curtailed by the Taliban in her home region of Swat. But implausibility is never an impediment to conspiracism. In 2016, when eight children were allegedly killed by rat attacks in Peshawar, according to the city's mayor, there was speculation that the rats had been specially bred or 'genetically modified in labs by countries hostile to Muslims such as the US'.[82]

Tales of 'abnormally large sized rats that seemed to have a taste for human flesh'[83] ignored logical explanations, such as uncovered sewage systems serving as a breeding ground for rats and the fact that rats are known to attack humans if the humans are unable to fend them off due to weakness or illness. Instead of seeking scientific explanations for attacking human infants, residents of Peshawar looked for the secret scheme behind the event. Some claimed that Afghan refugees had brought the large rats to Peshawar while others embraced the theory that the rats had been unleashed on the city as part of a foreign and anti-Muslim plot.

Conspiracist minds can apply their core belief to all fields, including sports. In 1987, British journalist Emma Duncan was surprised at the explanations offered for Pakistan's failure to perform well at cricket. The Pakistan team 'was knocked out of the cricket World Cup in the semi-finals' not 'just because the Australians were better than the Pakistanis'. Several theories were offered: 'One of the Pakistani players had been betting against his own team; the English umpires had favoured Australia because if England won its semi-final it would have to play against either Pakistan or Australia, and Australia was weaker; one of the Pakistani players was an employee of the company sponsoring the game, which had foisted him on to the team.'[84]

It is often instructive to track down the source of conspiracy theories to understand the method to their madness. The Middle East Media Research Institute (MEMRI) noted that the websites advancing the HAARP theory were 'also involved in conspiracy theories against Israel and India, and the tone of their content is pro-Pakistani military and pro-militant organizations'. These included websites identifying themselves with 'Zaid Hamid, a Pakistani demagogue who advocates Islamic revolution in South Asia and beyond'. One of them, called itself 'Takmeel' (meaning 'Completion')—an allusion to Pakistan being incomplete without expanded borders. According to MEMRI, the home page of Takmeel 'announces its plan to launch a radio station from the Indian capital, declaring: "Coming Soon – Radio Pakistan Delhi".'[85]

The notion that Pakistan as it exists today is incomplete has been part of the discourse of Pakistani ultra-nationalists since 1971. Instead of admitting to the failings of the ideology of Pakistan in holding on to erstwhile East Pakistan, some ideologues adopted the position that the loss of Bangladesh was only a temporary setback. Prominent among them was Mahmud Ali, a Bengali politician from Sylhet, who stayed behind in Pakistan after collaborating with the Pakistan Army during the 1971 civil war.

Ali was conferred the status of a minister of state by Bhutto and retained that position until his death in 2006 without actually serving in any cabinet.[86] He founded Tehrik-e-Takmeel-e-Pakistan (Movement for the Completion of Pakistan), which 'aimed at the completion of the ideological and geographical boundaries of Pakistan by making the whole of Punjab and Bengal part of Pakistan'.[87] Retaining Ali with a senior government title and providing him government resources to propagate an entirely fanciful idea provides some insight into the thinking behind such propaganda.

Beginning with the 1948 war, when Pashtun tribal lashkars were organized to seize control of the princely state of Jammu and Kashmir, Pakistani leaders have considered ideological propaganda and irregular warfare as important elements of their national strategy. Ideally, the propaganda about Pakistan being the axis of a global Islamic revival would gain support for Pakistan from Muslims around the world, especially in neighbouring countries including India.

Even if that objective is not achieved, it would keep Pakistanis enthused to contend with India, which the Pakistani elite fear their people might stop doing in the absence of religious and hyper-nationalist inspiration. Irregular warfare, involving fighters other than uniformed soldiers, is seen as a force multiplier in asymmetric competition.

According to Anatol Lieven, who is generally considered sympathetic to Pakistan, 'One reason why there are so many bizarre conspiracy theories in Pakistan is that there are so many conspiracies'.[88] But most conspiracies in Pakistan seem to be designed to convince Pakistanis that their country is the target of external conspiracies. In the era of social media, it is not unusual to find pictures on the Internet of Pakistanis dissenting from the official narrative about Pakistan's security with Stars of David, American flags or Hindu insignia painted across their foreheads. The patriotism of Pakistan's public figures is often measured by their attitude towards the country's external enemies and their support of Pakistan's army.

The trend of describing Islam, Pakistan and Pakistan's army as a holy trinity that must be protected against external and internal enemies has aggravated since Pakistan's foray into international jihad, beginning with the war against the Soviets in Afghanistan. But its roots go back to Pakistan's earliest days. The country's mainstream media has not hesitated to carry unproven and unprovable rumours and innuendo about Pakistanis undermining the country at the behest of foreign governments or because of ties with Jews and Hindus.

Charges of treason have often been used to discredit political opponents and dissidents throughout Pakistan's history though no one has been tried and convicted on the charge. Several people have gone from high office to being labelled traitors, only to be accused of acting against the national interest once again. Suhrawardy was described as a traitor for his post-Partition stance advocating protection of religious minorities and non-adversarial relations with India. That did not stop him from becoming prime minister in 1956 though he was forced from office within a few months.[89]

Similarly, Bengali leader A.K. Fazlul Haq, who was one of the movers of the 1940 resolution demanding Pakistan, was also described as an Indian agent when he called for free trade with India in 1954, as chief minister of East Bengal. He went on to become a member of the federal cabinet and governor of East Pakistan after hardening his stance on India.[90]

Pakistan's first military dictator, Ayub Khan, criticized the phenomenon of 'swapping labels'. He noted that 'yesterday's "traitors" were tomorrow's Chief Ministers, indistinguishable as Tweedledum and Tweedledee'.[91] But that did not stop him from treading the same path. Opposed by Jinnah's sister, Fatima, in a presidential election, Ayub did not shirk from suggesting that the sister of Pakistan's founder was surrounded by treasonous politicians. Ayub enlarged the intelligence services and expanded their role in certifying the patriotism of public figures. His successors, both civil and military, continued with the tradition.

An interesting case is that of Zulfikar Ali Bhutto, who served as a minister in Ayub Khan's military regime for eight years and became popular for promising a 'thousand-year war with India' as foreign minister. When he resigned, and formed the left-wing Pakistan Peoples Party (PPP) in 1967, reports suddenly surfaced about his mother having been born a Hindu and of Bhutto having sought to claim his father's property in India after Partition by asserting Indian citizenship. Bhutto became president of Pakistan, and later prime minister after the 1971 military debacle in East Pakistan, as the leader of the largest West Pakistani political party. As Pakistan's undisputed civilian ruler, Bhutto's patriotism was never questioned. Instead, Bhutto criticized Pashtun and Baloch leaders for collaborating with India and Afghanistan, citing intelligence reports similar to the ones which, only a few years earlier, had targeted him.

The saga did not end there. Bhutto's party won another election in 1977 but his opponents refused to accept the election results, leading to several months of street protests. During these protests, allegations of Bhutto having a Hindu mother and being an Indian agent resurfaced. They were amplified, without proof, after General Zia-ul-Haq toppled Bhutto's elected government and took the reins of power in a military coup. Zia released the Pashtun and Baloch leaders jailed by Bhutto and sought their support in discrediting Bhutto, who was executed in 1979 after a show trial ostensibly on charges of abetting a murder. Fabrications about his 'Hindu connection' were spread with even greater vehemence to justify his judicial murder.[92]

Zulfikar's daughter, Benazir Bhutto, was also portrayed as a 'national security risk' when she was poised to win the 1988 elections after Zia's death. Her army-backed rival, Nawaz Sharif, accused her of hobnobbing with the 'Jewish Lobby' in the United States to shut down Pakistan's nuclear weapons programme. Benazir Bhutto was ousted by the then president Ghulam Ishaq Khan two years later at the army's behest. By 1993, the shoe was on the other foot when Ishaq Khan dismissed Sharif's government on charges of corruption and putting Pakistan's security in jeopardy. Now Sharif stood accused of secret dealings with the US and India and rumours circulated about his romantic involvement with an Indian Muslim woman from Kashmir.[93]

Benazir Bhutto's second government, elected in 1993, was removed in 1997 leading to Sharif's return to office. Sharif was eventually overthrown in 1999 by General Pervez Musharraf in Pakistan's fourth military coup. Once again, the ousted prime minister's treason was whispered about without putting him on trial or sharing evidence. The pattern was repeated with the civilian government that followed Musharraf's ouster in 2008 and with the decision by Pakistan's Supreme Court to disqualify Sharif in 2017, after he had been elected to office again four years earlier. Although Sharif's latest disqualification resulted from investigation of the so-called Panama Papers, which exposed holders of offshore bank accounts, he was accused in social media of being an Indian agent. Rumours also swirled of his alleged investments in India and 'secret partnerships' with Indian businessmen.[94]

The cycles of discrediting leaders as 'traitors' or 'enemy agents' and occasionally allowing them to return to high office reveal a lot about Pakistan's political culture. Leaders of all ethnic-based political parties, representing Pashtuns, Baloch, Sindhi and Urdu-speaking Muhajir ethnicities, have been alternately declared enemies of the state and included in government at one time or another. The purpose of the exercise seems to be to create a permanent environment of fear and national insecurity, with the people constantly looking for saviours who would defend the country against external and internal foes.

The person or political party accused of sedition can return to the fold of patriotism by cutting a deal with the Pakistani establishment and ceding their independence. Neither the allegations of treason nor their sudden forgiveness are ever fully explained to the people. In some cases, direct intervention by the Supreme Court provides a fig leaf of legitimacy in the absence of a trial. Unlike other countries, where the apex court is only the court of final appeal in criminal matters, Pakistan's Supreme Court acts politically to directly make pronouncements in response to media articles or petitions by political rivals. One need not be convicted of disloyalty to the state after due process of law when innuendo, fabricated media reports and public comments by Supreme Court judges can suffice to tarnish reputations and cut public support.

Pakistan's history is often characterized by an overarching lack of transparency. In the last seventy years, all elected Pakistani prime ministers have either been assassinated, dismissed or forced to resign by heads of state or the judiciary with military backing, or deposed in coups d'état. Several troubling events in the country's history—including the assassination of its first prime minister, Liaquat Ali Khan; covert deals with foreign powers, including the United States, China, North Korea and some Arab countries; the circumstances leading to the 1965 war; the loss of East Pakistan; the insurgencies in Balochistan (1973–77 and 2004 to now); the military operations in Karachi (1992–2000 and 2015 to now); and the discovery of Osama bin Laden in Abbottabad and the secret US military operation to kill him—remain subjects of conspiracy theories because information about them (including reports of publicly announced inquiry commissions) has never been made public.

'Actual conspiracies spur conspiracy theories by stimulating real fears,' Daniel Pipes wrote in his book *The Hidden Hand: Middle East Fears of Conspiracy*, adding that 'the reverse holds true, as well: conspiracy theories beget conspiracies. Imaginary plots generate actual ones, actual ones generate imaginary ones, mutually reinforcing each other in an endless, and ever-deepening, cycle of irrationality.'[95] This sequence has been at work in Pakistan for decades. As a result, Pakistan is far from being a society that bases its conversations on facts or a democracy where the law takes its course, institutions work within their specified spheres, and elected leaders are voted in or out by the people.

6

'The Institution'

PAKISTAN'S PREOCCUPATION WITH SECURITY may have its roots in the fact that the military was the only fully functional institution inherited by the country at the time of the country's founding. The handicaps that Pakistan started out with are well known and widely documented. Khalid Bin Sayeed points out: 'Muslims lagged behind Hindus in administrative services, in commerce and finance, and in political leadership.'[1] The All-India Muslim League was woefully unprepared for running a country and some of its choices around the time of Partition had added to Pakistan's difficulties. Many of the new country's politicians and civil servants had to start from scratch, dealing with issues such as finding residential and office space in Karachi or Lahore. But the army was already a going concern in at least West Pakistan as the British Indian Army's Northern Command Headquarters were in Rawalpindi, which easily became Pakistan's General Headquarters.[2]

The League's leaders managed to get Pakistan on its feet with the help of what Lawrence Ziring described as 'the Civil–Military Complex'—the handful of British-trained Muslim civil servants and army officers with at least some experience in government. Among these, the army officers belonging to geographic Pakistan had an advantage as they had not migrated to the country from India, had well-established family and clan ties, and controlled a well-disciplined institution. Thus, the army was well positioned to emerge as the arbiter of Pakistan's destiny.

The Muslim League politicians made the original decision to turn Pakistan, in Suhrawardy's words, into 'a state which will be founded on sentiments, namely that of Islam in danger or of Pakistan in danger, a state which will be held together by raising the bogey of attacks'.[3] Their decision not only led to maintaining 'constant friction' with India[4] but also ended up conferring greater authority on the military. Once British officers handed over command to Muslim generals, squabbling politicians started turning to the army for advice and dispute resolution. Eventually, the army directly assumed power for the first time within eleven years of Independence. This, Ziring points out, 'ended the process of political bargaining in defining the direction of Pakistan' as Pakistan's first generation of primarily British-trained generals 'deferred to the experts, minimized the role of the politicians and tried to isolate the clerics'.[5]

To this day, the military remains the final authority on most policy issues in Pakistan and is euphemistically referred to as 'the institution', or 'the establishment'. It is argued that Pakistan's military has been largely responsible for saving the country from even greater chaos, given the venality of Pakistan's politicians and clerics. The military's contribution to Pakistan as it stands today is significant. But 'the institution' can also be blamed for perpetuating policies that should have been revised or abandoned long ago as well as for the failure of other institutions to grow independently and effectively.

The military's dominance over Pakistan's policy direction is structural, rooted in the circumstances of Pakistan's birth. The country had inherited almost one-third of British India's army but only 17 per cent of its revenue sources. Unlike politicians and clerics, military officers were disciplined and well trained, enabling them to execute decisions more methodically. But the military's political pre-eminence has made it difficult for Pakistanis to debate fundamental policy choices. Most nations raise an army proportionate to the size of threat to their security. In Pakistan's case, the magnitude of security threats has been expanded to match the size of an army inherited from the colonial era.

At Independence, Pakistan's army comprised the mainly Punjabi Muslim units of the British Indian Army. Most of its senior commanders were British, supported by a handful of Pakistani officers most of whom had not attained field rank in pre-Partition India. As Shuja Nawaz, author of *Crossed Swords: Pakistan, Its Army and the Wars Within* points out, not only Pakistan but its army were also created in a hurry. Some Muslim officers 'were quickly promoted, unfortunately some beyond their experience or capacity'[6] so that the British officers would not retain command indefinitely. Although the army was somewhat better organized than the civilian departments of government, it lacked crucial supplies and resources like all of Pakistan at the time.

The British defined the Pakistan Army in many ways, possibly including its Islamic orientation. India's leaders had no interest in siding with their former colonial master in the cold war that had begun but the British could still rely on the Pakistani component of the large force they had built during the Second World War. The first commandant of the Pakistan Military Academy (PMA), Brigadier Francis Ingall, was chosen for the job by the commander of British forces in India. Ingall started the tradition of naming the formations at the academy after Arab Muslim warriors and is still honoured as the academy's founder. Ingall Hall is the only building at the academy named after a non-Muslim. After Ingall, other British officers served as the academy's commandants until 1957. The Command and Staff College at Quetta had British commandants until 1954.

It is ironic that Christian officers from various parts of the British Commonwealth were training officers for an institution that would later describe itself as the 'soldiers of Islam'. Some of the most prominent self-proclaimed Islamists of the Pakistan Army—army chief Gen. Aslam Beg and ISI heads Lt Gen. Hamid Gul and Lt Gen. Javed Nasir—were trained at the time the PMA was commanded by Britishers. Similarly, Maj. Gen. Robert Cawthorne, an Australian officer of the British Indian Army, was the longest-serving head of Inter-Services Intelligence, from 1950 to 1959. The ISI's later positioning of itself as protector of Pakistan's Islamic identity seems inconsistent with the fact that its formative years involved command by a non-Muslim for nine years.

The limitations of its military machine at the time of Independence did not come in the way of the Pakistan government defining an expansive internal and external role for the army as early as 5 and 6 September 1947. According to Nawaz, 'the external role was defined in the anachronistic British imperial defence terms, to prevent aggression by a minor power while preparing to defend against a major power'.[7] Given the limited means of Pakistan, the army had to secure its share of these resources to survive as an institution—a struggle for survival within the struggle for survival of the new country.

Lieven argues that 'it was precisely because Pakistan's birth was so endangered that the new state came to attach such central importance to its military, and from the first gave the military such a disproportionate share of its resources'. He quotes Pakistan's first prime minister, Liaquat Ali Khan, who stated in 1948, 'The defence of the state is our foremost consideration. It dominates all other governmental activities.' According to Lieven, Pakistani leaders 'felt acutely endangered from within and without: from India, of course, but also from Afghanistan with its claim to Pakistan's Pathan territories, and equally importantly by internal revolt. This combination of threats led to the creation of what has been called Pakistan's "national security state".'[8]

Lieven compares Pakistan's security apparatus with the 'powerful national security establishment in India' and concludes that the Indian security endeavour is 'on a far smaller scale compared to the Indian state as a whole, and with a far smaller role for the uniformed military'. He recognizes the Pakistan military's role in Pakistan's obsession with security but reminds us 'that it is the job of militaries to be paranoid' and that this 'sense of strategic disadvantage and embattlement has been with the Pakistani military from the start'.[9] In his opinion, the military is Pakistan's only institution inherited from the British Raj that has proved resilient and effective. 'As the history of law, democracy, administration and education in Pakistan demonstrates, other British institutions in what is now Pakistan (and to a lesser extent India as well) failed to take root, failed to work, or have been transformed in ways that their authors would scarcely have recognized,' Lieven maintains.

Pakistanis often attribute the institutional sturdiness of the Pakistani military to the martial culture of Muslims in the region constituting Pakistan. Several British scholars, including Lieven, seem to agree with that explanation. 'The British military system,' Lieven writes, 'was able to root itself effectively because it fused with ancient local military traditions rather than sweeping them away (as was the case with education and law).' He acknowledges that 'the basis for the future Pakistani army' was laid in the loyalty of Punjabi Muslim soldiers to the British during the 1857 mutiny against the rule of the British East India Company. 'British racial prejudice,' he states, 'saw the tall, fair-skinned Punjabis and Pathans as "martial races", providing military material far superior to the smaller and darker peoples of the rest of India.'[10]

This analysis suggests that the Pakistani military started out with three advantages in comparison with other institutions of state. First, it inherited a disciplined and well-organized structure; second, it could call upon the nation to make sacrifices in its support because its purpose—defending the new country—was widely shared by the country's leaders and people; and third, it had a higher degree of ethnic homogeneity resulting from British racist recruitment policies. While politicians and civil servants squabbled, forming ethnic-based cabals, the newly promoted generals spoke the same language at home and had greater esprit de corps from the day they became Pakistanis. These advantages have translated into the army's dominance of Pakistan's decision making since its early days.

'Pakistan's history is one of conflict between an underdeveloped political system and a well-organized army,' Nawaz points out, adding that the army 'grew in numbers and political strength as a counter weight to a hostile India next door and in relation to the domestic political system'.[11] The first plot for a military coup was reported within four years of Pakistan's creation, in 1951, when Major General Akbar Khan allegedly conspired to overthrow Liaquat Ali Khan's government. Akbar Khan was dissatisfied with Liaquat's policy on Kashmir and was wary of a fledgling alliance with the United States. The 'Rawalpindi Conspiracy', as it is known, was also said to have sought support of communist poets and writers. It failed primarily because it did not involve the military's institutional decision to take over and did not have support of the highest-ranking army officers.[12]

The first successful military coup, in 1958, was made possible by the will of the army chief, Gen. Ayub Khan, and was supported by a collective decision among senior officers—a formula that has worked effectively in all subsequent coups and behind-the-scenes political actions of the military. Ayub Khan attributed the army's involvement in domestic affairs to the failings of Pakistan's political class, an explanation that continues to be invoked for military dominance until today. 'The army could not remain unaffected by the conditions around it,' Ayub wrote, adding, 'nor was it conceivable that officers and men would not react to all the political chicanery, intrigue, corruption and inefficiency manifest in every sphere of life'. According to him, he and other officers only acted as 'a patriotic and national army' in taking over the reins of power and in doing so they were merely responding 'to the thinking of the people in the country'.[13]

The same argument was invoked when Gen. Yahya Khan replaced Ayub Khan as president almost eleven years later, scrapping the constitution that had been written under the first military regime. The *Economist* described Ayub Khan's ouster and replacement by Yahya Khan in an editorial titled 'Tweedle Khan Takes Over',[14] noting that the Pakistan Army had become accustomed to wielding power and was developing an institutional 'group think' on political matters. Others pointed out 'the growing suspicion' among Pakistani civilians that 'whenever it was felt in General Headquarters that things were not going well or were not going according to the taste and opinion of senior officers, the armed forces (in effect the army alone) would move in or contrive to do so.'[15]

That 'political breakdown results in military intervention' is only one explanation for repeated military interventions in Pakistan's politics. Since political stability would result in reducing the military's role in domestic politics and might even influence the availability of resources for its pre-eminence in external security, it is not in the military's institutional interest to allow the political system to become stable. It is true that most military chiefs have opted to retire from command as professional soldiers, without yielding to the temptation of directly assuming power. But the army still insists that it must have a say in political matters as 'a patriotic and national army'. In doing so, it not only responds 'to the thinking of the people in the country' but also ensures that the people's thinking coincides (or at least appears to coincide) with the views of the army leadership.

One of the army chiefs who did not like to be tainted by politics, Gen. Jehangir Karamat, acknowledged that 'the military translates its potential into the will to dominate' in events of political breakdown or instability, leading to 'military intervention followed by military rule'. But Karamat states: 'As far as the track record of the military as rulers in the past is concerned, I am afraid it is not much better than the civilians.'[16]

Shuja Nawaz, whose brother Gen. Asif Nawaz served as army chief (1991–93), elucidates that the army's use of 'its significant coercive powers with the underlying threat of its military might to challenge the authority of the state and capture power time and again' has left 'the instruments of the state weakened'. In his words, 'The paradox that hobbled Pakistan's political development was that as the army grew in strength and size, it stunted the growth of the political system whose leaders either made no attempt to redress the power imbalance between the institutions of the state and that of the army, making the latter effectively the centre of power; or worse, they invited the army to settle political differences amongst themselves.'[17]

Nawaz notes that Pakistan has emerged as 'a persistent praetorian state with military or quasi-military rule for most of its life after independence from the British' wherein the army maintains 'patron-client relationships with the bureaucracy and with Islamist parties whom it used in its efforts to fight populist leaders in both East and West Pakistan and fuel the Kashmiri insurgency against Indian rule'.[18]

Pakistan is now caught in a vicious circle wherein fear of India (and other foreign enemies) enhances the army's prestige, which in turn enables the army to dominate the state while also making sure that external fears remain embedded in the Pakistani psyche. The military sustains its image by manipulating the flow of information to Pakistanis, ensuring the marginalization of visions of the national interest other than the one advanced by the armed forces.

The need for the army to control the nation psychologically was explained by Maj. Gen. Sher Ali Khan, who was Gen. Agha Mohammad Yahya Khan's minister for information and national affairs. Sher Ali observed that 'the reason the military was able to snatch the initiative from politicians after the fall of Ayub was not because of its fire power'. In a memorandum for Yahya Khan he said that the army could not shoot its way through the country's main thoroughfares without having 'a conflagration on our hands that no amount of fire power [sic] in our control' could handle. 'The strength of the army which enabled it to seize the initiative from incompetent politicians in March 1969,' Sher Ali argued, lay in its charisma.[19]

In Sher Ali's view, the army's charisma was 'a precious political resource' that 'existed because the mass of the people had not actually encountered the army directly'. They saw it as 'a mythical entity, a magical force, that would succor them in times of need when all else failed'. Preserving this charisma was important because if it was lost, it could not be easily retrieved. The people interacted frequently with the bureaucracy and the politicians and knew them to be corrupt and oppressive but they saw the army as 'the final guarantor of Pakistan and its well-being'.[20]

Sher Ali proposed that the army should not rule directly because regular contact with the people might lead them to think less of army officers who are 'fashioned by the Almighty from the same clay as other Pakistanis'. To conserve the military's charisma, the institution should maintain a facade of democracy and assume the role of referee in a political system characterized by 'a badly divided parliament and warring political parties'. Heeding Sher Ali's advice, the Yahya regime devoted a great deal of effort 'to supporting weak parties to ensure that they make a good showing' when Pakistan held a general election for the first time in 1970.[21] Denigrating and weakening civilian institutions has since then been an integral part of the Pakistan military's domestic strategy as is the building up of the army's image as the nation's only saviour.

Back-seat Driver

The role of the army as back-seat driver has resulted in poor civil–military relations throughout Pakistan's history since the 1970s. Finding civilian protégés who are content with having office but do not wield actual power has proved tough. The military has lost faith in civilian politicians installed by it after policy disagreements or the civilians' inability to remain popular. Most policy disagreements involve external relations or concerns that the civilians are being ineffective in managing the economy. After Gen. Musharraf's nine-year stint as military dictator, the military claims to have vowed never to take over. But a large propaganda machine continues to build the army's image at the expense of elected civilians. Although generally wary of upsetting the military, politicians and journalists sometimes expose the secretive machinations aimed at ensuring the military's supremacy in decision making.

The massive effort to build up Gen. Raheel Sharif, army chief from 2013 to 2016, as 'The chief who could be king'[22] is a case in point. An article with that title in the *Herald* described the phenomenon. 'Raheel Sharif's popularity grew out of the barracks and spread across Pakistan, making him more popular than any politician including Prime Minister Nawaz Sharif and Pakistan Tehreek-e-Insaf (PTI) chief Imran Khan,' the article said. Apparently, a mosque in Islamabad had been named after him in 2014 and 'his portraits could be spotted on the back of trucks and auto-rickshaws everywhere'. Banners and billboards featuring his image were put up in almost every major Pakistani city, particularly Karachi, where a military operation was under way against the Muttahida Qaumi Movement (MQM), the political party representing the Muhajir ethnic group.

According to report in the *Herald*, candidates contesting the 2015 local elections had put up Gen. Sharif's photos on their publicity material to attract voters. On social media, a #ThankYouRaheelSharif hashtag 'trended for months', ostensibly showing the nation's gratitude for the general's resolve to fight terrorists responsible for attacks in Pakistan's cities. 'The reasons for his popularity are not difficult to comprehend in times of rampant terrorism, insecurity, corruption and a general disappointment with politics,' the *Herald* wrote. Gen. Sharif was 'widely credited with improving security in the country in general and Karachi in particular' and praised 'for launching an anti-corruption drive, mostly focused against politicians'.[23]

Gen. Sharif's much-vaunted popularity did not last beyond his tenure as army chief. It vaporized after he retired and accepted the position of commander of a yet to be raised multinational Islamic force envisaged by Saudi Arabia. The appearance of his popularity had been choreographed by the military's propaganda arm—Inter-Services Public Relations (ISPR)—and the Inter-Services Intelligence (ISI). Aqil Shah, author of *The Army and Democracy: Military Politics in Pakistan,* pointed to 'relentless campaigns on news television channels and social media', that emphasized 'Raheel Sharif's "can do" leadership and "unwavering moral courage in the face of an existential threat" to Pakistan'. These campaigns, Shah observed, also compared the general to 'selfish, corrupt and dithering' politicians such as Nawaz Sharif and Asif Ali Zardari and glorified him as 'almost a superhuman being, an omniscient commander of the faithful'.[24]

Shah highlighted something widely known to journalists in Pakistan. 'The military's public relations machine—consisting of an expanded and restructured ISPR and the information management wing of the ISI headed by a major general or someone in an equivalent rank from the air force or the navy—routinely invest effort and money in constructing and maintaining a glorified public image of the armed forces,' he said. This machine uses social media, with hundreds of fake accounts and, in Shah's words, 'funds glitzy hyper-patriotic videos, songs and films, with the active collaboration of artists, actors, movie directors and writers'.[25]

The military's attention to the media as an instrument of controlling the people's thinking has grown along with the expansion of the Pakistani military. For years, ISPR was headed by an officer of the rank of colonel and like the public relations outfits of other countries, most of its staff comprised media professionals, not uniformed military. Its command was upgraded to brigadier rank in the late 1970s, only to be upgraded again in the 1990s. The head of ISPR is no longer a media man trained to don the uniform during a short stint at the military academy. It is a regular military officer of the rank of at least major general though

Gen. Sharif promoted his image builder, Asim Bajwa, to the rank of lieutenant general.

'The image of a nationalist soldier, who is highly professional, yet upholds the religious and cultural values of an Islamic republic, have fed the nationalist discourse,' says Ayesha Siddiqa, whose research into the Pakistan military's business ventures has earned her the military's hostility. She points out that 'the military has developed an extensive communication structure and a strategy to engage with the formal civil society and with society at large' to influence the national narrative and discourse. For example, the ISPR has been involved in financing the local film industry, theatre and an extensive radio network and, since 2007, the army has emerged as a major player in the media with 'its tentacles in all segments of the industry.' The military also maintains separate units to engage with radio, television and other forms of media.[26]

Siddiqa notes that the ISPR is 'known for intimidation such as directing television channels regarding their choice of news-programme anchors, and in certain cases, even their choice of guests'. The military is notoriously reticent about transparency regarding its influence over Pakistan's ostensibly open media. When human rights activist, Asma Jahangir, approached the Pakistan Supreme Court to demand information about television and radio channels run by the military, the court simply kept the petition pending.[27]

One of the most glaring examples of the military's effort to control Pakistan's narrative and discourse is its effort to revive Pakistan's film industry with propaganda as fiction. Pakistan's once vibrant film industry had fallen on hard times since the 1980s, losing viewers to India's Bollywood movies and home entertainment systems. From 2009, ISPR has helped Pakistani film producers in making 'films that did not challenge national interest, which translated as supporting a narrative that challenged the traditional elite, painting the military in bright colours, portraying India as an enemy and following the army line on sensitive issues'.[28]

Pakistani cinema has since been revived somewhat with movies such as *Waar* (Strike), produced in 2013, packed with action, fiery nationalism and demonization of India. Its storyline showed 'Indian villains team[ing] up with Islamist militants to plot spectacular attacks across Pakistan' and 'Pakistani security forces jump[ing] in and sav[ing] the day'.[29] Apart from blaming India for Islamist terrorism in Pakistan, the movie also suggested that opponents of the Kalabagh Dam project, opposed by Khyber Pakhtunkhwa and Sindh provinces because of how it might affect them, acted at India's behest. Another ISPR-supported film, *Maalik,* was banned by civilian authorities in 2016 because it glorified 'the idea of vigilante justice by a group of retired army officers' against corrupt politicians and feudal lords.[30]

Militaries throughout the world maintain a communications outfit and the existence of a public relations wing for Pakistan's armed forces is not unusual of itself. In times of war, the military's public outreach often includes propaganda and psychological warfare. What sets Pakistan apart is the ubiquity of the military's public relations effort and the fact that it remains on a war-footing more or less on a permanent basis. The US or Indian military helping a Hollywood or Bollywood war movie also differs from the Pakistani situation by virtue of its impact on the total amount of content available to the public. A dozen movies with militarist messages out of, say 1,700 Bollywood or 500 Hollywood films produced in a year, do not have the same weight as six ISPR-backed movies out of fifteen produced in Pakistan. Moreover, the armed forces of a democratic country are unlikely to be openly involved in promoting institutional political positions on domestic issues.

The Pakistani military not only ensures the dominance of its official perspective, it also actively attempts to silence all voices that might credibly challenge it. The ISI is responsible for delivering sticks and carrots to journalists. 'Any journalist who dares question the picture-perfect image of Raheel Sharif or the military's policies in, say, Balochistan can only do so at his or her own expense,' Aqil Shah pointed out, adding that the military viewed the media as an 'element of national power' essential to mould public opinion and generate support for its views on national security.[31]

There are many instances of the ISI's involvement in harassing or intimidating dissidents but its most extreme example is the story of Syed Saleem Shehzad, 'a journalist known for his exposés of the Pakistani military', whose body was discovered floating in the Upper Jhelum Canal in May 2011. Shehzad had been reported missing after failing to show up for a television interview in Islamabad. He had informed several of his colleagues that the head of the ISI's Media Wing had been harassing him to reveal his sources about a terrorist attack on a Pakistani airbase in Karachi a few days after US forces killed Osama bin Laden in Abbottabad.

Dexter Filkins, who researched Shehzad's murder for the *New Yorker* magazine, explained the context of the Pakistani reporter's elimination. 'Less than three weeks after the Abbottabad raid, the Army was humiliated a second time,' he wrote. 'A group of militants, armed with rocket-propelled grenades and suicide vests, breached one of the country's most secure bases, the Pakistan Naval Air Station-Mehran, outside Karachi, and blew up two P-3C Orion surveillance planes that had been bought from the United States. At least ten Pakistanis affiliated with the base died. The components of several nuclear warheads were believed to be housed nearby, and the implication was clear: Pakistan's nuclear arsenal was not safe.'[32]

'In barracks across the country, military officers questioned the competence of Pakistan's two most powerful men, Gen. Ashfaq Parvez Kayani, the chief of the army staff, and Gen. Ahmad Shuja Pasha, the chief of the Inter-Services Intelligence agency, or I.S.I.,' Filkins continued. 'Some officers even demanded that the Generals resign. Ordinary Pakistanis, meanwhile, publicly disparaged the one institution that, until then, had seemed to function.' Shehzad was caught up in this tumult because he 'wrote a sensational story for *Asia Times* Online, the website that employed him, saying that the attack on the Mehran base had been carried out by al Qaeda—not by the Pakistani Taliban, which had claimed responsibility. He said that the Mehran assault had been intended to punish the military for having conducted 'massive internal crackdowns on al Qaeda affiliates within the Navy'. A number of sailors had been detained for plotting to kill Americans, and one "was believed to have received direct instructions from Hakeemullah Mehsud"—the chief of the Pakistani Taliban.'[33]

Shehzad's autopsy report showed that he had 'died slowly and painfully, his rib cage smashed on both sides, his lungs and liver ruptured'. In Filkins's words, 'Someone, apparently, had intended to send a message by killing him. The media in Pakistan immediately suggested a culprit.' Filkins cited a report in the newspaper *Dawn* about journalists believing that Shehzad had been picked up by the ISI because of his story on the PNS–Mehran base attack.

The belief among Islamabad journalists of the ISI's involvement was so strong that 'an I.S.I. official made a statement denying that its agents had played any role in the killing', and describing Shehzad's death as 'unfortunate and tragic'. Then came the obligatory claim that 'baseless accusations against the country's sensitive agencies' were 'unfounded'. Filkins pointed out that in the decade since 2001, forty-six journalists had been killed in Pakistan 'and the I.S.I. had never before issued such a stark denial. The statement hardly quieted suspicion; in fact, it heightened it.'[34]

Shehzad was known for good contacts among Pakistan's various jihadi groups and had often written about links between Islamist militants and the armed forces, something officially denied by Pakistan. Although his reporting was often based on interviews with Islamist militants, the Pakistani military was never as annoyed with him as in the environment following the Abbottabad raid. Filkins observed that Shehzad 'had cultivated so many militants as sources' that 'he occasionally seemed to glorify the men who were carrying out suicide bombings and assassinations'.[35] But that was not the reason for the ISI's ire towards Shehzad. His reporting could interfere with two things important to the military—the national narrative that it had things under control and the American belief that it was their ally, however unreliable, in fighting terrorism—and he paid for that with his life.

Shehzad's case might have been the most egregious but it is not the only instance of use of force by the military in controlling the flow of information and ideas or enforcing its narrow view of patriotism and nationalism. In 2010, the *New York Times* reported: 'An investigative reporter for a major Pakistani newspaper was on his way home from dinner here on a recent night when men in black commando garb stopped his car, blindfolded him and drove him to a house on the outskirts of town. There, he says, he was beaten and stripped naked. His head and eyebrows were shaved, and he was videotaped in humiliating positions by assailants who he and other journalists believe were affiliated with the country's powerful spy agency.' The reporter, Umar Cheema, thirty-four, had written several articles for *The News* that were critical of the Pakistani army in the months preceding the attack.[36]

Cheema's investigative reports against civilian politicians, notably Asif Ali Zardari, had received scant attention from the military but three articles 'on delicate internal army problems' provoked the 'don't go there' reaction. According to the *New York Times*, the first of these 'reported on the sensitive issue of the court martial of two army commandos who refused to obey orders and join the assault on a radical mosque and school in Islamabad in 2007'; the second suggested that 'suspects in a major terrorist attack against a bus carrying ISI employees were acquitted because of the "mishandling" of the court case by the intelligence agency'; and the third 'described how Army House, the residence of the chief of army staff, was protected by 400 city police officers and not by soldiers, as required by law'.[37]

Cheema's decision to publicly describe what happened to him resulted in the discovery that other journalists and public figures had also been similarly harassed or warned by the ISI or other security services. The *New York Times* went on to report, 'The law minister in Punjab Province, Rana Sanullah Khan, said that in 2003, when he was an opposition politician and had criticized the army during the presidency of Gen. Pervez Musharraf, he was kidnapped and brutalized in a similar manner. In January [2010], in Islamabad, the home of Azaz Syed, a reporter for *Dawn*, the main English-language daily, was attacked by unknown assailants, days after he was threatened by supposed ISI agents over an investigative article he was researching related to the military. Kamran Shafi, a leading columnist and himself a former army officer who writes critically of the military, was harassed and his house was attacked last December by "elements linked to the security establishment", according to his own account.'[38]

Soon after the Shehzad murder, prominent author Ahmed Rashid, revealed that he had been threatened repeatedly by the ISI over the years, 'and was once warned personally by Musharraf' while he ruled Pakistan. Rashid's colleagues suggested that his prominence in the West had generally protected him but he had to be more careful, depending on the circumstances. 'There is a red line in Pakistan—there has always been a red line,' Rashid said, pointing out that the Shehzad murder had heightened the stakes for those treading closer to the military's red lines.[39]

New York Times reporter Carlotta Gall experienced first-hand the consequences of crossing the military's red line when she was beaten up in her hotel room during a visit to Quetta in 2006. Her Pakistani photographer was detained by her attackers, who belonged to the ISI. An officer told Gall that she was not permitted to visit the neighbourhood of Pashtunabad (where Afghans resided) and that it was forbidden to interview members of the Taliban. 'As they were leaving, I said the photographer had to stay with me,' she wrote, adding "He is Pakistani", the officer said. "We can do with him whatever we want." I knew they were capable of torture and murder, especially in Quetta, where the security services were a law unto themselves. The story they didn't want out in the open was the government's covert support for the militant groups that were propagating terrorism in Afghanistan and beyond.'[40] It is not surprising that few foreign reporters have dared to venture to Quetta or other places where Pakistan hides and trains jihadi terrorists attacking inside India or Afghanistan.

In addition to controlling and managing what Pakistanis know and discuss or what the rest of the world finds out about the country through mass media, the military has also focused its energies on micromanaging social media. ISPR and ISI use social media as part of the grand strategy of narrative building to create an echo chamber that discredits dissent, builds up hyper-patriotism, keeps alive the fear of Pakistan being constantly under threat, and even generates and spreads conspiracy theories. The strategy encourages large numbers of retired military officers to join Pakistani WhatsApp chat groups and maintain accounts of Facebook, Twitter and Snapchat. Centrally directed accounts, sometimes fake, heap scorn or abuse on anyone who disagrees with the military's views on Pakistan's policies or prospects. In 2017, several independent-minded bloggers were abducted and tortured before being released to leave the country.[41]

The military's charisma is protected not only by direct propaganda but also by the nurturing of a broad military family that includes children and grandchildren of military officers. Although 'military brat' is a widely known global phenomenon, the Pakistani version is particularly prominent in articulating the military view on every subject. Thus, an Army Public School's alumnus grows up almost brainwashed in his hatred of Pakistan's enemies as well as its politicians, accepts civilian inferiority as natural, even if he/she chooses to be a civilian, and generally sees the world from the same lens as the country's officers' corps is brought up to see. In recent years, army families have played a significant part in social media mobilization and lending support to pro-military politicians (such as former cricket star Imran Khan) and clerics.

Sometimes the overwhelming desire of the military to impose a single version of the country's past, present and future involves almost ludicrous methods. For example, the army tries hard to limit discussion of its performance in the wars of 1965 and 1971, the circumstances surrounding the 1999 Kargil conflict, or the details of its support for jihadi groups. But well-researched outside accounts remain available, which are then described as 'anti-Pakistan'. The result is a chasm in Pakistani perceptions of what happened and what the rest of the world regards as the real sequence of events.

Even when one of the army's own describes the past in less than glorious terms, efforts are made to limit the circulation of the damaging material. It is almost as if the institution's frailties and failings must be hidden not only from the world and Pakistani civilians but from itself. For instance, the army's general headquarters reportedly purchased all 22,000 copies of a detailed evaluation of the 1965 war, written by Lt Gen. Mahmud Ahmed, a former ISI chief.

The general had written the book after painstaking research and detailed cartography and thought publishing it forty years after the war would be useful for army officers and civilians. The GHQ, however, 'found the book published by Oxford University Press "too sensitive"', because it described the army's previously publicized victories as a myth. Musharraf, who was then army chief, 'directed the Army Book Club to immediately buy all copies, worth millions of rupees, directly from the publishers to stop it from being marketed'.[42] Preserving the myth was deemed more important even forty years after the fact than letting a senior general set right the historical record.

Keeping alive a mythology about military officers being superior in every way to their civilian counterparts is integral to the army's continued dominance of Pakistan. Military officers are better managers and administrators and generally more honest, according to legend, and reports of mismanagement, maladministration or corruption by military men is often protected from scrutiny. It is deemed equally important to fabricate accounts of how the rest of the world thinks very highly of Pakistani officers. Fake websites have been used to promote fake global rankings listing ISI as the world's best intelligence service and the Pakistan Army commander, Gen. Raheel Sharif, as the world's best commander.

Military intervention in politics is often accompanied by charges of widespread civilian corruption and politicians often protest that while they are periodically subjected to accountability, military officers are not. The military insists that it has an effective internal accountability system, though the general public seldom hears about a general going to prison the way politicians and civil servants are routinely incarcerated. Gen. Raheel Sharif responded to charges about the military not being accountable by announcing action against some senior officers. This involved forcing some generals to return 'ill-gotten wealth' to the treasury, forfeiting their seniority or benefits and forced retirement, none of which could be compared with the long pre-trial imprisonment endured by political leaders facing similar charges.[43]

Similarly, the army has never disowned the actions of its past commanders, including the military dictators, and has intervened to stop their trial or condemnation. Yahya and the generals who lost East Pakistan faced no charges, nor did the officers accused of atrocities against Bengalis. Zia's excesses remain unacknowledged. His successor, Gen. Aslam Beg, was not put on trial for diverting military funds towards handpicked politicians to influence the 1990 election even after the Supreme Court ordered that charges be filed against him. Musharraf acknowledged publicly that Gen. Sharif had 'helped him leave the country by keeping the [civilian] government from pressuring the courts' when he was put on trial for abrogating the constitution.[44]

The protection of the military's image has become a euphemism for maintaining the military's impunity. Welfare trusts run by the army, navy and air force own and manage fifty commercial enterprises in the country, which claim protection from criticism or questioning similar to that available to military as an institution. Defence Housing Authorities in virtually all major Pakistani cities sit on some of the country's best commercial and residential real estate. The military's commercial enterprises cover stud farms, sugar mills, restaurants, housing schemes, aviation services, private security companies, banking, insurance, oil and gas, wind energy, agricultural seed supplies and for-profit schools. In addition, the military also owns manufacturing facilities for apparel, cereals, fertilizer, cement, knitwear, shoes and woolens.[45]

Even if one accepts the legitimacy of the military engaging in business for the welfare of serving and retired military personnel, the Pakistani practice of folding discussion of these business activities into its national security discourse is very unusual. Tenant farmers at a military farm in Okara, protesting against transformation from sharecroppers to renters, found themselves facing charges of acting on enemy instigation. Tenants at the 17,000-acre grain and dairy, Okara Military Farms, refused to pay their rent and staged protests, including some that turned violent. Instead of treating it as industrial action, the army 'responded by cutting off water to the fields of rebellious tenants, sending troops to surround their villages and arresting hundreds of protesting farmers'.[46]

The *Washington Post* reported that at least seven villagers were killed between 2000 and 2003 in the farm stand-off and cited villagers' statements about being tortured. 'This is not an issue of human rights,' said Maj. Gen. Mahmud Shah, director general of the Remount, Veterinary and Farms Corps, which oversees Okara and twenty-three other military farms. 'This is a law-and-order situation.'[47] Since then, the farmers have been painted as 'enemies of the state'.[48]

Just as anyone questioning the military is assumed to be hand-in-glove with the state's enemies, anyone who is seen as upstaging or defeating India is adopted by the military as a hero. When Pakistan's cricket team beat India in the final of the International Cricket Council (ICC) Champions Trophy tournament in June 2017, army chief Gen. Qamar Javed Bajwa announced a reward for the winning team members out of the military's budget. The players were to go for the Umrah pilgrimage to Mecca at the army's expense, ostensibly because defeating India at cricket was somehow a national security need. 'Nothing beats "Team Work", Pakistan is a team against every threat', said the COAS, according to DG ISPR Maj. Gen. Asif Ghafoor.[49]

Ghafoor also articulated the military's view of its primacy in 'shaping the national narrative and to counter propaganda pushed by forces against Pakistan' while seeking the media's cooperation in this enterprise. 'If the international community says we have not done enough' against terrorism, he said, it had to be described as 'a politicized narrative' shaped by inimical forces 'including India'. According to Ghafoor, 'Media plays a big role in shaping the narrative, and I request the media to help shape Pakistan's narrative.' As the army's principal spokesperson, he laid out his institution's understanding of the relationship between security and narrative. 'When the state is united and will put forth a narrative, it would be more effective', he stated.[50]

Nuclear Pride

No nuclear-armed nation worries the rest of the world as much as Pakistan. But for Pakistanis possessing nuclear weapons is a matter of national pride, an unparalleled achievement that signifies the country's place under the sun. In his 2012 book, '*Eating Grass: The Making of the Pakistani Bomb*', Feroz Hassan Khan explains that Pakistan's nuclear programme is seen by Pakistanis as an integral part of 'the broad narrative of Pakistani nationalism'. According to this account, Pakistan's senior officials, young scientists and engineers overcame 'perennial political crises' and 'poor civil-military relations', because 'they were unwilling to allow India's strategic developments to go unanswered'. For Pakistanis, nuclear weapons are not just an instrument of deterrence or even national security. They are 'the most significant symbol of national determination and a central element of Pakistan's identity'.[51]

Khan cites the Pakistani narrative of 'enduring rivalry and strategic competition with India' that he says turned bitter after several wars and crises. According to this narrative, 'The last major war in 1971 resulted in humiliating military defeat and dismemberment of Pakistan, which simply reinforced its belief that its adversaries were determined to destroy the very existence of the new state. This perception united the nation state into a "never again" mind-set that found succor in the acquisition of a nuclear capability.'[52]

As a former senior officer in the Pakistan military's Strategic Plans Division where he served last as brigadier, Feroz Hassan Khan speaks with authority when he identifies the three important beliefs regarding nuclear weapons that define Pakistani strategic thought. 'First, nuclear weapons are the only guarantee of Pakistan's national survival in the face of both an inveterately hostile India that cannot be deterred conventionally and unreliable external allies that fail to deliver in extremis. Second, Pakistan's nuclear programme is unfairly singled out for international opposition because of its Muslim population. This feeling of victimization is accentuated by a belief that India consistently "gets away with" violating global non-proliferation norms. Third is the belief that India, Israel or the United States might use military force to stop Pakistan's nuclear programme. Today these three beliefs—nuclear necessity for survival, international discrimination against Pakistan and danger of disarming attacks—form the centre of Pakistani strategic thinking about nuclear weapons', he writes.

Given these essentially political or ideological convictions, Pakistan's leaders—its 'military, bureaucratic, and scientific establishment', according to Khan—remain committed to paying any political, economic or technical cost to reach or maintain their objective of a nuclear-armed Pakistan.[53] The Pakistani nuclear weapons programme is said to be India-specific and Pakistan is unlikely and unwilling to heed concerns about nuclear weapons expressed by the rest of the world. The consensus Pakistan view is that the world does not understand Pakistan's fears and aspirations in relation to India.

Most nuclear weapon powers see their weapons of mass destruction as a means of maintaining the status quo and as deterrents to bad behaviour on part of their enemies. Pakistan, on the other hand, developed its military nuclear programme primarily to advance its claim of parity with India and as a means to settle what it considers the unfinished business from the 1947 partition of the subcontinent. Pakistan is not content to consider nuclear weapons the ultimate protection against being overrun by a much larger India. It hopes to settle the Kashmir dispute by pressuring India at the sub-conventional level, through militants and terrorists, while ensuring that India cannot respond out of fear of a nuclear conflagration.

'If nuclear weapons are acquired by countries whose governments totter and frequently fall, should we not worry more about the world's destruction than we do now?' Kenneth Waltz had once wondered, adding, 'If nuclear weapons are acquired by two states that are traditional and bitter rivals, should that not also foster our concern?'[54] Pakistan's internal instability, its reputation as a terrorist incubator and its perennial conflict with India are all sources of concern for the international community. Pakistanis do not see things the same way. They insist that Pakistan's nukes are in safe hands, fully in control of its military, and directed where they should be—against an intransigent India that refuses to respect Pakistan.

For most international observers Pakistan presents a challenge to nuclear deterrence theory. As George Perkovich and Toby Dalton explained, 'Western deterrence theorists never contemplated a nuclear-armed adversary that tolerated or employed sub-conventional violence by proxy on the adversary's homeland.'[55] Instead of making Pakistan feel secure, possession of nuclear weapons has only added to its paranoia. The United States and Israel have been added to India as countries that might want to take Pakistan's nuclear weapons away. It does not matter that even the Soviet Union and the United States never contemplated taking away each other's nukes and the global norm has always been for nuclear-armed nations to accept that they can no longer fight one another.

It is not atypical for Pakistani officials and media personalities to include nuclear threats in their traditional bravado against India and other 'enemies of Islam'. Lt Gen. Hamid Nawaz Khan, who served as secretary for defence (2001–05) and minister of interior (2007–08) told a television audience after his retirement, 'We shouldn't wait for India to attack us. We should attack right away and nuke them if they appear to be readying for an attack.'[56] Majeed Nizami, editor-in-chief of the ultra-nationalist *Nawa-i-Waqt* newspaper group once famously declared that his fondest wish was to turn himself into a nuclear bomb and get dropped on India. 'Pakistan should not hesitate to use nuclear weapons to wrest Kashmir from India,' he declared without explaining how that might work out.[57]

Nizami's other pronouncements betrayed the lack of widespread understanding of the concept of nuclear deterrence among Pakistanis. 'India is Pakistan's eternal enemy,' he explained, adding, 'Unless we defeat it in a nuclear war, it will keep plotting conspiracies against Pakistan.' In his reckoning, shared often with the public through his mass media empire, Pakistan's 'missiles and nuclear bombs are superior to India's' so Pakistan should use weapons of mass destruction to tackle

India. 'Don't worry if a couple of our cities are also destroyed in the process', he said, as if that amounted to reassurance.[58]

Such extreme posturing is not limited to influential media personalities like Nizami. Defence Minister Khawaja Asif directed a nuclear threat to Israel on twitter in response to a fake news report that quoted Israeli defence minister threatening to 'destroy [Pakistan] with a nuclear attack'. Asif wrote, 'Israel forgets Pakistan is a nuclear state too.'[59] On a Pakistani television channel, Asif went farther and quoted the Quran in favour of holding forth a nuclear threat. 'Allah has said in the Qur'an, "The horses must be prepared", so we should always be completely prepared', Asif observed. 'If there is a threat to our security, or if anyone steps on our soil and if someone's designs are a threat to our security', Pakistan would not hesitate to use nuclear weapons. In another TV interview, the defence minister asserted that Pakistan's nuclear devices were not 'showpieces'. Pakistan would annihilate India if 'our safety is threatened', he declared even though there was no immediate provocation justifying his warning.[60]

Luckily, Pakistan's nuclear weapons are not controlled by retired generals like Hamid Nawaz Khan, newspaper editors like Nizami or even a jingoistic civilian defence minister. But such hardline views do reflect an influential segment of Pakistani national opinion and one cannot dismiss the significance of the sentiment it reflects. Moreover, Pakistan has tended to maintain ambiguity about its nuclear deterrence, avoiding official articulation of 'red lines' governing nuclear use. Although there has been some identification of the circumstances that might lead to Pakistani deployment of nuclear weapons more recently, the concept of deterrence as widely known to the rest of the world is still not fully understood or appreciated in the country.

Moreover, Pakistan has consistently refused to abjure 'first use' of nuclear weapons, based on its concerns about India's overwhelming conventional military superiority. The conditions that might lead Pakistan to the use of its nukes listed in January 2002 by Lt Gen. Khalid Kidwai, long-serving director of the Strategic Plan Division and virtual head of Pakistan's nuclear command structure, did not preclude scenarios where Pakistani misreading of Indian intentions might trigger a nuclear exchange.

According to Kidwai, Pakistan might resort to use of nuclear weapons if 'India attacked Pakistan and conquers a large part of its territory; India destroys a large section of Pakistan's land and air forces; imposition of a blockade to such an extent that it "strangles" transportation of vital supplies and adversely affects the "war-waging stamina" of the country; India pushes Pakistan into political destabilization or creates large-scale internal subversion'.[61] Two additional red lines unofficially postulated by other Pakistani officers include Indian crossing of the Line of Control (LOC) to an extent that threatens Pakistan's control over Azad Kashmir and Indian attack on any of Pakistan's power generation facilities or nuclear installations.[62]

Of these, 'India pushes Pakistan into political destabilization or creates large-scale internal subversion' are subjective concepts. Would the subcontinent face nuclear war if Pakistan's intelligence services assume, as they often do, that political instability in the country has been instigated by outsiders? Could domestic extremist groups, whether Islamist or ethnic nationalist, instigate a wider conflict ending in a nuclear exchange by stepping up internal subversion that Pakistan might blame on India? Nothing in the public discourse on Pakistani nuclear policy offers answers to these questions.

Given the India-centric nature of Pakistan's strategic plans, Pakistan's politicians and military officers seem to see nuclear weapons as 'a way to deter future conventional war with India that might threaten further territorial losses or even the survival of the state'.[63] Frustrated with Pakistan's continued use of sub-conventional warfare—militancy in Jammu and Kashmir and terrorism throughout the region—as an instrument of trying to alter the status quo, the Indians have pondered conventional military options. Pakistan's military leaders, on the other hand, have sought to maintain their sub-conventional option by invoking the prospect of first use of nuclear weapons to deter a conventional military threat.

Pakistan's nuclear brinkmanship seems designed to persuade the rest of the world to pressure India into resolving India–Pakistan disputes on Pakistan's terms to prevent nuclear conflict and proliferation. The testing of *Nasr*, a very short-range ballistic missile that Pakistan claims can be used for launching battlefield nuclear weapons and reports that

Pakistan was equipping its surface ships and diesel-powered electric submarines with nuclear tipped missiles exacerbated 'the dangers of miscalculated, inadvertent, or unauthorized use arising from delegated command and control'.[64] They were also effective in scaring US policymakers and some American scholars into arguing against policies that might constitute punishment for bad behaviour over supporting terrorists or undermining the international community's effort to stabilize Afghanistan.

'The rivalry between Pakistan and India is driven by historical, political, religious, psychological, and security factors,' George Perkovich argues while advancing the case for handling Pakistan with kid gloves. 'On balance, it is arguably fair to say that the Pakistani security establishment bears a disproportionate share of responsibility for the conflicts and crises of the Indo-Pak relationship and the inability of diplomacy to normalize it. But this is not the whole story, and, in any case, the fact of the rivalry means that if Pakistan is destined to be forever isolated while India is embraced, Pakistan will be less inclined to take steps that would be in India's and the rest of the world's security interest.'[65]

Such voices are, however, are being drowned out by calls for Pakistan's isolation as the means of forcing its hand over terrorism-related policies. The Pakistani paradigm of seeking strategic advantage by persisting with sub-conventional warfare in the shadow of nuclear weapons and Pakistan's insistence on seeking parity with India, seems to be marginalizing Pakistan from larger nuclear stability issues in what experts describe as 'the second nuclear age' (i.e., an era of multiple nuclear powers, following the 'first nuclear age' of five global nuclear-armed countries that culminated with the Non-Proliferation Treaty). The India–US nuclear deal, and US-backed efforts to secure Indian membership of the Nuclear Suppliers Group (NSG), point to a path for India's acceptance in the global nuclear community. Even after obstructing India's entry to the NSG, with China's help, Pakistan still has no path forward for its own admission to the nuclear restraint and management regimes.

Pakistan's embrace of tactical nuclear weapons (TNWs) creates a new tier of security problems even as it ostensibly enhances security against a potential conventional military strike. Pakistan now has to deal with heightened global concerns about an Islamist or jihadist takeover of the Pakistani state, armed not just with strategic but also with tactical nuclear weapons. Although Pakistani policymakers and scholars dismiss such concerns, they nonetheless persist.

Pakistan began developing low-yield, tactical battlefield nuclear weapons, such as the Nasr missile, to provide 'flexible deterrence options' in response to India's 'Cold Start' doctrine of conventionally striking back at Pakistan rather quickly in the event of terrorist attacks similar to the one conducted in Mumbai in November 2008. Nasr proponents argue that by maintaining 'a credible linkage between limited conventional war and nuclear escalation', the missile will deter India from carrying out its plan.[66]

Tactical weapons, like the Nasr, which has a short range of about 60 kilometres, could be forward-deployed near the Indo-Pakistan border, ready for access by field commanders in case of need. Giving field commanders quick access to nuclear weapons enhances operational readiness but it also involves devolution of command and control to local commanders. It could pose the risk of unauthorized or unnecessary use[67] though Pakistanis point out that, so far, their track record in acting responsibly with nuclear weapons is impeccable.

According to Pakistani scholar Mansoor Ahmed, arguments about TNWs being inherently destabilizing when deployed close to a border do not apply in Pakistan's case. 'Such risks relate to questions of "battle-space management, field security problems, and the probability that India would pre-emptively attack the weapon systems once they have been flushed out of peacetime storage", coupled with the possibility of rapid nuclear escalation leading to all-out nuclear war,' he explains. Ahmed insists that challenges encountered in optimally deploying TNWs—referred to as the Goldilocks dilemma—in South Asia are not similar to those faced during the NATO–Warsaw Pact confrontation in the cold war. 'Pakistan's situation fundamentally differs from the NATO dilemma because Pakistan claims to retain centralized control over all strategic and tactical nuclear weapons at all times, whereas the deterrent power of NATO's position derived from decentralized control,' he concludes.[68]

In the absence of greater information about the centralized nature of Pakistan's control of tactical weapons, Ahmed's assertion is insufficiently reassuring. The security of TNWs and their delivery vehicles is said to be more problematic than strategic weapons systems 'because of their relatively small size and portability'.[69] Jeffrey McCausland points to the inherent contradiction 'between the requirement for ensuring warhead security in peacetime and survivability in a crisis, and providing operational availability in wartime'. Given that this issue was a major dilemma for NATO force planners during the cold war, it remains unclear how Pakistan is likely to resolve it amidst the almost fanatical ideological hatred of India among the rank and file of its military.

In his book, Brigadier Feroz Hassan Khan has explained at some length the conceptual framework of Pakistan's arrangements for security of its strategic nuclear weapons without offering explicit details. He speaks of 'physical safety mechanisms and firewalls both in the weapon systems themselves, as well as in the chain of command'. According to him, 'No single individual can operate a weapon system, nor can one individual issue the command for nuclear weapon use. The NCA (National Command Authority) command and control system ensures that weapons can be operationally ready on short notice, yet unauthorized arming and/or use never takes place. Pakistan does not keep its nuclear weapons on hair-trigger alert. The nuclear weapons are few and probably kept in disassembled form; their components are reportedly stored separately, at dispersed sites. Keeping the weapons in a disassembled form, along with the use of authorization codes reduces the risk of capture or unauthorized use.'[70]

These arrangements are likely to be effective only in case of strategic weapons. Khan's explanation that 'Pakistan's arsenals are maintained in non-deployed form' might not necessarily extend to TNWs. According to Khan, Pakistan's National Command Authority 'maintains centralized control of the assets, and an elaborate system of security and the Security Division have installed safety measures that ensure the physical security of storage and transport'.[71] But it is unclear whether such elaborate centralized controls could be applied once tactical nukes are available for deployment along Pakistan's 2,897-km border with India.

As Michael Krepon points out, nuclear risks will grow significantly in the event of another India–Pakistan confrontation 'since tactical nuclear weapons are the least safe and secure in Pakistan's arsenal, and since these and longer-range, nuclear-capable launchers will be moved around in the midst of a serious crisis'. He laments that 'Pakistan's military leaders seem unpersuaded by arguments that mixing tactical nuclear weapons into conventional battle plans is a lousy idea'.[72] What then, if anything, can be done to encourage Pakistan to change its military and nuclear doctrines?

'The perceived need to counter Indian regional hegemony and putative conventional military advantages became the foundational impulse behind Pakistan's prior work on nuclear weapons,' Perkovich and Dalton explain. They note that 'the impulse endures, now wrapped in a narrative that nuclear weapons are the sole element of national power that will not only even the score with India, but also deter threats ranging from limited conventional war to existential conflict'. The allure of the bomb, they point out, has led Pakistan's national security managers to compete with—and in some important measures, to outcompete—India on nuclear weapon capabilities, even as Pakistan falls farther and farther behind India on nearly all other attributes of national power.

According to this view, 'The weaker Pakistan becomes as a state, the more Pakistan's military leadership in Rawalpindi seems to rely on nuclear weapons to bolster national security. And the weaker Pakistan becomes, the more the dangers associated with its growing stockpiles of nuclear weapons and fissile material will be compounded'.[73]

The pride Pakistanis associate with their country's possession of nuclear weapons notwithstanding, Pakistan's dependence on nukes reflects bourgeoning insecurity. The sense of security that accompanied nuclear deterrence for other countries, continues to elude Pakistan.

Living without Paranoia

Pakistan has sometimes been described as 'a paranoid state', one 'characterized by a pervasive distrust and suspiciousness of others'. Most of Pakistan's fears centre on India but in the eyes of its leaders and most of its people, others are not above conspiring against Pakistan. Experts on political paranoia have highlighted 'the determinant role' of a paranoid world view in some of the worst excesses in recent history. Adolf Hitler's Germany, Stalin's Soviet Union and Ayatollah Ruhollah Khomeini's Iran 'mobilized paranoid rage' against external enemies. Paranoid thinking also 'fuelled the fires that have caused tens of thousands of ethnic murders in the Balkans, in India and in Central Africa'.[74]

There may be some paranoid dynamic 'even in stable, democratic and humane societies', which might be deemed 'part of the human condition'. A certain amount of suspicion is probably necessary in politics, health and defence. But political paranoia might begin 'as a distortion of an appropriate political response but then far overshoots the mark'. Instead of focusing on dangers that exist, the paranoid starts inventing dangers and becomes 'the center of malevolent attention'.[75]

The paranoid mind sees 'conspiracy as the motivating force in history and the essential organizing principle in all politics'. For true believers, the conspiracy is 'already powerful and growing rapidly' and 'Time is short. They see themselves as the "few people who recognize the danger" who "must expose and fight the conspirators" before their "irreversible victory". They also believe that the conflict cannot be compromised or mediated. It is a fight to the death. The conspirators are absolutely evil, so, as the opponents of this evil power, members of the paranoid group see themselves as the force for good. Indeed, they acquire in their own eyes the role of the defenders of all that is good.'[76]

Those who see 'conspiracy as a universal political explanation' consider 'history and politics as completely rational and ultimately predictable, if only one has the key. In a world of uncertainty, the paranoid leader offers his followers certainty. The systematic world the paranoid creates in his fantasy is far more coherent than the real world.

Nothing happens that is not deliberately caused.'[77] It has been pointed out: 'The most powerful value of conspiracy thinking is to remove responsibility from the person or group believing itself to be the victim of the conspiracy.' Thus in the Middle East (as well as Pakistan), belief in conspiracies helps explain that the responsibility for backwardness of 'victims' lies with 'malevolent foreign factors', not with their own policies or action. 'Indeed, a central psychological motivation for conspiratorial thinking', write Robert Robins and Jerrold Post, 'is to serve as an antidote for the poisonous feeling of powerlessness'.[78]

In Pakistan's case, genuine threats to the country's viability at its inception have been wrapped into a state ideology that reflects all elements of state paranoia. Pakistanis deem their country central to the thinking and strategy of all its real and perceived enemies. They view their position in the comity of nations in grandiose terms, are hostile to anyone who refuses to see things the same way and live in constant fear of losing autonomy. Projection of Pakistan's own fears or weaknesses on to others is also commonplace. It is not unusual to hear Pakistanis talk about the weaknesses of India or even the United States instead of acknowledging their own. Former ISI chief, Hamid Gul, spoke of having 'all those resources, plans and techniques that are sufficient to break India into pieces,'[79] and the same "ambition" is also voiced often by ideologue Zaid Hamid.[80] Former army chief, Gen. Aslam Beg, asserted the need for 'fusion' between Pakistan and Afghanistan,[81]an idea described as 'greater Pakistan' by its proponents that extends the country's influence into the Middle East and Central Asia.[82]

Pakistan's policy towards Afghanistan is emblematic of political paranoia. Soon after Independence, Pakistan had reason to be wary of Afghanistan because of the influence of Pashtun nationalist sentiment. Then, Indian–Afghan support for Pashtun independence or merger with Afghanistan could have fuelled unrest in the border regions. The Soviet intervention, followed by US-supported jihad and the subsequent Afghan civil war subdued the prospective challenge to Pakistan from Pashtun nationalism or separatism. Now, Islamist extremists such as the Taliban pose a threat to both countries but Pakistan still looks at Afghanistan from the outdated prism of a potential Afghan–Indian pincer movement.

The history between the countries explains Pakistan's inflexibility in recognizing changed realities. It is true that Afghanistan had recognized Pakistan after initial reluctance because of its claim that the border drawn by the British in 1896—known as the Durand Line—had been unjustly imposed on Afghans by the British. According to Afghan nationalists, the British took Afghan territories, included them in British India and left them to Pakistan as continuation of that injustice, which divided Pashtuns. In the 1950s and '60s, Afghanistan's rhetorical support for 'Pashtunistan', a land encompassing all ethnic Pashtuns, justifiably irked Pakistan though it did not pose a serious security threat to Pakistan because of Pakistan's absolute military and numerical superiority. The Afghans maintained cultural, educational and economic ties with India but refused to side with it during the India–Pakistan wars of 1965 and 1971.

During the 1980s, Pakistan hosted large numbers of Afghan refugees and served as the staging ground of the anti-Soviet Afghan jihad, which resulted in the virtual evaporation of the idea of Pashtunistan. After the Soviet withdrawal and particularly after the collapse of the Soviet-installed Afghan government a few years later, Pakistan had an opportunity to reap the reward of goodwill it had generated by hosting millions of Afghans as refugees. The mujahideen who had been supported by Pakistan, the United States and most of the Muslim world were set to play a dominant role in Afghanistan's future. But instead of letting Afghan politics take its own course, Pakistan decided to play favourites among the mujahideen, instigating a brutal civil war.

'We have earned the right to have [in Kabul] a power which is very friendly toward us', Gen. Zia told American scholar Selig Harrison. 'We have taken risks as a front-line state and we will not permit a return to the pre-war situation, marked by a large Indian and Soviet influence and Afghan claims on our own territory.'[83] Efforts by his successors to try and instal a 'friendly' government in Kabul resulted in the brutal civil war among mujahideen factions, some of whom sought support from Arab extremists such as Osama bin Laden for their faction's supremacy. Kabul was virtually destroyed by the relentless rocket attacks mainly by Pakistan-backed forces of Gulbuddin Hekmatyar. But Pakistan did not get the government of its choice until it helped the rise to power of the Taliban—a puritanical movement of former madrasa students, which promised order amidst the chaos of civil war.

The Taliban's brutalities and disregard for human rights resulted in their failure to win international recognition. In the end, their government relied heavily on Pakistan, which hosted their sole embassy in the world though Pakistan was able to persuade two other countries, Saudi Arabia and the United Arab Emirates, to recognize the Taliban regime as Afghanistan's lawful government. Pakistani officials completely ignored warnings that the Afghan Taliban would inspire extremists in Pakistan who would someday challenge the writ of the state. The 9/11 terrorist attacks in the United States in 2001, planned by al-Qaeda from Afghanistan, resulted in the US threatening Pakistan as the US began military action to remove the Taliban from power.

Gen. Musharraf signed on as an American ally against the Taliban to evade America's wrath, and Pakistan voted for UN resolutions demanding their removal from power.[84] But Pakistan allowed Taliban leaders to regroup on its soil covertly, assuming that the Americans would leave Afghanistan soon after destroying al-Qaeda and global terrorist organizations, leaving Pakistan to instal a friendly government in Kabul once again.

For sixteen years since 9/11, Pakistan has aided the American forces in Afghanistan by providing logistical support while providing a haven to their enemies at the same time.[85] As a result of this dichotomy, some factions of Taliban have turned on Pakistan and attacked Pakistani civilian as well as military targets. Pakistan has lost America's trust as American critics accuse Pakistan of acting as arsonist and firefighter in Afghanistan at the same time.

After years of denial, Pakistan now argues that it does, indeed, support insurgents in Afghanistan, but it does so because of security concerns about Indian influence.[86] For outsiders, that excuse seems based on exaggerations and falsehoods. India has no offensive military presence in Afghanistan and there has never been any evidence that the Afghans are willing to be part of India's alleged plan for a two-front war with Pakistan. Afghanistan's president, Ashraf Ghani, asked India in 2016 to train Afghan military officers and repair military aircraft after frustration with Pakistan, which failed to fulfil promises of restraining the Taliban and forcing them to the negotiating table.

Pakistan's convoluted Afghan policy has lost it the goodwill of Afghans, which it earned by hosting millions as refugees in the 1980s. Pakistan's leaders often question Afghanistan's acceptance of economic assistance from India even though Pakistan does not have the capacity to provide such aid itself. For years, Pakistani officials falsely asserted that India had set up twenty-four consulates in Afghanistan, some close to the Pakistani border. In fact, India has only four consulates, the same number that Pakistan has, in Afghanistan.[87] Lying about easily verifiable facts is usually the tactic of governments fabricating a threat rather than ones genuinely facing one.

Instead of choosing the simpler option of befriending Afghanistan's government, Pakistan's policy has centred on trying to thrust a regime of its choice on Afghanistan. The diplomatic option of negotiating an agreement with Afghanistan on the extent of India's role there that would not threaten Pakistan has almost never been considered because Pakistan's military is unwilling to trust both the Afghans and the Indians. Ironically, Pakistan has failed repeatedly in offering evidence that India is running covert operations from Afghanistan against Pakistan in Balochistan. When the arrest of an alleged Indian spy was announced with much fanfare in March 2016, he was said to have entered Pakistan through Iran, not Afghanistan.[88]

For the paranoid mind, facts do not always matter. Pakistanis know in their hearts that their country is under threat and that is enough for them to gloss over detailed reasoning or demands for proof. The pre-eminence of the military in Pakistan's life accentuates its psychosis as the military is trained primarily to think in terms of defending the nation against threats, not for creating an environment conducive to its political or economic development. In his 1984 study, *The Pakistan Army*, Stephen

Cohen wrote, 'There are many armies that guard their nation's borders, there are those that are concerned with protecting their own position in society, and then there are those that defend a cause or an idea. The Pakistan Army does all three.'[89]

Twenty-two years later, in another book Cohen pointed out that 'For the foreseeable future, the army's vision of itself, its domestic role, and Pakistan's strategic environment will be the most important factors shaping Pakistan's identity.' In his view, 'Regardless of what may be *desirable*, the army will continue to set the limits on what is *possible* in Pakistan.'[90]

That, in many ways, summarizes the reason why Pakistan has had difficulty in conceiving its identity and direction beyond thinking of hard security and living with a permanent sense of insecurity. An army is a vital national institution but a nation is more than its army. It needs a vibrant economy, an educated and competitive workforce, as well as intellectual and scientific curiosity and creativity. Gen. Muhammad Musa, commander-in-chief of the Pakistan Army from 1958 to 1966 once told me that 'a soldier, by training, has little understanding of anything other than locating and liquidating enemies'.

A military-led national discourse has resulted in Pakistan's obsession with real and imagined enemies. Aided by conspiracy theories, Pakistanis are sometimes unable to plan realistically for their development or to find their rightful place in the world. Since patriotism is measured by vociferousness in hating the enemy, charlatans can advance self-interest by engaging in jingoist rhetoric. Only one course is open: that of opposing India at all cost and in every conceivable way, seeking Kashmir's accession to Pakistan as a priority, justifying Pakistani support for terrorists as necessary because of asymmetry of power, describing nuclear weapons in glowing terms and endorsing the views of the military.

Other options—such as normalizing ties with India even without resolving the Kashmir dispute, expanding regional trade as an element of economic growth, befriending Afghanistan instead of trying to impose Taliban on it and limiting nuclear weapons to basic deterrence—are rejected as attempts to undermine national interest.

Several Pakistani politicians have found that embracing the doctrine of national insecurity is the easy route to power. Zulfikar Ali Bhutto and Nawaz Sharif both started their political careers by hewing their views close to those of the military as a means of ascent. More recently, a similar strategy has been adopted by cricketer-turned-politician Imran Khan. Religious political parties and extremist sectarian groups too have flourished in an environment that encourages belief in Islam and Pakistan being in constant danger. Although nationalist frenzy is not a substitute for economic or educational attainment, even entrepreneurs and businessmen prefer to profit from the circumscribed setting. Notoriously corrupt real-estate magnates have grown rich by developing defence housing authorities and Bahria (meaning Navy) housing projects. Major business houses almost invariably seek military contracts as a means of maintaining ties to the nation's pre-eminent institution.

The insecurity paradigm allows individuals to get away with criminality while criminalizing those who dissent from the state narrative. Thus, Dr A.Q. Khan managed to illicitly sell nuclear technology to overseas buyers to enrich himself while projecting himself as Pakistan's saviour and the man who made its nuclear weapons programme possible.[91] Similarly, Dawood Ibrahim, a notorious gangster from Mumbai, could set up his underworld operations in Karachi with official patronage because he had struck against India in shape of the 1993 Mumbai Stock Exchange bombings.[92] On the other hand, Nobel laureate Malala Yusafzai has to live abroad because her stated views and beliefs do not fully coincide with the paranoid Pakistani world view.

A glaring example of military-backed uber-patriotism interfering with pragmatic economic decision making relates to the large gold and copper mines in Reko Diq, Balochistan. Like most Third World countries, Pakistan had signed a contract to extract the copper and gold with a multinational mining corporation. In January 2015, the military magazine *Hilal* published an article by Samar Mubarakmand, described as 'an eminent scientist who led the team of scientists and engineers to conduct Pakistan's nuclear tests at Chagai in May 1998'. The article titled 'Destined Towards a Rich Pakistan: Reko Diq Mineral Resources' suggested that Pakistan did not need to pay a foreign company to extract its minerals and that scientists who succeeded in making nuclear weapons for Pakistan could also make it rich by developing its natural resources.

Letting foreigners develop mines, Mubarakmand argued, would be against Pakistan's national interest. 'There would be no possibility of knowing how much mineral wealth has actually left Balochistan,' he wrote, warning that '95% of Reko Diq assets would leave the country with a meagre 5% of their value available' to Balochistan and Pakistan. The nuclear scientist clearly indicates the effect of involving foreigners: 'No industry based on indigenously produced cheap copper would be established in Balochistan, eliminating the possibility of providing hundreds of thousands of jobs to the local people. The province would remain poor and prone to extremist activities.' His proposed solution was 'the beginning of mining and refining activity with Pakistan's own human resources'.[93]

Mubarakmand's pitch was received well by the military as well as xenophobic civilians. Balochistan has long been a troubled province and, in the official Pakistani view, easy prey to the usual foreign suspects. Therefore, the contract of the Tethyan Copper Company (TCC), which had the mining licence for Reko Diq, was cancelled. Soon after Mubarakmand's article Prime Minister Nawaz Sharif declared that Pakistan would soon be able to 'break the begging bowl' with the help of the Metallurgical Corporation of China (MCC). The Chinese are, in Pakistani folklore, more mindful of Pakistan's interests and security needs than westerners and can be trusted to never have any truck with the Indians.[94]

By August 2017, Pakistan had failed to take out even an ounce of Reko Diq's copper or gold and faced the prospect of more than $11 billion in penalties for cancelling TCC's contract. TCC had been bought by the Chilean global mining giant, Antofagasta, which took the breach of contract to the World Bank's International Centre for Settlement of Investment Disputes (ICSID), which ruled against Pakistan's breach of contract.[95] The case should serve as a reminder why military officers and nuclear scientists with a greater claim to patriotism may not be the best persons to make decisions about commercial mining or understanding the inviolability of international contracts.

For Pakistan to evolve differently than it has since its inception, it is necessary to change its national narrative away from paranoia. That does not mean Pakistan should not be mindful of potential threats along its borders or should ignore the likelihood of external enemies fomenting trouble inside the country. All it means is a restoration of balance within Pakistani society about understanding what is or is not a threat. A proportionate understanding of threats requires not only freer debate than is allowed in Pakistan but also requires inputs from professions other than soldiering. National security threats must be examined without the tinge of an ideology of fear or the taint of conspiracy theories and mass media hysteria.

Most experts recognize the value of professional soldiers and military officers but almost all of them warn against praetorian tendencies. Eric Nordlinger wrote, 'Military officers are professional managers of force and violence' who 'direct the application of force and violence to enhance national security in the face of potential and actual threats ranging from subversion to all-out conventional warfare'. He likened them to 'other professionals' such as doctors, lawyers, teachers, engineers and scientists and emphasized that 'they place a high value upon autonomy, exclusiveness and expertise'.

According to Nordlinger, 'Heightened professional expertise may engender interventionist dispositions when civilian governments are preforming inadequately.'[96] This engenders praetorianism, which 'refers to a situation in which military officers are major predominant political actors by virtue of actual or threatened use of force'.[97] Pakistan has become an entrenched praetorian state where the military now not only protects national security but defines national interest autonomously of elected civilians and does not countenance any interpretation of national interest other than the one it institutionally advances.

Professional military officers are expected to have the 'right to decide questions of military strategy, the requirements for recruitment into the military academy and officer corps, the content of the training curriculum, the criteria governing promotion, promotions themselves, and the assignment of officers to particular responsibilities and units'.[98] An army with professional officers can be very effective in its well-defined realm but if it insists on making all critical national policy decisions, the result is the psychosis of insecurity that appears to characterize Pakistan.

Pakistan must have a national purpose other than strategic or symbolic competition with India and its institutional strength should not just be the strength of its military. Its citizens should be able to choose between various alternative paths for their country, not be bogged down with a narrow ideological prism that isolates Pakistanis from the mainstream of global thinking.

7

Warriors, not Traders

IF, AS PRESIDENT CALVIN Coolidge said in 1925, 'the chief business of the American people is business', the principal preoccupation of Pakistanis is ideology and defending their nation against real and imaginary threats. Economic considerations have always been deemed secondary in Pakistan's policy priorities, important only to the extent of finding resources for greater goals such as securing Kashmir, facing the 'Indian threat' or reviving Islam's lost glory. A nation's economic output reflects the aggregation of the productivity of its individuals and it is enriched, as Adam Smith put it, 'by the economic prosperity of its people'.[1]

Pakistan's history, however, is a chronicle of a government demanding sacrifice for belief and nation rather than of fostering individual free enterprise that produces collective success. When the *Forbes* magazine published its annual list of billionaires for 2017, the list comprising 2,043 names did not include a single person from Pakistan.[2] Similarly, Pakistani companies seldom make it to various lists ranking corporate brands recognized around the world, or even in Asia. The only Pakistani to ever make the *Forbes* billionaires list, Mian Muhammad Mansha, joined the world's billionaires club in 2010 after selling half his shares in the Muslim Commercial Bank but fell off the list the very next year.[3]

Speculation was that Mansha did not like the publicity that came with being on the *Forbes* list. Although some Pakistanis are not past flaunting their wealth, acknowledging legally acquired fortunes is not always easy. Successful businessmen can face threats from any number of sources—the government commanding taxes, politicians and clerics asking for donations, kidnappers demanding ransoms and journalists engaging in blackmail or abusing an entrepreneur because they simply do not understand business. That fear of extortion deters Pakistani entrepreneurs against public pride in generation of wealth has become an integral part of the capitalist ethic.

Conventional wisdom in Pakistan suggests that the country is endowed with natural wealth and a productive people, with a flourishing informal economy that is simply not reflected in statistics. Another common explanation for Pakistan's relatively uninspiring economic performance is that the country's riches are regularly plundered by corrupt politicians and civil servants, making it seem poorer than it is. Every military intervention in Pakistan's politics has been predicated on the assumption that an honest general can help recover the billions of dollars siphoned from the economy and stashed in bank accounts abroad, though no large-scale repatriation of stolen Pakistani wealth has so far occurred.

Still, it is not unusual for Pakistanis to talk about overseas property and 'billions of dollars' in Swiss accounts that would, if brought back, help Pakistan become collectively wealthy.[4] Instead of offering concrete suggestions for economic policy, politicians rail against the alleged corruption of their opponents and offer the promise of prosperity based on 'bringing back the nation's looted wealth'. Little effort is made to understand the economic explanations for flight of capital or why corruption in Pakistan does not result in local capital formation as it does in countries like South Korea or China.

Corruption is indeed endemic in Pakistan but it is not the only explanation for Pakistan's economic problems. Pakistanis generally avoid critical examination of issues such as why the per hectare yield of its major crops is almost half of most other countries, why Pakistanis consume 34 per cent less calories on average than the rest of the world, or why the value of Pakistan's cotton textile exports is less than that of Bangladesh while Pakistan is the world's fourth largest cotton producer and Bangladesh produces negligible amount of cotton?[5] Fulmination against corruption has become the economic equivalent of conspiracy theories explaining the country's insecurity. In popular sentiment, just as conspiracies have made Pakistan weak and vulnerable, its destined economic greatness has been thwarted by corruption, not poor policy choices.

In fact, the Pakistani state has sustained itself for seventy years with external assistance and borrowed money, fostering a national culture of borrowing and living beyond the means. The entrepreneurship of some Pakistanis notwithstanding, Pakistan operates generally on the assumption that God—and others—will provide for both the individual and the nation, without Pakistanis having to concern themselves too much, as Americans do, with 'producing, buying, selling, investing and prospering in the world'.[6]

Most commentary and discussion in Pakistan relates to ideological, political or security concerns and the country's prominent economists either work for international financial institutions or otherwise find recognition abroad. Pakistani economist Nadeem Ul Haque, who spent most of his working life at the International Monetary Fund, seemed surprised when he analysed the content of Pakistani newspapers and found that Urdu newspapers devoted a meagre 3 per cent of their headline space to economic matters while English newspapers covered economic matters in less than 2 per cent of their output.[7]

The lack of focus on economic issues identified by Haque in 1994 has worsened since the advent, in 2002, of multiple television channels as the principal news medium for Pakistanis. Television news in Pakistan is overwhelmingly about political jousting, Islamic sloganeering, conspiracism and occasional incitement against Pakistan's external enemies, mainly India and the United States. Economic issues are seldom discussed and periodic harangues against corruption or rising prices lead viewers to believe that affluence of nations is somehow a function only of reining in malfeasance and price controls. According to Haque, Pakistan's limited economic conversation is 'not about understanding relationships between key variables, uncovering agent and agency behaviour, delineating the role of policy, or debating market or government failure'. It focuses on 'mindless number pronouncements' and arbitrary targets for growth in various sectors set by the government.[8]

Even internationally, Pakistan is viewed almost exclusively from a security lens without too much attention to economic trends. Every now and then, the potential for quick gains in the relatively small stock market arouses interest of international traders. But, as Teresita Schaffer complained in a 2011 article, 'Pakistan-watchers tend to focus on political and security issues' when 'they need to start thinking as well about the economy, the outlook for which is grim over the next several years'. Pakistan's economic problems, she argued, 'resulted from the long-standing failure of the Pakistani government to invest in its people, or from more mundane mismanagement of vital sectors, such as energy'.[9]

Most of Pakistan's economic woes, however, reflect deep structural problems, some dating back to the country's founding. That they are seldom discussed, let alone addressed, indicates the country's single-minded emphasis on its ideological concerns at the expense of common sense economic decisions. Pakistanis often point out that the country and its inhabitants are in a better economic condition today than they were at the time of Pakistan's creation. This is, of course, an indisputable fact. Pakistan's nominal GDP has risen from $3.8 billion in 1947 to $284 billion in 2016 while per capita income rose from $100 to $1,468 over the same period. The annual rate of economic growth has averaged 5 per cent in the first six decades of Pakistan's existence and stands at 3.6 per cent for the last ten years.

Since 1947, Pakistan's economy has had years of high economic growth as well as ones with a dismal growth rate. But higher growth has coincided with the flow of concessional resources from international donors and could just as easily be lost if these external inputs are taken away. Moreover, Pakistan remains a net importer of goods and services and its industrialization has not expanded sufficiently. Nor has the country shown sufficient promise in technological innovation or adapting to higher technology.

Growth in Pakistan's agriculture in recent years has been lacklustre but has at least kept pace with the growth in rural population, according to Schaffer. Industrial growth, on the other hand, has lagged behind the growth of cities.[10] Bad planning and worse policy has resulted in electricity outages, several hours a day in many places, which impedes industrial productivity. Moreover, Pakistan's population continues to grow at 2.4 per cent annually, which means that it has more children to feed, clothe and educate, in addition to providing sanitation and health care. As many as 44 per cent children between the ages of five and sixteen are out of school[11] while the country has less than one hospital bed (0.6, to be exact) per 1000, reflecting the generally poor state of education and health care. A young population can be an economic advantage if it can be productively employed but, in Pakistan's case, the large youth bulge represents millions of potentially uneducated, unemployed and unhappy young people.

The ratio between tax collection and GDP as well as between exports and GDP for Pakistan is among the lowest in the world. This means that the government faces a persistent shortage of revenue and the country confronts a perennial shortage of foreign exchange. Pakistan collects taxes equal to only 12.4 per cent of its GDP, which is lower than countries like Sri Lanka (13 per cent), India (16 per cent), Indonesia (15 per cent), Malaysia (14 per cent), Thailand (17 per cent), Philippines (14 per cent), and South Korea (16 per cent).[12] Pakistan ranked amongst the bottom seventh (155th rank) out of 161 countries for its exports to GDP Ratio (10.59 per cent) which is better than only six countries—Tajikistan, Yemen, Ethiopia, Sudan, Afghanistan and Burundi.[13] Pakistan's exports have been declining, both in absolute terms and as a percentage of GDP.[14] The country is deemed to have 'an extremely low "export orientation"' and merchandise exports account for barely 7 per cent of GDP, having declined from around 14 per cent of GDP in the early years of the millennium.[15]

Meekal Ahmed, another Pakistani economist who spent most of his life at the IMF, lamented that Pakistan's 'economy has, for the past few decades, lurched from one financial crisis to the next. At the heart of the problem has been poor management of public finances and deep-seated, unresolved structural issues in the economy that bad management and poor governance have exacerbated. The consequences of this secular decline in economic governance are plain to see: macroeconomic instability, high inflation, poor public services, criminal neglect of the social sectors, widespread corruption, crippling power outages, growing unemployment, deepening poverty and a deteriorating debt profile.'[16] According to him, each Pakistani economic crisis has been 'a caricature of the previous one with an economic boom, typically fuelled by official aid inflows, followed by bust which ends in a severe balance of payments crisis'.[17]

Ahmed joined other Pakistani economists in complaining that most Pakistani rulers, except Ayub Khan, showed little interest in economic matters. For Ayub, economic development was one of several planks in the edifice of the unified Pakistani nation he hoped to build. 'He placed the Planning Commission under the President's Secretariat and himself became the Chairman', staffing the Commission 'with some of Pakistan's best and brightest economic minds'. Under him, 'Pakistan was considered to be a "model of development" and "aid-effectiveness".'[18] But, as Ishrat Husain points out, Ayub's policies resulted in 'the paradoxical combination of the biggest growth rates in Pakistani history and large increases in income inequality, inter-regional differences and the concentration of economic power. While the period had strong macroeconomic management, it paved the way for a series of problems that were exacerbated in subsequent regimes.'[19]

But Ahmed's observation that Pakistani rulers lacked interest in economic matters is insufficient to explain the country's erratic economic history. Not only did Ayub Khan's much vaunted successful macroeconomic management fail to convert Pakistan into a self-sustaining economic powerhouse, subsequent periods of aid-fuelled growth also did not maintain momentum. In 1960, when Pakistan's nominal GDP was $3.7 billion, Thailand's nominal GDP at $2.76 billion was less than Pakistan's and South Korea's $3.9 billion was only a hair breadth ahead. By 2016, South Korea's nominal GDP had risen to $1.4 trillion and Thailand had grown into a $406 billion economy while the size of Pakistan's economy hovered at $284 billion. Neither Thailand nor South Korea became richer by discovering vast reserves of oil or some other natural resource. They utilized the factors of production—land, labour, capital and entrepreneurship—in an effective way to produce wealth while Pakistan was clearly unable to do so.

The best and the brightest Pakistanis still prefer the stability of a permanent government or foreign job to the gains of entrepreneurship; Pakistan's farmers remain unable to generate higher yields per acre but are disinterested in land reform or adopting technology; industrialists still persist with spinning yarn from raw cotton than taking risks and investing in making new value-added products; the stock market's base remains narrow as few individuals are willing to save and invest; and the financial sector remains limited in its scope compared with its peers in other countries.

Pakistan's recurrent economic crises are partly the product of general disdain towards pursuit of economic activity in a culture that extols the virtues of the warrior more than that of the trader. Pakistan's founders introduced Pakistan to the rest of the world as a nation of warriors and emphasized its strategic location while seeking external economic assistance. That pattern has endured over the years. Pakistan has suffered on account of wars with India, Islamist terrorism and local insurgencies but it cannot simply describe itself as a victim of others' strategic decisions. Successive Pakistani leaders made the choice of depending on foreign aid while building military capacity, ignoring the fundamentals of economics. Land reform and sustained modernization of agriculture, training of a skilled workforce, and nurturing of innovation or entrepreneurship has so far not been a significant part of Pakistan's evolution.

In February 1948, Jinnah recorded a radio talk to introduce Pakistan to the people of Australia. He described Pakistanis as 'mostly simple folk, poor, not very well educated and with few interests beyond the cultivation of their fields'. But then he addressed what he saw as the key to addressing Pakistan's poverty. Pakistanis, he insisted, 'come of hardy, vigorous stock, and I think without boasting I can claim that they are brave. They made good soldiers, and have won renown in many battles. They have fought side by your side in two world wars.' This gave them a claim on external support in Jinnah's view and he said he did 'not believe that anyone from abroad who gives a helping hand would have reason to regret it'. According to him, the fact that the 'greater part of the world's jute is grown in East Bengal' gave Pakistan 'the great benefit of earning large sums of foreign exchange', which would be 'very valuable to us in setting up and expanding our industries'. Pakistan was 'short of capital and technical knowledge; but given a little time, and here and there a friendly hand, these deficiencies should be made good'.[20]

This, in a nutshell, was the economic plan of Pakistan's founding father. West Pakistan's warriors would be the attraction for Western capital and technical knowledge while East Pakistan's jute would earn foreign currency that would help the country's industrialization. Instead of economic considerations, foreign policy and being home to warriors who proved their mettle fighting alongside the British in two world wars were deemed enough as building blocks of the country's economy. By the time Liaquat, as prime minister, arrived in the United States in 1950 on his first official visit, he 'stressed his nation's strategic position and the fighting qualities of her anti-Communist Muslim warriors' to seek American aid.[21] That approach has worked for Pakistan to the extent of keeping it going thus far but is proving inadequate for transforming it into an Asian economic tiger.

Misplaced Priorities

Before Pakistan's creation, Muslim League propaganda spoke of the 'treacherous Hindu bania'—a reference to the trading caste among the Hindus. 'The political ideology which is generally styled by its adherents as the Indian Nationalist viewpoint ought in truth to be called the Aryo-Dravidian Hindu Imperialist doctrine,' wrote El Hamza in his 1941 treatise '*Pakistan: A Nation*'. According to him, the banias had become important in Indian politics due to their numerical strength and 'their occupation of the most fertile Indian plain, the Ganges valley'. They produced wealth but were overrun by 'the ambitious military leaders from across the Western Himalayas', who assimilated the 'war-like quasi-nomadic Aryan tribes' of the subcontinent's north-west by converting them to Islam.[22]

In this telling of the story of Pakistan's origins, its Muslim warriors had nothing in common with the banias of the Gangetic plain. Added to it was the quirk pointed out by Pakistani historian K.K. Aziz that most Muslims 'of any importance' in the subcontinent traced their ancestry to immigrants 'from Yemen, Hijaz, Central Asia, Iran, Ghazni or some other foreign territory'. Aziz noted that not only was it 'a false claim', it affirmed Afghan, Mughal and Muslim exclusiveness. The claim that ancestors of most Muslims accompanied or followed invading armies belied the claim of Islam's widespread acceptance in India. But its more significant impact was to tie Pakistan, the homeland of Muslims, to Arab, Turkish, Persian and Afghan Muslim warriors and 'leaders, thinkers or scholars' associated with them.[23] Interestingly, there was little mention of merchants and traders while making the case for Pakistan even though Islamic history speaks of Prophet Muhammad as the most honest among merchants of his time and lists prominent pioneers of Islam, such as the third Caliph Usman, as traders.

The historic record shows that while the All-India Muslim League invoked religious, geographic, historic and even racial arguments in favour of its demand for Pakistan, it did not think it important to offer an economic rationale. That has not prevented some Pakistani writers from claiming, as Shahid Javed Burki does, that 'Economics was the basis of Pakistan's creation'. According to Burki, 'Pakistan was created not because its founding fathers thought that "Islam was in danger" but for entirely economic reasons.' He goes on to attribute the rise of extremism also to economic and political reasons. Those who follow extremist ideologies, Burki insists, 'are not fighting a war of faith with the Pakistani state or the West. These people resent their exclusion from political and economic systems—both dominated by narrow elites—and some of them have opted for extreme violence as the preferred form of expression.'[24]

Such historic revisionism is strongly contested by serious scholars. 'One might expect that the leaders of the movement for Pakistan would have articulated a vision for economic development', writes American academic Christopher Candland, noting the view that 'Muslims, particularly in Bengal and elsewhere in eastern India, embraced the movement for Pakistan as a struggle against economic exploitation'. But he only found 'Sentiments in favor of the economic development of the Muslim community through industrialization' that were 'sprinkled through speeches, resolutions and documents of the All-India Muslim League'. In his opinion, 'Jinnah and other Muslim League leaders had no firm plans, much less ideological moorings, for the desired nature or direction of the Pakistani economy other than that it should grow and that Pakistan needed to industrialize.'[25]

According to Candland, the All-India Muslim League last offered details of its social programme in a 1937 resolution 'which called for economic reforms, including the fixing of a minimum wage and maximum daily working hours, improving health and hygiene, clearing slums and abolishing usury and debt'.[26] When the Indian National Congress established a Planning Commission 'to chart the pattern of economic development in independent India', the League created a Planning Committee and tasked it to focus on areas that would be part of Pakistan. The Committee's work did not go beyond issuing a first draft of an economic plan, and it did not even produce a final draft report.[27]

Pakistan's founders did not think seriously about economics beyond voicing fear of economic deprivation at the hands of 'the economically dominant Hindu community'. They dismissed doubts about Pakistan's economic and financial viability by describing them as 'hostile Hindu propaganda' and made little effort to explain how they would overcome any potential economic disadvantages of Partition. Chaudhry Mohammad Ali narrated Jinnah's response in December 1943 to British journalist Beverly Nichols's question, 'Are the Muslims likely to be richer or poorer under Pakistan?' Jinnah's response was emotive. 'The Muslims are a tough people, lean, and hardy. If Pakistan means that they will have to be a little tougher, they will not complain. But why should it mean that? What conceivable reason is there to suppose that the gift of nationality is going to be an economic liability?'[28]

The entire debate about the need for a separate homeland was cast in political and ideological terms, and the only concern deemed valid related to Hindu 'conspiracy'. When, in 1946, an interim government comprising representatives of major political parties was being created, the Congress offered the finance portfolio to the Muslim League, which coveted defence or home affairs. The Muslim League saw it as a ruse, instead of as an opportunity to lay the economic foundations of strong Pakistan, assuming that the Congress had offered the finance portfolio 'because of the proverbial Muslim inability to handle matters like Finance' and because the 'Congress thought they would make fools of themselves'.[29] In the end, Liaquat became head of finance in the interim government ahead of Independence and the League celebrated when he was able to present united India's last budget, disproving lack of Muslim proficiency in budget making.

Liaquat was assisted in formulating the 1946 budget by Malik Ghulam Muhammad, a chartered accountant at the Indian Railways and Chaudhry Mohammad Ali, an officer of British India's Audit and Accounts Service. Both men later played an important part in Pakistan's formative years. Ghulam Muhammad became Pakistan's first finance minister and went on to become Governor-General while Mohammad Ali headed the country's civil service and later served as prime minister. As accountants, both concerned themselves with managing receipts and expenditures without showing much wisdom. Both were also anti-Hindu and pan-Islamist ideologues. Mohammad Ali even headed the Nizam-e-Islam Party (Party for Islamic System) in his latter days.

The bitterness engendered by Partition, the dispute over Kashmir and India's reactions paved the way for the paradigm Liaquat and his two accountants advocated for Pakistan. Once war started in Kashmir, anti-Pakistan hardliners in India could argue that transferring Pakistan's share of undivided India's assets amounted to arming or funding an adversary in the middle of war. India withheld Pakistan's share of assets located in India, further aggravating the paucity of resources stemming from Pakistan's weak industrial and revenue base. Pakistan was allocated a 17.5 per cent share in the assets and liabilities of British India. Cash balances were held by the Reserve Bank of India (RBI), which held back the transfer of Rs 750 million for months. Pakistan's share of 165,000 tonnes of arms, ammunition and other military material was also withheld.[30]

Pakistan's leaders had already decided to look for aid from the West, integrate Pakistan with the Muslim Middle East and stop viewing the subcontinent as a single economic unit. Soon after Independence, Mir Laik Ali, a former adviser to the princely state of Hyderabad, arrived in Washington to seek a $2 billion loan for Pakistan. Jinnah was already explaining Pakistan's geostrategic significance to American reporters, arguing that just as the US 'was now bolstering up Greece and Turkey, she should be much more interested in pouring money and arms into Pakistan'.[31]

Jinnah's warning that the whole world would be menaced 'If Russia walks in here' was quoted in the US alongside assertions by other government officials to the effect, 'Surely America will build our army' or 'Surely America will give us loans to keep Russia from walking in.' Critics noted the persistent Pakistani 'hope of tapping the US Treasury' and 'wondered whether the purpose was to bolster the world against Bolshevism or to bolster Pakistan's own uncertain position as a new political entity'.[32] Although the Americans were slow to respond to Pakistan's entreaties for aid, Liaquat and his team stuck to their strategy. Pakistan would effectively delink its economy from India, seek Western aid to industrialize and pay for its military and work on building an economic bloc of Islamic countries.

Until Western aid started flowing in, things were bound to remain tough and national pride was expected to make up for any sense of economic disadvantage. When Ghulam Muhammad presented Pakistan's first budget, it was designed to show a small surplus in both revenue and trade. Seventy-five per cent of the federal budget was allocated for national defence,[33] primarily to cover salaries and establishment costs of the large army inherited from the Raj. There was no allocation for education and little money for law enforcement, civil administration and health care. On Pakistan's first anniversary of Independence, Jinnah spoke of 'economic manoeuvres' by Pakistan's enemies aimed at fulfilling prophecies 'that Pakistan would be left bankrupt'. Still, the founder took pride—'Our first budget was a surplus one; there is a favourable balance of trade, and a steady and all-round improvement in the economic field.'[34]

Pakistan's second budget promised higher wages for government employees, remissions for the poor and more taxes on luxuries. Although

defence was still the priority, this time some spending was also envisaged for education, research, industries, agriculture and a major housing project for refugees who had come in from India. Once again, a nominal surplus of Rs 600,000 was shown, partly in one-upmanship with India. Alongside *Dawn*'s banner headline praising Ghulam Muhammad for producing a surplus budget for Pakistan was the one declaring 'But India has a deficit of Rs 14.79 crores' pointing to the Rs 147 million gap in India's projected revenue and expenditure.[35] Pakistanis were expected to feel good that in their eternal competition with Hindu India, their Muslim finance minister had somehow drafted a better budget.

Meanwhile, Pakistani efforts to woo the United States in bailing it out economically continued with little initial success. The plea for $2 billion in loans resulted in $10 million in funding from the War Assets Administration—0.5 per cent of the original request. However, soon after Indian prime minister Jawaharlal Nehru's visit to Washington in 1949, President Harry Truman approved an invitation for Liaquat that George McGhee, assistant secretary of state for Near East Asia, delivered in person before the year's end during a visit to the region. Ghulam Muhammad was the first Pakistani official to meet McGhee and his first request was that the United States should appear to treat Pakistan at par with India.

McGhee related in his memoirs that to Ghulam Muhammad it was 'of the utmost importance' that Liaquat was accorded a reception equal to what Nehru received.[36] Muhammad also attempted to convince the United States of the importance of creating an Islamic economic bloc, an idea Jinnah originally introduced. McGhee responded by pointing out that Islamic countries' economies were not complementary. Cooperation between countries producing more or less similar goods from primitive agricultural economies, he pointed out, would not yield substantial gains. 'I did not believe that religion in itself provided a basis for a separate economic grouping,' McGhee wrote.[37]

That did not discourage the ideologues in Karachi from moving forward with their original plans. Although McGhee had pooh-poohed the plan for an Islamic economic bloc, he did hold out some promise of

US aid. Pakistan went ahead and hosted an Islamic economic conference on its own, and plans to break away from India economically continued to be discussed. Of these, the break from India was the most complex to execute. Chaudhry Mohammad Ali pointed out that under the British 'Free trade within the whole area, a single tariff, a unified system of currency and credit, and a network of railways and telegraphs had helped to integrate the economy.'[38] But because 'trade and industry of the subcontinent was in Hindu or British hands', the ideological imperative was to rapidly industrialize Pakistan and to economically disconnect India as soon as possible.

At Independence, West Pakistan manufactured cotton yarn while East Pakistan's principal products were jute and tea. Cotton from West Pakistan went to mills in Ahmedabad and Bombay, while jute from East Pakistan fed the mills in Calcutta. But Ghulam Muhammad refused to join Britain and India when they devalued their currencies in 1949, leading to suspension of India–Pakistan trade.[39] India's decision had effectively made it possible for the Pakistani ideologues to break the interlinked economies.

As it turned out, the potential disruptive effect of losing traditional markets was contained by the 'Korean boom'—the global rise in the price of commodities resulting from the Korean War. Pakistan could sell its jute and cotton to buyers other than India for a higher price, absorbing the effect of losing the Indian market. Candland says, 'Maintaining an overvalued currency allowed Pakistan to receive higher prices for (not completely market driven) exports, while reducing the cost of imported machinery and capital goods'. It enabled implementation of the Industrial Policy Document of 1948 that proposed state-led industrialization and described it as a 'state imperative'.[40]

State-led industrialization coupled with the search for foreign aid, became the mainstay of Pakistan's economic strategy until 1971. Significant amount of foreign aid started flowing in from 1954 onwards, after Pakistan joined US-led military alliances. In addition to US bilateral assistance, international financial institutions such as the World Bank and the Asian Development Bank also started financing projects and concessional credit became more readily available for industrialization. The process picked up speed during the decade-long military regime of Ayub Khan, which provided macroeconomic stability without paying too much attention to political or social considerations.

Ayub brought in American economists such as Gustav Papanek, Emile Despres, Lionel Hanson, David Bell and Richard Mallon to work in the Planning Commission. The main goal of Ayub's economic development strategy, Candland points out, was capital accumulation. The private capitalist's function was expected to be to reinvest profits and savings while the government 'encourage[d] the private sector through a variety of incentives with little or no curb on profits'. It was assumed that while the landlords, the middle classes and wage earners did not save, capitalists saved and that saving alone could bolster domestic investment. This strategy was characterized as the 'functional inequality' approach. 'Western economists advising the Pakistan government argued that economic growth required an inequitable but temporary concentration of wealth.'[41]

The Ayub era marked the expedient implementation of the industrialization strategy initiated immediately after Independence. That strategy focused on building 'a public sector that would be the foundation for private sector development' while reserving 'energy, armaments and some transportation and communications for exclusive development by the government'. There was also emphasis on exporting agricultural products. Although Pakistan described itself as a market-oriented economy, it developed a large public sector under this policy. By 1950, the government had set up the Pakistan Industrial Development Corporation (PIDC) to establish public sector industries, which were transferred to the private sector once they were viable.[42]

Several Muslim families prominent in trading before Pakistan's creation became industrialists through this transfer of ownership. 'The creation of an industrial elite in Pakistan was not the product of a long history of indigenous economic development,' Candland points out. It was 'the product of the post-independence political elite's strategic efforts to foster an indigenous capitalist class'.[43] The government's support of private companies with 'soft loans and generous credit from public sector institutions with very little oversight' created an incestuous connection between the business community, politicians and civil servants. It not only fostered a culture of corruption but also led to Pakistan's businessmen being averse to long-term investment while pursuing short-term profits.[44]

By the mid-1960s, twenty-two families of industrialists controlled 70 per cent of manufacturing and 90 per cent of the banking and insurance sectors. State-run and donor-funded enterprises such as the Industrial Development Bank of Pakistan (IDBP) and the Pakistan Industrial Credit and Investment Corporation (PICIC) provided liberal credit to help these private businesses. Pakistan's new industrial class 'was formed largely of a small group of refugee families who had previously been traders in India, and who were able to discern the new industrial profit opportunities'. The politically dominant landlords had almost no role in industrial development.[45] There was also no one from East Bengal among the twenty-two families though one family from Calcutta (the Ispahani family) had made East Pakistan their headquarters after Partition and stayed on in Bangladesh after its independence.

The new industrialists took over profitable enterprises set up by the government while unprofitable and unsold factories continued to be operated in the public sector. Pakistan witnessed economic growth but with great concentration of wealth in a few hands. 'Growth philosophy argued that in the initial stages of economic development some concentration of income and wealth in a few hands was necessary,' Meekal Ahmed explains, adding that Pakistan's economic planners thought that they could tackle considerations of equity and income distribution at a later stage of the country's development. But he also notes that the strategy had other flaws. Some of the industries were protected by high tariff barriers and generated 'negative value-added' once their inputs and outputs were valued at world prices rather than at distorted domestic prices.

According to Ahmed, 'Factor price distortions, including an overvalued exchange rate had led to the choice of highly capital-intensive techniques of production, generating little employment per unit of capital and output.' Although Pakistan had grown economically, its growth 'had been distorted in terms of factor proportions and allocative inefficiencies.

More importantly it had exacted a high price in terms of inter-personal and more ominously inter-wing disparities in income and wealth.'[46] Regional disparities paved the way for East Pakistan's separation while the impoverishment of the many led to the rise to power of Zulfikar Ali Bhutto's left-leaning government.

Bhutto nationalized major industries, shipping, banking and insurance, thereby weakening the twenty-two families. But Pakistan's political economy did not shift drastically away from that of an elitist state. Although it has been several decades since Bhutto's removal from power in the July 1977 military coup, his decision to nationalize private businesses (many of which were built with state finances) continues to be cited by some as a reason for the risk aversion of Pakistan's business community. But Ahmed argues that 'Nationalization was by and large well-received by the people' as a means of 'redressing the evils of concentration of wealth and wide disparities in income'. He also praised Bhutto's decision to devalue the Pakistan rupee and bring it closer to its 'equilibrium' value.

According to Ahmed, 'The years of clinging to an artificially appreciated rate of Rs 4.76 per US dollar which was propped up by tight controls on foreign exchange and which created many distortions in the economy were finally over.' Bhutto's government handled the 1973 oil price shock by seeking short-term financing from the International Monetary Fund (IMF) and got it without stringent conditionality. 'To be fair to Mr Bhutto,' Ahmed writes, 'the gods were not kind to him. Each year brought a drought or a flood—negative domestic exogenous shocks—which hurt growth' and caused inflation.

Bhutto kept the economy afloat, however, by 'securing financing from friendly Islamic countries (including $500 million from Shah of Iran) and the Gulf, as well as an emerging new phenomenon: rising workers' remittances which were becoming an important source of financing the external accounts'.[47] The dependence on remittances and the discovery of new sources of external funding from Muslim countries helped Bhutto's successors, beginning with Zia, to maintain economic growth though they now spoke of privatization instead of nationalization.

In his study of Pakistan's elitist growth model, Ishrat Husain points out that Pakistan's governments since 1947 have been dominated by the 'same constellation of landlords, industrialists, traders, politicians, military and civil bureaucrats and some co-opted members of the religious oligarchy and professional and intellectual groups'. He was puzzled by the fact that the model endured through various forms of government attempted in Pakistan—'democratic, nominated, directly or indirectly elected, dictatorial'—and different ideological pronouncements of the governments in power.[48]

'Markets are normally associated with efficiency and are found to be impervious to the considerations of equity and distribution,' Husain asserted. 'The state is usually thought of in terms of ensuring equity and access to opportunities. But under an elitist model, where both economic and political power are held by a small coterie of elites, the market is rigged and the state is hijacked in order to deliver most of the benefits of economic growth to this small group. The markets therefore produce inefficient outcomes that are detrimental to the long-term sustainability of growth and the state, through its actions, exacerbates the inequities in the system.'[49]

Thus, while Pakistan has generally been protected from 'external shocks such as adverse terms of trade, disruption of access to world markets, debt crisis, or the collapse of the Soviet bloc', its domestic factors have shaped its economic paradoxes. Although the Pakistani economy has grown at an average annual rate of 5 per cent, it seems unable to handle the expansion of its urban population from 17 per cent in 1947 to the current almost 40 per cent;[50] its agriculture remains dominated by the same four crops that were important at Independence;[51] its manufacturing remains centred on textiles;[52] and its human development lags behind many in its neighbourhood.[53]

Rent-Seeking and Dutch Disease

The hallmark of Pakistan's economy is rent-seeking, defined in the dictionary as 'the fact or practice of manipulating public policy or economic conditions as a strategy for increasing profits'. According to Husain, 'Large-scale private entrepreneurs in Pakistan have been

protected from the forces of market competition and have been provided ample rent-seeking opportunities by government policies.' Pakistan's industrialists have been protected from external competition, which might enhance 'technology and innovation, efficient use of resources, and managerial and organizational skills'.[54]

Moreover, since the 1980s, nationalized commercial banks and development financial institutions have been employed 'as a source of political patronage—to reward the loyal followers of the government or to win over the adversaries'.[55] Thus, many borrowers appearing as industrialists in bank loan documents borrowed with the intention of never returning their loans and were never interested in sustained manufacturing.

Just as Pakistan's elite engages in rent-seeking behaviour at the domestic level, Pakistan has acted as a rentier state at the international level. Political scientists define a rentier state as one 'which derives all or a substantial portion of its national revenues from the rent of indigenous resources to external clients'. Although most rentier states depend on a single natural resource, such as oil, Pakistan has been able to parlay its strategic location into a resource and has become dependent on foreign aid. Having relied on the United States for the last seventy years, there appears to be a tendency among Pakistan's policymakers to show a preference for China as the country's new economic patron.

Hazem Beblawi and Giacomo Luciani point out that the economy of a rentier state 'relies on a substantial external rent', making it less important for it to develop 'a strong domestic productive sector'. Only 'a small proportion of the working population is actually involved in the generation of the rent' and 'the state's government is the principal recipient of the external rent'.[56] Each of these characteristics of rentierism applies to Pakistan's pursuit of US assistance that began with the country's founding generation (Jinnah, Liaquat and Ghulam Muhammad), flourished under its military rulers (Ayub, Zia and Musharraf) and has persisted under elected leaders who continued to seek assistance while promising to break the proverbial begging bowl.

Pakistan's history reveals a pattern of seeking foreign economic assistance in return for security and foreign policies favourable to the aid-providing patron. Even before Independence, Pakistan made a pitch for US military and economic aid in early interactions with American diplomats. The US ambassador to India, Henry F. Grady, reported Jinnah's hope that the 'US would aid Pakistan in its many problems',[57] after their meeting in July 1947. Pakistani visitors to Washington, most frequent among them being Finance Minister Ghulam Muhammad, demanded attention as the world's largest independent Muslim country while 'seeking aid for the new state'.[58] As prime minister, Liaquat spoke of Pakistan's usefulness as a bulwark against communism and dangled the prospect of Pakistani troops participating in the Korean War.

In recent years, as Americans questioned the usefulness of their aid amid increasing divergence in strategic interests, Pakistanis have retorted by complaining that the United States failed to reward Pakistan sufficiently for its contributions during the cold war. This is often a reference to Pakistan providing an intelligence base to the CIA near Peshawar during the 1960s and Pakistan's role as the staging ground for the anti-Soviet jihad in Afghanistan during the 1980s. But Pakistan's attitude even in 1947–48, when it had yet to do anything for America and still expected huge inflows of US cash, commodities and arms simply because of its strategic location, confirms the rentier approach of its elites.

There was little discussion among Pakistanis, however, about possible reductions in the size of the army that was inherited from the British so as to lower the fiscal deficit. Furthermore, Pakistani leaders prioritized the political necessity of avoiding Indian dominance over the economic need to retain regional markets for agricultural products. They also rejected ideas of a customs union or closer economic cooperation with India. Instead, Pakistan's leaders convinced themselves that they deserved special consideration from America and, thus, they devoted their energies to securing aid from US leaders.

Initially, the United States refused to embrace the plan for sustaining Pakistan economically and militarily through large amounts of aid. There were no buyers in Washington at the time for the conception of the new country as the 'pivot of the world', as Jinnah had described it.

But instead of re-evaluating their expectation of aid as panacea, Pakistan redefined it to seek 'some sort of Marshall Plan'[59] for the Middle East and Pakistan. The argument was that every country needed assistance from outside 'in the earlier stages of its development' and Middle Eastern nations were no exception. It was 'the duty, and should be the privilege, of more advanced countries, and particularly the USA to assist them'.[60]

Interestingly, although Pakistan was a South Asian country, its appeals for assistance were based on describing it as an extension of the Middle East. The Muslim League media also raised the spectre that Pakistan may turn against the United States if its needs were not met. In a bid to be noticed by US diplomats, local newspapers ran articles to induce guilt among American diplomats for not being helpful to a struggling nation whose leaders were so favourably disposed towards their country. Foreign Minister Zafrullah Khan made this argument when he said that the 'well-known friendship of Pakistan toward the US and Pakistan's obvious antipathy to the Russian ideology would seem to justify serious consideration by the US government of the defence requirements of Pakistan'.[61]

Pakistan's efforts paid off with the election of Gen. Dwight D. Eisenhower as the thirty-fourth president of the United States in 1952. His aides spoke of plans for 'bringing strategically situated Pakistan into the free world's defense system' and for 'building a Pakistani army and eventually locating American airfields there'.[62] The new Secretary of State, John Foster Dulles, hoped that 'the strong spiritual faith and martial spirit of the people' of Pakistan 'make them a dependable bulwark against communism'.[63]

Pakistan's ambassador to the United States, Muhammad Ali Bogra, calculated that Pakistan could secure economic and military aid by portraying Pakistan as a front-line state in the battle against communism. He told Americans that Pakistan's army was the only army in the region willing to fight Soviet influence and incursions. That there was no significant Soviet influence in the region hardly mattered to men like Dulles, who were eager to implement their grand global strategy. Within months of Eisenhower's inauguration, Ghulam Muhammad—now Governor-General—decided to appoint Bogra as prime minister, hoping that his standing in Washington would help with Pakistan's quest for aid.

Pakistani leaders saw external alliance as a means of addressing domestic issues and of building their economy. They were all too willing to privately discuss joining a US-led military alliance as long as assurances of arms and aid accompanied it. They also sought US support in Pakistan's conflicts with Afghanistan and India though the US did not always see regional issues from Pakistan's prism. Pakistan joined the South-East Asia Treaty Organization (SEATO) even though it was not geographically a part of South-East Asia and later became part of the Baghdad Pact and the Central Treaty Organization (CENTO). With that began an aid relationship that has lasted several decades, notwithstanding frequent Pakistani disquiet over American demands and American concerns about Pakistan's double-dealing.

Between 1948 and 1953, the United States had provided only $121 million in economic assistance to Pakistan. Between 1954 and 2017, the cumulative amount of US economic and military assistance has risen to $45.147 billion, including food aid under Public Law 480 (which enabled Pakistan to pay for American wheat in local currency) and Coalition Support Funds (which reflected reimbursement for the cost of military operations against terrorists beginning in 2002).[64] US assistance has spiked in three periods, during each of which Pakistan was ruled by a military dictator. The first phase of large-scale aid disbursement occurred under Ayub Khan (1958–69), the second under Zia-ul-Haq (1977–88), and the third under Pervez Musharraf (1999–2008). Under Ayub, Pakistan offered the Americans listening posts targeting the Soviet Union and China; the Zia era saw the arming, training and launching of Afghan mujahideen against the Soviet Union; and Musharraf benefited from helping the US in their war effort in Afghanistan in the aftermath of 9/11.

There is also a correlation between Pakistan's economic growth and the availability of external aid over the years. US aid has often been augmented by concessional loans from other developed countries, eighteen of whom formed the Aid to Pakistan Consortium that was later renamed the Paris Club. US support also influenced lending decisions of the IMF, World Bank and other institutions. On several occasions,

Pakistan's usefulness to the US in the strategic realm determined the lenders' decision to provide debt relief.

During the Ayub era, Pakistan received an average of $277 million annually in US aid alone.[65] That assistance peaked at $2.8 billion in 1962, enabling economic growth to reach 8.7 per cent for 1963—the highest growth rate under the Ayub regime.[66] 'It is true that foreign aid at that time mostly in the form of outright grants and PL 480 grain shipments paid for in rupee counterpart funds and thus non-external debt-creating fuelled much of the growth,' writes Meekal Ahmed. He explains, 'By supplementing domestic savings, aid allowed Pakistan to invest more than might have otherwise been possible with domestic resources alone.' He also acknowledges, 'The external environment was exceptionally benign.'[67]

Even Shahid Javed Burki, who tends to be more defensive about Pakistan's economic performance than Ahmed, acknowledges, 'Pakistan's foreign policy in the 1960s paid rich dividends in the form of large amounts of concessional resource flows.' According to him, 'In terms of the proportion of GNP as well as real flows per head of the population, foreign aid during this period was greater than it had been in the 1950s and greater than it was to be in the 1970s and 1980s.' Burki concedes the adverse side of the large inflow of assistance. 'Although it certainly contributed to the remarkable growth in GNP during the 1960s,' he writes, 'it also dampened the rate of domestic savings.' He conditionally joins those who attribute Pakistan's low domestic savings rates to 'the negative impact of easy access to foreign capital flows', noting that it cannot 'be easily ruled out'.[68]

Between 1977 and 1988, Pakistan's average annual growth under Zia was 6.6 per cent when the government received an average of $394 million in aid per year from the Americans.[69] In Ahmed's words, 'Zia's regime represented the second episode of aid-fueled growth' but 'His economic policies were otherwise unremarkable and devoid of any bold initiative.' The Zia regime pursued an 'ultra-conservative approach' and 'had an aversion to changing the economic status quo'. Once, the government was forced into 'a three-year arrangement with the IMF because of balance of payments difficulties', but the arrangement 'was abandoned' without completion or substantive economic reforms.[70]

The picture under Musharraf was no different. Between 2000 and 2008, Pakistan's average annual growth was 4.6 per cent[71] while the government received an average of $1.2 billion[72] per year of bilateral American assistance and $190 million[73] in IMF disbursements. After announcing support for the US in its war against terrorism in 2001, the Paris Club rescheduled $12.5 billion in loans owed to several countries. Pakistan also completed an IMF restructuring programme for the first time since 1988 but this might have been made possible only by 'massaging the data'. According to Ahmed, 'Pakistan had earlier confessed to cooking the fiscal books and showing a lower fiscal deficit than the true one. A fine was paid and Pakistan returned some money to the IMF quietly, raising questions about poor book-keeping, open to 'discreet and deft manipulation'.[74]

The Musharraf regime rejoiced over breaking the begging bowl and regaining economic sovereignty. The government, Ahmed says, 'embarked on a hasty and ill-conceived dash for growth', comforted by 'a significant level of foreign exchange reserves, sharply rising workers' remittances, upgrades by rating agencies, large inflows of foreign private direct and portfolio investment, new bond flotation, and plentiful aid'. Growth was attained during this period but not by increases in investment and exports; it was based on consumption and imports. This led to 'speculative bubbles' in 'the real estate sector, the stock market and commodities such as gold', and the mirage of consumption-led growth and prosperity ended with the rise in global oil prices and the 2008 global financial crisis.[75]

Just as generous external assistance has fuelled the expansion in Pakistan's economy in certain years, its years of lowest economic growth have often been ones when aid has trickled instead of flowing, and most of these have come under civilian rule. The Ayub boom ended with a series of events culminating in the independence of Bangladesh, the rise to power of Zulfikar Ali Bhutto and a decline in concessional Western funding; the ostensible economic take-off under Zia terminated with a crash-landing amid differences between Pakistan and the US over Pakistan's nuclear programme resulting in sanctions under the Pressler Amendment that deprived the alternating civil governments of Benazir Bhutto and Nawaz Sharif during the 1990s of generous aid; and the illusion of prosperity created by Musharraf was followed by diminished growth and relative austerity under civilian leaders.

Foreign and national security policy was instrumental in securing large amounts of aid under Ayub, Zia and Musharraf but Pakistan also paid an economic price for pursuing policies divergent to those of its principal patron, the United States. Military assistance was suspended in 1965 when Ayub went to war with India, the Pressler sanctions resulted from Pakistan's pursuit of nuclear weapons and the post-Musharraf tensions resulted from Pakistan's decision to continue supporting the Taliban in Afghanistan. But Pakistan's economy muddled through during lean aid periods through borrowing from the IMF or with contributions from Gulf Arab states, especially Saudi Arabia.

Air Marshal Nur Khan, a war hero and former Pakistan air force chief, had once likened Pakistan's aid dependency to 'taking opium'. Speaking to an American diplomat soon after the loss of East Pakistan in December 1971, he said, 'Instead of using the country's own resources to solve the country's problems, the aid craver, like the opium craver, simply kept on begging to foreigners to bail him out of his difficulties.' Nur Khan proposed 'a Chinese-style austerity programme' for Pakistan although he doubted if 'many Pakistanis had the conviction and dedication to put up with the sacrifice that such a programme would entail'.[76]

Since that comment was made, China has embraced a free-market economy resulting in rising national wealth and higher standards of living for the Chinese people. But in Pakistan, despite repeated setbacks because of the craving for aid, no serious effort has ever been made to deal with that addiction. Pakistan's low domestic resource mobilization reflected in a narrow tax base and its precarious foreign exchange position repeatedly force its leaders to seek external funding. Instead of figuring out how to improve productivity and expand exports, Pakistani leaders have been content with borrowing from one source to settle debts of another, or sought rollover and rescheduling of debts. Some non-aid solutions to the country's perennial balance of payments crisis have been reliance on remittances, initiated under Zulfikar Bhutto, and the 'no-questions-asked' foreign currency deposits (FCDs) scheme offered by the first Nawaz Sharif government (1990–93).

The price of remittances has been the emigration from the country of talented professionals as well as large numbers of unskilled workers willing to undertake hard work. Remittances have helped Pakistan pay for imports, repay foreign debts, and show sufficient foreign exchange earning to qualify for more loans but they have also led to social and economic distortions. As the smartest- and hardest-working Pakistanis move abroad to earn and send hard currency to their families, the availability of a quality workforce in Pakistan has shrunk. The beneficiaries of remittances in villages and small towns often tend to live off their foreign-based productive family member's largesse and do not always engage in productive economic activity.

Remittances have fuelled consumption without necessarily bolstering investment. According to critics, remittances do not always contribute to economic growth in remittance-receiving countries. 'No nation can credibly claim that remittances have funded or catalyzed significant economic development,' says an IMF report.[77] In Pakistan's case, remittances have increased consistently even when the growth rate has been slow. They have mainly provided hard currency to pay for imports and contributed to overall growth by adding to consumption.

While the idea of paying for imports through remittances has lasted for several decades since it was first embraced in the 1970s, Pakistan's other initiatives to procure foreign exchange have not proved so durable. Of these, the FCD scheme that allowed Pakistanis to convert illegal or undeclared income into dollar accounts, without fear of legal retribution, started in 1991 and ended in 1998. Its demise occurred when the government froze hard currency withdrawals and repaid everyone the value of their deposits in Pakistani rupees to deal with the foreign currency crisis created by sanctions imposed after Pakistan's nuclear tests in 1998.

Other schemes to deal with diminution in concessional flow of foreign funds have veered from the dangerous to the comical. In early 1991, soon after the US invoked the sanctions under the Pressler Amendment, 'Pakistan's army chief and the head of its intelligence agency proposed a detailed "blueprint" for selling heroin to pay for the country's covert military operations.' The proposal was revealed by none other than the then prime minister Nawaz Sharif. In an interview to the *Washington Post*, Sharif claimed that three months after his election as prime minister in November 1990, Gen. Aslam Beg, the then army chief of staff, and Lt Gen. Asad Durrani, then head of the Inter-Services Intelligence (ISI), had told him that 'large-scale drug deals' could help pay for the money needed by the armed forces for national security–related covert foreign operations. Sharif claimed he stopped the two generals' 'blueprint' from going into effect.[78]

In his second stint as prime minister (1997–99), Sharif himself came up with a plan to get rid of foreign debt through voluntary contributions and donations by Pakistanis at home and abroad. He launched the Prime Minister's National Debt Retirement Programme with the slogan 'Qarz Utaro Mulk Sunwaro' ('Pay off the Debt, Improve the Country') amid much nationalist chest-thumping on 27 February 1997. The idea was that a little sacrifice by every Pakistani, especially those living and earning abroad, could help pay off Pakistan's national debt that was more than $63 billion at the time.[79] People were invited to follow in the footsteps of the companions of Prophet Muhammad who gave their life's savings while preparing for one of early Islamic history's legendary battles.

Many people donated their savings, including women giving away their personal jewellery, while others put money into high-profit, special bank deposits to help the national treasury. But the gimmick did little to dent Pakistan's massive debt. In addition to $32 billion owed to foreign creditors, Pakistan owed $23 billion to domestic lenders at interest rates of 12 per cent to 18 per cent. Another $3 billion would accrue in interest or service charges on that debt by the year's end.[80]

The prime minister and his advisors refused to heed criticism that a country's debt cannot be paid down by a donations campaign.

In the end, the new programme collected only $178.4 million, of which non-refundable donations were only $28 million. Qarz-e-Hasana—an Islamic form of lending whereby the borrower returns the money if he can but is forgiven if he cannot—brought in another $1.6 million while profit-bearing term deposits (on which the government would have to pay some return) raised $148.8 million.[81] Patriotic exhortations had failed to be a match for realistic economic considerations. Pakistan was soon back where it had started, turning to the United Arab Emirates, China, the World Bank, the Asian Development Bank and the IMF for borrowing in hard currency.

It is true that civilian governments in Pakistan have tended to be poorer macroeconomic managers because of political considerations that do not always bother military regimes. But the story of better economic management by dictators covers up the fact of greater aid availability and is often narrated primarily by Pakistani civil servants serving at international financial institutions (IFIs). Beginning with Ayub's long-serving finance minister Muhammad Shoaib, who was associated with the World Bank, several Pakistani bureaucrats have worked in the IFIs and have acted as a bridge between their country and the Bretton Woods system. Some have ended up as finance ministers, State Bank governors, and Planning Commission heads, usually in military regimes and one, Moeen Qureshi, even became interim prime minister. Their main contribution to Pakistan has been in helping to negotiate more aid or concessional loans.

The description of Pakistan's economic history by IFI officials of Pakistani origin sometimes glosses over the flaws of the country's aid-dependent economic model because the authors' relevance stems mostly from serving as intermediaries between Pakistan and the donor agencies. But in recent years, frustration in Western capitals with Pakistan's policies, especially in relation to jihadi terrorism, and the global perception of Pakistan as a problem state has diminished the ability of Pakistanis to indefinitely portray hopeful scenarios to continue receiving large amounts of Western assistance. This explains Pakistan's increasing desire in recent years to turn to China, though it is unclear how Chinese aid will act as a catalyst for indigenous growth where Western aid failed without Pakistanis changing their fundamental outlook in economic matters.

The Pakistani response to threats of an aid cut in retaliation against its terrorism policies, especially over the last decade, have usually comprised bravado or defiance in addition to suggesting that Pakistan does not really need Western aid or that the volume of aid is insignificant. Pakistan neither acknowledges its support for terrorist groups that attracts aid-related threats nor admits its heavy reliance on foreign concessional funds. Some Pakistani officials have argued that US aid to the country since 9/11 has been nothing other than meagre compensation for the country's losses due to terrorism.

That argument was first made by Asif Zardari after succeeding Musharraf as Pakistan's president in 2008. He said that Pakistan had become a breeding ground for Islamist militants because of its involvement, first in the US-led effort against the Soviet Union and now in the American fight against terrorism. Pakistan had suffered direct losses to its economy to the tune of $70 billion because of terrorism, he declared, adding that the 'international community owes it to Pakistan to support it in the fight against militant mindset'.[82] Zardari also came up with the slogan 'Trade, not aid', claiming that Pakistan would not need aid if it was given preferential trade access by the European Union and the United States.[83] The EU relaxed tariffs for several categories of Pakistan's textiles though that did not significantly alter Pakistan's trade imbalance after an initial boost in exports. It was ironic that even in promising to end aid dependence, Pakistan's leaders sought trade on easier terms instead of retooling their economy to expand trade as many other countries have been able to do.

By 2016, Pakistani officials had revised the notional cost of losses caused by terrorism upward to $118 billion.[84] No one outside of Pakistan, certainly no serious economist, accepted the argument that a country should be given a greater helping hand because of estimated losses accruing from past policies pursued with earlier assistance. By now Nawaz Sharif was prime minister for a third time beginning his term in 2013. After the massive floods in 2010 that displaced twenty million people, Sharif (then opposition leader) had criticized the Zardari government for seeking international aid and insisted that Pakistan had 'sufficient resources to rebuild millions of homes, buildings and bridges destroyed in the worst floods in 80 years'.[85] Once in office, he and other leaders of his party persisted with anti-aid and anti-dependence grandiloquence though the government continued to seek aid and received an IMF bailout and Pakistan never turned down the aid or the conditions it was offered.

After the election of Donald Trump as US president, increased public criticism of Pakistan in the US was followed by the type of angry statements that have become familiar over the years. Shahid Khaqan Abbasi, who had taken over as prime minister after Sharif was disqualified by the Supreme Court from holding public office, said it would be counterproductive for the United States to sanction Pakistani officials or further cut military assistance. He reasoned that reduction in aid to Pakistan by the US 'would hurt both countries' fight against militancy'.[86] This echoed the view expressed by many Pakistani public figures that the United States, not Pakistan, is the real beneficiary of its assistance to Pakistan. The argument was disingenuous at best and could be summarized as follows: 1) The US offers assistance as an incentive to Pakistan for changing its policies; 2) The US should not speak of reducing or cutting aid in retaliation for Pakistan not changing the policies it was supposed to change; 3) The US would get hurt because Pakistan would continue to follow policies that the US objects to, which Pakistan was already following while receiving the aid.

In addition to adopting an attitude suggesting aid as entitlement, Pakistani leaders sometimes downplay the importance of aid to Pakistan or act as if aid conditionality is somehow an attack on Pakistan's national honour. For example, Sharif's brother, Shahbaz, described the 'so-called' US financial help as exaggerated. 'The exaggerated comments being made in the national and international discourse regarding the US aid to Pakistan are tantamount to rubbing salt into the wounds of Pakistanis suffering terrorism, poverty and backwardness,' he said. According to the younger Sharif, 'no foreign aid is acceptable at the cost of our national sovereignty and honour' and it was 'time Islamabad closed the chapter' of American aid.[87]

Cricketer-turned-politician Imran Khan has, in recent years, played to populist sentiment against the United States just as Zulfikar Bhutto and Nawaz Sharif had done before him. 'Pakistan must detach itself from American influence and pull out of the "war on terror" in order to create prosperity and achieve regional peace,' he said soon after the elder Sharif's disqualification in 2017. 'Sadly, our ruling elite took dollars from the Americans and went into this war,' Khan told a British newspaper, adding emotional comments like 'Aid cripples the country'; 'It enslaves the country'; 'You are dictated decisions from abroad'; and 'It has created such hatred in our society. It has created turmoil.'[88] But Khan offered no alternative plan for arming Pakistan's military or paying for its foreign debts and imports, the actual reasons for Pakistan's aid and debt craving.

Arguments downplaying the significance of aid in Pakistan's military and economic evolution are not limited to politicians. Media commentators often make similar points. 'One cannot consider military assistance as a favour to Pakistanis,' an article in *Dawn* argued in 2012 amidst American criticism of Pakistani policy. The author went on to say that US military assistance had 'been instrumental in reinforcing Pakistani armed forces against the civilian governments'. According to him, 'The American military and economic assistance offered to General Zia in early 80s and later to General Musharraf since 2002 are examples of how American funds have strengthened military dictators against civilian setups in Pakistan.'[89]

He then went on to make what has become another familiar argument among Pakistanis. Citing the size of the Pakistan economy ($175 billion at the time) and the average US bilateral assistance in the preceding ten years ($825 million annually since 2002), the author cited remittances by Pakistani expatriates (an average $1 billion each month in 2011) to point out that remittances mattered more than US aid. 'I would argue that Pakistan's economy owes much more to what the expatriates contribute than what comes in charity from the United States,' he wrote without explaining why, for decades, Pakistan's economic managers still sought aid if it was not really needed.[90]

Such sentiments against foreign pressures over aid are not new. In 1967, Ayub Khan had titled his political autobiography *Friends Not Masters*. The book's Urdu version was titled *Jis rizq say aati ho parvaz mein kotahi* ('Livelihood that impedes flying to greater heights')—a line from poet-philosopher Muhammad Iqbal extolling the virtue of living and soaring like an eagle. Ayub had been embarrassed by US suspension of military assistance and concessional sales during the 1965 war against India. Instead of acknowledging that he had violated the terms of US military aid in initiating the war, Ayub joined the chorus of blaming the aid provider for not respecting the recipient. He wrote, 'People in developing countries seek assistance, but on the basis of mutual respect; they want to have friends not masters.'[91]

Fifty years and several other threats and aid suspensions later, Pakistan continues to nurture a sentimental opposition to aid, while seeking foreign assistance remains an integral part of the economic strategy pursued by successive governments, both military and civilian. There are reasons Pakistan's economic managers have not given up on external aid despite rising remittances. Although remittances enhance the country's foreign exchange reserves, they are spent by millions of individuals and do not enhance the government's treasury. Only aid provides budget support in hard currency and can be used for buying military equipment that Pakistan constantly needs.

'Most of Pakistan's needs,' said a newspaper article explaining Pakistan's reliance on aid, 'are of an urgent nature and cannot be postponed. Mobilizing resources, bringing back the billions parked abroad and broadening the tax net are all easier said than done.' Although the governor of the State Bank of Pakistan has publicly said that '$25 million are illegally taken abroad each day', Pakistan has not been able to get a single dollar repatriated from the much-talked-about illegal overseas holdings. According to the author of the article, 'The drive to broaden the tax base has also failed to take off. Out of over 31,000 notices that were recently sent by the Federal Board of Revenue, two-thirds were returned undelivered, and less than 500 people filed their income tax returns.'[92]

In a similar vein, a former secretary of the Karachi Chamber of Commerce and Industry wrote a letter to the editor stating that the 'trade not aid' argument was a myth. 'Ideally, trade not aid must be the significant component of our economic policy,' he observed, noting the 'pitfalls' of aid. But he went on to say that Pakistan's 'wide resource gap amidst growing socio-economic requirements' made aid 'inevitable or inescapable for a developing country like Pakistan'. According to him, 'The Second-World-War-ruined economies of Germany and Japan soon assumed the posture of developed and forward-looking economies through the assistance of the World Bank and IMF which came into existence after the war.' The author praised India for effectively utilizing aid to be 'now included among the 10-most-developed countries of the world.'[93]

Aid could lead to Pakistan's economic development, the author of the letter argued, but was not helping due to 'mismanagement and corruption' and 'the rapid growth in population'. He blamed terrorism and the energy crisis for undermining investment and resulting in a precarious economy. In his view, 'the solution of "trade not aid" appears to be without any substance, having no relevance with the ground reality and must be termed as a myth'. The letter ended with calls to give priority to economics over politics and for 'good governance combined with the rule of law'.[94] There was, as often, no effort to acknowledge the quantum of aid already received since Independence, nor an explanation for why it failed to create a self-propelling economy.

Some economists, notably S. Ehtisham Ahmad and Azizali Mohammed, have explained the distortions in Pakistan's economy in terms of 'Dutch disease'—the phenomenon of a single resource bringing an influx of foreign currency, depressing other exports and generally making the economy inefficient.[95] The term 'Dutch disease' was coined by the *Economist* magazine in 1977 to explain the Dutch economy's difficulties after the discovery of large natural gas reserves. It is often applied to problematic economies of countries that depend on a single commodity, such as oil or natural gas. 'Commodity-rich countries tend to struggle,' explains the *Economist* because commodity prices fluctuate and most economies need back-up industries. Most developing countries dependent on a single resource 'had low growth rates during the 1970s and 1980s'. Moreover, 'when the commodities run out, there will be little left to sustain an economy'.[96]

Ehtisham Ahmad and Azizali Mohammed argued that 'the influx of US assistance' had 'created a Dutch Disease-like effect', on Pakistan 'except that the country lacks oil, and trades on its geographical importance'.[97] Aid provided in return for Pakistan's military strategic cooperation had 'distorted incentive structures in Pakistan and weakened the desire for self-reliance' like that created by dependency on a single commodity in case of other countries afflicted with 'Dutch disease'. According to the two economists, fluctuations in Pakistan's geopolitical importance have made Pakistan's economy increasingly vulnerable. The impact of large inflows of aid during periods of high geostrategic importance have created 'a rentier-class dependent on "external handouts", supporting sixty-five-year-old "infant" industries that are unable to compete given a level playing field with efficient producers in East Asia, or even Bangladesh'.[98]

According to this view, 'The congruence of interests between the landed aristocracy and industrial elites, politicians and rent-seeking bureaucrats endangers growth, as well as effective service delivery and maintenance of personal and household security.' Ahmad and Mohammed warn that the 'internal dynamics of this process are not sustainable' and note the 'periodic waning of direct US interest in the region, e.g., in the late 1970s, and after the withdrawal of the Soviets from Afghanistan in the late 1980s and the subsequent collapse of the USSR'. They point out that notwithstanding the Pakistani establishment's sense of being treated unfairly, 'Pakistan was not completely cut off and IMF programs were instituted, with US support.' Thus, the multilateral donors' 'Exceptionally favorable conditionality and flexibility in giving waivers on not meeting even soft conditionality standards, have led successive Pakistani governments to treat lightly the fundamental issue of domestic resource mobilization measures that underpinned each program.'[99]

Thus, 'weak civilian governments vying for popularity, and military governments without political support seeking legitimacy' sought external assistance, depended on the few beneficiaries of that assistance for financial and political support, and avoided critical reforms. Virtually every Pakistani government has 'resisted raising domestic resources by failing to expand the tax base, modernizing tax administration and closing preferences and loophole, among other essential reforms required to run a modern state'. Although '11 out of 12 IMF programs since 1988 were abandoned in the middle or scrapped altogether—and the country has become known as a "start-stop adjuster",' the IMF continues to periodically bail Pakistan out for political reasons.

Noting a similar pattern with World Bank assistance, Ahmad and Mohammed observe that 'Neither the World Bank, nor the IMF (for that matter), raised alarms in a timely manner especially in the period around 2005/6, as the tax reforms were gutted by a favorite government allied to the War on Terror.' They justifiably lamented disappointing development outcomes '[d]espite the promise of an abundant land, with water, irrigation and natural resources, a large and hard-working population, and an ancient civilization, and significant inflows of foreign capital' over several decades in Pakistan.[100]

A Productive Future?

Pakistan views itself as a strategically located country needed by the world's major powers and as home to descendants of mighty Muslim warriors. This view of the self, coupled with the dominance of a narrow elite, accounts for Pakistan's inability to address its periodic economic crises. Instead of recognizing the national economy as the total of the nation's productive capacity, Pakistan's leaders see it as something they need to manage top-down with foreign subsidies, which they believe Pakistan is entitled to as rent for its strategic location. Although the country has a young, potentially industrious population, it has spent its first seventy years living off aid, accumulating debt and maintaining an expansive government that dominates its economic life.

Speaking in December 2016, IMF's managing director Christine Lagarde summarized Pakistan's economic difficulties after 'significant fiscal consolidation' under the latest IMF programme. Pakistan's public debt, at about 19 trillion rupees or 65 per cent of GDP, remained high. 'This debt needs to be serviced and, at current levels, the interest bill is larger than Pakistan's entire development budget,' Lagarde noted, adding that the debt could be reduced only by increasing revenue and reducing expenditures. Pakistan 'collects little more than half of what is estimated as a feasible amount' in taxes and other revenue. 'This means continued efforts are needed to bring more people into the tax net and ensure that all pay their fair share,' she said.[101]

It is also important to reduce losses of public enterprises, which stand at more than two-thirds of the government's Income Support Programme for the poor. 'Private investment in Pakistan today accounts for only 10 per cent of the economy,' Lagarde said, while the average in emerging markets is about 18 per cent. According to her, 'Pakistan's exports are about 10 per cent of GDP; emerging markets' exports are nearly four times as high. So here too, Pakistan can do better. Higher public investment in infrastructure can help.'

Lagarde proposed that Pakistan build 'fiscal and external cushions to be adequately prepared for future economic shocks'. To that end she recommended 'structural reforms in the energy sector, and tax policy and administration; ending losses in public enterprises; and making a sustained effort to improve governance and foster a dynamic and export-oriented private sector. In parallel, added focus on strengthening health, education, closing the gender gap and providing social protection can ensure that gains in living standards are widely shared.'[102]

Comments such as these by Lagarde have been made before without resulting in the comprehensive re-examination of Pakistan's economic alignment that is being advocated. Nadeem Ul Haque, the Pakistani economist, notes that Pakistani society and media are generally 'uninterested in reforms, economic development and growth'. Pakistani national discourse and intellectual space remain preoccupied with real and imagined security issues or challenges to the survival of Pakistan and the world's Muslims.

Although several economists question Pakistan's heavy military spending, Haque insists that is less of a problem. In his view 'countries can choose their own levels of defense provided they allow serious forces of economic growth and development to be unleashed'. The real problem for Haque is that 'Pakistan is not growing and developing because we as a people do not accept change'. The populace at large, and even its thought leaders, do not understand 'what the continued low rankings of Pakistan in global indicators such as "competitiveness" and "cost of doing business" means'.[103]

In Pakistan, however, popular understanding of economics is often limited to discussion of the country's geostrategic location as a resource that the world cannot ignore, the concerns of the salaried class about the cost of living, and complaints about 'massive corruption' that are aired but never redressed. The preoccupation with national security makes it difficult to propose economic solutions to economic problems.

The subject of trade with India is taboo unless it is accompanied by a resolution of the Kashmir dispute. Privatization of large loss-making state enterprises, such as Pakistan Steel, and Pakistan International Airlines (PIA), has often been contemplated but shelved due to 'national security concerns'. Xenophobic nationalism interferes with travel facilities for foreign businessmen and corporate executives as well as with large investment projects like the Reko Diq copper and gold mines.

Haque and others have highlighted the shortcomings of the country's 'economic software'—the ability to govern and manage Pakistan's resources. Pakistan's lack of investment in its human capital has been a recurrent theme in much of the analysis of Pakistan's economy in at least the past two decades. Ishrat Husain lamented Pakistan's struggle to 'carve out institutions, almost from scratch, that were basic to the running of the economy, and the administration of law and order, justice and security'. He points out that 'for various reasons, principally the threat from neighbouring India, the defence forces were strengthened more than other institutions affecting civilian life' and that 'the human capital base of Pakistan is much weaker in relation to its economic growth performance and compared to its neighbours in the region'.[104]

The weakness of the human capital base is both quantitative and qualitative. Low school enrolment, higher dropout rates at secondary school level and lower literacy rates than other South Asian countries reduce the size of the pool from which the country might draw skilled personnel. But even those lucky enough to make it to a tertiary level of education do not always receive an education comparable to other countries. Only four Pakistani universities were among the world's top 1,000 institutes listed in the Times Higher Education World University Rankings in 2017, three less than the previous year. Of the four, only Quaid-i-Azam University (QAU) was among the top 500 universities.[105]

Pakistan, which has 188 public or private universities, compared unfavourably with countries in geographic proximity. While only four of those was ranked among the top 1,000 universities, the Times list included thirty institutions from India, sixty from China, fourteen from Iran, sixteen from Turkey, five from Saudi Arabia, eight from Malaysia, seventy-one from Japan, twenty-seven from South Korea, twenty from Taiwan and six from Hong Kong.[106]

At least part of Pakistan's quality of education problem stems from its ideological orientation. The goal of education in Pakistan is not to enable critical thinking but to produce skilled professionals capable of applying transferred information instead of being able to think for themselves. To produce soldiers, engineers and doctors indoctrinated with a specifically defined Islamic ideology, the country has ignored liberal arts and social sciences.

Students in Pakistan are taught to look at the world through the prism of Pakistani Islamo-nationalism and often tend to shut themselves off from knowledge that might not be relevant. Even the engineers and doctors are not always innovative because of the general milieu that values conformity and maligns unusual ideas. The average Pakistani student is brought up on a mix of dogma and mythology that does not encourage respect for facts or empiricism. Textbooks suggest that 'Islam was the "crowning factor" in the establishment of Pakistan which is "not a geographical entity but an ideology which reflects a unique civilization and culture". It was a "revolt" against insidious efforts to impose "Hindu nationalism on the Muslims and their culture".'[107]

Learning that 'Pakistan came to be established for the first time when the Arabs under Muhammad bin Qasim occupied Sind and Multan', as one textbook suggests, breeds an attitude in which self-glorification is more important than self-assessment. The same textbook says: 'By the 13th century Pakistan had spread to include the whole of northern India and Bengal and under the Khiljis, Pakistan moved further southward to include a greater part of Central India and the Deccan.' Historian Ayesha Jalal mocked this particular textbook for 'Pakistan's habit of showing up after every second or third sentence,' citing how the author mentioned the assertion of 'the spirit of Pakistan' by Shaikh Ahmed Sirhindi in the sixteenth century in response to Mughal emperor Jalaluddin Akbar's syncretic religious policies.[108]

That Pakistan did not exist when Akbar reigned from 1556 to 1605 seems to make no difference. Nor does the fact that the Mughal emperor Aurangzeb's death in 1707 preceded Pakistan's birth by 240 years when students are told that 'Under Aurangzeb the Pakistan spirit gathered in strength' and that 'his death weakened the Pakistan spirit'.[109] The pervasiveness of distortions of history and the tendency to discuss even the sciences in the context of Islam's glory or Pakistan's security, crafts a mind that sees things not as they are but as it would like them to be. The consequence of using education as a tool of ideological indoctrination has been to undermine the quality of Pakistani education. Although Pakistan has produced many individuals who have done path-breaking work in the sciences and even social sciences, these are the exceptions, not the norm.

The products of an educational straitjacket, Pakistan's government officers prefer maintaining the status quo while entrepreneurs and business managers remain in short supply. 'All indicators suggest that our assets such as Railways, PIA, educational institutions, power generation and irrigation can all be managed better for increased productivity, increased growth and more employment,' Haque insists. But that can only be done through 'complex reforms involving all tiers of government and society and they need much research and discussion', which is missing in Pakistan.

As an example, Haque speaks of 'the power of vibrant and creative cities that foster entrepreneurship and are ever changing' even as they are 'densely populated, allow for high-rise and mixed-use construction, and discourage excessive reliance on cars'. Such cities in other parts of the world have been tied to increases in individual and national productivity, fostering of creativity and nurturing of entrepreneurship. Pakistani 'cities are highly over-regulated' and are 'the opposite of what this international evidence is suggesting'. Haque advocates 'quality policies and programs' that lower transaction costs and improve public service delivery instead of remaining stuck with an urban sprawl that limits the growth of the individual.[110]

In Haque's opinion, donor-supported austerity has added to Pakistan's already starving public services. The quality of public services 'declined as schools were unable to afford books, hospitals medicines and police the tools for their work'. Furthermore, the shortage of cash led to postponement of 'much-needed maintenance of critical assets such as railways, transmission lines, roads, generation companies'. Pakistan's public sector assets such as the railways and the power generation and distribution networks have not been maintained properly for years and are 'being run by people least interested in productivity (more worried about perks)'.[111]

To cut back on government expenditures, Haque bemoans, the government cut off funding of libraries and other social infrastructure leading to fragmentation of Pakistani society. As a result, 'all global measures of trust and social capital show sharp declines in Pakistan'.[112] Haque proposes heavier investment in human capital and a move away from austerity of the type proposed by donor agencies in pursuit of short-term targets. Pakistan must unleash the productive energies of its own populace, withdraw the traditional privileges of the elite and take a long-term view of its economic development.

One of Haque's arguments—supported by others—pertains to changing the incentive structure of Pakistan's public servants. Pakistan's civil service, judiciary and military have their origins in the colonial institutions set up by the British. As the top ranks of these institutions were filled by Britishers, the colonial government had to offer many perquisites to attract capable individuals to move from the United Kingdom to live and work in the subcontinent. Military officers were housed in purpose-built homes in cantonments, a swath of land around a garrison that was completely managed by the military. Civil servants were also given large houses to live in, along with being provided chauffeured transportation and personal servants. These perks enabled the colonial officer to live differently and aloof from the native population.

Pakistan inherited large estates of Government Officers' Residences (GOR) and cantonments, which now fall in the heart of major cities and comprise expensive real estate. Civil and military officers still retain domestic servants paid for by the exchequer and every branch of government maintains a fleet of cars, in addition to paying for drivers and fuel, for officials. The size of a government residence and car increases with the increase in rank.

Since the 1960s, public land has also been allocated for housing 'colonies' sold to military officers on below-market prices, followed by similar schemes for civilian bureaucrats and judges. But if the original reason for the perquisite system was to make service in hot and humid British India attractive for Europeans, what justification is there for retaining it seventy years after Independence? Haque, among others, suggests that the government should get out of managing real estate or transportation fleets for its officers, monetize all compensation and raise revenue by selling off its property at market prices. In addition to privatizing the still vast industrial holdings of the government, privatization since 1991 notwithstanding, a dramatic decision on divesting property retained for officials' perks would reduce the government's intrusion in the workings of the market.

Ishrat Husain is another prominent Pakistani economist who believes that Pakistan needs '[a]n effective and capable state combined with properly regulated and well-functioning markets in a competitive environment'. In his view, Pakistan's model of elitist growth must be replaced by the model of shared growth. The traditional roles of the market and the state must be restored so that competitive markets organize the production of goods and services while the government focuses on providing 'a legal and regulatory framework that only governments can provide' and attend to 'tasks such as investing in infrastructure, providing essential services to the poor, and maintaining security, law and order and a judicial system that is fair and enforces private contracts promptly'.[113]

'Pakistan's critical natural resources are the large reservoir of irrigation water and the fertile land of the Indus valley', Husain states, noting that Pakistan has not efficiently utilized this resource. He holds '[t]he mispricing of water, the political economy of water allocation, and the inefficient management of the system' for not allowing the change in the composition of Pakistan's agricultural products or a rise in productivity.[114] In addition to strengthening Pakistan's human capital base and improving governance, any new visualization of Pakistan would inevitably involve better utilization of water and modernization of Pakistani agriculture. Mahbub-ul-Haq, known for developing the Human Development Index with Indian economist Amartya Sen, often pointed out as early as the 1980s that Pakistan needed to diversify its crops and look at fruits, vegetables and flowers as potentially new cash crops.

Husain explains that '[t]he strategy for bringing about improved governance in the context of Pakistan would involve the breakup of the monopoly of economic and political power that has been amassed by a small class of politicians, large businessmen, military and civil service officers, professionals and zamindars [landlords]'. Pakistan's 'locus of power' is 'tilted in favour of entrenched interest groups' and many, including Husain, have proposed 'a reduction in their power' though few practicable suggestions have surfaced.

Husain describes the following 'main ingredients of the agenda for governance and institutional reform': 'improving the quality and performance of civil services; restructuring the organization of the federal, provincial and district governments; revamping the mechanism for delivery for basic public goods and services; strengthening key institutions engaged in economic governance; introducing checks and balances in the system by building up the capacity and authority of certain institutions of restraint'.[115] Almost all would-be Pakistani reformers fail in proposing what might compel the entrenched powerful interests to relinquish or share some of their power.

Currently, Pakistan's optimism about its future revolves around China's strategic interest in the country manifested in the China–Pakistan Economic Corridor (CPEC), a more-than-$44-billion package of projects aimed at modernizing Pakistan's infrastructure and improving connectivity with China as well as the rest of Asia through China's One Belt One Road (OBOR) project. The size of CPEC investments is about 16 per cent of Pakistan's 2016 GDP. While some 'early harvest' projects, totaling $28 billion, would be completed within the next few years, the rest of CPEC investments in energy and transport infrastructure financed by China are not scheduled to be completed before 2030.

For China, CPEC is part of its global plan to deploy the excess capacity of its huge infrastructure companies as well as to absorb some of its surpluses, but for Pakistan it presents an opportunity for economic growth and infrastructure expansion. Ironically, CPEC is seen by Pakistanis not purely in economic terms but as a security guarantee of China's commitment to their country. Once again, the historic pattern of insecurity and presumption of global strategic centrality seem to be at work. The centerpiece of CPEC is the port of Gwadar, on the Balochistan coast of the Arabian Sea, and Pakistani social media often carries future maps showing China and Pakistan exercising influence all over the Middle East and the Indian Ocean region from this strategic location.

Gwadar was first offered for development to the Americans by Pakistan's defence secretary in 1972, soon after the separation of Bangladesh. Then, Pakistan had said it 'would be willing to make land and port facilities available for US use' along the Arabian Sea coast 'including (from west to east) Jiwani, Gwadar, Sonmiani Bay, Karachi and area South and east of Karachi'. Even then, the Pakistani view was that the United States 'might be interested in developing [a] port such as Gwadar which could be important for economic development of that region of Pakistan'.[116] Thus, the notion that a foreign power can be induced to help Pakistan project power as well as develop economically while developing naval facilities for its own use is not new. The Americans passed on the 1972 offer and it took several decades to get the Chinese interested in the scheme. So far, China insists that CPEC has purely economic aims, while Pakistanis continue to assume that it is a strategic project that would enhance the country's security.

The difference of perception over ultimate goals notwithstanding, CPEC does offer an economic way forward to Pakistan just as the flow of US and other Western assistance did in the country's early history.

But unless the issues burdening Pakistan's economy discussed earlier are addressed, the CPEC boom might also end in a familiar bust.

According to an IMF report, $10 billion of CPEC's early harvest projects would develop road, rail and port infrastructure while another $18 billion (almost 6 per cent of GDP) is allocated to energy projects provided through Foreign Direct Investment (FDI). Some CPEC priority projects that are already under way contributed to increases in FDI, imports of machinery and industrial materials and the government's external financing in 2015–16. 'Financing modalities vary across sectors and projects,' noted the IMF report. 'In the energy sector, power plant projects will be funded through FDI by Chinese firms with commercial loans borrowed from Chinese banks. These firms will operate as independent power producers (IPPs) and have their electricity sales guaranteed through pre-negotiated power purchase agreements including guaranteed tariffs. In the transport sector, financing will be provided by the Chinese government and state banks mostly as concessional loans.'[117]

Although CPEC is likely to increase Pakistan's current account deficit because of increases in imports of machinery, industrial raw materials and services, it could have a considerable positive impact on Pakistan's economy if implemented as envisaged. According to the IMF, CPEC is 'expected to add significant power-generation capacity within the next few years, and subsequent energy projects could further expand the capacity over the long term', mitigating 'Pakistan's chronic electricity load-shedding problem'.[118] That would help domestic economic activities and exports. Transport infrastructure projects would improve domestic and international market access. But over the long term, CPEC would be advantageous only if the economic activity it generates in Pakistan helps service the debt generated by the projects and pays for the profits of Chinese companies that would go out of the country.

Sceptics are not sure that CPEC will transform Pakistan's economy as expected. *The Economist* described it in January 2017 as part of 'Pakistan's misguided obsession with infrastructure', pointing out that Pakistan's first motorway between Lahore and Islamabad built twenty years ago 'still has a desolate feel'. The '$1.2 billion white elephant' has been unable to generate traffic sufficient to pay for its costs, disproving the belief that 'investment in infrastructure is a foolproof way of boosting the economy'. The newspaper listed other underused facilities, such as airports 'many of which are modern and spacious'. In its view, 'Pakistan's infrastructure is underused because the economic boom it was meant to trigger has never arrived.'

Even after staving off a balance-of-payments crisis, achieving some measure of macroeconomic stability, trimming the budget deficit, benefiting from lower oil prices and witnessing a 50 per cent rise in the stock market since the end of 2015, concerns about Pakistan's economic prospects lingered. Foreign and domestic investors, said the *Economist*, had been put off by terrorism and insurgency. 'The country is also held back by inefficient and often cartelized industries, which have fallen behind rivals in India and Bangladesh,' it continued, adding, 'Exports, 60 per cent of which are textiles, have been shrinking for years. Much more needs to be done to create an educated workforce. Almost half of all those aged five to 16 are out of school—25m children.'[119]

Pakistan's needs are, as the World Bank puts it, 'better nutrition, health and education'. *The Economist* cited Lijian Zhao, a Chinese diplomat, as saying that China is all too aware that Pakistan needs more than just big-ticket infrastructure if it is to flourish. He praised 'the efforts of Britain and other countries to improve Pakistan's "software", such as education and the rule of law', explaining that 'China's expertise is hardware'.[120] It is not China's fault that it is helping Pakistan with the economic hardware of infrastructure just as it was not primarily America's lapse that it helped Pakistan secure concessional flows of capital. The responsibility for failing to lay the foundations of Pakistan's long-term prosperity lies with Pakistan's political and thought leaders. They are the ones who have built national pride around religion, nuclear weapons and a military equipped with foreign assistance while seeing no dishonour in constant supplication.

8

Avoiding the March of Folly

IN HER BOOK *THE March of Folly*, American historian Barbara W. Tuchman analyses the phenomenon of governmental folly and obstinacy, which she found 'noticeable throughout history regardless of place or period'. Folly, as defined by her, is 'the pursuit by governments of policies contrary to their own interests'.[1] Although Tuchman did not include Pakistan in her monumental study of governmental folly, Pakistan's history offers ample evidence bearing out her definition.

To imagine a future for Pakistan different from its past, it is important to recognize the various wrong turns taken by its leaders. Falsification of history and pretending that all is well except for the machinations of enemies create a mirage of success that does not exist. Assuming that there is no alternative path for 210 million people except to cling to an inflexible ideology either breeds delusional expectations or hopelessness. Reimagining Pakistan as a federation reflecting the will of its peoples while pursuing pragmatic policies might end its tenacious fragility.

The resilience of Pakistan and Pakistanis, disproving predictions of imminent collapse over seven decades, should not lead to hubris. Just as governmental folly unfolds over time, so do its consequences. Resilience over a period is no guarantee of protection forever from the cumulative results of folly. The Soviet Union fought bravely against Nazi invasion and proved resilient for forty-five years of the cold war. It could not, however, survive the failings of its misdirected economic policies, notwithstanding possession of nuclear weapons, a large military and a ubiquitous security service focused on crushing dissent. Yugoslavia defied predictions of Balkanization for seventy years; its eventual breakdown occurred just when its rulers assumed it had coalesced into a stale state.

In view of the tendency in Pakistan to view all unfavourable scrutiny and commentary as a conspiracy, it is important to note that pointing out fragility is not the same as desiring it. One can wish and pray for the best for Pakistan and its people while sharing worrisome observations about its trajectory. Analysis that highlights grim results of bad policies also implies the prospect of better outcomes with a different course of action.

In varying degrees, Pakistan has been a victim of all four kinds of misgovernment that have been identified by Tuchman as manifesting in human history, 'often in combination'. The first of these is tyranny or oppression, 'of which history provides so many well-known examples that they do not need citing'. Historic examples for the second, 'excessive ambition', include 'Athens' attempted conquest of Sicily in the Peloponnesian War, Philip II's of England via the Armada, Germany's twice-attempted rule of Europe by a self-conceived master race', and 'Japan's bid for an empire of Asia'. The third type of misrule is 'incompetence or decadence', exemplified by 'the late Roman Empire, the late Romanovs and the last imperial dynasty of China'.[2]

It is not difficult to identify combinations of oppression, excessive ambition and incompetence in the conduct of the Pakistani state since its inception. But it is the fourth kind of misgovernment, 'folly or perversity', to which Tuchman devotes detailed attention. 'Self-interest is whatever conduces to the welfare or advantage of the body being governed,' she writes, adding that 'folly is a policy that in these terms is counter-productive'. While examining 'folly', Tuchman identifies several case studies—from the Trojans' decision to take the wooden horse carrying enemy Greek soldiers inside their walled city to America's conduct during the Vietnam War—based on three criteria: first, the policy adopted 'must have been perceived as counter-productive in its own time, not merely by hindsight'; second, 'a feasible alternative course of action must have been available'; and third, 'the policy in question should be that of a group, not an individual ruler, and should persist beyond any one political lifetime'.[3]

Applying the criteria of folly to Pakistan, it is not difficult to understand how its policies over the decades reflect a series of imprudent choices, notwithstanding the availability of viable options. 'All misgovernment is contrary to self-interest in the long run, but may actually strengthen a regime temporarily,' Tuchman points out. In her view, folly lies in the 'perverse persistence in a policy demonstrably unworkable or counter-productive'.[4] Take the example of Pakistan's decision to be an ideological Islamic state instead of embracing a secular constitution. Successive Pakistani leaders, both civil and military, have persisted with that choice even after the loss of erstwhile East Pakistan, frequent internal discord, the rise of Islamist terrorism within the country and the spectre of international isolation or falling behind other countries. The poor track record of theocracies or of other ideological states in the modern era has not inspired a review of Pakistan's Islamist predilection.

Similarly, Pakistan has consistently refused to allow its diverse ethnic groups to maintain their national character, insisting instead that they merge their identity into Pakistan.

Pakistan's leaders created a national narrative based on religion that was bound to spawn extremist interpretations even though they were warned against it. They also attempted to impose as national language the language of a minority (Urdu) instead of recognizing the right of all its ethnic groups to retain their languages. The Bengalis were the first to revolt against efforts to erase their identity and the Baloch are currently in open revolt for the third time since Pakistan's creation. Pashtun, Seraiki and Sindhi nationalism also continues to surface with varying degrees of support despite official suppression. Even the Urdu-speaking Muhajir community now insists on recognition as a separate nationality, instead of allowing itself to be submerged in a Punjabi-led Pakistan.

Pakistan has paid scant attention to ethnicity- and language-based nationalism in other countries to understand why suppression of language or culture and efforts at forced integration are doomed to fail. Spanish rulers have failed to obliterate Catalan identity despite concerted efforts since 1716, and especially under the Franco dictatorship (1939–75); Scotland has reasserted its nationalism, overcoming union with England since 1707; and the Kurds refused to become Turks or Iraqis despite restrictions and repression since the 1920s. Pakistanis have constantly forgotten that offers of autonomy and recognition of linguistic and cultural separateness is often a better option than imposing greater centralization by force.

Similarly, after inheriting a large army from the British Raj, Pakistan has continuously maintained a larger military than its own resources allowed. It has sought foreign aid and borrowed heavily to pursue hostility towards a larger neighbour without winning any of the wars it has fought. The military (and most civilians) consider securing Kashmir a national objective at the expense of strengthening the country as it is.

Pakistan has failed to invest in educating its expanding population, traded military and intelligence cooperation for external assistance, failed to build a self-sustaining economy and evolved as a militarist and militant state to wield asymmetric influence in its region. Instead of befriending the governments in Afghanistan, Pakistan has spent considerable blood and treasure to try and instal a government of its choice in Kabul, prolonging conflict along its north-western frontier and dragging in foreign powers. Instead of viewing nuclear weapons as ultimate guarantors against a foreign invasion, Pakistan has seen them as weapons of pride that confer higher international status and allow the country to demand resolution of disputes on its terms.

Each of these policy choices has been made despite caution being voiced at the time about their counterproductivity. Viable alternatives were identified but ignored and the policy contrary to self-interest persisted under different leaders and governments.

Tuchman speaks of folly that 'belongs to the category of self-imprisonment in the "we have no alternative" argument and in the most frequent and fatal of self-delusions—underestimation of the opponent'.[5]

'We have no alternative' is an argument often heard in Pakistan. Whether it is military intervention in politics, support for jihadi terrorism, or refusal to change attitudes towards Afghanistan and India, it is argued that Pakistan has no other course open to it than the one it already follows. Underestimation is also a frequent part of the Pakistani elite's collective assessment, whether the opponent is India, the Bengali nationalists, jihadi extremists, impatience of Western governments with broken promises, or even the impact of poor social indicators on Pakistan's national power.

Psychologists, beginning with Irving Janis, use the term 'groupthink' for the phenomenon that has dominated Pakistani decision making. 'Groupthink' is defined by the *Meriam Webster Dictionary* as 'a pattern of thought characterized by self-deception, forced manufacture of consent and conformity to group values and ethics'. In his study of the trend toward disastrous decisions of national policy, Janis determined that groupthink did not represent stupidity nor could it be attributed merely to the emotional state of individuals. He pointed out that those who led the United States into the Bay of Pigs invasion 'comprised one of the greatest arrays of intellectual talent in the history of the American Government'. They just 'displayed the typical phenomena of social conformity that are regularly encountered in studies of group dynamics among ordinary citizens'.[6]

In Janis's view, America's 'failure to be prepared for the attack on Pearl Harbor, the Korean War, and the escalation of the Vietnam War' were all victims of "groupthink"'.

In his case studies of the fiascos, Janis found 'powerful social pressures' at work to silence any dissident who 'begins to voice his objections to a group consensus'. He found 'shared illusions' and 'group norms that bolster morale at the expense of critical thinking' at work.[7]

'One of the most common norms,' Janis writes, 'appears to be that of remaining loyal to the group by sticking with the policies to which the group has already committed itself, even when those policies are obviously working out badly and have unintended consequences which disturb the conscience of each member.'[8]

According to Janis, 'The symptoms of groupthink arise when the members of decision-making groups become motivated to avoid being too harsh in their judgements of their leaders' or their colleagues' ideas.' They soften their objections or criticism to appear amiable and 'seek a complete concurrence on every important issue, with no bickering or conflict to split the cozy, "we-feeling" atmosphere'.[9]

Most significantly, whenever there is greater 'amiability and esprit de corps' among 'members of a policy-making in-group, the greater the danger that the independent critical thinking will be replaced by groupthink, which is likely to result in irrational and dehumanizing actions directed against out-group'.[10]

Janis identifies eight symptoms of groupthink. The first of these, 'Invulnerability', comes from the illusion that no major harm is possible or likely. It provides 'some degree of reassurance about obvious dangers', creates over-optimism, increases willingness to take extraordinary risks, and results in failure to "respond to clear warnings of danger"'.

The second groupthink symptom is 'Rationale', the collective construction of rationalizations 'in order to discount warnings and other forms of negative feedback'.

The third, 'Morality', stems from a belief in 'the inherent morality of their in-group,' which 'inclines the members to ignore the ethical and moral consequences of their decisions'. The fourth, 'Stereotypes', leads to assumptions about enemies that 'they are so evil that genuine attempts at negotiating differences with them are unwarranted, or they are too stupid or too weak to deal effectively with whatever attempts the in-group makes to defeat their purposes, no matter how risky the attempts are'.[11]

The other four symptoms of groupthink identified by Janis are 'Pressure, Self-Censorship, Unanimity', and what he calls 'Mindguards'. The concurrence-seeking norm is reinforced by pressuring 'any individual who momentarily expresses doubt about any of the group's shared illusions or who questions the validity of the arguments supporting a policy alternative favored by the majority'; groupthink victims 'avoid deviating from what appears to be group consensus' and self-censor their concerns or doubts.

After pressuring others to change their views or keep quiet about their misgivings, it is easy for groupthink victims to assume that everyone agrees with them. Janis writes: 'Victims of groupthink sometimes appoint themselves as "Mindguards" to protect the leader and fellow members from adverse information that might break the complacency they shared about the effectiveness and morality of past decisions.'[12]

It is not difficult to find the symptoms of groupthink as the dominant factor in Pakistani decision making. The belief, frequently reinforced with propaganda that Pakistan is a special country blessed by Allah that is destined to come to no harm generates feeling of invulnerability that has not eroded even after frequent crises and the loss of half the country. Pakistani leaders rationalize their actions, sometimes even after disastrous consequences and insist on their inherent morality without regard for evidence to the contrary.

Stereotyping Pakistan's myriad enemies—from India to Israel, the United States and ethnic nationalists—is also easily spotted in Pakistani leaders' behaviour over the years, as is the tendency to pressure dissidents, censor qualms, demand unanimity of a 'national narrative', and to appoint mindguards against independent thinking.

Pakistan's history of groupthink began with the leaders of the All-India Muslim League refusing to heed concerns of other Muslim leaders about Partition's implications for the subcontinent's Muslims. Advice by British officials relating to division of assets, accession of princely states and economic viability of the new country's government were similarly ignored. After Independence, Suhrawardy and others who advocated secularism and regional autonomy were marginalized as Pakistan's first-generation leaders proceeded to build Pakistani identity on a religious basis and laid the foundations of an economy dependent on foreign assistance.

Once the army fully took charge, its esprit de corps enhanced the potential for groupthink. Air Marshals Asghar Khan and Nur Khan considered the infiltration of guerillas into Kashmir in 1965 as a blunder that would lead to war without any prospect of victory. But Ayub Khan and his closest advisors assumed the war would remain confined to Jammu and Kashmir, would result in a Pakistani victory and would not escalate into full-fledged war along the border with India.

The dissidents proved right. India attacked Pakistan after Pakistani infiltration into Kashmir and Pakistan lost much blood and treasure without any gains. Those who blundered into war had to be content with celebrating the soldiers' sacrifices and Pakistan's ability to survive. Although the war had been initiated for decisive victory in Kashmir, it ended with a peace agreement brokered by the Soviet Union that restored the status quo.

The 1971 loss of East Pakistan tops Pakistan's list of fiascos. General Yahya Khan's military regime misread the prospects of various political parties in general elections. Once the people of East Bengal had voted overwhelmingly for the Awami League, West Pakistani leaders should have understood the mood of their country's eastern wing. The governor of East Pakistan, Admiral Syed Ahsan, and the commander of the Pakistani garrison there, Lt Gen. Sahibzada Yaqub Khan, both advised against using force to overturn the outcome of elections. Yahya Khan and other generals seemed unwilling to transfer power to the Awami League despite its overwhelming electoral victory and assumed that killing or arresting several thousand party activists would end the Bengali challenge.

Ahsan lamented the anti-Bengali bias of the military leadership and the fact that East Pakistan was completely unrepresented in decision making. He and Yaqub were removed from their positions over their advocacy of talks with the Awami League instead of trying to militarily put it down. In his statement before the Hamood-ur-Rahman Inquiry Commission, Ahsan spoke of 'the high tide of militarism' and 'open talk of a military solution according to plan' when he flew to Rawalpindi after the elections. 'I was caught quite unaware in this atmosphere for I know of no military solution which could possibly solve whatever crisis was supposed to be impending in the minds of the authorities,' he said.[13]

The decision to start military operations led several months later to war with India and the surrender of Pakistan's eastern command against the advice of erstwhile East Pakistan's governor, 'the only sane voice in the government' at the time. Ahsan's description of a meeting in Rawalpindi on 22 February 1971—a few days before the military operation—serves as a reminder of the pitfalls of groupthink. The meeting, presided by Yahya Khan, was attended by provincial governors and martial law administrators along with other military and the civilian officers of the intelligence services. Ahsan 'was the only non-army governor and the only retired officer in the midst of active service men'.[14]

'I was the only person, though a non-Bengali, who had to represent the sentiments of seventy million Bengalis to a completely West Pakistani generalship,' Ahsan told the Inquiry Commission months later. 'During the past 17 months, in meetings and conferences, my brief ran counter to the cut-and-dried solutions of West Pakistan representatives and civil servants. The president invariably gave decisions which accommodated East Pakistan's viewpoint, at least partially. This made me unpopular with my colleagues who probably thought I was "difficult" at best and "sold" to the Bengalis at worst.'[15]

Writing about the six Catholic popes of the European Renaissance era whose decisions and actions paved the way for the Protestant Reformation, Tuchman wrote, 'Disregard of the movements and sentiments developing around them was a primary folly.' Her words apply equally to West Pakistani leaders' attitude towards East Pakistan. 'They were deaf to disaffection, blind to the alternative ideas it gave rise to, blandly impervious to challenge, unconcerned by the dismay at their misconduct and the rising wrath at their misgovernment, fixed in refusal to change, almost stupidly stubborn in maintaining a corrupt existing system.'[16]

The 'Illusion of permanence, of the inviolability of their power and status' and the conviction that 'challenges could always be suppressed' are as visible in Pakistani behaviour in Bangladesh as Tuchman found it in the conduct of the Papacy in the fifteenth and early sixteenth century. West Pakistani leaders also overlooked, to their peril, the experience of Britain in relation to its American colonies in the eighteenth century. 'Britain's self-interest' at the time 'was clearly to maintain her sovereignty, and for every reason of trade, peace and profit to maintain it with goodwill and by the voluntary desire of the colonies.' The British could have offered the colonies representation in the British parliament, conceded the colonies' right to be consulted before imposition of taxes, or granted autonomy while retaining nominal sovereignty.

Instead, the British insisted on their right to tax the colonies and, in the process, instigated the War of American Independence. 'Finally, it came down to attitude,' Tuchman says. 'The attitude was a sense of superiority so dense as to be impenetrable. A feeling of this kind leads to ignorance of the world and of others because it suppresses curiosity.'

She also comments on 'the terrible encumbrance of dignity and honor; of putting false value on these and mistaking them for self-interest; of sacrificing the possible to principle, when the principle represents "a right you know you cannot exert"'. The British 'persisted in first pursuing, then fighting for an aim whose result would be harmful whether they won or lost'[17] just like the Pakistanis did in Bangladesh at great cost.

Governmental folly often involves refusing to pay attention to facts and ignoring history. If there were lessons to be learnt from the East Pakistan/ Bangladesh fiasco, Pakistan's civil and military leaders did not learn them. Instead of recognizing the inadequacy of the two-nation theory, religious ideology and brute force in keeping the country together, the break-up was rationalized as the result of Indian hostility, malfeasance of Pakistani politicians, and the geographic remoteness of the eastern wing.

A contiguous Pakistan, it is now argued, is less vulnerable to centrifugal forces as long as it maintains a strong intelligence apparatus. By this logic, garrisons in all parts of the country and the ability to move troops more efficiently guards against a repetition of what happened in Bangladesh; Although the subcontinent's Muslims are now citizens of three countries rather than two, Pakistan's individuality continues to be based on the two-nation theory and the idea of implacable hostility toward Hindus and other 'enemies of Islam'. Patterns of politics and administration in Pakistan changed little after the separation of East Pakistan. With East Pakistani Hindus out of the equation, the proportion of non-Muslims in the population declined to less than 3 per cent, shrinking further the constituency for secular politics.

Thus, Pakistan continued its long trek of folly. Although the military handed over power to civilian politicians, the new civilian leadership weakened itself by adopting authoritarian methods. Zulfikar Ali Bhutto preferred to silence critics within his own party rather than listen to their advice. His decision to quell rebellion in Balochistan with the army's help and his conceding space to Islamists by giving in to some of their demands paved the way for the army's return to power in 1977.

The new military ruler, Gen. Zia-ul-Haq, combined brutality with obscurantism and saw himself as the man who would end all uncertainty about Pakistan's ideology and direction. He executed Bhutto, against the advice of many, assuming that he could rule Pakistan unchallenged while Islamizing it. Not only did Bhutto's execution fail to finish off his Pakistan Peoples Party, it polarized the country's politics for the next three decades. Islamization sowed seeds of violence and communal hatred that are still producing a bitter harvest.[18]

The venality of Pakistani politics after the Zia era, the failure of civilian governments to tame the military or the intelligence services while earning a reputation for politicians as inherently corrupt, the continued support for jihadi terrorism in Kashmir and Afghanistan despite blowback in Pakistani cities, the military misadventure in Kargil and the renewed use of force to put down Baloch, Sindhi and Muhajir ethnic nationalism are all examples of folly born out of groupthink. It is almost as if in Pakistan, as Tuchman puts it, 'the power to command frequently causes failure to think; that the responsibility of power often fades as its exercise augments'.[19]

'The overall responsibility of power is to govern as reasonably as possible in the interest of the state and its citizens,' Tuchman asserts. According to her it is the duty of those who lead or govern 'to keep well-informed, to heed information, to keep mind and judgement open and to resist the insidious spell of wooden-headedness. If the mind is open enough to perceive that a given policy is harming rather than serving self-interest, and self-confident enough to acknowledge it, and wise enough to reverse it, that is a summit in the art of government.'[20] Pakistan has been unfortunate that its leaders and rulers have repeatedly chosen ideological wooden-headedness over pursuit of reasonable and viable options.

Fragility, Control and Resilience

What should one make of the fact that Pakistan continues to endure even after the recklessness and lack of wisdom of its leaders? After all, it is somewhat enigmatic that a country whose future has been seen by others as shaky since its inception has also shown hardiness and managed to survive. Does Pakistan's resilience in the face of adverse predictions over the last seven decades mean that those seeing it as fragile or crisis prone are wrong? There could be underlying strengths in the Pakistani national character that historians, social scientists and economists probably ignore. The critics could simply be prophets of doom and gloom, unable to understand cultural factors for Pakistan's buoyancy, if not outright hostile to the idea of Pakistan. But it could also just be the nature of state stagnation, decline or failure that its timeline cannot be accurately forecast.

It is important to remember that the future of states and nations is not preordained. Historians can draw parallels between the past and the present and draw conclusions for the future; other social scientists might observe a country's trajectory, notice whether it is moving upward or not, and identify the factors that might improve its prospects or lead to further deterioration. Critical examination of Pakistan's conduct and pointing out its shortcomings do not amount to predicting its imminent collapse; responding to all critique with 'predictions of collapse have been proved wrong' is a straw-man argument.

Pakistan could muddle through for many years without addressing any of its many paradoxes or fault lines. But that does not eliminate the seven major inconsistencies and contradictions or the five significant fissures that plague. Pakistan's paradoxes are: 1) it is a new country in a region where other countries draw on ancient history; 2) it is a South Asian state aspiring to be part of the Middle East; 3) it has adopted a radical version of Islamic orthodoxy as a state ideology even though its people's practice of Islam is generally based on heterodox Sufism; 4) it has generally allied itself to the West while being suspicious of, and being suspected by, Western nations; 5) its political tradition is largely authoritarian even as it speaks of itself as a democracy; 6) it is a nuclear weapons power but still remains insecure; and 7) even in periods of foreign-funded economic growth, it is unable to attain internal political or economic stability.

Pakistan must also contend with five critical fault lines: 1) the division between its military and civilians; 2) the ideological divide between those seeking greater Islamization and those aspiring for a tolerant homeland of Muslims run as a normal democracy; 3) ethnic cleavages between and within its provinces; 4) the gap between rich and poor; and 5) irredentism caused by the overlap of its ethnic groups with one or the other of neighbouring countries.

Poor policy responses to these paradoxes and fissures are often at the heart of Pakistan's predicament. Its prospects could improve if its leaders revisit some of their fundamental assumptions and deal with the reasons for its being crisis prone. But the obstinate refusal to consider reform proposals and the insistence on rewriting history rather than learning from it have trapped Pakistan in a vicious circle. Instead of acknowledging bad decisions and moving away from them, Pakistan's policymakers deny their bad choices; they then make further wrong decisions to support their denial, with further consequences and further denials. It is, based on the criteria defined by Tuchman, classic folly.

Most reasonable people prefer reform over revolutionary upheaval. It is, therefore, important to recognize that even when things appear outwardly calm, nations might be simmering under the burden of misgovernment. The collapse of states has almost never been predicted with accuracy and the fact of avoiding breakdown for any length of time does not mark the end of vulnerability. Wisdom requires paying attention to signs of deterioration as soon as they manifest themselves because continued existence despite fragility can lead to false expectations. An examination of recent state collapse would better illustrate that point.

Other than Pakistan, which lost one wing but survived as a country with half its former territory and population, two other states—the Soviet Union and Yugoslavia—have fractured in the second half of the twentieth century. Both were multi-ethnic states, held together by an ideology rather than other characteristics of nationhood. Of these, the Soviet Union was built as a successor to the Russian Empire and was created by the Bolsheviks in 1922 in the hope of welding disparate ethnicities into a monolith through a centralized political system and economy. Yugoslavia—literally the land of South Slavs—was born at the end of the First World War when territories of the Austro-Hungarian empire where Croats, Slovenes, and Bosniaks lived were joined with the Serbian kingdom.

Pakistan resembles Yugoslavia in terms of being based on the idea of a common uniting thread (race for Yugoslavia, religion for Pakistan) unifying otherwise disparate people. It is also similar to the Soviet Union by virtue of the expectation that a shared belief system or ideology can result in the emergence of a monolithic nation under a centralized state. The experience of both the Soviet Union and Yugoslavia can help Pakistan avoid the hazards they succumbed to, making it possible for Pakistan to be imagined differently.

The Soviet Union adopted communism as its ideology, became a totalitarian state and was fully controlled by the communist leadership with the help of an efficient intelligence service—the Committee for State Security (KGB). If, as political psychologists say, '[t]he paranoid lives in a world of danger, as the center of malevolent attention', the Soviet Union was the quintessential 'paranoid state'.

In their book, *Political Paranoia: The Psychopolitics of Hatred,* American academics Robert S. Robins and Jerrold Post listed the seven elements of paranoia. 'Extreme suspiciousness is one of the principal components of the paranoid syndrome,' they note, adding that its other features are 'centrality, grandiosity, hostility, fear of loss of autonomy, projection and delusional thinking'.[21] All of these elements manifested themselves in Soviet state policy. Its surveillance apparatus 'employed about 480,000 full-time agents to oversee a nation of 280 million, which means there was one agent per 5,830 citizens'.[22]

In addition to controlling dissent and suppressing subversion, the state security apparatus also helped build and sustain a 'national narrative' much as the ISI does in Pakistan. According to David Satter, who served as the *Financial Times*'s Moscow correspondent from 1976 to 1982, 'The KGB was the invisible animating force responsible for everything in the Soviet Union that appeared to occur automatically, from the votes by acclamation in factory meetings to the all-pervasive silence that provided the backdrop for them.' He points out that it was important for the Soviet regime 'to force its citizens to demonstrate their "happiness"' as justification for 'the claim to have created a society characterized by voluntary unanimity'.[23]

The KGB acted as scriptwriter and director of 'the country's ideological play' and forced 'Soviet citizens to play their assigned roles'. It ensured conformity in society 'by placing everyone under surveillance with the help of a network of informers so dense that there was not a club, apartment building, or work brigade without one and making sure that anyone showing political independence was fired from his job'. It camouflaged its actions 'by pretending to act within the framework of a "democratic" ideology', and 'took whatever measures were necessary to suppress the handful of exceptions who had the courage publicly to dissent'.[24]

In the words of an American military analyst, 'The KGB was the glue holding together the totalitarian state that was the USSR.' It was not a good intelligence organization '[i]f a good intelligence agency is defined as having the ability to gather and analyze information that enhances the government's understanding of its adversaries'. It just 'ensured the political submission of the citizenry and eliminated subversive elements, real or imagined' through its 'omnipresence and omniscience'.[25]

A similar scheme of maintaining the state through an overbearing security and propaganda apparatus was implemented by the Soviet-installed German Democratic Republic in East Germany between 1949 and 1990. Its State Security Service, generally known as 'the Stasi' earned the reputation for effectiveness and ruthlessness comparable to the Nazi Gestapo. The Stasi employed one secret policeman per 166 East German, beating the Gestapo's ratio of one officer for 2,000 people. Adding regular informers, the Stasi had at least one spy watching every sixty-six citizens while part-time moles took the ratio to one informer per 6.5 citizens. According to one expert, 'It would not have been unreasonable to assume that at least one Stasi informer was present in any party of ten or twelve dinner guests.'[26]

The Stasi's principal function was to ensure security and continuity of the East German regime. By the time the regime collapsed in 1990, it had 102,000 full-time officers and non-commissioned personnel working for it, including 11,000 members of the State Security Ministry's own special guards regiment. Between 1950 and 1989, a total of 274,000 persons served in the Stasi. 'The Stasi was much, much worse than the Gestapo, if you consider only the oppression of its own people,' according to Simon

Wiesenthal of Vienna, Austria, who has been hunting Nazi criminals for half a century. 'The Gestapo had 40,000 officials watching a country of 80 million, while the Stasi employed 102,000 to control only 17 million.'[27]

Stasi also 'complemented the propaganda efforts' of the East German Communist Party, 'regularly supplied various levels of party and state with so-called atmospheric reports' about citizens' opinions, and dealt with 'non-aligned citizens' who 'might disseminate their negative attitudes to others'. It was responsible for 'the struggle for the minds and hearts of the people' and used force to bring under control anyone 'lacking commitment' to the official perspective.[28]

Stasi tried to control dissemination of all information in the country and prevented public appearances by the regime's opposition. In the process, it failed to gain insight into the motives of the East German system's critics and widened the gap between the state and its critics.[29] Would-be reformers became radicals after being driven underground and Stasi was ill-prepared and ill-equipped to deal with the situation when the iron curtain and the Berlin Wall were swept aside.

Although Pakistan is not a totalitarian state like the Soviet Union or communist East Germany, the ISI's role in trying to impose 'a false version of reality' and its 'proclivity for creating illusions'[30] differ little from the Soviet or East German circumstances.[31] Instead of engaging in intelligence gathering and analysis, agencies like ISI, KGB and Stasi end up defining national interest, identifying and punishing those among the citizenry who do not conform to that definition, and engage in a vast array of activities aimed at maintaining a particular ideologically driven narrative without regard for facts that might disprove it.

In addition to imposing an ideology and developing institutional mechanisms of control, the Soviet Union also attempted to alter demographic patterns as a means of enforcing national unity. Beginning under Stalin, large numbers of Russians were relocated to territories inhabited by other nationalities and some ethnic groups were moved outside their traditional homeland. That effort was not unlike the settlement of Punjabis in Sindh and Balochistan resulting from grants of parcels of land, especially for retired military personnel, though Pakistan has not yet adopted forced mass resettlement of the Soviet kind.

In the end, the Soviet effort to assimilate everyone into a Russianized communist state failed. The non-Russian ethnic groups, comprising more than half the Soviet population, resisted loss of their identity for the entire seven decades of the Soviet Union's existence. Similarly, East Germans did not lose their German-ness just because of being indoctrinated with communist ideology. Forty years of brainwashing and intrusive domestic surveillance proved ineffective in the end. When the opportunity presented itself, East Germans preferred to link up with their capitalist-democratic ethnic kin in West Germany than choosing association with Slavic communists living to their east.

Another important element of the Soviet experience was its positioning itself as the only rival to the United States much like Pakistan sees itself as the only barrier to India's hegemony in South Asia. As one of the two superpowers emerging from the debris of the Second World War, the Soviet Union decided to compete with the United States in every sphere at great expense. In the initial years, Soviet efforts to be America's equal appeared somewhat realistic. The Soviets acquired nuclear weapons, developed a space programme, supported communist parties across the world and presided over a vast global propaganda network. But gradually the state's needs began to exceed its economic capacity and the cost of the arms race led to Soviet economic decline.

Mikhail Gorbachev, who took over as the Soviet Union's last leader in 1985, openly recognized the country's economic and political problems. His policy of glasnost (openness), which was accompanied by a programme of economic reform known as perestroika (restructuring), failed to save the centralized, ideological state. Ironically, until Gorbachev admitted the need for rebuilding the Soviet state, even Western experts had assumed that the Soviet system was improving and that conditions of life were better for the masses. In a book edited by US scholar (and later National Security Adviser) Zbigniew Brzezinski that appeared in 1969, only six out of fourteen articles considered 'collapse as a serious possibility although not immediately'.[32]

Seymour Martin Lipset explained that most experts on the Soviet Union relied on Soviet data, which led to the conventional wisdom by the 1970s 'that the Soviet GNP was some 60 per cent of the American'. Westerners with right-wing or anti-communist leanings believed the worst about the Soviet Union but those with a left-liberal orientation processed available information without 'the view that economic statism, planning, socialist incentives would not work'. Moreover, most scholars focused on explaining how the Soviet system operated and avoided questioning the dysfunctional aspect of its very foundations. In other words, they 'took the fact of the USSR's long-term existence for granted'.[33]

One of the most prescient and scathing critiques of the Soviet system came from a Soviet emigre, Andrei Amalrik, in his 1970 essay 'Will the Soviet Union Survive Until 1984?' He argued that those 'who most benefited from the system, largely the educated professionals, want democratic reforms, greater freedom, and the rule of law' while 'the workers without rights, the collective farmers, all exhibit "pervasive discontent" with their lot'. Amalrik forecast that 'a halt or even a reversal in the improvement of the standard of living (such as was to occur from the seventies on) would arouse such explosions of anger, mixed with violence, as were never before thought possible'.[34]

In Amalrik's view, the Soviet Union was under threat because of the 'ossification' of the system. He saw the regime becoming 'progressively weaker and more self-destructive' and unable to 'hold down the forces of nationalism' in Eastern Europe. The regime could be toppled by 'any event which undermined domestic stability', according to Amalrik who anticipated a breakdown in the Soviet Union by the 1980s.[35] Gorbachev's rise to power, and his attempts to admit the system's mistakes in an effort to reform them fulfilled Amalrik's projections. In the end, the Soviet Union disintegrated on 25 December 1991, when Russian leaders decided to save their empire's core by letting go its accretions.

It is significant that most Western academics as well as the intelligence agencies of most of the world's major powers did not foresee the collapse of the Soviet Union or even its likelihood before its occurrence. There was a similar failure to anticipate the end of East European communist regimes. Amalrik, the émigré with a visceral understanding of his country, did better in understanding the forces at work in the Soviet Union than most outside journalists, social scientists and economists.

The break-up of Yugoslavia, which began in 1991, took outsiders by as much surprise as the collapse of the Soviet Union and its Eastern bloc. It marked the 'demise of the very Yugoslav idea—that is, the political philosophy that all south Slavs should live and feel that they belong in a single state'.[36] The various ethnicities or nationalities that had come together in Yugoslavia, first in 1919 and then again after the Second World War, decided to reassert their identities at a time when the rest of the world was not paying attention.

A writer for *Vanity Fair* saw Yugoslavia viable and flourishing just before its cracks, papered over for decades, became visible again. 'Yugoslavia had tourism, heavy industry; it was a food-surplus nation. Its new freeways linked the rest of the European community with Greece, Turkey and the export markets of the Middle East. The totems of an emerging consumer society were everywhere: new gas stations, motels, housing developments and discos and sidewalk cafes in the villages. Most impressive were the large private houses covering the roadside hills. Before the killing started practically everybody, it seems, was just finishing a new house, or had just bought a new car.'[37]

The Yugoslav elite's relative prosperity and the apparent success of integration under Josip Broz Tito, made most observers oblivious to the country's fault lines. Tito, a charismatic Croat, had led Yugoslav resistance to the Nazis and had gone on to rule the country for thirty-five years. He pursued a modified communist ideology, attempted to be fair to all of Yugoslavia's ethnicities and positioned himself as a bridge between the Eastern and Western blocs during the cold war. Strategic location trumped economic criteria in ensuring flow of resources into Yugoslavia just as it has done in Pakistan's case. Tito's 'system of government was intricate and complex, but designed to be manifestly fair'.[38]

British journalist Christopher Bennett observed that in the years before the country unravelled, 'Yugoslavs could, and did, walk tall in the world boasting of the cultural diversity which made their common country unique.' Tito acquired enormous international prestige and took full advantage of his country's geopolitical position, 'sandwiched between East and West and yet independent'. As a result, 'Yugoslavia had many friends. It hosted a number of notable international competitions, including the 1984 Winter Olympics in Sarajevo, and each year hundreds of thousands of foreign tourists flocked to its many holiday resorts, especially those on the Adriatic coast.'[39]

But critics and 'prophets of doom' had recognized Yugoslavia's fragility and fissures based on historic factors for some time. The speculation increased after Tito's death in 1980. Although there were solid reasons for concern about the future of 'an artificial creation', both Yugoslav elites and their friends abroad brushed them aside. They argued that the country had a large military and a unified electrical grid; its civil servants had a significant rate of intermarriage across ethnic groups; its textbooks and media had created a cohesive South Slav identity; and its international importance meant that it could always rely on external resources to bolster its economy. Based on these factors it was not difficult to take the endurance of the idea of Yugoslavia for granted.

Underneath this surface calm and behind the denials of trouble by Yugoslavia's leaders, lay a powder keg. 'The north was comparatively wealthy, the south poor, and the gap between rich and poor enormous,' writes Bennett. 'Per capita income in Slovenia, the richest federal state, was about six times greater than in Kosovo, the poorest. Serbs, Montenegrins, and Macedonians were Orthodox and had lived under Ottoman rule, while Croats and Slovenes were Catholic and had lived within the Hapsburg Empire.'[40]

They may all have been South Slavs but the people of Yugoslavia had other identities, which surfaced rather quickly and brutally once confrontation between their leaders began.

Vesna Pesic, a liberal Serbian politician and intellectual, spoke of Yugoslavia's failure to become a political community—'a nation-state whose identity conceptually and structurally transcended the various nations that it comprised'. Just as Pakistan is dominated by Punjab, the Yugoslav state 'was dominated by Serbian institutions'. Serbs were prominent in its military, political leadership and civil service. 'Serbia believed that it had the right to speak in the name of all Yugoslav peoples and to influence decisively the form of the state in conformity with Serbian national interests,' Pesic stated, adding that 'anything less than a centralized state would deprive Serbia of its dominant role in ruling the new country'.[41]

If the words Yugoslavia, Serb and Serbia are replaced by Pakistan, Punjabi and Punjab in Pesic's remarks, they could easily pass off for comments by Baloch, Sindhi, Pashtun or Muhajir politicians from Pakistan.

Still, none of the differences among Yugoslavs was inescapable and it was not the country's fate to break up. But the desire to believe only the positive while ignoring negative trends blinded Yugoslavs and their friends abroad to the country's underlying fragilities. Pakistan could possibly do better by not allowing its resilience narrative to become an excuse to reject examination of its weaknesses. Instead of relying on ideology as national unifier, strategic location as ticket to the flow of external resources, and a strong military and intelligence service as guarantor of its continued survival, Pakistanis need to examine their history and problems realistically and dispassionately.

To end its march of folly, Pakistan needs to reassess its core beliefs about a religion-based polity, reconsider the notion of permanent conflict with its larger neighbour, recreate political institutions to reflect its ethnic diversity and rebuild its economy without reliance on the largesse of others. Only then would it be able to reliably get rid of the spectre of failure or fragility and low international standing by all non-military benchmarks.

A New Nationalism

At the heart of Pakistan's dysfunction is its evolution as an ideological elitist state. The ideology had been crafted to respond to circumstances surrounding a new country's relatively sudden birth, which had transformed millions of Muslim subjects of the British Indian Empire into Pakistanis overnight. The creation of Pakistan was the result of a political deadlock between two political parties—the Indian National Congress and the All-India Muslim League—who had competed for support from communally separate electorates.

Franchise at the time was limited to 15 per cent of British India's population. Although the Muslim League won an overwhelming majority of Muslim votes in the 1946 election that helped it press the claim for Pakistan, it could not be certain that passions during one election cycle would suffice to create a new nation where none had previously existed.

'Nowhere has the lack of consensus over the meaning of Pakistan and its ambiguous relation to Islam surfaced more sharply than in doubts over the definition of "the Pakistani",' observes Farzana Shaikh, in her book *Making Sense of Pakistan*. According to her, Muslims who came from India, 'sought to establish their pre-eminence as "real" Pakistanis by comparing their migration to the archetypal Muslim exodus (hijrat) led by Prophet Muhammad to establish the first Islamic community in seventh-century Arabia. On the other hand, there prevailed the political logic of so-called "sons of the soil", who appealed to their demonstrable (if sometimes imagined) roots in the regions of Pakistan.' There were also 'two opposing ideas of political belonging that had informed the idea of Pakistan: the first, resting on an ideational construction of a natural Muslim community, the second on the notion of a locally negotiated national community'.[42]

Pakistan's first military ruler, Ayub Khan, cogently summarized the dilemma of identity that confronted Pakistanis soon after Independence. 'Till the advent of Pakistan, none of us was in fact a Pakistani,' he wrote, 'for the simple reason that there was no territorial entity bearing that name.' Before 1947, 'our nationalism was based more on an idea than on any territorial definition. Till then, ideologically we were Muslims; territorially we happened to be Indians; and parochially we were a conglomeration of at least eleven, smaller provincial loyalties.'[43]

Appeals to religious sentiment, therefore, were aimed at diluting the 'smaller provincial loyalties' and create a clearly defined Pakistani identity. But the ideology of Pakistan that has been fostered in the past seventy years has had two major consequences. First, it opened the door for endless debates and schisms around Islam that prevent discussion of more pressing and practical governance issues; second, it conflated an Islamic Pakistani nationalism with anti-Indianism, putting Pakistan in foreign and national security policy straitjacket.

The report of the judicial inquiry commission, led by Justice Munir, convened in July 1953 after that year's anti-Ahmadi riots had rightly foreseen the strains that would result from trying to transform Pakistan into an Islamic ideological state. 'The commission interviewed almost all leading clerics and found that they often considered each other's beliefs incompatible with Islam,' observes Farahnaz Ispahani in her book *Purifying the Land of the Pure: A History of Pakistan's Religious Minorities*. Islamists of various sects and persuasions 'wanted Pakistan to become an Islamic state' but 'their visions of such a state differed significantly. They seemed to agree only on their contempt for and opposition to non-Muslims.'[44]

According to the Munir Commission, no one who had 'given serious thought to the introduction of a religious State in Pakistan' had failed to realize 'the tremendous difficulties with which any such scheme must be confronted'. It pointed out that before Partition 'even Maulana Abul Ala Maududi of Jamaat-i-Islami was of the view that the form of Government in the new Muslim State, if it ever came into existence, could only be secular'.[45] Although a consensus has been imposed with the help of the military over the last several decades that Pakistan must be an Islamic state, the issue remains, 'which version of Islam should the state adopt in becoming Islamic?'

Meanwhile, several economic and social decisions remain hostage to theological considerations. The civil and military elite that needs the 'ideology of Pakistan' to retain its dominance is not always religiously observant, creating an environment of officially sanctioned hypocrisy in implementing the diktats of the clerics. For instance, Pakistan bans open sale or consumption of alcohol even though large amounts of alcohol continue to be smuggled in and sold illegally.[46] In addition to the loss of revenue that smuggling entails, driving alcohol consumption underground breeds criminality just as it did during the Prohibition era in the United States.[47]

Because the law does not recognize that Pakistanis buy, sell and consume alcohol in the quantities they do, the state pretends that alcohol-related illness also does not exist. Reports of alcoholism or alcohol addiction are handled by private charities because they are not officially acknowledged.[48] For years, Pakistan also denied it had any incidence of HIV/AIDS even as the problem ballooned to affect possibly 200,000 people.[49] Clearly, Pakistani society is far from pious but must pretend that it abides by Islam's injunctions to keep alive the myth of its being Islamic. The religious foundation of its nationalism interferes with Pakistan being able to formulate public policy in certain areas.

The other pillar of Pakistani nationalism, anti-Indianism, is less open to ambiguity than defining the Islamic rules for the state but is no less problematic. Leading Pakistani thinker Khaled Ahmed lamented, 'Pakistani nationalism comprises 95 per cent India hatred. They call it Islam because that is how we learn to differentiate between ourselves and India.'[50] That hatred leads to unrealistic competition, asymmetric warfare and the embrace of conspiracy theories.

In real terms, Pakistan is hardly India's rival. India's population is six times larger than Pakistan's while its economy is ten times bigger. Notwithstanding problems of poverty and corruption (which Pakistan also faces), India's $2 trillion economy has managed consistent growth since the 1990s whereas Pakistan's $284–$304 billion economy tends to grow only in spurts and in times of greater donor support. Over time, the economic gap between the two neighbours will only widen.

Instead of resenting India, Pakistan could stake a claim to its own share of prosperity. The two-way trade between India and China stands at $72 billion even though the two countries are often considered rivals. The volume of India–Pakistan trade is a measly $2 billion. Instead of tapping the potential of trade with India, Pakistan refuses to open it because of its 'ideological rivalry' and the unsettled dispute over Jammu and Kashmir. This deprives Pakistan of a large market and encourages smuggling of Indian products or their import through third countries, which only makes it more expensive. The government loses customs revenue in the process.

The discord between India and Pakistan also holds back the entire South Asian region, home to around 1.7 billion people living in eight countries—Afghanistan, Bangladesh, Bhutan, India, Maldives, Nepal, Pakistan and Sri Lanka. The combined GDP (at nominal rates) of these countries stands at US $2.9 trillion and it is the least integrated region in the world. Intra-regional trade comprises only 5 per cent of total trade of South Asia's eight countries. There are few flights between the region's capitals and road and rail links are in poor condition or non-existent.

This is in stark comparison to the ASEAN (Association of South-East Asian Nations) region, home to 650 million people, ten countries and a combined GDP of US $2.6 trillion, where 25 per cent of all trade involves neighbours. Half of all trade under the North American Free Trade Agreement (NAFTA) that binds Canada, the United States and Mexico takes place within the region, as it does in the European Union. If Pakistan sheds its obsession with resolving the Kashmir dispute before opening trade relations with India, it could become a major beneficiary of a South Asian free trade.

While most matter-of-fact considerations point to the need for normalizing Pakistan's relations with India, its state ideology and national narrative impede normalization. It is not difficult to see why Pakistan's founding generation might have needed an ideology to get through the trauma of Partition. All of them were born, and grew up, as Indians and many did not belong to the territory that had become Pakistan. They needed an explanation for the difficult transition that the birth of a new country entailed. Pakistan's 'artificially demarcated frontiers' led to a 'desperate quest for an officially sanctioned Islamic identity'[51] and the 'ideology of Pakistan' was deemed the solution.

The more westernized segment of Pakistani society, which includes most military officers, have always been more committed to the anti-Indian component of the national ideology than its religious part. That has led to the assumption that, concessions to Islamist sensibilities notwithstanding, power in Pakistan would never actually be wielded by religious leaders and clerics. But that assumption could be tested as Islamist militant groups are brought into the political mainstream—a policy initiated with military support in 2017—and military officers, politicians and civil servants with Islamist leanings rise within the structure of power. Pakistan could slide further down the path of rejecting modernity and seeking revival of a distant 'glorious Islamic past' as a result of how it defines its national identity.

Pakistan's emphasis on religion is primarily a function of the desire to erase identities derived from ethnicity, culture and language, which have often been considered the basis of nationalism. 'Pakistan originally comprised five major ethnolinguistic groups, whose unity Liaquat Ali Khan signified with a clenched fist,' Stephen Cohen wrote, explaining the evolution of Pakistan's ideological nationalism. Bengalis were 'an absolute majority in the new state, although the poorest' and they were the first ones to fight to leave Pakistan and seek an independent Bangladesh. Punjabis, Sindhis, Baloch and Pashtuns all lived in their respective regions in West Pakistan with varying degrees of commitment to the idea of Pakistan.[52]

The predominately Urdu-speaking migrants from India, 'the Muhajirs (named after the migrating companions of Prophet Muhammad),' became the 'sixth important group' after Partition. They had 'experienced the greatest hardships when the new state was created' and were 'the best-educated and most pro-Pakistan' element among Indian Muslims. 'East Punjabis (who also had to leave their homes and flee to Pakistan)' were another such group.[53]

According to Cohen, 'The leaders of the new state assumed that Jinnah's leadership and a common faith would override any differences between the major ethnolinguistic groups.' Support for the idea of Pakistan had been 'tepid among Sindhis, Pashtuns, and Baloch', making ethnolinguistic differences a real concern. North Indian Muslims, who had strongly supported the creation of Pakistan, were mostly left behind in India. Only 'the leadership and the professional classes' undertook the 'harrowing migration after partition'. Pakistan's leaders 'developed an ethnolinguistic-nationalist narrative' that 'begins with a glorious precolonial state-empire when the Muslims of South Asia were politically united and culturally, civilizationally and strategically dominant. In that era, ethnolinguistic differences were subsumed under a common vision of an Islamic-inspired social and political order.'[54]

In this description, 'the divisions among Muslims that did exist were exploited by the British, who practised "divide-and-rule" politics, displacing the Mughals and circumscribing other Islamic rulers'. The Hindus, the story goes on, 'were the allies of the British, who used them to strike a balance with the Muslims; many Hindus, a fundamentally insecure people, hated Muslims and would have oppressed them in a one-man, one-vote democratic India'. The demand for Pakistan 'united these disparate pieces of the national puzzle, and Pakistan was the expression of the national will of India's liberated Muslims'. Cohen is struck by the fact that this storyline 'barely acknowledged Pakistan's separatist and autonomist movements' and showed 'remarkable continuity' before and after Pakistan's own division in 1971.[55]

Since Independence, Pakistan's rulers and ideologues have generally 'stressed the importance of a strong center and criticized the idea of greater provincial autonomy'. Cohen cites Jinnah, who 'spoke of a Pakistan that was not Bengali, Baloch, Punjabi, Sindhi, or Pashtun, but a new nation, exhorting his listeners to remember the lessons of 1,300 years ago, when Islam came to India and unified it: "You have carved out a territory, a vast territory. It is all yours: it does not belong to a Punjabi or a Sindhi or a Pathan or a Bengali. It is all yours. You have got your Central Government where several units are represented. Therefore, if you want to build yourself up into a nation, for God's sake give up this provincialism."'[56]

Cohen notes that 'Ayub Khan was intolerant of regionalism, and as a military man saw the need for a strong center to hold the country together'. General Yahya Khan risked the loss of erstwhile East Pakistan rather than accept greater provincial autonomy. Zulfiqar Ali Bhutto also 'pursued a tough state-centric policy, moving forcefully against the Baloch and triggering a rebellion among a powerful linguistic group, the Mohajirs'. When Zia was asked about the prospect of 'a multinational Pakistan in which the Baloch, Pashtun, Sindhis and Punjabis would be entitled to local self-rule, he expressed his dismay at "this type of thinking. We want to build a strong country, a unified country. Why should we talk in these small-minded terms? We should talk in terms of Pakistan, one united Pakistan."'[57]

Pakistan's tolerance of its ethnolinguistic groups does not go beyond the constitution and official statements. Since Independence, 'every Pakistani leader, whether from the Punjab or a less populous province, has vehemently opposed "nationalist" or ethnolinguistic sentiments, which they consider a threat to the state'. Pakistan's leadership fears 'ties between India or Afghanistan and disloyal Pakistani ethnolinguistic communities'. Ironically, Pakistan's founding document, the 1940 Lahore Resolution of the All-India Muslim league, said that 'the independent state it called for should have "constituent units" that would be "autonomous and sovereign"'.[58]

Pakistan's establishment sees 'calls for national self-determination or autonomy by ethnolinguistic minorities' as 'calls for separate statehood, and the breakup of Pakistan' instead of considering them 'part of a bargaining game' seeking 'greater autonomy'. The fear is rooted in the experience of the demand for Pakistan. Historians have pointed out that the demand for Pakistan also started out as an instrument of bargaining for special protections for the subcontinent's Muslims but ended with the creation of a new country.

'While the movement for Pakistan had been built upon a shared antagonism toward Hindus, Pakistanis today are not uniformly anti-Indian,' Cohen stresses. For ethnic minorities, the 'fear of India is offset by fear of domination by other Pakistanis. In the 1960s the deepest fault line had an east–west orientation, as Bengalis came to regard the Punjabi–Muhajir Establishment and the military as stifling. Since 1971 the fault lines have become more diffuse.' The Baloch, Pashtun, Muhajir and Sindhi groups resent the dominant Punjab but their 'connections to the land' and the idea of Pakistan differ. The Baloch, Sindhis and Pashtun 'have histories that can be traced back one or two millennia, and others, such as the Muhajirs, are newcomers to Pakistan.

Like Yugoslavia, being part of the same country for seventy years has changed ethnic and cultural balances due to internal migration in Pakistan. The country's ethnic groups also 'have a different relationship with the dominant Punjab. Some are fairly close, such as the Pashtuns; others, such as the Baloch, were alienated to the point of open warfare, with the Sindhis and Muhajirs having a mixed history. Some of these groups are entangled in mutual enmity, usually involving Punjabis as the third side of the triangle. Sindhis, like the Bengalis, resent the Muhajir–Punjabi nexus but are also pressed upon by the Baloch; the Baloch have been subjected to in-migration from Pashtuns; and the Muhajirs have come to regard Sindhis and Punjabis as threats to their identity and prosperity.'[59]

Instead of acknowledging ethnic differences and resolving them through constitutional arrangements, Pakistan's imagining of national identity relied on the 'nexus between power and bigotry'. In the words of Ayesha Jalal, 'Proclaiming itself an "Islamic state" created on the bedrock of a non-territorially defined Muslim nation or ummah, the architects of Pakistan embraced the idea of the nation state without conceding space to territorial nationalism in their official ideology.' The country's educational system and narration of history 'became hooked to official concocted national soporifics early on'.

Rewriting history 'from an Islamic point of view' became a priority for 'the managers of the state' during Pakistan's earliest days 'and has since been refined to a bureaucratic art by national research societies and central or provincial textbook boards'.[60] But Jalal notes that it 'has not resolved the problem of identity posed by the demographic fact of more Muslims in the subcontinent living outside the territory of the much-vaunted homeland for India's Muslims'.[61]

'The dilemmas of imagining a coherent Pakistani nation,' Jalal points out, have not ended with the 'improbable array of conjuring tricks, and some somersaults on the tight rope of historical memory'. Despite conjuring 'ingenuity in argument', Pakistan has been unable to overcome 'regional and linguistic diversities which have resisted being melted down to fit the monolithic moulds of the state's Islamic identity'.[62]

Pakistan's ideology has not really enhanced its functionality even if it helped its first generation get through the transition of seeing themselves as Pakistanis. A favourable international environment, specifically Pakistan's cold war alliance with the West, enabled the country to sustain hostility towards India and to justify its Islamic orientation as a barrier to communism. The current dependence on China might pay for anti-Indianism for a few more years but is unlikely to help Pakistan overcome its fundamental contradictions.

The rise in recent years of Hindutva in India will probably feed the 'ideology of Pakistan' for a few more years by setting up an oppositional idea to confront. In the end, Pakistan would still need a new basis for its nationalism that is based on reality rather than engineered narratives of history and aspiration. Currently, ideological reasons dictate that Pakistan remain implacably hostile to India, maintain an expensive military and support jihadi terrorist organizations. But the cost of these policies has debilitating effects like failing to invest in education that develops critical thinking, being less globally connected and losing the economic benefits of being a friendly destination for tourists or investors.

Like other states that defined themselves only through ideology, Pakistan cannot expect to go on forever on the strength of hatred or fear of 'the other' without the debilitating effects of such animosity. Nor can it expect its international alignments to constantly bail it out of domestic political and economic setbacks. Pakistan is already plagued with political paranoia and many of its citizens 'believe that a vast and subtle conspiracy exists to destroy their way of life'—Islam, whatever the form or sect of Islam they might belong to. Paranoids do not function well as global citizens and, considering the complexity of sectarian and theological arguments, Pakistan is likely to only descend further into intra-Islamic feuds.

The description of 'the paranoid's view of history' offered by scholars of the phenomenon often applies to many Pakistani politicians, as well as religious and thought leaders. Their view, backed by the powerful state security machinery, is that corruption or weak leadership are Pakistan's major issues, not the pursuit of an ideological abstraction.

Given Pakistan's demographic profile, an overwhelming majority of Pakistanis does not hate or fear Hindus, India, Jews, Americans or Pakistan's other supposed enemies because of personal experiences. There is little contact between young Pakistanis with 'the enemies' for them to have sentiments about them. Psychologists agree that prejudice is learned behaviour and in Pakistan's case, it has methodically been nurtured as the bedrock of Pakistani national identity. Dealing with militarism and support for militancy, as well as their social, political and economic effects, requires amplification of Pakistani voices that question its national narrative and offer an alternative one.

Pakistan's multi-ethnic reality, prospect of conflict and fear of disintegration should encourage Pakistanis to seriously examine other states facing similar concerns and emulate successful models. Pakistan could learn, for example, from Belgium, which has a relatively brief history as a country, comprises three ethnic groups (Flemish, Walloons and Germans), and has neighbours with overlapping ethnolinguistic groups.

Just as there had been no Pakistan before 1947, there was no state called Belgium until 1830. The territory that now comprises Belgium was previously the Southern Netherlands and had been the battlefield of conflict involving France, Germany and the Netherlands. It was controlled by Spain (1556–1714) and the Austro-Hungarian empire (1714–94) before being occupied and annexed by France (1794–1814). At the Congress of Vienna, marking the end of the Napoleonic era, Belgium ended up being merged in the United Kingdom of the Netherlands. The Belgians revolted against Dutch rule in 1830, creating a completely new sovereign country.

Although Belgium had been born out of revolt against the Dutch king William I, Belgians did not embrace nationalism marked by hatred towards the Dutch. The religious difference between Belgium's Catholic majority and the Protestants of the Netherlands also was not made the basis of antipathy towards 'the other'. There was no attempt to invent a past, suggesting that Belgium had always existed as an idea, if not as a country, or to suggest that Protestant–Catholic differences made it impossible for the two communities to ever live under the same flag or at peace with one another.

Instead, Belgium recognized its multi-ethnic, multilingual reality by having multiple official languages and granting equal rights to all ethnic groups. By the time it was seventy years old, in 1900, Belgium had become a highly industrialized country that took advantage of its position at the crossroads of European commerce and diplomacy. Since then, it has survived German occupation during two world wars to occupy a central position in the European Union and NATO.

The inflated national ego of Pakistanis might balk at comparison with Belgium, which is much smaller than Pakistan. But Belgium's relatively brief history, its multi-ethnicity, its historic and ethnic overlap with neighbouring countries, and its size relative to possible regional rivals offer a model for an alternative imagining of Pakistan. Belgium's population at eleven million is one-sixth of France's sixty-six million people,[63] the same proportion that exists between Pakistan and India though Belgium's $466 billion GDP is one–fifth of France's

$2.5 trillion economy, whereas India's economy is ten times larger than Pakistan's. In some ways, Pakistan's desire to compete militarily and otherwise with India is like Belgium deciding to become France's permanent rival.

If France or Germany are too big to handle, couldn't Belgium have maintained hostility at least with the Netherlands? At seventeen million, the population of Netherlands is only six million citizens more than Belgium's and the difference in size of the two countries' GDP (Belgium $466 billion, Netherlands $771 billion) is also not that large.[64] But both Belgians and the Dutch were smart enough not to consider themselves nations of warriors that need conflict. Even after the bitter experience of German occupation during the two world wars, Belgium did not consider warping its nationalism into a narrative of hatred and fear.

If Pakistan's leaders decide that they want to change the country's direction on a permanent basis, several examples from recent history could be identified for them to emulate. The rise of Germany and Japan from the ashes of the Second World War and China's turn away from Mao Zedong's hardline communism towards Deng Xiaoping's economic modernization show the way for changing national narratives. The willingness of China and Taiwan to engage with one another even though neither recognized the legitimacy of the other for a quarter-century offers a way out for the India–Pakistan dispute over Jammu and Kashmir. Let us examine some of these exemplars.

Even after the catastrophe of US nuclear attacks on Hiroshima and Nagasaki, 'Japan's grand narrative showed remarkable resilience'.[65] Although as much as a quarter of Japan's capital stock had been destroyed in war, the country's 'huge pre-war investment in human capital—skills and training—was there to be exploited in rebuilding the nation'.[66] Instead of resisting new ideas and arguing that old policies failed only because they were not implemented effectively, Japan's leaders acknowledged their blunders. Emperor Hirohito accepted full responsibility for Japan's wartime decisions and renounced his status as God-King. As a result, 'From the ashes of war rose a nation hungry and anxious to rebuild and an elite united by an unprecedented consensus on Japan's future course.'[67]

In Germany, a defeated nation dealt with the humiliation of occupation but with a willingness to question its own attitudes. In surveys commissioned by Gen. Lucius D. Clay of the US, almost a third of Germans 'persisted in anti-democratic and anti-Semitic sentiments; two-thirds denied even partial responsibility for the rise of anti-Semitism. Yet a substantial majority admitted that the German population as a whole should bear some blame or guilt for Nazi crimes.'[68] The process of overturning the belief system inculcated by the Nazis was complex but its advocates, both foreign and German, persisted. 'It was in the 1960s,' writes one observer, 'when a new generation of Germans began asking their parents "What did you do in the Third Reich?" that the real transformation began and New Germans sensitive to their recent history emerged.'[69]

Admittedly, occupying forces played a role in the post-war transformation of Germany and Japan but China's decision to abandon ideological confrontation with the West and embark on a multi-decade modernization programme was completely indigenous. Its architect was Deng Xiaoping, who had been ridiculed during the Cultural Revolution as a 'Capitalist Roader' and removed from office. Deng used his 1979 trip to the United States to spread, through Chinese state media, 'images of American life that helped to inspire Chinese desires for growth, entrepreneurship and Western consumer goods'.[70]

Within a decade, China had effected 'a 180-degree change of direction from Mao's last years', moving away 'rapidly from ideological dogmatism toward eclectic pragmatism, from extreme totalitarianism toward liberalized authoritarianism, from a command economy toward "market socialism", and from autarkic isolationism toward international interdependence'.[71] China froze all its conflicts to economically catch up with the world's major producing nations.

In the words of one China watcher, 'As Deng said, "it does not matter if a cat is black or white so long as it catches the mouse", it no longer matters if an economic policy is capitalist or socialist, in other words, as long as it results in economic growth.'[72] China's annual economic growth rate averaged 9.7 per cent from 1989 until 2017 and reached an all-time high of 15.4 per cent in 1993. China negotiated the return of Hong Kong from British to Chinese sovereignty in 1997 by promising to retain the region's political and economic autonomy. China sought enhanced partnership with Western nations it had blamed in the past for historic wrongs. Its trade relationships completely ignored political considerations and disputes. Two-way annual trade with Taiwan, which China considers a renegade province, and India, with whom it shares a disputed border, stands at around $200 billion and $71 billion respectively.[73]

Although critics believe that China changed itself only to be able to accumulate resources to fight another day, China's ability to modify itself shows the way for effecting fundamental transformation. China retained its large military and intelligence apparatus, along with the commercial enterprises run by the Peoples Liberation Army, but it did not persist with zero-sum ideological stances or conflicts with neighbours.

Pakistan could adopt a new course just as Germany and Japan did after 1945 and China after 1989. It could begin by allowing discussion of alternative imaginings of Pakistan that are not bound by its narrowly defined ideological parameters. Pakistan's military officers might need to do the greatest rethinking. Their institution has played a significant role in defining Pakistan as it stands. A younger generation of soldiers is having to fight jihadi militants attacking the Pakistani state, after an earlier team of generals nurtured the jihadis. Instead of mainstreaming groups deemed terrorists by the rest of the world, Pakistan would do better by allowing secular advocates of ethnic nationalisms and supporters of normal relations with Afghanistan and India into the national mainstream.

Instead of a narrow definition of patriotism that excludes all serious deliberation about alternative paths for the country, Pakistan's military could begin reflecting on why the alternative paths may actually lead to a better future. There is, however, no sign that such rethinking is under way. A weak civil society, aided by the international community, is struggling to make Pakistanis aware of the country's deeper malaise. There are no major national political figures on the horizon who might wean Pakistan away from illusions and conspiracy theories towards a realistic assessment of its prospects and potential. Isolation and alienation from most of the developed world could serve as a wake-up call but, for the moment, a strategic embrace from China and Russia is serving as a distraction.

Meanwhile, the poor social indicators and low international rankings receive little attention in Pakistan's national discourse. Pakistan has survived for seventy years, defying predictions to the contrary, and the assumption that the same will remain true forever is the usual response of those who refuse to imagine a future for Pakistan different from its relatively short past.

Pakistan's excessive focus on survival and resilience—and its direction being set by men trained only to think of security—may have sowed the seeds of its myriad problems. Pakistan could continue to survive as it has done so far and defy further negative predictions. But if it does not grow economically sufficiently, integrate globally and remains mired in ideological debates and crises, how would its next seven decades be any different from the past seventy years?

9

Afterword

SOON AFTER *REIMAGINING PAKISTAN* was published, Pakistan started undergoing several changes though none could be described as a fundamental shift in the national direction. Nawaz Sharif, ousted as prime minister by the Supreme Court, was imprisoned and a controversial election in July 2018 resulted in Imran Khan becoming prime minister. Khan was hailed as Pakistan's saviour by some and seen as an inexperienced and dimwitted demagogue by others. But everyone could see the hand of the all-powerful military in most political and economic developments.

Within a few months of Khan's selection, Pakistan witnessed a sharply devalued rupee, greater dependence on foreign largesse, lower credit rating and even less democracy than before. Although Khan had garnered support by promising to build 'Naya Pakistan' (New Pakistan), he and his supporters represented the Pakistani elite's desire to change the country's fortunes without changing any of the fundamental assumptions and attitudes that have brought Pakistan to its current state.

To cobble together a majority in parliament, Khan had to bargain with traditional politicians, compromising the principles he supposedly espoused. Independent members of the elected national assembly were bought over with inducements as were members of the Punjab provincial assembly. In both houses, Khan's Pakistan Tehrik-e-Insaf (PTI) was short of a majority. In Punjab, the PTI was not the single largest party but still formed the government. Khan had to include in his cabinet, people he once called 'daku' (robber), including the Musharraf-era Punjab chief minister, Chaudhry Pervaiz Elahi, against whom Khan had initiated a loan write-off complaint.

But compromise is an essential part of politics and Khan did what is essential for success and survival in politics. That is the reason people like me predicted that the rhetoric about 'Naya Pakistan' will amount to little as it has on several earlier occasions. The Pakistani establishment and its apologists wanted the world to believe that Khan's triumph was the result of the rise of a younger generation of Pakistanis. These young nationalists have been brought up on propaganda about how corrupt civilian politicians have deprived Pakistan of its rightful place under the sun.

As a celebrity who built a cancer hospital in his mother's memory after winning the 1992 Cricket World Cup, Khan was the perfect messenger of Pakistani hyper-nationalism—charismatic and untainted by corruption. Of course, when one has never been in public office, one cannot be accused of misusing public funds. Still the Pakistan Muslim League-Nawaz (PML-N) and the Pakistan Peoples Party (PPP) received nineteen million votes between them, compared to sixteen million votes for PTI, in the 2018 election.

The military has been the anchor for the ship of state in Pakistan since 1951. But after the collapse of the military regime headed by General Pervez Musharraf in 2008, it was assumed that the generals had learnt that soldiers alone cannot ensure a country's progress. Instead of assuming power directly, they seemed willing to share responsibility for running the country with elected politicians. The politicians pushed for greater control over policymaking in the last decade. The eighteenth amendment to Pakistan's Constitution enhanced the authority of the provinces, giving them greater control over economic resources.

Relations between Pakistan's generals and politicians have never been smooth under dyarchy or dual control. There was always deference to the military's concerns in foreign policy and matters pertaining to national security. But politicians sought greater say in areas that are the exclusive domain of civilians in most countries. The two generals succeeding Musharraf as chief of the army staff went to great lengths to keep up appearances of constitutional governance and civilian rule. Many around the world have bought into the idea of gradual democratization of Pakistan and it might yet happen.

When General Qamar Bajwa became the army chief in November 2016, he decided that Pakistan could not afford to be pulled in different directions by the military and the civilians. There is considerable potential in stable civil–military relations and Bajwa expressed a desire to make Pakistan 'a normal country.' Unlike General Raheel Sharif, he did not want a personality cult for himself nor did he focus solely on getting an extension in his three-year tenure, as General Ashfaq Kayani had preferred.

Although he received a three-year extension as his tenure drew to a close in November 2019, Bajwa's interest was in correcting the country's course from General Headquarters (GHQ) through parliament and civilian institutions. 'The military and the civilian government are on one page' became the new mantra.

The courts, especially the Supreme Court headed by Justice Saqib Nisar, gave judgments that advanced the military's greater objectives and judges who failed to toe the line were sidelined or removed. The media was tightly controlled and the general heading Inter-Services Public Relations (ISPR) became the virtual czar over the flow of information to Pakistan's citizens.

But after installing Imran Khan as the prime minister through an election that did not offer a level playing field to his rivals, the military effectively reverted Pakistan to where it was before the 2008 election that resulted in Musharraf's removal from office. It is interesting that many of Khan's ministers and close advisers are all individuals who held government positions under Musharraf.

As is often the case with well-laid-out plans of absolute control, Pakistan's current dispensation has had its share of setbacks. Justice Nisar's successor as chief justice waited until the last few weeks of his tenure to deliver a series of judgments that challenged Bajwa's plans. The extension of Bajwa's tenure as army chief by three years was determined as not covered by any existing law. The Supreme Court allowed a six-month extension to enable a legal fix, forcing Bajwa and Khan to try and secure enough votes in both houses of parliament for new legislation or even a constitutional amendment.

The army's perceived right to intervene in politics was also dealt a judicial blow by a decision convicting General Pervez Musharraf to death for treason over his suspension of the Constitution in 2007. Although Musharraf was safely in Dubai, with no prospect of extradition, the sentence created a chink in the military's armour of patriotism and divided the nation between supporters and opponents of the army's primacy in Pakistan's political life.

Historically, treason was an offense attributed to dissident Pakistanis by Pakistan's generals. This was the first time a former army chief was being described by a court as a traitor for violating the Constitution, which Generals Zia and Musharraf had described in the past as 'a piece of paper' that could be discarded in the national interest.

The military's spokesman rushed to Musharraf's defence, asserting that a man who commanded Pakistan's army could never be described as guilty of treason. A chorus of voices from the civilian side chimed in. There was some talk of condemning the judge heading the bench that convicted Musharraf as insane. Soldiers were photographed putting up anonymous posters hailing Musharraf as a hero.

The decision against Musharraf can be reversed under a new chief justice, after a fresh compromise and an appeal. But the damage to the military's precious charisma as the uber-institution of Pakistan has already been done.

The Pakistani military, like all militaries, is motivated by patriotism and its plan for effectively remaining in charge stems from several wrong assumptions. It assumes that diverse opinions and policy prescriptions are damaging for Pakistan; that politicians and independent thinking civilians are untrustworthy and lacking in national spirit; and that learning from the past means determining whom to blame rather than figuring out what those mistakes might have been.

There has been a remarkable consistency in the core beliefs and thoughts of Pakistan's top military commanders. General Bajwa said at one point that Pakistan was the target of 'a hybrid campaign', in which 'our own people' are major protagonists. This way of thinking assumes that the normal exchange of ideas in a democracy is undesirable. Pakistan's first military ruler, Field Marshal Ayub Khan, spoke in a similar vein and most army chiefs since then have insisted on shutting down debate about what really ails Pakistan.

While the military leadership waged war against alternative narratives, Pakistan was put on the grey list of the UN's Financial Action Task Force (FATF) that deals with money laundering and terrorist financing. Pakistan also ended up on the United States of America's 'countries of concern' list in relation to religious freedom. The country's low ranking in most international indicators—its low literacy (which fell by 2 per cent over the last four years) and poor human capital—are issues that get little mention and even less attention in the national discourse.

In international relations, deteriorating ties with the United States and India were put down to those countries' arrogance. In the view from Islamabad, there is smugness about the 'all-weather friendship' with China coupled with the assumption that Pakistan's strategic location makes it so important that some combination of powers would always be available as the country's allies.

Pakistanis drew comfort when US president Donald Trump invited Imran Khan to the White House even after accusing Pakistan of not doing 'a damn thing for us' and Khan replying with a list of costs incurred by Pakistan on behalf of the United States. The US needs Pakistan's help in negotiating a deal with the Taliban that paves the way for military withdrawal from Afghanistan. The Trump administration is ready for a transactional arrangement, but diplomatic re-engagement is not the same thing as revival of past levels of friendship.

In case of India, Khan's supporters couldn't even get comfort from a formal meeting. Relations between the two neighbours went into an unprecedented downward spiral after a major terrorist attack in Jammu and Kashmir in February 2019 though strains had emerged right from the start of Khan's tenure as prime minister. Even before the Pulwama terrorist attack and India's retaliatory strike inside Pakistani territory, the Indian government had argued that it would only talk to Pakistan after it ends support for terrorism. Pakistan's gesture of returning the pilot of an Indian plane that fell inside territory controlled by Pakistan, amid hostilities beginning with the Pulwama attack, proved insufficient for revival of dialogue.

In addition to concerns about external pressures, there was anxiety about the state of the economy. This resulted in the appointment of technocrats as managers of the economy along with the creation of a National Development Council, with the army chief as a member. Pakistan secured its thirteenth bailout since the 1980s from the International Monetary Fund (IMF)—a loan of $6 billion—subject to tough conditions. Pakistan's repeated knocks on the IMF's door come whenever the country faces a balance of payments crisis. Pakistan has borrowed from the IMF eighteen times since 1972. Compare that with only ten IMF loans for Bangladesh in the same period.

Pakistan's IMF borrowings since 1972 ran to an estimated $19 billion, while Bangladesh's dealings with the IMF were a modest $2.7 billion. With rising exports, Bangladesh has not sought help from the IMF since 2015. Turning to the IMF is the economic equivalent of a sick individual being in intensive care. Considering that Pakistan has spent twenty-two years in the last three decades in the IMF's intensive care, the country's economy obviously suffers from some serious ailment. Pakistan's leaders, however, remain preoccupied with mitigating only the symptoms of the latest bout of illness.

In addition to help from the IMF, loans and deposits were sought from China, Saudi Arabia, Qatar and United Arab Emirates (UAE) to help stave off a budgetary and foreign-exchange crisis. The indebtedness to these countries affected Pakistan's ability to conduct an independent foreign policy. Khan joined the leaders of Malaysia and Turkey in September 2019 to announce the creation of a new grouping of Muslim countries only to skip the first summit of the grouping he founded in December at Saudi Arabia's behest.

There was no understanding among the men who rule Pakistan that economic performance is often linked to political stability and predictability as well as all the other things—like higher literacy, quality of education, human capital, openness to new ideas, social trust, ease of travel—that they do not wish to discuss.

Middle-class Pakistanis had cheered when Imran Khan promised that he would transform the prime minister's house into a university (which has not yet happened) and reduce expenses on catering for official events (which also awaits fulfilment). But there is little understanding that catering expenses are a drop in the bucket of Pakistan's huge deficit, and the gimmick of transforming a residential building into a university might end up incurring significant costs.

For several decades, salaried Pakistanis—soldiers, civil servants, doctors and engineers often employed by the government and their offspring who have grown up in government residences and cantonments—have bought into a simplified national narrative. Pakistan, they are told, is a special country created by God and endowed with natural wealth and productive people. The common explanation for Pakistan's relatively uninspiring economic performance is that the country's riches are regularly plundered by corrupt politicians and bureaucrats, making it seem poorer than it is.

Every military-backed intervention in Pakistan's politics has been predicated on the assumption that an honest leader can help recover the billions of dollars siphoned off from the economy and stashed away in bank accounts abroad, although no large-scale repatriation of stolen Pakistani wealth has ever occurred. It is not unusual for Khan's supporters to talk about overseas property and 'billions of dollars' in Swiss accounts that would, if brought back, help Pakistan become collectively wealthy.

Of course, there is no pot of gold stashed abroad by 'corrupt politicians' that can be brought back to the country to make it prosperous. Corruption is an important issue but handling it selectively, by targeting opposition politicians, is hardly a silver bullet for solving Pakistan's problems. This narrative does not address economic explanations for the flight of capital or why corrupt Pakistanis move their capital abroad instead of investing it at home like similarly corrupt individuals in South Korea or China.

A nation's performance depends on sensible policies, not rhetoric and God's special endowments. The malaise diagnosed in *Reimagining Pakistan* still requires comprehensive remedy and none of the vicissitudes since the book first appeared in hardcover suggest that the process of reimagining has so far begun.

Notes

Introduction

1 See, for example, Francesca Marino and Beniamino Natale, *Apocalypse Pakistan: An Anatomy of 'the World's Most Dangerous Nation*, Delhi: Niyogi Books, 2014; Hasnain Kazim, *Inside Pakistan: The Most Dangerous Country in the World*, London: Haus Publishing, 2018.
2 See, for example, Jamil Gardezi, *Pakistan: The Unstable State*, Lahore: Vanguard Books, 1983; 'Pakistan as the fifth most unstable country,' *Dawn*, 13 June 2010, https://www.dawn.com/news/873602 (accessed on 17 December 2017).
3 See, for example, Robert Cassidy, 'Islamabad: Incubator for Islamist Insurgents, Inc.', *Real Clear Defense*, 31 January 2017, https://www.realcleardefense.com/articles/2017/02/01/islamabad__incubator_for_islamist_insurgents_inc_110726.html (accessed on 17 December 2017); Daniel Markey, *No Exit from Pakistan: America's Tortured Relationship with Islamabad*, Cambridge, UK: Cambridge University Press, 2013, p. 30.
4 'On "high alert": Pakistan listed 10th on fragile states index', *The Express Tribune*, 28 June 2014, https://tribune.com.pk/story/728189/on-high-alert-pakistan-listed-10th-on-fragile-states-index/ (accessed on 17 December 2017).
5 Mohammad Hanif, 'Pakistan, land of the intolerant', *The New York Times*, 19 October 2017, https://www.nytimes.com/2017/10/19/opinion/pakistan-muslims-ahmadis.html?_r=0 (accessed on 17 December 2017).

6 Richard Leiby, 'Book review: "Magnificent Delusions" by Husain Haqqani, on US–Pakistan relations', *The Washington Post*, 22 November 2013.
7 Carl Schurz, *The Reminiscences of Carl Schurz*, Volume III, New York: The McClure Co, 1907, p. 336.
8 Richard Leiby, 'Book review: "Magnificent Delusions" by Husain Haqqani, on U.S.-Pakistan relations'.
9 Marina Ottaway, *Democracy Challenged: The Rise of Semi-Authoritarianism*, Washington, DC: Carnegie Endowment for International Peace, 2002, pp. 5–8.
10 David R. Mares, 'The National Security State', in Thomas Holloway (ed.), *A Companion to Latin American History*, New York: Wiley, 2011, pp. 386–87.
11 F.S. Aijazuddin, 'Be forewarned', *Dawn*, 16 November 2017.

1: A Resilient 'International Migraine'?

1 British Embassy, Washington, Letter to Foreign Office, 1 June 1950, UK National Archives, Documents Online 35/2981, cited in Dennis Kux, *The United States and Pakistan: Disenchanted Allies*, Washington, DC: Woodrow Wilson Center Press, 2001, p. 36.
2 'Global Opposition to US Surveillance and Drones, but Limited Harm to America's Image', Chapter 4: 'How Asians View Each Other', Pew Global Attitudes Survey, 2014, Washington, DC: Pew Research Center, 2014, http://www.pewglobal.org/2014/07/14/chapter-4-how-asians-view-each-other/ (accessed on 5 July 2017).
3 'Pakistan second "most unpopular country" in the world: Poll', AFP, 24 May 2013, https://tribune.com.pk/story/553830/pakistan-second-most-unpopular-country-in-the-world-poll/ (accessed on 5 July 2017).
4 Remarks by President Donald Trump on the Strategy in Afghanistan and South Asia, Fort Myer, Arlington, Virginia, 21 August 2017, https://www.whitehouse.gov/the-press-office/2017/08/21/remarks-president-trump-strategy-afghanistan-and-south-asia (accessed on 24 August 2017).
5 Eric Levenson and Sophia Saifi, 'Pakistan rejects "insinuations" in Trump's Afghanistan speech', CNN, 24 August 2017.
6 Interview of Madeline Albright on *Fox News*, 2 December 2009, https://www.youtube.com/watch?v=gQhwDj5KWNU (accessed on 5 July 2017).

7 Speech by Huseyn Shaheed Suhrawardy on 6 March 1948, 'Constituent Assembly of Pakistan debates: Official Report, 1946-1956,' Karachi: Manager, Governor-General's Press and Publications, 1950–56, pp. 262–63.

8 Ayesha Jalal, *The State of Martial Rule*, Cambridge, UK: Cambridge University Press, 1990, p. 16.

9 Ibid.

10 Ibid.

11 Tom Treanor, 'The Home Front', *Los Angeles Times*, 23 March 1943.

12 K.L. Gauba. *Consequences of Pakistan*, Lahore: Lion Press, 1946, pp. 169–73.

13 Nawab Dr Nazir Yar Jung (ed.), *The Pakistan Issue*, Lahore: Sh Muhammad Ashraf, pp. 102–03.

14 Ibid., pp. vii–xii.

15 'To the Americans', editorial, *Dawn*, 13 September 1948.

16 Yelena Biberman, 'How we know what we know about Pakistan: *New York Times* news production, 1954-71', *Modern Asian Studies*, October 2017, pp. 18–20.

17 Ibid.

18 Ibid.

19 Carlotta Gall, *The Wrong Enemy: America in Afghanistan, 2001-2014*, Boston: Houghton Mifflin Harcourt, 2014, p. xv.

20 Ibid., p. xvi.

21 Raza Khan, 'Pakistanis appalled at US Congressmen's views, says Rabbani', *Dawn*, 14 July 2016.

22 'UK, US statements on missing persons "extremely inappropriate": Rabbani', *Pakistan Today*, 16 January 2017, https://www.pakistantoday.com.pk/2017/01/16/uk-us-statements-on-missing-persons-extremely-inappropriate-rabbani/, (accessed on 5 July 2017).

23 'Pakistan wants credit for terror fight, not money, Gen Qamar tells CENTCOM chief', *The Express Tribune*, 19 August 2017, https://tribune.com.pk/story/1485291/want-acknowledgement-sacrifices-terror-war-gen-qamar-tells-centcom-chief/ (accessed on 24 August 2017).

24 Drazen Jorgic, 'Despite rising economy, Pakistan still hampered by image problem,' Reuters, 19 July 2016.

25 Population Division, *Population Graphs*, United Nations Department of Economic and Social Affairs, 2016.

26 World Bank Open Data, *Pakistan Life expectancy at birth, total (years)*, Washington, DC: World Bank, 2016.

27 'Pakistan's Development Journey: 1947-2001', in *Social Development in Pakistan: Annual Review, 2001*, Karachi: Oxford University Press, 2002, p. 8.

28 World Bank Open Data, *Pakistan Adult literacy rate, population 15+ years, both sexes (%)*, Washington, DC: World Bank, 2016.

29 'Literacy in India', Census 2011, np., nd., http://www.census2011.co.in/literacy.php (accessed on 17 December 2017).

30 'Literacy Trends in Pakistan', UNESCO, March 2002, p. 6, http://www.unesco.org.pk/education/life/nfer_library/Reports/4-39.pdf (accessed on 27 March 2017).

31 Kaiser Bengali, 'History of Educational Policy Making and Planning in Pakistan, Working paper series #40—1999', Sustainable Development Policy Institute, 1999, https://www.sdpi.org/publications/files/W40-History%20of%20Educational%20Policy%20Making.pdf (accessed on 28 March 2017).

32 'Education', UNESCO Institute for Statistics, United Nations Educational Social and Cultural Organization 2017.

33 World Bank Open Data, *Pakistan Adult literacy rate, population 15+ years, both sexes (%)*, Washington, DC: World Bank, 2016.

34 'Education Index 2016', Human Development Report, UNDP, http://hdr.undp.org/en/content/education-index (accessed on 5 July 2017).

35 Riazul Haq, 'Literacy rate in Pakistan slips by 2%', *The Express Tribune*, 26 May 2017, https://tribune.com.pk/story/1419396/economic-survey-literacy-rate-pakistan-slips-2/ (accessed on 5 July 2017).

36 'Education Index 2016', Human Development Report, UNDP, http://hdr.undp.org/en/content/education-index (accessed on 5 July 2017).

37 'Key Indicators for Asia and the Pacific 2014', Asian Development Bank, p. 72, https://www.adb.org/sites/default/files/publication/43030/ki2014-mdg2.pdf (accessed on 27 March 2017).

38 'Net enrolment rate, secondary, both sexes (%)', World Bank Data, http://data.worldbank.org/indicator/SE.SEC.NENR?locations=PK (accessed on 27 March 2017).

39 'Pakistan—Education and Literacy 2015', UNESCO, http://uis.unesco.org/country/pk (accessed on 27 March 2017); 'Nepal—Education and Literacy 2015', UNESCO, http://uis.unesco.org/country/np (accessed on 27 March 2017).

40 'A growing number of children and adolescents are out of school as aid fails to meet the mark', UNESCO, Policy Paper 22/Fact Sheet 31, July 2015, http://www.uis.unesco.org/Education/Documents/fs-31-out-of-school-children-en.pdf (accessed on 27 March 2017).

41 Kashif Abbasi, '22.6m Pakistani children still out of school: report', *Dawn*, 9 March 2017.

42 '263 Million Children and Youth Are Out of School', UNESCO Institute for Statistics, UNESCO, 15 July 2016 http://uis.unesco.org/en/news/263-million-children-and-youth-are-out-school (accessed on 7 July 2017).

43 Ishrat Husain, *Pakistan: The Economy of an Elitist State*, Karachi: Oxford University Press, 1999, p. xvi.

44 'The Hidden Crisis: Armed Conflict and Education', UNESCO, 2011, p. 43.

45 'GDP per capita—Pakistan et al.', World Bank, http://data.worldbank.org/indicator/NY.GDP.PCAP.CD/countries?order=wbapi_data_value_2012+wbapi_data_value&sort=desc (accessed on 30 June 2017).

46 'Competitiveness rating—primary education enrollment rate', World Economic Forum 2014-15, http://reports.weforum.org/global-competitiveness-report-2014-2015/rankings/#indicatorId=ENROL1NET (accessed on 15 June 2017).

47 'Government expenditure on education, total (percentage of GDP)', World Bank, http://data.worldbank.org/indicator/SE.XPD.TOTL.GD.ZS?locations=PK (accessed on 14 June 2017).

48 'The Hidden Crisis: Armed Conflict and Education', UNESCO, 2011, p. 147, http://unesdoc.unesco.org/images/0019/001907/190743e.pdf (accessed on 14 June 2017).

49 Ibid., p. 148.

50 'Urban population (percentage of total)', World Bank, http://data.worldbank.org/indicator/SP.URB.TOTL.IN.ZS?locations=PK (accessed on 1 July 2017).

51 'Health Expenditure, public (percentage of GDP)', World Bank, http://data.worldbank.org/indicator/SH.XPD.PUBL.ZS?locations=PK (accessed on 1 July 2017).

52 'Federal Budget 2015-16: Budget in Brief', Finance Division (Government of Pakistan), June 2015, http://www.finance.gov.pk/budget/Budget_in_Brief_2015_16.pdf (accessed on 27 March 2017).

53 Emma Luxton, 'By 2060, this country will have the world's largest population', 20 September 2016, https://www.weforum.org/agenda/2016/09/the-countries-with-the-biggest-populations-from-1950-to-2060/ (accessed on 17 December 2017).

54 'The largest armies in the world based on active military personnel in 2017', Statistical Portal, https://www.statista.com/statistics/264443/the-worlds-largest-armies-based-on-active-force-level/ (accessed 17 December 2017).

55 'List of Countries by projected GDP (nominal) as per IMF Economic Outlook', Statistic Times, 23 April 2017, http://statisticstimes.com/economy/countries-by-projected-gdp.php (accessed 17 December 2017).

56 'List of Countries by projected GDP (PPP basis) as per IMF Economic Outlook', Statistic Times, 23 April 2017, http://statisticstimes.com/economy/countries-by-projected-gdp.php (accessed 17 December 2017).

57 'Pakistan Country Profile – Economy', CIA World Factbook, USA, Central Intelligence Agency, 2016.

58 Ibid.

59 Ibid.

60 Ibid.

61 'Poverty: 60.3% Pakistanis living on $2 a day', *The Express Tribune*, Karachi, 4 August 2015.

62 'Global Competitiveness Index', World Economic Forum, http://reports.weforum.org/global-competitiveness-index/country-profiles/#economy=PAK (accessed on 27 March 2017.

63 Faseeh Mangi and Chris Kay, 'Half a Million Jobs Lost as Textile Crisis Hits Pakistan's Economy', Bloomberg, 20 September 2016, https://www.bloomberg.com/news/articles/2016-09-20/a-deserted-karachi-factory-signals-pakistan-s-textile-crisis (accessed on 28 March 2017).

64 Figure for 2014 from 'Tax revenue (percentage of GDP)', World Bank, http://data.worldbank.org/indicator/GC.TAX.TOTL.GD.ZS?locations=PK (accessed on 29 March 2017).

65 Figure for 2015 from 'GDP growth (annual percentage)', World Bank, http://data.worldbank.org/indicator/NY.GDP.MKTP.KD.ZG?locations=PK (accessed on 28 March 2017).

66 Figure for 2015 from 'Population growth (annual percentage)', World Bank, http://data.worldbank.org/indicator/SP.POP.GROW?locations=PK (accessed on 28 March 2017).

67 'The Global Human Capital Report 2017: Preparing people for the future of work', Geneva, Switzerland: World Economic Forum, 2017, pp. vii–viii.

68 'Pakistan—Human Development Report 2016', UNDP, 2016, http://hdr.undp.org/sites/all/themes/hdr_theme/country-notes/PAK.pdf (accessed on 29 March 2017).

69 Pankaj Ghemawat, Steven A. Altman, *DHL Global Connectedness Index*, Bonn, Germany: Deutsche Post DHL Group, October 2016.

70 Hassan Maheen, 'Development Advocate Pakistan', *UN Development Programme Pakistan,* Islamabad: UNDP, September 2016.

71 'A new ranking of every country's citizenship', *The Economist*, 2 June 2016.

72 J.J. Messner (ed.), *Fragile States Index*, 2015, Washington, DC: The Fund for Peace, 2016, http://library.fundforpeace.org/library/fragilestatesindex-2015.pdf (accessed on 3 June 2017).

73 'Country Data and Trends: Pakistan in 2016: Ten-year Trend', *Fragile States Index*, Washington, DC: The Fund for Peace, 2017, http://fsi.fundforpeace.org/2016-pakistan (accessed on 3 June 2017).

74 Iftikhar Khan, '84 pc of population lacks access to safe drinking water', *Dawn*, 8 March 2017.

75 Kathy Gannon and Katy Gaile, 'Study: Arsenic poisoning a risk for 50M in Pakistan', Associated Press, 24 August 2017.

76 Preface by Guy Wint, Oxford, 1966. Arif Hussain, *Pakistan: Its Ideology and Foreign Policy*, London: Frank Cass & Co, 1966, p. xi.

77 Ibid.

78 Lawrence Ziring, *Pakistan, the Enigma of Political Development,* Folkestone, UK: WM Dawson & Co, 1980, p. 248.

79 Ibid, p. 249.

80 Ibid.

81 Ibid.

82 Telegram from Consul General [India] Macdonald to the Secretary of State, 8 March 1947, *Foreign Relations of the United States (FRUS)*, Volume III (1947), pp. 149–50.

83 'Better Off in a Home,' *Time,* 25 August 1947.

84 Ibid.

85 Ibid.

86 *House of Commons Debates*, 10 July 1947, col. 2445.

87 *House of Commons Debates*, 16 July 1947, col. 809.

88 Hans J. Morgenthau, 'Military illusions', *The New Republic*, 19 March 1956, pp. 14–16.
89 Ibid.
90 Ibid.
91 Abdul Sattar, *Pakistan's Foreign Policy: 1947-2005, A Concise History*, Karachi: Oxford University Press, 2005, p. 8.
92 Abdus Sattar, 'Fifty Years of the Kashmir Dispute: The Diplomatic Aspect', in Suroosh Irfani (ed.), *Fifty Years of the Kashmir Dispute*, Muzaffarabad: University of Azad Jammu and Kashmir, 1997, pp. 11–12.
93 Shahid Javed Burki, *Pakistan: A Nation in the Making*, Boulder, CO: Westview Press, 1986, p. 201.
94 Ibid., pp. 199–200.
95 Maleeha Lodhi (ed.), *Pakistan Beyond the Crisis State*, New York: Columbia University Press, 2011, p. 2.
96 Ibid.
97 Laurence Léveillé, 'Lodhi: Though a weak state, Pakistan has a strong society', *The Chautauquan Daily*, 24 July 2012.
98 Ibid.
99 Ibid.
100 Ishrat Husain, 'How Green is My Valley?', *The News* (Pakistan), 13 August 2012.
101 Ibid.
102 G. Allana, 'Reflections on Statistics', in H.B. Khokhar, *20 Years of Pakistan*, Karachi: H.B. Khokhar, 1967, p. 99.
103 Ibid.
104 Ibid.
105 Maleeha Lodhi (ed.), *Pakistan Beyond the Crisis State*, p. 2.
106 Ibid.
107 Irfan Husain, 'Karachi Literature Festival has transitioned smoothly to London but is it overambitious?' *Dawn*, 29 May 2017, https://images.dawn.com/news/1177691 (accessed on 3 June 2017).

2: Faith, Grievance and Special Purpose

1 O.H.K. Spate, 'Partition of India and Prospects for Pakistan', *Geographical Review*, Vol. 38, No. 1, January 1948, pp. 5–29.
2 Document 73: Round of Interview between Rear Admiral Viscount Mountbatten of Burma and Mr Gandhi and Khan Abdul Ghaffar

Khan, Mountbatten Papers, Viceroy's Interview, No 30, 4 April 1947, in Nicholas Mansergh and Penderel Moon (eds), *Constitutional Relations between Britain and India: The Transfer of Power, 1942-47, Volume X: The Mountbatten Viceroyalty and Formulation of a Plan, 22 March—30 May 1947*, London: Her Majesty's Stationery Office, 1981, p. 120.

3 El Hamza, *Pakistan: A Nation*, Lahore: Muhammad Ashraf, 1941, p. 114.

4 Ibid., pp. 124–25.

5 Ibid., pp. 25–28.

6 Ibid., p. 33.

7 Ibid., pp. 37–39.

8 Mohammad Ayub Khan, *Friends Not Masters: A Political Autobiography*, Karachi: Oxford University Press, 1967, p. 187.

9 F.K. Khan Durrani, *The Meaning of Pakistan*, Lahore: Islamic Book Service, 1944, pp. vii–viii.

10 Ibid., pp. ix–xii.

11 Ayesha Jalal, *The State of Martial Rule: The Origins of Pakistan's Political Economy of Defence*, Cambridge, UK: Cambridge University Press, 2007, p. 20.

12 Dr Afzal Iqbal, *Islamisation of Pakistan*, Delhi: Idarah-I Adabiyat-I Delhi, 1984, p. 38.

13 Ibid.

14 Ibid., p. 207.

15 Ibid., p. 38.

16 Cemil Aydin, *The Idea of the Muslim World: A Global Intellectual History*, Cambridge, MA: Harvard University Press, 2017, p. 180.

17 William Philips, *Ventures in Diplomacy*, Boston: The Beacon Press, 1952, pp. 373–74.

18 Paul Julian Hare, *Diplomatic Chronicles of the Middle East: A Biography of Ambassador Raymond A. Hare*, Ann Arbor, Michigan: University of Michigan Press, 1993, pp. 41–43.

19 Ibid.

20 Document 130: Record of Interview between Rear Admiral Viscount Mountbatten of Burma and Mr Hossain Imam, Mountbatten Papers, Viceroy's Interview No. 53, 12 April 1947, in Nicholas Mansergh and Penderel Moon (eds), *Constitutional Relations between Britain and India: The Transfer of Power, 1942-47, Volume X: The Mountbatten Viceroyalty and Formulation of a Plan, 22 March—30*

May 1947, London: Her Majesty's Stationery Office, 1981, pp. 209–10.

21 Document 203: Minutes of Viceroy's Seventh Miscellaneous meeting, Mountbatten Papers, 3 April 1947, in Nicholas Mansergh and Penderel Moon (eds), *Constitutional Relations between Britain and India: The Transfer of Power, 1942-47, Volume X: The Mountbatten Viceroyalty and Formulation of a Plan, 22 March—30 May 1947*, London: Her Majesty's Stationery Office, 1981, p. 380.

22 Document 64: Minutes of Viceroy's Seventh Staff Meeting, Mountbatten Papers, April 1947, in Nicholas Mansergh and Penderel Moon (eds), *Constitutional Relations between Britain and India: The Transfer of Power, 1942-47, Volume X: The Mountbatten Viceroyalty and Formulation of a Plan, 22 March—30 May 1947*, London: Her Majesty's Stationery Office, 1981, pp. 100–01; Document 43: Note by Field Marshal Sir C. Auchinleck on communal affiliation of Officers in the Indian Army, Mountbatten Papers, Official Correspondence Files: Armed Forces, Indian, Vol. I, Part I., undated, March 1947, in Nicholas Mansergh and Penderel Moon (eds), *Constitutional Relations between Britain and India: The Transfer of Power, 1942-47, Volume X: The Mountbatten Viceroyalty and Formulation of a Plan, 22 March—30 May 1947*, London: Her Majesty's Stationery Office, 1981, pp. 62–63; Document 215: Mr Abell to Rear Admiral Viscount Mountbatten of Burma (R/3/1/189: f138), 16 June 1947, in Nicholas Mansergh and Penderel Moon (eds), *Constitutional Relations between Britain and India: The Transfer of Power, 1942-47, Volume XI: The Mountbatten Viceroyalty Announcement and Reception of the 3 June Plan, 31 May—7 July 1947*, London: Her Majesty's Stationery Office, 1982, pp. 418—19; Document 329: Field Marshal Viscount Montgomery to General Simpson (via Viceroy and India Office. Telegram R/3/1/82: f 8-9), New Delhi, 24 June 1947, in Nicholas Mansergh and Penderel Moon (eds), *Constitutional Relations between Britain and India: The Transfer of Power, 1942-47, Volume XI: The Mountbatten Viceroyalty Announcement and Reception of the 3 June Plan, 31 May—7 July 1947*, London: Her Majesty's Stationery Office, 1982, p. 607.

23 Document 64: Minutes of Viceroy's Seventh Staff Meeting, Mountbatten Papers, April 1947, in Nicholas Mansergh and Penderel Moon (eds), *Constitutional Relations between Britain and India: The Transfer of Power, 1942-47, Volume X: The Mountbatten*

Viceroyalty and Formulation of a Plan, 22 March—30 May 1947, London: Her Majesty's Stationery Office, 1981, pp. 100–01.

24 Document 329: Field Marshal Viscount Montgomery to General Simpson (via Viceroy and India Office. Telegram R/3/1/82: f 8-9), New Delhi, 24 June 1947, in Nicholas Mansergh and Penderel Moon (eds), *Constitutional Relations between Britain and India: The Transfer of Power, 1942-47, Volume XI: The Mountbatten Viceroyalty Announcement and Reception of the 3 June Plan, 31 May—7 July 1947*, London: Her Majesty's Stationery Office, 1982, p. 607.

25 *Star of India*, 1 August 1947. Cited in Venkat Dhulipala, *Creating a New Medina: State Power, Islam and the Quest for Pakistan in Late Colonial North India*, Delhi: Cambridge University Press, 2015, p. 446.

26 Document 64: Minutes of Viceroy's Seventh Staff Meeting, Mountbatten Papers, April 1947, in Nicholas Mansergh and Penderel Moon (eds), *Constitutional Relations between Britain and India: The Transfer of Power, 1942-47, Volume X: The Mountbatten Viceroyalty and Formulation of a Plan, 22 March—30 May 1947*, London: Her Majesty's Stationery Office, 1981, pp. 100–01.

27 Document 231: Mr Liaquat Ali Khan to Rear Admiral Viscount Mountbatten of Burma, Mountbatten Papers, Official correspondence files, Interviews (2), 17 June 1947, in Nicholas Mansergh and Penderel Moon (eds), *Constitutional Relations between Britain and India: The Transfer of Power, 1942-47, Volume XI: The Mountbatten Viceroyalty Announcement and Reception of the 3 June Plan, 31 May—7 July 1947*, London: Her Majesty's Stationery Office, 1982, pp. 449–50.

28 Chaudhri Muhammad Ali, *The Emergence of Pakistan*, Lahore: The Services Book Club, 1988, pp. 251–52.

29 Abdus Sattar, 'Fifty Years of the Kashmir Dispute: The Diplomatic Aspect', in Suroosh Irfani (ed.), *Fifty Years of the Kashmir Dispute*, Muzaffarabad: University of Azad Jammu and Kashmir, 1997, pp. 11–12.

30 Ibid.

31 Shuja Nawaz, *Crossed Swords: Pakistan, Its Army and the Wars Within*, Karachi: Oxford University Press, 2008, pp. 20–21.

32 Ibid., pp. 27–28.

33 Document 506: Viceroy's Personal Report No. 11 (L/PO/6/123: ff 155-62), 4 July 1962, in Nicholas Mansergh and Penderel

Moon (eds), *Constitutional Relations between Britain and India: The Transfer of Power, 1942-47, Volume XI: The Mountbatten Viceroyalty Announcement and Reception of the 3 June Plan, 31 May—7 July 1947*, London: Her Majesty's Stationery Office, 1982, pp. 898–900.

34 Ibid.

35 See Yaqoob Bangash, *A Princely Affair: The Accession and Integration of the Princely States of Pakistan, 1947-1955,* Karachi: Oxford University Press, 2015.

36 Maj. Gen. (Retd) Akbar Khan, *Raiders in Kashmir*, Karachi: National Book Foundation, 1970, pp. 8–18.

37 L.F. Rushbrook Williams, *The State of Pakistan*, London: Faber and Faber, 1966, pp. 33–50.

38 Telegram from the Embassy in Pakistan to the Department of State, 'Subj: Meeting with Bhutto', *Foreign Relations of the United States (FRUS), 1969–1976,* Volume XI, *South Asia Crisis, 1971*, 20 December 1971, Document 328, pp. 859–60.

39 L.F. Rushbrook Williams, *The State of Pakistan*, pp. 139–40.

40 Ayesha Jalal, *The Struggle for Pakistan: A Muslim Homeland and Global Politics*, Cambridge, MA: Belknap Press of Harvard University, 2014, pp. 384.

41 Ibid.

42 Ibid., p. 389.

43 Mubarak Ali, 'In Search of Identity', *Dawn*, 7 May 2000.

44 Speech by Liaquat Ali Khan on 4 May 1950, National Press Club, Washington, DC, in Liaquat Ali Khan, *Pakistan: The Heart of Asia, Speeches in the United States and Canada May and June 1950 by Prime Minister of Pakistan*, Cambridge, MA: Harvard University Press, 1950, p. 11.

45 Mahammad Ayub Khan, *Friends Not Masters: A Political Autobiography*, pp. 196–97.

46 Ibid.

47 Ibid.

48 See, for example, Fazal Muqeem Khan, *Pakistan's Crisis in Leadership*, Islamabad: National Book Foundation, 1973, p. 1.

49 Alyssa Ayres, *Speaking Like a State: Language and Nationalism in Pakistan*, Cambridge, UK: Cambridge University Press, 2009, p. 6.

50 Waheed-uz-Zaman, 'Editor's Note,' in *The Quest for Identity* (Proceedings of The First Congress on the History and Culture of

Pakistan held at the University of Islamabad, April 1973), Islamabad: University of Islamabad Press, 1974, p. i.

51 Husain Haqqani, *Pakistan Between Mosque and Military*, Washington: Carnegie Endowment for International Peace, 2005; (updated and revised) Delhi: Penguin India, 2016.

52 'Pakistan Datasheet: Sectarian violence in in Pakistan since 1989', South Asian Terrorism Portal, http://www.satp.org/satporgtp/countries/pakistan/database/sect-killing.htm (accessed on 31 July 2017).

53 'Pakistan Datasheet: Shias killed in Pakistan since 2001', South Asian Terrorism Portal, http://www.satp.org/satporgtp/countries/pakistan/database/Shias_killed_Pakistan.htm (accessed on 31 July 2017).

54 'Pakistan Datasheet: Terrorist related violence Pakistan since 2003', South Asian Terrorism Portal, http://www.satp.org/satporgtp/countries/pakistan/database/casualties.htm (accessed on 31 July 2017).

55 Arnold J. Toynbee, 'Pakistan as a historian sees her', in *Crescent and Green: A Miscellany of Writings on Pakistan*, London: Cassell & Co Ltd, 1955, p. 2.

56 Ibid.

57 Speech by Huseyn Shaheed Suhrawardy on 6 March 1948, *Constituent Assembly of Pakistan Debates: Official Report, 1946-1956*, Karachi: Manager, Governor-General's Press and Publications, 1950–56, pp. 262–63.

58 Ibid.

59 'Quaid-i-Azam Muhammad Ali Jinnah's Presidential Address to the Constituent Assembly of Pakistan at Karachi, 11 August 1947', *Quaid-i-Azam Muhammad Ali Jinnah, Speeches and Statements as Governor-General of Pakistan 1947–48*, Islamabad: Government of Pakistan, Ministry of Information and Broadcasting, Directorate of Films and Publications, 1989, p. 42.

60 Ibid.

61 Sri Prakasa, *Pakistan: Birth and Early Days*, Meerut: Meenakshi Prakashan, 1965, pp. 83–84.

62 Benedict Anderson, *Imagined Communities: Reflections on the Origin and Spread of Nationalism*, London: Verso, 1983.

63 'Pakistan: The Next Generation 2009,' report by the British Council of Pakistan, Islamabad, November 2009.

64 Ian Stephens, *Pakistan,* London: Ernest Benn Limited, 1964, p. 25.

3: Ideological Dysfunction

1 Sune Engel Rasmussen and Kiyya Baloch, 'Student's Lynching Sparks Rare Uproar in Pakistan over Blasphemy Killings', *The Guardian*, 26 April 2017.
2 Haseeb Bhatti, 'Mashal's father asks SC to relocate daughters to Islamabad citing "security threats" at home', *Dawn*, 7 June 2017.
3 Ibid.
4 'Mob kills man, burns corpse for desecrating Quran,' Associated Press, 4 July 2012.
5 Ibid.
6 'Lawyers Shower Roses for Governor's Killer', *Dawn*, 5 January 2011.
7 Carlotta Gall, 'Assassination Deepens Divide in Pakistan', *The New York Times*, 5 January 2011.
8 'Executed Pakistani hailed as hero of Islam for supporting blasphemy law', Reuters, 1 March 2016.
9 Adil Pasha, 'Mumtaz Qadri's Shrine: In Memory of Salmaan Taseer's Assassin', *Dawn*, 27 December 2016.
10 Farzana Shaikh, *Making Sense of Pakistan*, New York: Columbia University Press, 2009.
11 Erik H. Erikson, *Young Man Luther*, New York: WW Norton & Co., 1962.
12 Khalid Bin Sayeed, *The Political System of Pakistan*, Boston: Houghton Mifflin Co., 1967, pp. 172–73.
13 Faisal Devji, *Muslim Zion: Pakistan as a Political Idea*, Cambridge, MA: Harvard University Press, 2013, p. 3.
14 Venkat Dhulipala, *Creating a New Medina: State Power, Islam and the Quest for Pakistan in Late Colonial North India*, Delhi: Cambridge University Press, 2015, p. 4.
15 Muhammad Ishaq Sandelvi, *Islam ka Siyasi Nizam, Jis Mein Islam Ke Siyasi Nizam Ka Asasi Khaka Pesh Kiya Gaya Hai* (Political System of Islam: Presenting the outline of the political system of Islam), Azamgarh, 1957. Cited in Venkat Dhulipala, *Creating a New Medina,* p. 233.
16 Venkat Dhulipala, *Creating a New Medina*, p. 355.
17 Ibid., p. 360.
18 Ishtiaq Ahmed, *The Punjab Bloodied, Partitioned and Cleansed: Unravelling the 1947 Tragedy through Secret British Reports and*

First-Person Accounts, Karachi: Oxford University Press, 2012, pp. 83–84.

19 Lionel Carter, *Punjab Politics, 1st January 1944–3rd March 1947: Last Years of the Ministries, Governor's Fortnightly Reports and other Key Documents*, New Delhi: Manohar, 2006, p. 145.

20 Refers to Muslim League leader, Sir Firoz Khan Noon who later became prime minister of Pakistan,1957–58.

21 Lionel Carter, *Punjab Politics*, p. 160.

22 Ibid., p. 171

23 Venkat Dhulipala, *Creating a New Medina*, p. 360.

24 Ibid.

25 Letter from Mahmudabad to Jinnah, 3 December 1945, Z.H. Zaidi (ed). *QA Papers, Vol. 12, 1 August 1945 – 31 March 1946*, pp. 375–76. Cited in Venkat Dhulipala, *Creating a New Medina*, p. 446.

26 'Quaid-i-Azam Muhammad Ali Jinnah's Presidential Address to the Constituent Assembly of Pakistan at Karachi, 11 August 1947', *Quaid-i-Azam Muhammad Ali Jinnah, Speeches and Statements as Governor-General of Pakistan 1947–48*, Islamabad: Government of Pakistan, Ministry of Information and Broadcasting, Directorate of Films and Publications, 1989, p. 42.

27 Ibid.

28 'Quaid-i-Azam lays stress on need for technical training', *Dawn*, 19 April 1948.

29 Khalid Bin Sayeed, *The Political System of Pakistan*, pp. 183–84.

30 Safdar Mahmood, *Constitutional Foundations of Pakistan*, Lahore: Jang Publishers, 1990, p. 52.

31 Ibid., p. 10.

32 Speech by Ishtiaq Hussain Qureshi on 16 December 1948, *Constituent Assembly of Pakistan Debates: Official Report, 1946-1956*, Karachi: Manager, Governor-General's Press and Publications, 1950–56, pp. 225–26.

33 Speech by Azizuddin Ahmed on 16 December 1948, *Constituent Assembly of Pakistan Debates: Official Report, 1946-1956*, Karachi: Manager, Governor-General's Press and Publications, 1950–56, pp. 225–26.

34 Speech by Syed Abdul Basher Mahmud Husain on 17 March 1950, *Constituent Assembly of Pakistan Debates: Official Report, 1946-1956*, Karachi: Manager, Governor-General's Press and Publications, 1950–56, pp. 103–05.

35 Reply by Fazlur Rehman on 7 April 1951, *Constituent Assembly of Pakistan Debates: Official Report, 1946–1956*, Karachi: Manager, Governor-General's Press and Publications, 1950–56, pp. 964–65.
36 Speech by Liaquat Ali Khan on 7 March 1949, *Constituent Assembly of Pakistan Debates: Official Report, 1946–1956*, Karachi: Manager, Governor-General's Press and Publications, 1950–56, pp. 1–7.
37 M. Rafique Afzal, *Pakistan: History and Politics, 1947-1971*, Karachi: Oxford University Press, 2001, p. 99.
38 'Rally around Islam, rally around Quran–Ashmawy's clarion call to Pakistanis', *Dawn*, 7 April 1948.
39 Aslam Siddiqui, *Pakistan Seeks Security*, Karachi: Longmans Green, 1960, p. 89.
40 Ibid., pp. 82–83.
41 Ibid., pp. 88–89.
42 Toheen Ahmed, 'Muhammad Asad: The Story of a Story of a Story', *Criterion Quarterly*, Vol. 6, No. 1, http://www.criterion-quarterly.com/muhammad-asad-the-story-of-a-story-of-a-story/ (accessed on 1 July 2017).
43 Leonard Binder, *Religion and Politics in Pakistan*, Berkeley: University of California Press, 1961, p. 97.
44 Nadhr Ahmed's 1956 survey quoted by Jamal Malik, *Colonialization of Islam: Dissolution of Traditional Institutions in Pakistan*, Lahore: 1996, p. 180. The number could have been even fewer. According to other estimates in 1957–58, Pakistan had only 119 seminaries with 4,790 regular students.
45 'Pakistan's radical madrassas retain clout despite crackdown', *The Washington Times*, 2 February 2016.
46 *Pakistan: Madrassas, Extremism and the Military*, International Crisis Group Asia Report No 36, Islamabad/Brussels, 29 July 2002, pp. 1–3.
47 Ibid.
48 'Djinn Energy', *FAS Project on Government Secrecy*, 29 October 2001, https://fas.org/sgp/news/secrecy/2001/10/102901.html (accessed on 3 July 2017).
49 Leonard Binder, *Religion and Politics in Pakistan*, pp. 184–93.
50 Ibid.
51 Ibid.
52 Ibid.
53 Ibid.

54 Ibid.
55 I.H. Qureshi, *Pakistan: An Islamic Democracy*, Lahore: Institute of Islamic Culture, 1951, p. 2.
56 Ibid., p. 3.
57 Ibid., p. 8.
58 Leonard Binder, *Religion and Politics in Pakistan*, p. 192.
59 Ibid., p. 98.
60 Herbert Feldman, *From Crisis to Crisis: Pakistan 1962-1969*, London: Oxford University Press, 1972, p. 42.
61 *Report of the Court of Inquiry constituted under Punjab Act II of 1954 to enquire into the Punjab Disturbances of 1953*, Lahore: Government Printing, Punjab, 1954, p. 1.
62 Ibid., p. 2.
63 Ibid., pp. 201–02.
64 Ibid., pp. 213–18.
65 Ibid., pp. 231–32.
66 Mohammed Ayub Khan, 'Pakistan Perspective', *Foreign Affairs,* New York, July 1960, p. 549.
67 Altaf Gauhar, *Ayub Khan: Pakistan's First Military Ruler*, Karachi: Oxford University Press, 1996, p. 93.
68 Mohammad Ayub Khan, *Friends Not Masters: A Political Biography*, Karachi: Oxford University Press, 1967, pp. 196–97.
69 Ibid.
70 Ibid.
71 Huseyn Shaheed Suhrawardy, 'Political Stability and Democracy in Pakistan', *Foreign Affairs*, Vol. 35, No. 3, April 1957, p. 425.
72 Ibid.
73 S.M. Burke, *Pakistan's Foreign Policy – An Historical Analysis*, London: Oxford University Press, 1973, p. 252.
74 'Appendix IX: The Ruet-e-Hilal Controversy', Herbert Feldman, *From Crisis to Crisis: Pakistan 1962-1969*, pp. 287–88.
75 Ayesha Khan, 'Policy-making in Pakistan's population programme', *Health Policy and Planning Journal*, Oxford University Press, Vol. 11, No. 1, 1996, p. 31.
76 A.H. Nayyar and Ahmad Salim, *The Subtle Subversion – The State of Curricula and Textbooks in Pakistan*, Islamabad: Sustainable Development Policy Institute, 2003, p. 3.
77 Mohammad Ayub Khan, *Friends Not Masters,* p. 172.

78 Ibid.
79 Ibid., p. 183.
80 Election Commission of Pakistan, *Report on the General Elections Pakistan 1970-71*, Vol. 1, Karachi: Election Commission of Pakistan, 1972.
81 Ibid.
82 Herbert Feldman, *The End and the Beginning: Pakistan 1969-1971*, Karachi: Oxford University Press, 1975, pp. 46–47.
83 Khadim Hussain Raja, *A Stranger in My Own Country: East Pakistan Crisis 1969-71*, Karachi: Oxford University Press, 2012.
84 Transcript of Telephone Conversation between President Nixon and His Assistant for National Security Affairs [Kissinger], San Clemente, California, 29 March 1971, *Foreign Relations of the United States,* Volume XI (1969–1976), pp. 35–37.
85 Telegram 165, from American Embassy Islamabad to State Department, 'Admiral Ahsan on Events in East Pakistan', dated 17 August 1971, in Roedad Khan, *American Papers: Secret and Confidential, India, Pakistan, Bangladesh, Documents 1965-1973*, Karachi: Oxford University Press, 1999, p. 643.
86 Telegram 959, from the Consulate General in Dacca to the Department of State, 28 March 1971, *Foreign Relations of the United States,* Volume E-7 (1969–1976), pp. 1–2.
87 Sydney Schanberg, 'An Alien Army Imposes Its Will: East Pakistan', *The New York Times*, 4 July 1971.
88 Michael Hornsby, 'President Yahya Dashes Hopes of Reconciliation', *The Times* (London), 3 July 1971.
89 For detailed analyses of the East Pakistan crisis, please see: Hasan Zaheer, *The Separation of East Pakistan: The Rise and Realization of Bengali Muslim Nationalism*, Karachi: Oxford University Press, 1994; Rao Farman Ali Khan, *How Pakistan Got Divided*, Lahore: Jung Publishers, 1992; Kamal Matinuddin, *Tragedy of Errors: East Pakistan Crisis, 1968-71*, Lahore: Wajidalis, 1994; Khadim Hussain Raja, *A Stranger in My Own Country: East Pakistan, 1969-1971*, Dacca: University Press Limited, 2012; Gary J. Bass, *The Blood Telegram: Nixon, Kissinger and a Forgotten Genocide*, New York: Alfred Knopf, 2013.
90 John H. Gill, 'An Atlas of the 1971 India-Pakistan War: The Creation of Bangladesh', Washington, DC: National Defense University, Near East South Asia Center for Strategic Studies Occasional Paper, 2004.

91 Charles Mohrs, 'Dacca Captured: Guns Quiet in Bengali Area but War Goes on at Western…', *The New York Times*, 16 December 1971.

92 Malcolm Browne, 'West to Fight On: Yahya Calls for Help but Vows to Battle "Alone If We Must"', *The New York Times*, 16 December 1971.

93 Malcolm Browne, 'The People Went to Mosques to Pray and Weep: India-Pakistan', *The New York Times*, 19 December 1971.

4: Islamist Rage

1 See Mubashir Hasan, *The Mirage of Power: An Inquiry into the Bhutto Years 1971-1977*, Karachi: Oxford University Press, 2000; also see Rafi Raza, *Zulfikar Ali Bhutto and Pakistan 1967-1977*, Karachi: Oxford University Press, 1997.

2 Anwar Syed, 'Pakistan in 1976: Business as Usual', *Asian Survey*, Vol. 17, No. 2, February 1977, pp. 1261–63.

3 Ibid.

4 Mubashir Hasan, *The Mirage of Power*, p. 256.

5 William Richter, 'The Political Dynamics of Islamic Resurgence in Pakistan', *Asian Survey*, Vol. 19, No. 6, June 1979, pp. 551–52.

6 Ibid.

7 Marvin Weinbaum, 'The March 1977 Elections in Pakistan: Where Everyone Lost', *Asian Survey*, Vol. 17, July 1977, No. 7, p. 614.

8 *Pakistan Times*, 18 April 1977, cited in William L. Richter, 'The Political Dynamic of Islamic Resurgence', *Asian Survey*, Vol. 19, No. 6, June 1979, p. 552.

9 Lt Gen. Jahan Dad Khan, *Pakistan Leadership Challenges*, Karachi: Oxford University Press, 1999, p. 158.

10 'The Offences Against Property (Enforcement of Hudood) Ordinance', Punjab Police, 10 February 1979.

11 National Legislative Bodies / National Authorities, Pakistan: Ordinance No. VII of 1979, Offence of Zina (Enforcement of Hudood) Ordinance, 1979, 10 February 1979.

12 Rahat Imran, 'Legal Injustices: The Zina Hudood Ordinance of Pakistan and Its Implications for Women', *Journal of International Women's Studies*, Vol. 7, No. 2, 2005, pp. 78–100.

13 Ibid.

14 See, for example, Nicholas D. Kristof, 'A Woman's Work Earns Her Enemies', *The New York Times*, 8 April 2007; Kayleigh Lewis, 'Rape

victims in Pakistan are risking everything for justice', *The Independent (UK)*, 19 February 2016; Seth Mydans, 'In Pakistan, Rape Victims Are the "Criminals"', *The New York Times*, 17 May 2002.

15 Hasan Akhtar, 'Daily prayer for officials in Pakistan', *Times* [London], 28 January 1978.

16 The President on Pakistan's Ideological Basis, Address by President General Zia-ul-Haq at the inauguration of Shariat Faculty at the Quaid-i-Azam University, Islamabad, 8 October 1979, Islamabad: Ministry of Information and Broadcasting, n.d., p. 2, cited in C.G.P. Rakisits, 'Center-Province Relations in Pakistan under President Zia: The Government's and Opposition's Approaches', *Pacific Affairs*, Vol. 61, No. 1, 1988, p. 79.

17 President Zia-ul-Haq's interview to Ian Stephens, 6 January 1979, in *President of Pakistan General Mohammad Zia-ul-Haq: Interviews to Foreign Media*, Islamabad: Government of Pakistan, undated, Vol. II, pp. 2–6.

18 Catherine Piggott, 'Pakistan moves to "Islamize" justice system', *The Ottawa Citizen*, 15 August 1990.

19 'Human Rights Commission of Pakistan Annual Report 2015', Islamabad: Human Rights Commission of Pakistan, 2016, http://hrcp-web.org/publication/book-genre/annual-reports/ (accessed on 20 August 2017).

20 Stephanie Palo, 'A Charade of Change: Qisas and Diyat Ordinance Allows Honour Killings to Go Unpunished in Pakistan', *U.C. Davis Journal of International Law and Policy*, Vol. 15, No. 1, 2008.

21 Molly Moore and John Ward Anderson, 'Islamic Law – and Zeal – Rise to Challenge Secular Politics in Pakistan', *The Washington Post*, 21 October 1992.

22 Raza Khan, '"Lightly beating" wife permissible, says CII's proposed women protection bill', *Dawn*, 26 May 2016.

23 Ibid.

24 Kalbe Ali, 'Who is Khadim Hussain Rizvi?' *Dawn*, 3 December 2017; Salman Masood, 'Pakistani Cleric's supporters block an entrance to Islamabad', *The New York Times*, 12 November 2017.

25 'Capitulation,' *Dawn*, Editorial, 28 November 2017.

26 Anthony D. Smith, *Theories of Nationalism*, New York: Harper & Row, 1971, pp. 20–23.

27 McKim Marriott, 'Cultural Policy in the New States', in Clifford Geertz (ed.), *Old Societies and New States: The Quest for Modernity in Asia and Africa*, New York: The Free Press, 1963, pp. 43–45.

28 Dennis Kux, *Disenchanted Allies – The United States and Pakistan 1947-2000*, Washington, DC: Woodrow Wilson Center Press, 2001, pp. 242–44.

29 Iqbal Akhund, *Trial and Error: The Advent and Eclipse of Benazir Bhutto*, Karachi: Oxford University Press, 2000, pp. 59–60.

30 Richard M. Weintraub, 'Mob Storms US Facility in Pakistan; At Least Five Killed as Police Open Fire on Moslem Protesters', *The Washington Post*, 13 February 1989.

31 Ibid.

32 Husain Haqqani, 'Muslim Rage is about politics, not religion', *Newsweek*,1 October 2012.

33 Mike Collet-White, 'Rushdie says writers losing influence in West', Reuters, 28 September 2012.

34 Jon Boone, 'Pakistan explodes in fury as south Asia's Muslims join anti-US protests', *The Guardian* (UK), 21 September 2012.

35 'Protests across Pakistan against anti-Islam film', AFP/*Dawn*, 14 September 2012.

36 Husain Haqqani, *Pakistan Between Mosque and Military*, Washington, DC: Brookings Press, 2005, p. 139.

37 Nadeem Farooq Paracha, 'The heart's filthy lesson', *Dawn*, 14 February 2013, https://www.dawn.com/news/786019 (accessed on 17 December 2017).

38 Farhan Bokhari, 'Women, sport and Islam: Dispatches', *Financial Times*, 13 July 1996.

39 'Women protest in Pakistan', *The New York Times*, 4 July 1988.

5: Insecurity and Jihad

1 Michael T. Kaufman, 'Pakistan's Islamic Revival Affects All Aspects of Life', *The New York Times*, 13 October 1980.

2 Aslam Siddiqui, *Pakistan Seeks Security*, Lahore: Longman & Greens, 1960, Preface.

3 Jinnah's speech reported in *The Statesman*, 25 October 1947.

4 A.R. Siddiqui, *The Military in Pakistan: Image and Reality*, Lahore: Vanguard, 1996, p. 107.

5 Speech by Zulfikar Ali Bhutto, 'India's Aggression', Speech in the UN Security Council, New York, 22 September 1965, http://www.bhutto.org/1957-1965_speech49.php (accessed on 5 August 2017).

6 Ibid.

7 Ibid.

8 Ibid.

9 Ibid.

10 Speech by Zulfiqar Ali Bhutto, 'My country beckons me', Speech in UN Security Council, New York, 15 December 1971, http://www.bhutto.org/1970-1971_speech46.php (accessed on 5 August 2017).

11 Ibid.

12 President Zia-ul-Haq's interview to Joseph Kraft, 11 March 1981, cited in *President of Pakistan General Zia-ul-Haq: Interviews to Foreign Media,* Vol. IV, Islamabad: Directorate of Film and Publications. Ministry of Information and Broadcasting, Government of Pakistan, p. 79.

13 Alastair Jamieson, 'Did Pakistan TV Debate Prompt Burning of Yoga Center?', NBC News, 10 March 2014.

14 Shamil Shams, 'Water scarcity in Pakistan – A bigger threat than terrorism', *Deutsche Welle*, 7 February 2017, http://www.dw.com/en/water-scarcity-in-pakistan-a-bigger-threat-than-terrorism/a-37444480 (accessed on 27 June 2017).

15 Mehreen Zahra-Malik and Asim Tanveer, 'Pakistani Islamists Use Floods to Turn Opinion against India', Thomson Reuters, 16 September 2014, https://www.reuters.com/article/uk-southasia-flood-militants/pakistani-islamists-use-floods-to-turn-opinion-against-india-idUKKBN0HB2LY20140916 (accessed on 27 June 2017).

16 'US puts $10m bounty on Lashkar-e-Taiba's Hafiz Saeed', BBC, 3 April 2012, http://www.bbc.com/news/world-asia-india-17594018 (accessed on 20 June 2017).

17 'US says Salahuddin is a "global terrorist"', Deutsche Welle, 26 June 2017, http://www.dw.com/en/us-says-salahuddin-is-a-global-terrorist-will-it-impact-kashmir/a-39435894 (accessed on 27 June 2017).

18 'Hindus responsible for Terrorism, CJ Says', *Daily Times*, 17 March 2010.

19 Jawaharlal Nehru, 'Education is Meant to Free the Spirit of Man', Convocation address by Jawaharlal Nehru to AMU students on 24 January 1948, New Delhi: Government of India, 1948.

20 Shahbaz Rana, 'General Raheel sends clear message to hawkish India', *The Express Tribune*, 1 September 2016.

21 Mufti Ghulam Farid Haqqani, *Pakistan aur afvaaj-e-Pakistan ka tazkira Quran aur Ahadith mein* (Urdu), Peshawar: Darul Ifta wal Qaza, undated, p. 21.

22 Anatol Lieven, *Pakistan: A Hard Country,* London: Allen Lane, 2011, pp. 187–89.

23 Pakistani security analyst Zaid Hamid, '[After Constantinople] Prophet Muhammad's Second Hadith Is Regarding Ghazwa-e-Hind, That The Army Which Would Capture India Would Go to [Conquer] Israel', *MEMRI* (Middle East Media Research Institute), 24 May 2012, Special Dispatch No.4749, https://www.memri.org/reports/pakistani-security-analyst-zaid-hamid-after-constantinople-prophet-muhammads-second-hadith (accessed on 18 June 2017).

24 Ibid.

25 Bilal Khan, 'The Bilad-e-Khurasan in Making', Research Paper, 30 March 2008, https://islamreigns.wordpress.com/tag/bilad-e-khurasan/ (accessed on 12 June 2017).

26 Muhammad Yousuf Khan, *Islam main Imam Mehdi Ka Tassawar* ('Concept of Mahdi in Islam), Lahore: Jamia Ashrafia, p. 240; Bilal Khan, 'The Bilad-e-Khurasan in Making'.

27 Hind and Hindustan are Arabic and Persian names for India.

28 Taken from Sunan an-Nasa'i 3175, Book 25, Hadith 91, Vol. 1.

29 Taken from Sunan an-Nasa'i 3173, Book 25, Hadith 89, Vol. 1.

30 Example of the Hadith referring to Ghazwa-e-Hind claiming to be from Sahih Hadith.

31 Lashkar-e-Taiba founder Hafiz Saeed, 'Speech at public rally on Kashmir Solidarity Day', 5 February 2011, in 'Addressing Public Rally in Lahore, Lashkar-e-Taiba Founder Hafiz Muhammad Saeed Tells India: "Quit Kashmir or Get Ready to Face a War"', *MEMRI*, Special Dispatch No. 3626, 1 March 2011.

32 Zaid Hamid video of 10 April 2012 in 'Pakistani Security Analyst Zaid Hamid: "[After Constantinople] Prophet Muhammad's Second Hadith Is Regarding Ghazwa-e-Hind"', *MEMRI* Special Dispatch No 4749, 24 May 2012.

33 Maulana Waris Mazhari, 'Countering Pakistani Terrorists' Anti-India Propaganda', 26 January 2009, http://indianmuslims.in/countering-pakistani-terrorists-anti-india-propaganda/ (accessed on 15 June 2017).

34 Ibid.

35 Ibid.

36 Ibid.

37 Ibid.

38 Ibid.

39 Ibid.

40 Ibid.

41 Statement by Qari Hussain Ahmed included in a TTP video tribute to the slain commander Ahmed, released in December 2013. 'TTP Video Pays Tributes To Slain Commander Qari Hussain Ahmed', *MEMRI,* Special Dispatch No. 5576, 24 December 2013.

42 Abu Rumaysah, 'In Pursuit of Territory: The Benefits of Living Under Khilafah', *Ihaye Khilafat: The Voice of Tehreek e Taliban Pakistan, Striving for Global Khilafah*, October 2014, Issue No. 1.

43 'IMU Launches Urdu-Language Magazine, Battle of Hind', *SITE Intelligence*, Jihadist News, 15 January 2014.

44 IMU video on Ghazwa-e-Hind, *MEMRI,* Jihad and Terrorism Threat Monitor (JTTM), Weekend Summary, Special Announcements No. 307, 24 May 2014.

45 Kashmir's Dukhtaran-e-Millat on al-Qaeda, *MEMRI,* Jihad and Terrorism Threat Monitor (JTTM) Weekend Summary, Special Announcements No. 269, 7 December 2013.

46 Turkestan Islamic Party on Ghazwa-e-Hind, *MEMRI,* Jihad and Terrorism Threat Monitor (JTTM) Weekend Summary, Special Announcements No. 300, 12 April 2014.

47 'AQIS Clarifies Targets of Karachi Naval Yard Attack as U.S., Indian Navies', *SITE Intelligence*, Jihadist News, 30 September 2014.

48 'Islamic State Leader Abu Bakr al-Baghdadi Encourages Emigration, Worldwide Action', *SITE Intelligence* Jihadist News, 1 July 2014.

49 'Ansar al-Tawhid in the Land of Hind Pledges to IS, Repeats IS Spokesman's Call for Attacks', *SITE Intelligence*, Jihadist News, 6 October 2014.

50 'Al-Isabah Media Releases Audio of Pledge from Fighter in India to IS', *SITE Intelligence*, Jihadist News, 15 November 2014.

51 'Ansar al-Tawhid in the Land of Hind Eulogizes Slain Indian Fighter in Video', *SITE Intelligence*, Jihadist News, 13 October 2014.

52 Islamuddin Sajid, 'Hafiz Saeed Khan: The former Taliban warlord taking ISIS to India and Pakistan', *International Business Times*, 19 January 2015.

53 'Alleged TTP Fighter Offers Support to ISIS', *SITE Intelligence*, Jihadist News, 25 June 2014.

54 'Caliphate and Jihad Movement in Pakistan Pledges to IS, Claims Attacks', *SITE Intelligence*, Jihadist News, 10 July 2014.

55 'Jihadist Says Leader of Pakistani Jihadi Group Jundallah Pledged to IS', *SITE Intelligence*, Jihadist News, 19 November 2014.

56 'AQIS Bangla Video Calls Bangladeshi Muslims to Battlefield, Shows Base of Fighters', *SITE Intelligence*, Jihadist News, 29 November 2014.

57 Animesh Roul, 'The Threat from Rising Extremism in the Maldives', *CTC Sentinel*, 27 March 2013.

58 Jason Burke, 'Al-Qaida leader announces formation of Indian branch', *The Guardian*, 4 September 2014, https://www.theguardian.com/world/2014/sep/04/al-qaida-leader-announces-formation-indian-branch (accessed on 30 June 2017).

59 Ibid.

60 *Ihya-e-Khilafat Magazine*, Issue 1, Introduction, p.1, https://archive.org/details/IhyaEKhilafat (accessed on 1 May 2017).

61 Sabrina Tavernise, 'US Top Villain in Pakistan's Conspiracy Talk', *The New York Times*, 25 May 2010.

62 Steve Coll, 'Intrigue Permeates Pakistan; A Political Culture of "Shadow games"', *The Washington Post*, 15 December 1991.

63 Ibid.

64 Michael J. Wood, Karen M. Douglas and Robbie M. Sutton, 'Dead and Alive: Beliefs in Contradictory Conspiracy Theories', *SAGE Journals Social Psychological and Personality Science*, Vol. 3, Issue 6, 25 January 2012, pp. 767–73.

65 See, for example, Asif Haroon Raja, 'Is Panama gate a foreign conspiracy to derail Pakistan?' *Pakistan Tribune*, 21 July 2017, http://paktribune.com/articles/Is-Panama-gate-a-foreign-conspiracy-to-derail-Pakistan+-243325.html (accessed on 24 July 2017).

66 Declan Walsh, 'Pakistani media publish fake WikiLeaks cables attacking India', *The Guardian* (UK), 9 December 2010.

67 Ibid.

68 Michael J. Wood, Karen M. Douglas and Robbie M. Sutton, 'Dead and Alive'.

69 C.R. Sunstein and A. Vermeule, 'Conspiracy Theories: Causes and Cures', *Journal of Political Philosophy*, Vol. 17, Issue 2, June 2009, pp. 202–27.

70 Ibid.

71 Michael Baumann, 'Rational Fundamentalism? An Explanatory Model of Fundamentalist Beliefs', *Episteme*, Vol. 4, No. 2, 2007, pp. 150–66.

72 Jonathan Vankin, *Conspiracies, Cover-Ups and Crimes*, New York: Paragon House, 1991.

73 Kathleen Taylor, 'Has Kim Jong-Il Brainwashed North Koreans?' *The Guardian*, 20 December 2011, www.theguardian.com/commentisfree/2011/dec/20/kim-jong-il-brainwashed-north-koreans (accessed on 1 May 2017).

74 Jon Boone, 'Pakistani PM Nawaz Sharif names new chief of army staff', *The Guardian* (UK), 26 November 2016.

75 Khaled Ahmed, 'The mind of the generals', *The Indian Express*, 18 February 2017.

76 Ibid.

77 Ibid.

78 Ibid.

79 'What is the wildest conspiracy theory pertaining to Pakistan?' *Herald*, 19 June 2015.

80 'Pakistani Websites Accuse CIA of Causing Pakistan Flooding: US Research Program HAARP is being Used in Pakistan [to Cause Artificial Floods]'; 'They Can't Win a War with Nuclear-Armed Pakistan ... So They Have Other Ways to Do It', *MEMRI*, Special Dispatch No.3194, 27 August 2010.

81 Shamil Shams, 'Malala Yousafzai – honored abroad, maligned at home', *Deutsche Welle*, 11 April 2017, http://www.dw.com/en/malala-yousafzai-honored-abroad-maligned-at-home/a-17932794 (accessed on 1 May 2017).

82 Tim Craig and Haq Nawaz Khan, 'As giant rats menace Pakistan, conspiracy theories swirl', *The Washington Post*, 5 April 2016, https://www.washingtonpost.com/world/asia_pacific/as-giant-rats-menace-pakistan-conspiracy-theories-swirl/2016/04/05/48332714-f779-11e5-958d-d038dac6e718_story.html?utm_term=.517f1f3025c3 (accessed on 8 August 2017).

83 Ibid.

84 Emma Duncan, *Breaking the Curfew: A Political Journey through Pakistan*, London: Michael Joseph, 1989, p. 33.

85 Ibid.

86 'Veteran leader Mahmud Ali passes away', *Dawn*, 18 November 2006.

87 '6th death anniversary of Mahmud Ali today', *The Nation* (Pakistan), 17 November 2012.

88 Anatol Lieven, 'Inside Pakistan's spy network,' *New Statesman* (UK), 12 May 2011.

89 Khalid Bin Sayeed, *Pakistan: The Formative Phase*, Ann Arbor, MI: University of Michigan Press, 1960, pp., 390, 429–31.

90 Ibid., p. 390.

91 Muhammad Ayub Khan, *Friends Not Masters: A Political Autobiography*, Karachi: Oxford University Press, 1967, p. 55.

92 Stanley Wolpert, *Zulfi Bhutto of Pakistan: His Life and Times*, Ann Arbor, MI: University of Michigan Press, 1993.

93 See Husain Haqqani, *Pakistan Between Mosque and Military*, Washington: Carnegie Endowment for International Peace, 2005, pp. 199–260.

94 Mansoor Malik, 'Jindal's unannounced visit, talks with PM fuel speculation', *Dawn*, 28 April 2017.

95 Daniel Pipes, *The Hidden Hand: Middle East Fears of Conspiracy*, New York: St. Martin's Griffin, 1998, p. 347.

6: 'The Institution'

1 Khalid Bin Sayeed, *Pakistan: The Formative Phase*, Ann Arbor, MI: University of Michigan Press, 1960, p. 5.

2 Stephen Cohen, *The Pakistan Army*, Berkeley: University of California Press, 1984; Shuja Nawaz, *Crossed Swords: Pakistan, Its Army and the Wars Within*, Karachi: Oxford University Press, 2008, pp. 26–27.

3 Speech by Huseyn Shaheed Suhrawardy on 6 March 1948, *Constituent Assembly of Pakistan Debates: Official Report, 1946-1956*, Karachi: Manager, Governor-General's Press and Publications, 1950–56, pp. 262–63.

4 Ibid.

5 Lawrence Ziring, *Pakistan in the Twentieth Century*, Karachi: Oxford University Press, 1997, p. 148.

6 Shuja Nawaz, *Crossed Swords*, p. 29.

7 Ibid., p. 34

8 Anatol Lieven, *Pakistan: A Hard Country*, London: Allen Lane, 2011, p. 176.

9 Ibid.

10 Ibid., pp. 177–78.

11 Shuja Nawaz, *Crossed Swords*, p. xxvii.

12 Ibid., pp. 82–83.

13 Muhammad Ayub Khan, *Friends Not Masters: A Political Autobiography*, Karachi: Oxford University Press, 1967, p. 58.

14 'Tweedle Khan Takes over', *The Economist*, 29 March 1969.
15 Herbert Feldman, *The End and the Beginning: Pakistan 1969-71*, Karachi: Oxford University Press, 1975, pp. 2–3.
16 Cited in Shuja Nawaz, *Crossed Swords*, pp. xxvii–xxviii.
17 Ibid., p. xxix–xxx.
18 Ibid.
19 Roedad Khan, 'The Role of the Military-Bureaucratic Oligarchy', *Dawn*, 25 August 2001.
20 Ibid.
21 Ibid.
22 Nasir Jamal, 'Raheel Sharif: The Chief who could be king', *The Herald*, 5 December 2016.
23 Ibid.
24 Ibid.
25 Ibid.
26 Ayesha Siddiqa, *Military Inc: Inside Pakistan's Military Economy,* New Delhi: Penguin Random House, 2017, pp. 328–31.
27 Ibid.
28 Ibid.
29 Mehreen Zahra-Malik, 'New blockbuster movie shows why Pakistan loves to hate India', Reuters, 25 October 2013, http://www.reuters.com/article/entertainment-us-pakistan-waar-idUSBRE99O0CM20131025 (accessed on 18 August 2017).
30 Ayesha Siddiqa, *Military Inc: Inside Pakistan's Military Economy*, New Delhi: Penguin Random House, 2017, pp. 328–31.
31 Nasir Jamal, 'Raheel Sharif: The Chief who could be king'.
32 Dexter Filkins, 'The Journalist and the Spies: The murder of a reporter who exposed Pakistan's secrets', *The New Yorker*, 19 September 2011, https://www.newyorker.com/magazine/2011/09/19/the-journalist-and-the-spies (accessed on 24 July 2017).
33 Ibid.
34 Ibid.
35 Ibid.
36 Jane Perlez, 'Pakistani Journalist Speaks Out After an Attack', *The New York Times*, 24 September 2010.
37 Ibid.
38 Ibid.
39 Dexter Filkins, 'The Journalist and the Spies'.

40 Ibid.

41 See, 'I was tortured beyond limits: Pakistani blogger Ahmad Waqass Goraya', *The Indian Express*, 10 March 2017, http://indianexpress.com/article/world/i-was-tortured-beyond-limits-pakistani-blogger-ahmad-waqass-goraya-4563002/ (accessed on 24 July 2017); also, Rabia Mehmood, 'Pakistan's violent cyberspace: No place for dissent', Al Jazeera, 16 January 2017, http://www.aljazeera.com/indepth/opinion/2017/01/pakistan-violent-cyberspace-place-dissent-170115132256152.html (accessed on 24 July 2017).

42 Amir Mir, 'Musharraf buys all copies of sensitive '65 war book', *DNA*, 1 October 2006.

43 Shamil Shams, 'A spotlight on the Pakistani military's corruption', *Deutsche Welle*, 22 April 2016.

44 'Raheel Sharif "helped me out" in leaving Pakistan: Musharraf', *Dawn*, 20 December 2016.

45 Amir Wasim, '50 commercial entities being run by armed forces', *Dawn*, 21 July 2016.

46 John Lancaster, 'Fighting an Army's Empire', *The Washington Post*, 29 June 2003.

47 Ibid.

48 Saad Sarfaraz Shaikh, 'How Okara farmers have become the latest "enemies" of the state', *The Herald*, 23 August 2016.

49 'Army chief "announces Umrah" for CT 2017 winners', *Dunya News*, 19 June 2017.

50 'DG ISPR seeks media's support in shaping national narrative', Geo TV, 21 August 2017, https://www.geo.tv/latest/154653-asif-ghafoor-askks (accessed on 23 August 2017).

51 Feroz Hassan Khan, *Eating Grass: The Making of the Pakistani Bomb*, Stanford, CA: Stanford University Press, 2012, pp. 2–3.

52 Ibid.

53 Ibid., p. 6.

54 Kenneth Waltz, 'The Spread of Nuclear Weapons: More May Be Better', *Adelphi Papers* (171), London: International Institute for Strategic Studies, 1981.

55 Toby Dalton and George Perkovich, 'India's Nuclear Options and Escalation Dominance', Washington, DC: Carnegie Endowment for International Peace, May 2016, p. 8, http://carnegieendowment.org/files/CP_273_India_Nuclear_Final.pdf (accessed on 1 May 2017).

56 Cited in speech by Pervez Hoodbhoy, 'Pakistani Nuclear Weapons Program', presented at a meeting in New York City sponsored by the Lawyers Committee on Nuclear Policy and *The Nation*, 14 July 2009, http://lcnp.org/disarmament/ (accessed on 1 March 2017).

57 Majeed Nizami cited in *Nawa-i-Waqt*, 5 November 2008.

58 Majeed Nizami's speech at an event in his honour, cited in *Nawa-i-Waqt*, 24 June 2010.

59 'Khawaja Asif directs nuclear threat at Israel after reading fake news', *The Express Tribune*, 25 December 2016.

60 'Pakistan Threatens a Nuclear War with India', *Toronto Sun*, 4 October 2016.

61 Vernie Liebl, 'India and Pakistan: Competing Nuclear Strategies and Doctrines', *Comparative Strategy*, 6 April 2009, pp. 154–63, http://www.tandfonline.com/doi/pdf/10.1080/01495930902799731?needAccess=true (accessed on 1 May 2017).

62 Ibid.

63 Toby Dalton and George Perkovich, 'India's Nuclear Options and Escalation Dominance'.

64 Manpreet Sethi, 'India and the Nuclear Order: Concerns and Opportunities', in Toby Dalton, Toghan Kassenova and Lauryn Williams (eds), *Perspectives on the Evolving Nuclear Order*, Washington, DC: Carnegie Endowment, 2016, p. 79.

65 George Perkovich, 'Civil nuclear cooperation with Pakistan: Prospects and Consequences', Testimony before the House committee on Foreign Affairs, 8 December 2015, p. 2, http://carnegieendowment.org/files/Formatted_George_Perkovich_testimony.pdf (accessed on 1 May 2017).

66 Jaganath Sankaran, 'The Enduring Power of Bad Ideas: Cold Start and Battlefield Nuclear Weapons in South Asia', *Arms Control Today*, Vol. 44, No. 9, November 2014, p. 16.

67 Ibid.

68 Mansoor Ahmed, 'Pakistan's Tactical Nuclear Weapons and their Impact on Safety', Washington, DC: Carnegie Endowment for International Peace, 30 June 2016, http://carnegieendowment.org/2016/06/30/pakistan-s-tactical-nuclear-weapons-and-their-impact-on-stability-pub-63911 (accessed on 1 May 2017).

69 Jeffrey McCausland, 'Pakistan's Tactical Nuclear Weapons: Operational Myths and Realities', in Michael Krepon, Joshua White, Julia Thompson and Shane Mason (eds), *Deterrence Instability*

and Nuclear Weapons in South Asia, Washington, DC: Stimson Center, 2016, p. 167, https://www.stimson.org/sites/default/files/file-attachments/Deterrence_Instability_WEB.pdf (accessed on 1 May 2017).

70 Feroz Hassan Khan, *Eating Grass*, p. 332.

71 Ibid., p. 384.

72 Michel Krepon, 'Upending the stalemate between India and Pakistan', Stimson Center, 3 November 2015, https://www.stimson.org/content/upending-stalemate-between-india-and-pakistan (accessed on 1 May 2017).

73 Toby Dalton and Michael Krepon, 'A Normal Nuclear Pakistan', Washington, DC: Stimson Center and Carnegie Endowment for International Peace, 2015, pp. 7–9, http://www.stimson.org/sites/default/files/file-attachments/NormalNuclearPakistan.pdf (accessed on 1 May 2017).

74 Robert S. Robins and Jerrold Post, *Political Paranoia: The Pyschopolitics of Hatred*, Yale: Yale University Press, 1997, pp. 1–2.

75 Ibid., pp 3–4.

76 Ibid.

77 Ibid., p. 38.

78 Ibid., pp. 39, 40.

79 Elizabeth Roche, 'Hamid Gul, former ISI chief who nurtured the Taliban, dies at 79', Livemint, 17 August 2015, http://www.livemint.com/Politics/BRnD7Ka9hy26Bs9RASPubK/Hamid-Gul-Pakistans-projehad-exISI-chief-dies.html (accessed on 19 December 2017).

80 Anatol Lieven, *Pakistan: A Hard Country*, London: Allan Lane, 2011, pp. 188–89.

81 Mirza Aslam Beg, 'What has to be, has to be', *The Nation* (Pakistan), 8 October 2013.

82 Gauher Aftab, 'A Greater Pakistan,' *The Nation* (Pakistan), 17 September 2017, http://nation.com.pk/17-Sep-2017/a-greater-pakistan (accessed 17 December 2017).

83 Zia-ul-Haq's interview with Selig Harrison, published in *Le Monde Diplomatique*, cited in Steve Coll, *Ghost Wars: The Secret History of the CIA, Afghanistan, and Bin Laden, from the Soviet Invasion to September 10, 2001,* New York: Penguin Books, 2004, p. 175.

84 Pervez Musharraf, *In the Line of Fire: A Memoir*, New York: Simon & Schuster, 2006, pp. 201–03.

85 'Statement for the Record by General John Nicholson, Commander US Forces-Afghanistan before Senate Armed Services Committee', 9 February 2017, https://www.armed-services.senate.gov/imo/media/doc/Nicholson_02-09-17.pdf (accessed 17 December 2017); Elisabeth Bumiller and Jane Perlez, 'Pakistan's Spy Agency Is Tied to Attack on U.S. Embassy', *The New York Times*, 22 September 2011; 'Haqqani network is a "veritable arm" of ISI: Mullen', *Dawn*, 22 September 2011 https://www.dawn.com/news/660878 (accessed 17 December 2017).

86 See General Musharraf's interview to *The Guardian*: Jon Boone, 'Musharraf: Pakistan and India's backing for "proxies" in Afghanistan must stop,' *The Guardian*, 13 February 2015, https://www.theguardian.com/world/2015/feb/13/pervez-musharraf-pakistan-india-proxies-afghanistan-ghani-taliban (accessed 17 December 2017); also Sartaj Aziz's interview: 'Fighting militancy: Why should we antagonise all groups, asks Aziz,' *The Express Tribune*, 18 November 2014, https://tribune.com.pk/story/792914/fighting-militancy-why-should-we-antagonise-all-groups-asks-aziz/ (accessed 17 December 2017).

87 Anwar Iqbal, 'Indian role in Afghanistan overestimated in Pakistan: Olson', *Dawn*, 22 June 2016.

88 Syed Ali Shah, '"RAW officer" arrested in Balochistan', *Dawn*, 24 March 2016; Salman Masood and Hari Kumar, 'Pakistan Sentences Indian Spy to Death for Operating Terrorism Ring', *The New York Times*, 10 April 2017.

89 Stephen Cohen, *The Pakistan Army*, p. 86.

90 Stephen Cohen, *The Idea of Pakistan*, Washington, DC: Brookings Institution Press, 2006, p. 97. Emphasis in the original.

91 William Langewiesche, 'The Wrath of Khan', *The Atlantic*, November 2005, https://www.theatlantic.com/magazine/archive/2005/11/the-wrath-of-khan/304333/ (accessed 17 December 2017); Adrian Levy and Catherine Scott-Clark, *Deception: Pakistan, the United States, and the Secret Trade in Nuclear Weapons*, New York: Walker & Co, 2007.

92 Adrian Levy and Catherine Scott-Clark, *The Exile: The Stunning Inside Story of Osama bin Laden and Al Qaeda in Flight*, New York: Bloomsbury, 2017.

93 Samar Mubarakmand, 'Destined Towards a Rich Pakistan: Reko Diq Mineral Resources,' *Hilal* (English), January 2015.

94 'Huge reserves of iron ore, copper to help break begging bowl: PM', *Dawn*, 12 February 2015.

95 'World Bank tribunal rules against Pakistan in Reko Diq project case', *Dawn*, 21 March 2017.

96 Eric Nordlinger, *Soldiers in Politics*, Upper Saddle Ridge, NJ: Prentice Hall, 1977, p. 51.

97 Ibid., p. 1.

98 Ibid., p. 47.

7: Warriors, Not Traders

1 Adam Smith, *An Inquiry into the Nature and Causes of the Wealth of Nations*, 1776, Library of Economics and Liberty, http://www.econlib.org/library/Smith/smWN13.html (accessed on 1 July 2017).

2 Kerry Dolan, 'Forbes 2017 Billionaires List', *Forbes*, 20 March 2017, https://www.forbes.com/sites/kerryadolan/2017/03/20/forbes-2017-billionaires-list-meet-the-richest-people-on-the-planet/#14f7324a62ff (accessed on 23 March 2017).

3 Claire O'Connor, 'Billionaire drop-offs: Who Didn't Make the Cut?', *Forbes*, 9 March 2011, https://www.forbes.com/sites/clareoconnor/2011/03/09/billionaire-drop-offs-who-didnt-make-the-cut/#42e734482249 (accessed on 23 March 2017).

4 See, for example, this statement of Pakistan's finance minister at Khawar Ghumman, '$200bn of Pakistan in Swiss banks: Dar', *Dawn*, 10 May 2014.

5 'Pakistan far behind the world in per acre yield', *The Nation* (Pakistan), 18 March 2011, http://nation.com.pk/business/18-Mar-2011/pakistan-far-behind-the-world-in-per-acre-yield (accessed on 24 March 2017).; 'Cotton Production by Country in 1000 480 lb. Bales', Index Mundi, http://www.indexmundi.com/agriculture/?commodity=cotton (accessed on 13 September 2017).

6 Calvin Coolidge, thirtieth president of the United States, Address to the American Society of Newspaper Editors, Washington, DC, 17 January 1925, http://www.presidency.ucsb.edu/ws/?pid=24180 (accessed on 6 September 2017).

7 Nadeem Ul Haque and Arif Sheikh, 'Concerns of Intelligentsia in Pakistan: Content Analysis of Newspapers', *Economic and Political Weekly*, Vol. 29, No. 24, 11 June 1994, p. 1483.

8 Nadeem Ul Haque, 'Doing away with the defunct', *Pakistan Today*, 18 July 2014.

9 Teresita C. Schaffer, 'Pakistan's broken economy', *Foreign Policy*, 15 March 2011, http://foreignpolicy.com/2011/03/15/pakistans-broken-economy/ (accessed on 25 March 2017).

10 Ibid.

11 Kashif Abbasi, '22.6m Pakistani children still out of school: report', *Dawn*, 9 March 2017.

12 Aisha Ghaus-Pasha, 'Can Pakistan Get Out of the Low Tax to GDP Trap', *The Lahore Journal of Economics,* 'Development Challenges in the New Decade', Vol. 15 (Special Edition), September 2010.

13 'Exports, percent of GDP – country rankings', Global Economy Rankings based on World Bank data, http://www.theglobaleconomy.com/rankings/Exports/ (accessed on 1 July 2017).

14 'Textile, clothing exports decline', *Dawn*, 24 February 2017.

15 Sakib Sherani, 'Reviving Pakistan's exports', *Dawn*, 28 April 2017.

16 Meekal Ahmed, 'An Economic Crisis State?', in Maleeha Lodhi (ed.), *Pakistan: Beyond the Crisis State*, New York: Columbia University Press, 2011, p. 169.

17 Ibid.

18 Ibid.

19 Ishrat Husain, *Pakistan: The Economy of an Elitist State,* Karachi: Oxford University Press, 1999, p. 7.

20 'Quaid-i-Azam Muhammad Ali Jinnah's Broadcast talk to the people of Australia', Recorded on 19 February 1948.

21 S.M. Burke and Lawrence Ziring, *Pakistan's Foreign Policy: An Historical Analysis*, Karachi: Oxford University Press, 1990, pp. 123–24.

22 El Hamza, *Pakistan*: *A Nation*, Lahore: Muhammad Ashraf, 1941, p. 114.

23 K.K. Aziz, *The Murder of History: A critique of history textbooks used in Pakistan*, New Delhi: Renaissance Publishing House, 1998, pp. 98–99.

24 Shahid Javed Burki, 'Economics was the basis of Pakistan's creation', *Express Tribune*, 12 January 2015.

25 Christopher Candland, 'Poverty and Inequality: Persistent Effects of Pakistan's Formative Development Model', in Roger Long(ed.), *A History of Pakistan*, Karachi: Oxford University Press, 2015, pp. 743–44.

26 Ibid.
27 Ian Talbot, 'Planning for Pakistan: The Planning Committee of the All India Muslim League, 1943-46', *Modern Asian Studies*, Vol. 28, No. 4, 1994, pp. 875–89; also see, Khalid Shamsul Hasan (ed.), *Quaid-e-Azam's Unrealized Dream: Formation and Working of the All India Muslim League Economic Planning Committee*, with Background Material and Notes, Karachi: Shamsul Hasan Foundation for Historical Studies and Research, 1991.
28 Chaudhri Muhammad Ali, *The Emergence of Pakistan*, Lahore: Services Book Club, 1988, pp. 332–34.
29 Khalid Bin Sayeed, *Pakistan: The Formative Years, 1857-1948*, Karachi: Oxford University Press, 1968.
30 Abdus Sattar, 'Fifty Years of the Kashmir Dispute: The Diplomatic Aspect', in Suroosh Irfani (ed.), *Fifty Years of the Kashmir Dispute,* Muzaffarabad: University of Azad Jammu and Kashmir, 1997, pp. 11–12.
31 Margaret Bourke-White, *Halfway to Freedom: A report on the new India in the words and photographs of Margaret Bourke-White*, New York: Simon & Schuster, 1949, p. 93.
32 Ibid.
33 'Liaquat asks Army for Social Service and Sacrifices', *Dawn,* 10 April 1948.
34 'Quaid-e-Azam Muhammad Ali Jinnah's Message to the Nation on the occasion of the first Anniversary of Pakistan', 14 August 1948, 'Documents', Pakistan Horizon, Pakistan Institute of International Affairs, Vol. 30, No. 1 (First Quarter, 1977), pp. 170–255.
35 'Pakistan's second surplus budget', *Dawn*, 1 March 1949; 'But India has a deficit of Rs 14.79 crores', ibid.
36 George McGhee, *Envoy to the Middle World: Adventures in Diplomacy*, New York: Harper & Row, 1983, p. 91.
37 Ibid.
38 Chaudhri Muhammad Ali, *The Emergence of Pakistan*, pp. 332–34.
39 Christopher Candland, 'Poverty and Inequality: Persistent Effects of Pakistan's Formative Development Model,' in Roger Long, *A History of Pakistan*, Karachi: Oxford University Press, 2015, pp. 751–52.
40 Ibid.
41 Ibid., pp. 757–58.
42 Ibid., pp. 759–60.
43 Ibid., pp. 761–62.

44 Ibid., p. 763.
45 Angus Maddison, *Class Structure and Economic Growth: India and Pakistan since the Moghuls*, London: Allen and Unwin, 1971, p. 139.
46 Meekal Ahmed, 'An Economic Crisis State?', pp. 171–72.
47 Ibid., p. 173.
48 Ishrat Husain, *Pakistan: The Economy of an Elitist State*, pp. xii–xiii.
49 Ibid.
50 Michael Kugelman (ed.), *Pakistan's Runaway Urbanization: What Can Be Done?*, Washington, DC: The Wilson Center, 2014.
51 John Mcquaid, 'How to revitalize Pakistan's agricultural sector and rural economy', International Food Policy Research Institute, 12 December 2016, http://www.ifpri.org/blog/how-revitalize-pakistans-agricultural-sector-and-rural-economy (accessed 17 December 2017).
52 M. Aftab, 'Pakistan's textile industry goes on war path, as exports shrink', *Khaleej Times*, 25 June 2017, https://www.khaleejtimes.com/business/economy/pakistans-textile-industry-goes-on-war-path-as-exports-shrink (accessed 17 December 2017).
53 India ranks at 131, Bhutan at 132, Bangladesh at 139, Nepal at 144, and Pakistan at 147: '2016 Human Development Report: International Human Development Indicators', Human Development Reports, United Nations Development Programme, http://hdr.undp.org/en/countries (accessed 17 December 2017).
54 Ishrat Husain, *Pakistan: The Economy of an Elitist State*, pp. xii–xiii.
55 Ibid., p. 346.
56 Hazem Beblawi and Giacomo Luciani, 'The Rentier State in the Arab World', in Giacomo Luciani, *The Arab State*, London: Routledge, 1990, pp. 87–88.
57 US Embassy, New Delhi, Cable to State Department, 11 July 1947, *Foreign Relations of the United States* (*FRUS)* Volume III, 1947, pp. 161–62.
58 George McGhee, *Envoy to the Middle World*, p. 91.
59 'American Aid', editorial, *Pakistan Times*, 3 July 1948.
60 Ameen K. Tareen, 'Pakistan and the Marshall Plan', *Dawn*, 5 September 1949.
61 US Embassy, Karachi, Cable to State Department, 2 January 1948, 845F.001/1-248, Department of State Records, National Archives, National Archives Catalog, https://www.archives.gov/research/catalog (accessed 5 January 2017).

62 Latif Ahmed Sherwani, *Pakistan, China and America*, Karachi: Council for Pakistan Studies, 1980, p. 50.

63 Ibid.

64 'Overseas Loans and Grants: Obligations and Loan Authorizations, July 1, 1945–September 30, 2015', US Agency for International Development Report, Washington, DC: USAID, 2016, p. 145, http://pdf.usaid.gov/pdf_docs/PBAAF100.pdf (accessed on 1 July 2017).

65 Ibid.

66 Nancy Birdsall, Wren Elhai and Molly Kinder, 'Beyond Bullets and Bombs: Fixing the US Approach to Development in Pakistan', Report of the Study Group on a US Development Strategy in Pakistan, Washington, DC: Center for Global Development, July 2011; 'Pakistan: GDP Growth (Annual % Change), 1960-2017', World Development Indicators, The World Bank, https://data.worldbank.org/indicator/NY.GDP.MKTP.KD.ZG?locations=PK (accessed on 13 September 2017) and https://www.cgdev.org/files/1425136_file_CGD_Pakistan_FINAL_web.pdf (accessed on 13 September 2017).

67 Meekal Ahmed, 'An Economic Crisis State?', pp. 170–71.

68 Shahid Javed Burki. *Pakistan: A Nation in the Making*, Karachi: Oxford University Press, 1986, p. 124.

69 'Overseas Loans and Grants: Obligations and Loan Authorizations, July 1, 1945–September 30, 2015', US Agency for International Development Report, Washington, DC: USAID, 2016, p. 145, http://pdf.usaid.gov/pdf_docs/PBAAF100.pdf (accessed on 1 July 2017); World Development Indicators, ' Pakistan: GDP Growth (Annual % Change)', The World Bank *2017 (1960-2017)*.

70 Meekal Ahmed, 'An Economic Crisis State?', pp. 173–74.

71 World Development Indicators 'Pakistan: GDP per Capita % Change', World Bank 2017.

72 'Overseas Loans and Grants: Obligations and Loan Authorizations, July 1, 1945–September 30, 2015,' US Agency for International Development Report, Washington, DC: USAID, 2016, p. 145, http://pdf.usaid.gov/pdf_docs/PBAAF100.pdf (accessed on 2 July 2017).

73 'Pakistan: Transactions with the Fund from May 1, 1984 – August 31, 2017', International Monetary Fund, https://www.imf.org/external/np/fin/tad/extrans1.aspx?memberKey1=760&endDate=2017-09-14&finposition_flag=YES (accessed on 3 July 2017.

74 Meekal Ahmed, 'An Economic Crisis State?', p. 178.

75 Ibid., p. 181.

76 Telegram from American Consulate, Lahore to Secretary of State, 'Views of Air Marshal (Retd) Nur Khan on current situation', 22 December 1971, in Roedad Khan, *American Papers: Secret and Confidential, India, Pakistan, Bangladesh, Documents 1965-1973*, Karachi: Oxford University Press, 1999, pp. 757–58.

77 'Remittances and growth: Gone missing: Why has the growth in remittances not led to growth in GDP?', *The Economist*, 1 August 2014, https://www.economist.com/blogs/freeexchange/2014/08/remittances-and-growth (accessed on 3 July 2017).

78 John Ward Anderson and Kamran Khan, 'Heroin plan by top Pakistanis alleged', *The Washington Post*, 12 September 1994.

79 Huzaima Bukhari and Ikramul Haq, 'Qarz burhao, mulk bigarho', *Business Recorder*, 30 August 2013, http://fp.brecorder.com/2013/08/201308301226398/ (accessed on May 5 2017).

80 Anwar H. Syed, 'Pakistan in 1997: Nawaz Sharif's Second Chance to Govern', *Asian Survey*, Vol. 38, No. 2, February 1998, p. 122.

81 'Money for debt retirement not misused: PML-N', *Dawn*, 30 August 2010.

82 '$70 bn loss suffered in terror war: Zardari', *Dawn*, 31 October 2011.

83 'Need for trade, not aid, Zardari tells visiting US Congressman', *Express Tribune*, 8 November 2011.

84 '"War on terror" has cost Pakistan $118bn: SBP', *Dawn,* AFP, 19 November 2016.

85 Dean Nelson, 'Pakistan does not need western aid, opposition leader claims', *The Telegraph* (UK), 15 August 2010.

86 Drazen Jorgic, 'Pakistan PM warns US sanctions would be counter-productive', Reuters, 11 September 2017.

87 'Shahbaz for end to dependence on aid', *The News* (Pakistan), 5 October 2009.

88 Sune Engel Rasmussen, 'Pakistan must reject US aid and exit the war on terror, says Imran Khan', *The Guardian* (UK), 1 August 2017.

89 Murtaza Haider, 'Can Pakistan survive without US aid?' *Dawn*, 15 February 2012.

90 Ibid.

91 Mohammad Ayub Khan, *Friends Not Masters: A Political Autobiography*, Karachi: Oxford University Press, 1967.

92 Ahmad Saeed, 'Can Pakistan do without foreign economic aid?' *Dawn*, 4 November 2013.

93 Ibid.

94 Ibid.

95 'What Dutch disease is, and why it's bad', *The Economist*, 5 November 2014, https://www.economist.com/blogs/economist-explains/2014/11/economist-explains-2 (accessed on 5 July 2017).

96 Ibid.

97 S. Ehtisham Ahmad and Azizali Mohammad, 'Pakistan, the United States and the IMF: Great game or a curious case of Dutch Disease without the oil?', London School of Economics Asia Research Centre Working Paper 57, 2012, http://www.lse.ac.uk/asiaResearchCentre/_files/ARCWP57-AhmadMohammed.pdf (accessed on 7 July 2017).

98 Ibid.

99 Ibid.

100 Ibid.

101 Christine Lagarde, 'Pakistan and Emerging Markets in World Economy', speech given during Lagarde's visit to Pakistan, 24 October 2016, Islamabad: IMF Pakistan Office, 25 October 2016.

102 International Monetary Fund, 'Lagarde Calls on Pakistan to Build on Progress and Seize Opportunity to Complete Economic Transformation', IMF Press Release No.16/467, Islamabad: IMF Pakistan Office, 25 October 2016.

103 Nadeem Ul Haque, 'The Much needed Space for Growth Reforms', *Pakistan Today*, 26 November 2013, https://www.pakistantoday.com.pk/2011/12/26/the-much-need-space-for-growth-reforms/ (accessed 22 June 2017).

104 Ishrat Husain, *Pakistan: The Economy of an Elitist State*, pp. 338–90.

105 Ahsan Raza, 'With just 4 universities in top 1,000, Pakistan falls in world rankings this year', *Dawn*, 5 September 2017.

106 Muhammad Faisal Kaleem, 'Three Pakistani varsities out of world ranking', *Daily Times* (Pakistan), 6 September 2017, http://dailytimes.com.pk/islamabad/07-Sep-17/three-pakistani-varsities-out-of-world-ranking (accessed on 6 September 2017).

107 Ayesha Jalal, 'Conjuring Pakistan: History as Official Imagining', *International Journal of Middle East Studies*, Vol. 27, No. 1, February 1995, pp. 78–79.

108 Ibid.

109 Ibid.

110 Nadeem Ul Haque, 'The Much-needed Space for Growth Reforms', *Pakistan Today*, 26 November 2013, https://www.pakistantoday.com.pk/2011/12/26/the-much-need-space-for-growth-reforms/ (accessed 22 June 2017).

111 Nadeem Ul Haque, 'Fiscal arithmetic and economy of shortages', *Pakistan Today*, 14 December 2013, https://www.pakistantoday.com.pk/2013/12/14/fiscal-arithmetic-and-economy-of-shortages/ (accessed 22 June 2017).

112 Ibid.

113 Ishrat Husain, *Pakistan: The Economy of an Elitist State*, pp. xii, 344.

114 Ibid., pp. 49–50.

115 Ishrat Husain, 'Retooling Institutions', in Maleeha Lodhi (ed.), *Pakistan: Beyond the Crisis State*, New York: Columbia University Press, 2011, pp. 152, 154.

116 Telegram 2213 from the Embassy in Pakistan to the Department of State, 'GOP suggestion of military collaboration with U.S., including availability of military facilities in Pakistan', 10 March 1972, *Foreign Relations of the United States*, 1969–1976, Volume E–7, Documents on South Asia, 1969–1972, This is an electronic only volume available on the website https://history.state.gov/historicaldocuments/frus1969-76ve07 (accessed on 5 December 2017).

117 'Pakistan: Twelfth and Final Review Under the Extended Arrangement, Request for Waivers of Non-observance of Performance Criteria, and Proposal for Post-Program Monitoring-Press Release; Staff Report; and Statement by the Executive Director for Pakistan', Islamabad: International Monetary Fund, October 2016, https://www.imf.org/en/Publications/CR/Issues/2016/12/31/Pakistan-Twelfth-and-Final-Review-Under-the-Extended-Arrangement-Request-for-Waivers-of-44327 (accessed on 22 August 2017).

118 Ibid.

119 'Pakistan's misguided obsession with infrastructure', *The Economist*, 19 January 2017.

120 Ibid.

8: Avoiding the March of Folly

1 Barbara Tuchman, *The March of Folly: From Troy to Vietnam*, New York: Ballantine Books, 1984, p. 4.

2 Ibid., p. 5.
3 Ibid.
4 Ibid., p. 33.
5 Ibid., p. 25.
6 Irving Janis, *Groupthink: Psychological Studies of Policy Decisions and Fiascoes*, Boston: Wadsworth, 1982, pp. vii, 7–8.
7 Ibid., pp. 71–72.
8 Ibid.
9 Irving Janis, 'Groupthink', in Harold J. Leavitt, Louis R. Pondy and David M. Boje (eds), *Readings in Managerial Psychology*, Chicago: University of Chicago Press, 1989, p. 440.
10 Ibid., p. 441.
11 Ibid., pp. 442–47.
12 Ibid.
13 Ardeshir Cowasjee, 'Gen. Agha Mohammad Yahya Khan,' *Dawn*, 17 September 2000, https://www.dawn.com/news/1072331 (accessed on 1 August 2017).
14 Ibid.
15 Ibid.
16 Barbara Tuchman, *The March of Folly*, pp. 125–26.
17 Ibid., p. 230.
18 See Robert Wirsing, Shahid Javed Burki and Craig Baxter, *Pakistan Under The Military: Eleven Years of Zia-ul-Haq*, Colorado: Westview Press, 1991; Hasan Askari Rizvi, *The Military and Politics in Pakistan*, Lahore: Progressive Publishers, 1974; Robert Wirsing, *Pakistan's Security Under Zia*, New York: Palgrave Macmillan, 1991; Hasan Abbas, *Pakistan's Drift into Extremism: Allah, the Army, and America's War on Terror*, New York: Routledge, 2004; Owen Benett Jones, *Pakistan: Eye of the Storm*, New Haven: Yale University Press, 2003; Roger Long, *A History of Pakistan*, Karachi: Oxford University Press, 2015; Husain Haqqani, *Pakistan between Mosque and Military*, Washington: Carnegie Endowment for International Peace, 2005.
19 Barbara Tuchman, *The March of Folly*, p. 32.
20 Ibid.
21 Robert S. Robins and Jerrold Post, *Political Paranoia: The Psychopolitics of Hatred*, New Haven, CT: Yale University Press, 1997, p. 1.

22 John O. Koehler, *Stasi: The Untold Story of the East German Secret Police*, Boulder, CO: Westview Press, 1999, http://www.nytimes.com/books/first/k/koehler-stasi.html?mcubz=1 (accessed on 1 August 2017).
23 David Satter, *Age of Delirium: The Decline and Fall of the Soviet Union*, New Haven, CT: Yale University Press, 2001, pp. 214–15.
24 Ibid.
25 Aaron Bateman, 'The KGB and Its Enduring Legacy', *The Journal of Slavic Military Studies*, Vol. 29, No. 1, 2 January 2016, pp. 24–25.
26 John O. Koehler, *Stasi: The Untold Story of the East German Secret Police*.
27 Ibid.
28 Andreas Glaeser, 'Power/Knowledge Failure: Epistemic Practices and Ideologies of the Secret Police in Former East Germany', *Social Analysis*, Vol. 47, No. 1, Spring 2003, pp. 4–5.
29 Ibid.
30 Ibid.
31 See Hein Kiessling, *Faith, Unity, Discipline: The Inter-Service-Intelligence (ISI) of Pakistan*, London: Hurst, 2016; Owen Sirrs, *Pakistan's Inter-Services Intelligence Directorate: Covert Action and Internal Operations*, New York: Routledge, 2016; S.K. Datta, *Inside ISI: The Story and Involvement of the ISI in Afghan Jihad, Taliban, Al-Qaeda, 9/11, Osama Bin Laden, 26/11 and the Future of Al-Qaeda*, New Delhi: Vij Books, 2014; Usama Butt, *Pakistan's Elite Secret Service: The ISI, Global Security and the War on Terror*, London: Pluto Press, 2014; Bruce Riedel, *Deadly Embrace: Pakistan, America, and the Future of the Global Jihad*, Washington, DC: Brookings Press, 2011.
32 Seymour Martin Lipset and Gyorgy Bence, 'Anticipations of the Failure of Communism (Scholarly list of those who predicted fall)', *Theory and Society*, Vol. 23, No.2, Special Issue on the Theoretical Implications of the Demise of State Socialism, April 1994, pp. 169–210.
33 Ibid.
34 Ibid.
35 Ibid.
36 Christopher Bennett, *Yugoslavia's Bloody Collapse: Causes, Course and Consequences*, New York: New York University Press, 1995, p. viii.

37 Quoted in ibid., p. 1.
38 Ibid., pp. 5–7.
39 Ibid.
40 Ibid.
41 Vesna Pesic, 'Serbian Nationalism and the Origins of the Yugoslav Crisis', *Peaceworks* No 8, Washington, DC: United States Institute of Peace, 1996, pp. 5–21.
42 Farzana Shaikh, *Making Sense of Pakistan*, New York: Columbia University Press, 2009, pp. 46–66.
43 Mohammed Ayub Khan, 'Pakistan Perspective', *Foreign Affairs*, New York, July 1960, p. 549.
44 Farahnaz Ispahani, *Purifying the Land of the Pure: A History of Pakistan's Religious Minorities*, New Delhi: HarperCollins India, 2015, pp. 57–58.
45 Ibid.
46 Mohammed Hanif, 'Pakistan Has a Drinking Problem', *The New York Times*, 2 December 2016.
47 'Murree with a curry: alcohol sales boom in "teetotalitarian" Pakistan', AFP, 12 September 2016.
48 Charles Haviland, 'Pakistan battles growing alcohol addiction', BBC News, 16 September 2013.
49 M.A. Abdullah and B.T. Shaikh, 'Confusion and denial: need for systems thinking to understand the HIV epidemic in Pakistan', *Journal of Ayub Medical College Abbottabad*, Vol. 26, No. 3, July–September 2014, pp. 396–400.
50 Husain Haqqani, *India v Pakistan: Why Can't We Just be Friends?*, New Delhi: Juggernaut, 2016, p. 159.
51 Ayesha Jalal, 'Conjuring Pakistan: History as official imagining', *International Journal of Middle East Studies*, Vol. 27, No. 1, 1995, pp. 73–74.
52 Stephen Cohen, *The Idea of Pakistan*, Washington, DC: Brookings Press, 2004, p. 203.
53 Ibid.
54 Ibid.
55 Ibid., p 205.
56 Ibid., quoting Akbar S. Ahmed, *Jinnah, Pakistan and Islamic Identity: The Search for Saladin*, London: Routledge, 1997, p. 236.
57 Ibid., quoting Owen Bennett-Jones, *Pakistan: Eye of the Storm*, New Haven, CT: Yale University Press, 2002, p. 110.

58 Ibid., p. 206.
59 Ibid., p. 206.
60 Ayesha Jalal, 'Conjuring Pakistan', p. 77.
61 Ibid.
62 Ibid.
63 'Belgium: World Bank Data', https://data.worldbank.org/country/Belgium (accessed on 17 December 2017); 'France: World Bank Data', https://data.worldbank.org/country/france (accessed on 17 December 2017).
64 'Netherlands: World Bank Data', https://data.worldbank.org/country/netherlands (accessed on 17 December 2017).
65 David Williams, *Japan: Beyond the End of History*, Tokyo: Routledge, 1994, pp. 135–36.
66 Ibid.
67 Ibid.
68 Greg Rienzi, 'Other nations could learn from Germany's efforts to reconcile after WWII', *Johns Hopkins Magazine*, Johns Hopkins University, 2008.
69 Victor Sebestyen, 'Exorcising Hitler: The Occupation and Denazification of Germany by Frederick Taylor – review', *The Guardian* (UK), 23 April 2011.
70 Joshua Kurlantzick, 'After Deng: On China's Transformation', *The Nation*, 17 October 2011, https://www.thenation.com/article/after-deng-chinas-transformation/ (accessed on 1 July 2017).
71 A. Doak Barnett, 'Ten Years After Mao,' *Foreign Affairs*, Fall 1986, https://www.foreignaffairs.com/articles/asia/1986-09-01/ten-years-after-mao (accessed on 1 August 2017).
72 Catherine H. Keyser, 'Deng Xiaoping,' Weatherhead East Asian Institute at Columbia University: *Asia for Educators*, http://afe.easia.columbia.edu/special/china_1950_leaders.htm (accessed on 1 August 2017).
73 Sophia Yan, 'Trade has turned China and Taiwan into "frenemies"', CNN, 5 November 2015, http://money.cnn.com/2015/11/05/news/china-taiwan-trade-economy/index.html (accessed on 17 December 2017); 'The People's Republic of China: Trade Facts', United States Trade Representative, https://ustr.gov/countries-regions/china-mongolia-taiwan/peoples-republic-china (accessed 17 December 2017).

Index

Abbasi, Maj. Gen. Zaheerul Islam, 151, 152
Abbasi, Shahid Khaqan, 228
Abbasids, 106, 134
Abbottabad raid by United States, 112, 159, 172–73
Abdullah, Sheikh, 49
accession of princely states, 48–49
adultery (Zina laws), 100
Afghan refugees in Pakistan, 153, 191
Afghanistan, 2, 62, 157, 163, 185, 194, 203, 267, 270, 277
  jihadi militants, 112, 133–36, 139–45, 151, 175, 254
  mujahideen factions, 191
  NATO forces, 138
  Pakistan's policies, role in war, 3, 13, 60, 114–15, 132, 190–93, 220, 223, 247
  support for Pashtun independence, 190
  Soviet occupation, 29
    withdrawal, 232
    anti-Soviet war, 76, 100, 134, 156, 191, 218
    United States' intervention after 9/11, 29, 138–40, 192, 220, 227
agricultural production in Pakistan, 30, 202, 216
Ahmad, Mirza Ghulam, 81
Ahmadi issue, anti-Ahmadi riots, 56–57, 80–83, 84, 97–98, 100, 111, 118, 150, 265–66
Ahmed, Khaled, 151, 267
Ahmed, Mahmud, 177
Ahmed, Meekal, 203, 214–15, 221–22
Ahsan, Syed Muhammad, 92, 251–52
Aid to Pakistan Consortium (Paris Club), 220, 222
Akbar, Mughal emperor, 237
Albright, Madeline, 4–5
alcoholism in Pakistan, 266
Ali, Chaudhri Muhammad, 45, 208, 212
Ali, Mahmud, 154–55
Ali, Mir Laik, 210
Ali, Mubarak, 53
Aligarh Muslim University, 68, 129
Allana, Ghulam Ali, 30–31
All-India Muslim League, 7–8, 23, 27, 33–35, 38–40, 42–46, 47–49, 57, 66–68, 75, 77, 150, 160, 206–09, 250, 264
  Lahore Resolution, 270–71
al-Baghdadi, Abu Bakr, 135, 140–44
al-Banna, Hasan, 40
al-Hindi, Maulvi Abdul Rehman, 142
al-Husseini, Al-Haj Amin, Grand Mufti of Palestine, 40, 73, 132, 139, 141
al-Isabah, 142–43

al-Kanadi, Abdul Rahman, 140
al-Kuwaiti, Zubeir, 144
al-Qaeda, 133–35, 138–42, 144–45, 192, 172
al-Qaeda in the Indian Subcontinent (AQIS), 141, 144–45
al-Turkistani, Abu Muhammad, 140
al-Wafa Foundation for Media Production, 143
al-Zawahiri, Ayman, 140–42, 144–45, 151
American war of independence, 252
Andarabi, Asiya, 140
Anderson, Benedict, *Imagined Communities*, 59
Ansar al-Tawhid al-Hind (Supporters of Monotheism in India), 142
Arab Muslim Brotherhood, 73, 75
Arabic language, 72–73
Arabs, 26, 54, 107, 135, 138, 236
Art of Living Foundation, 127
Aryo-Dravidian race, 36–37
Asad, Muhammad, 74–75
Ashmawy, Sheikh Saleh, 73
Ashraf, Sheikh Muhammad, 35
Asia Bibi, 65
Asian Development Bank, 213, 226
Asif, Khawaja, 183
Association of South-East Asian Nations (ASEAN), 268
Atlee, Clement, 24
Aurangzeb, 237
Austro-Hungarian empire, 256, 274
authoritarianism, 116, 123
Awami League, 90, 92–93, 251
Azzam, Mufti Abuzar, 140
Azad Kashmir, 184
Azad, Abul Kalam, 8
Aziz, K.K., 207
Aziz, Lt Gen. Shahid, 151–52

Baghdad Pact, 113, 220
Bahria (Navy) housing projects, 195
Bajwa, Qamar Javed, 13–14, 179
balance-of-payments crisis, 243
Balochistan, 16, 17, 26, 33, 68, 90, 148, 171, 195–96, 259
Balochs, 53, 96, 106, 157–58, 269, 270, 271
  ethnic nationalism, 159, 254, 264
Bangladesh (East Pakistan), 1, 21, 28, 31, 51, 54, 59, 200, 214, 241, 243, 252–53, 267
  economy and population control, 22
  formation of (Bangladesh war), 92–95, 96, 107, 110, 117, 126–27, 147, 157, 159, 270
  Mukti Bahini (Liberation army), 93, 94
  Surrender of Pakistan army to the joint forces of India and Bangladesh, 51, 94
banking system, 29
Barelvis, 104, 105
Barkley, Alben S., 1
Beblawi, Hazem, 217
Beg, Aslam, 121, 162, 178, 190, 225
Belgium, 273–75
Bell, David, 213
Bengali Muslims, 36, 37, 93
Bengalis, 36, 92, 123, 271
Bhutan, 139, 267
Bhutto, Benazir, 110–11, 121, 146, 155, 157–58, 222
Bhutto, Zulfiqar Ali, xiii, 51, 90–91, 95–100, 118–19, 124–27, 130, 157, 195, 215, 222–23, 228, 253–54, 270
Bin Laden, Osama, 2, 60, 112, 138–41, 159, 172, 191
bin Maryam, Isa, 136
blasphemy, 63–65, 100, 102–05, 109, 119
Blood, Archer, 93
Bogra, Muhammad Ali, 219
Boundary Commission, 41
Bretton Woods system, 226
British
  divide-and-rule politics, 269
  Indian armed forces, 43, 161
  Indian Army, 45, 85, 160, 161, 162

military system, 163–64
British Commonwealth of Nations, 24
Brzezinski, Zbigniew, 260
bureaucracy, 26, 55, 59, 166, 167
Burki, Shahid Javed, 28, 207, 221

Caliphate and Jihad Movement, 143, 144
capitalism, 75, 78
caste exclusionism and untouchability of the orthodox Aryo-Dravidian Hindu, 36
Cawthorne, Maj. Gen. Robert, 162
Central Institute for Islamic Research, 87
Central Treaty Organization (CENTO), 113, 220
Chagai nuclear tests (1998), 195
Cheema, Umar, 174
China, 4, 114–15, 126, 141, 142, 159, 200, 220, 217, 226, 236, 275, 278
economy, 223, 276
India relations, 185, 267, 277
conflict (1962), 10, 124, 185
support for Pakistan, 55, 60, 61, 90, 185, 226, 240–43, 272
China-Pakistan Economic Corridor (CPEC), 240–42
Chinese Communist party, 114
civil-military relations, 168
Coalition Support Funds, 220
cold war, 26, 56, 113, 162, 186, 187, 218, 244, 262, 272
command and control system, 187
communal riots on eve of Partition, 27, 31
communication links, 29
communism, 56, 75, 218, 219, 257
conspiracism, conspiracy theories, 146–59, 201
Constantinople, 132–33
Constituent Assembly, 23, 40, 44, 57, 58, 67–69, 71–72, 78–79, 82, 91, 120
Constitution of Pakistan (1962), 86, 101, 165
corruption, 5, 63, 149, 177, 195, 200, 214, 231, 267
Council of Islamic Ideology (CII), 103
court system, 116–19
creation of Pakistan, xiii, 5–8, 9, 22, 24, 26, 30, 33, 35, 37–38, 50, 52–53, 56, 58, 60, 65, 69, 89, 101, 107, 111, 122, 125, 129, 131, 150, 163–64, 202, 206–07, 213, 246, 264, 269, 271
current account deficit, 242

Darul Uloom Deoband, 67, 79, 137, 138
Daulat, Hafiz Quran, 143
Daulatana, Mumtaz, 81
Defence Housing Authorities, 178, 195
demographic profile of Pakistan, 18, 20, 33–34, 273
Deng Xiaoping, 275–76
Despres, Emile, 213
Devji, Faisal, 66
Dhaka Stock Exchange, 15
Dhulipala, Venkat, 66
dismemberment, 89–95
domestic resource mobilization, 232
drinking water and sanitation in Pakistan, 20–21
Dulles, John Foster, 219
Duncan, Emma, 154
Durand Line, 190
Durrani, Asad, 225
Durrani, Fazal Karim Khan, 37–38

East and West Pakistan. *See also* Bangladesh
estrangement and war, 89, 92–95
power equation, 70, 84
economic development, 20, 86–87, 193, 213, 231, 238, 241
economic disparities between rich and poor, 17
economic system, 22, 78, 207
economy, 18, 29, 30–31, 60, 199–208, 212–16, 267, 275

rent seeking and Dutch disease, 216–33
education, 116, 235–37, 243, 247
Egypt, 73, 141
Muslim Brotherhood, 40
Eisenhower, Dwight D., 219
energy crisis, 231
entrepreneurship, 201, 204–05, 237, 276
Erikson, Erik, 66
ethnic groups, identities, 6, 7, 32, 37, 53, 59–60, 86, 168, 246, 256, 259–60, 263, 271
ethnolinguistic differences, 269–72
nationalism, 54, 60, 107
rights, 55
European Renaissance, 252
European Union, 227, 268, 274

Family planning, 88
Farland, Joseph, 51
Fazlullah, Mullah, 139
Federal Board of Revenue, 230
Feldman, Herbert, 91
film industry in Pakistan, 170–71
folly and obstinacy, 244–78
foreign currency deposits (FCDs) scheme, 224
Foreign Direct Investment (FDI), 242
foreign journalists in Pakistan, 10–13
foreign policy, 74, 86, 146, 206, 221
Fragile States Index (formerly Failed States Index), 20
fragility, control and resilience, 254–64

Gall, Cartlotta, 12, 175
Gandhi, Indira, 126
Gandhi, Mohandas Karamchand, 23, 34
Ganges Valley, 36–37
Gauba, K.L., 8
Gauhar, Altaf, 84
geo-strategic relevance of Pakistan, 19
German Democratic Republic (GDR), 260
Germany, 114, 189, 231, 245, 274
post-war transformation, 274, 276
Gestapo, 258–59
Ghafoor, Asif, 105, 179
Ghani, Ashraf, 115, 192
Ghazwa-e-Hind Hadith, 132, 135–42, 145–46
Ghulam Muhammad, Malik, 209–11, 217, 218, 219
Glancy, Sir, Bertrand, 67–68
global community of Muslims, 66
Global Connectedness Index, 19
global imagination about Pakistan, 1–2
Goldilocks dilemma, 186
Gorbachev, Mikhail, 260–61
Government Officers' Residences (GOR), 238–39
Greece, 210, 262
debt crisis, 114
gross domestic product (GDP) of Pakistan, 18, 19, 202–04, 234
'Groupthink', 248–50, 254
Gul, Hamid, 151, 152, 162
Gwadar, 241

Habib, Habibullah, 143
Hamid, Syed Zaid, 132–33, 137, 154, 190
Hamood-ur-Rahman Inquiry Commission, 251–52
Hamza, El, *Pakistan, A Nation*, 35–36, 37, 206
Hanif, Mohammed, 64
Hanson, Lionel, 213
Hapsburg Empire, 263
Haq, A.K. Fazlul, 156
Haq, Mahbub-ul-, 240
Haq, Zia-ul-, xiii, 54, 75–76, 99–102, 104, 110, 116, 118, 121, 127, 151, 157, 178, 191, 215, 217, 220–23, 229, 254, 270
Haqqani Network, 2, 151
Haqqani, Mufti Ghulam Farid, 131–32
Haque, Nadeem Ul, 201, 234–35, 237–39
Hare, Raymond, 41

Hari Singh, Maharaja of Kashmir, 49
Hasan, Mubashir, 97
Hassan, Mufti, 143
healthcare expenditure in Pakistan, 18
Hekmatyar, Gulbuddin, 191
High Frequency Active Auroral Research Program (HAARP), 153, 154
Hindus, Hinduism in India, xiii, xiv, 21, 22, 25, 31, 36, 49, 54, 101, 107, 128–30, 141, 145, 160, 211, 212, 236, 272
Hindu–Muslim relations, x, 8, 31, 34–41, 57, 69–70, 89, 101, 104, 109, 116, 122, 124–25, 128, 130–32, 136–37, 141, 145, 147, 150, 152, 155–57, 206, 208–09, 253, 271, 273
Hindus and Sikhs in Pakistan, 31, 35, 37, 40, 57, 93, 107
Hirohito, Emperor of Japan, 275
history, falsification of, 244
history and Pakistan, 4, 5, 9, 11, 14, 22, 25, 26, 29, 31, 38, 46, 50, 53, 59, 60, 65, 66, 67, 69, 80, 88–89, 106–08, 113, 118, 122–25, 130, 148, 156, 159, 164, 168, 190, 199, 204, 207, 213, 217, 226, 237, 241, 244, 250, 266, 272–75
Hitler, Adolf, 189
honour killings, 14, 102, 116
Hudood Ordinance, 1979, 100
Human Development Index, 19, 240
human flight and brain drain, 20
human rights and 'rule of law' in Pakistan, 13, 20, 29, 170, 179
Husain, Ishrat, 17, 29–30, 32, 204, 216, 235, 239
Hussain, Raja Khadim, 91

Ibrahim, Dawood, 195
ideological confusion, 83
ideological dysfunction, 63–95, 264
ideological indoctrination, 116, 237
ideological nationalism, 52, 62, 269
ideology of Pakistan, 22, 40, 53, 55, 61, 96, 101, 107, 116–17, 154, 265–66, 268, 272
Ijtihad, 78–79
Ilmuddin, 109
image and reality, 14–32
Income Support Programme, 233
India, 25, 27, 43, 101, 240, 269–70
  China, relations, 10, 90, 124, 267, 277
  Cold Start, 186
  diversity, 24–25
  economic development, 208–10
  higher education, 236
  Hindutva movement, 107, 128–29, 272
  literacy rate, 16
  pre-independence, British India, xiv, 1, 5–8, 36–40, 40–43, 46, 47–49, 113, 209, 239, 260, 264
  support for Pashtun independence, 190
  skill development, 19
  hegemony in South Asia, 260
  tax collection and GDP, 203
  United States, relations, 10, 185
India and Pakistan: conflict, hostile relations, x, xiii, xiv, 2, 13, 21–22, 29, 32, 36, 46, 48, 53–60, 62, 74, 88–89, 90–92, 95, 97, 106–08, 113–15, 117, 121–46, 146–59, 161–64, 166, 170–71, 175, 179, 180–88, 188–97, 199, 201, 205–07, 211, 218, 220, 235, 243, 247, 253, 265, 267–68, 270–72, 275
  war, 1947–48, 49, 50
  war 1965, xi, 87, 124, 159, 176–77, 191, 223, 229, 250
  war 1971, 51, 92–94, 176, 191, 251
Indian National Congress, 33, 34, 42, 47, 208, 209, 264
Indian Muslims, 8, 23, 141–42, 145, 269–70
Indus Valley, 36–37
Indus Waters Treaty, 127–28
Industrial Development Bank of Pakistan (IDBP), 214

Industrial Policy Document (1948), 212
industrialization, 84, 202, 206, 208, 212–13
infrastructure
  of roads, 29
  underused, 242–43
Innocence of Muslims, 111
insecurity, 5, 29, 52, 58, 61–62, 121–59, 168, 188, 194–95, 197, 200, 241
Intelligence Bureau (IB), 146
international assistance, 2, 11, 13, 19, 31, 60–61, 84, 114, 204–06, 210, 212, 217–23, 226–33
international community, 19, 115, 179, 181, 185, 227, 277
International Cricket Council (ICC), 179
international discourse on Pakistan, 4, 228
international financial institutions (IFIs), 201, 212, 226
International Monetary Fund (IMF), 152, 201, 203, 215, 220–24, 226, 227, 232, 233, 242
Inter-Services Intelligence (ISI), 12, 101, 132, 136, 146, 150, 152, 162, 169, 171–75, 177, 225, 257, 259
Inter-Services Public Relations (ISPR), 105, 169–71, 175
'Invulnerability', 249
Iqbal, Afzal, 39
Iqbal, Muahammad, 79
Islam, x, xiv, 8, 9, 36–40, 51, 54–59, 63–64
  Pakistan, a laboratory of, 65–71
  sects, 57
Islamic, Islamist
  concept of 'Ijma' (consensus), 78
  empires, 106
  enterprise, secular management, 77–84
  extremists/terrorists, 7, 15, 56, 61–62, 246
  fundamentalism, 8
  ideology and economic development, 86–87
  integrity for Pakistan, 94
  law, 70, 78–79, 101–03
  nationalism, 22, 37, 60, 84–89
  orthodoxy, 255
  radical ideology, 32, 53–54, 59–62
  rage, 96–120
  Socialism, 77–78, 90
Islamic Movement of Uzbekistan (IMU), 139–40
Islamic State of Iraq and al-Sham (ISIS), 133–35, 139, 140–45
Islamization, xiii, 56, 76, 97, 99–100, 102–03, 117, 121, 254, 255
Israel, 122, 133
  do not support Pakistan's nuclear programme, 182
Ittehad-e-Tanzeemat-e-Madaris, 76

Jahangir, Asma, 170
Jalal, Ayesha, 6–7, 39, 52, 236, 272
Jamaat-e-Islami (JI), 75, 79, 87, 90, 110, 138, 266
Jamaat-ul-Ahrar, 139
Jamia Hafsa Urdu Forum (JHUF), 140
Jamiat Ulema Islam (JUI), 67, 79, 90
Jamiat Ulema Pakistan (JUP), 90
Jamiat ul-Ulema-i Hind, 138
Jammu and Kashmir, 126
  Pakistan claim over, 48–50, 148, 247
Jan, Taher, 140
Japan, 114, 236, 245
  economy, 231
  post-war transformation 275–76
Jiang Zemin, 115
Jihad Fi Sabeelillah, 99
jihadi terrorism, jihadi terrorist groups, 2–3, 4–5, 12, 28, 56, 60, 62, 76, 95, 100, 112, 115, 121–59, 173, 175, 176, 186, 226, 228, 231, 243, 247–48, 254, 273, 277
  sponsorship of, 2–3, 4, 12–13, 60, 130, 134, 181, 184, 194

Jinnah, Muhammad Ali, xiii, 6–10, 13, 23–24, 25, 26, 32, 33–35, 39–42, 43–44, 45–46–48, 50, 53, 56, 58, 63, 67–68, 69–70, 79, 82, 85, 109, 120, 123–24, 156, 205, 208, 210–11, 217–18, 269–70
Junagadh, 124
Jundallah (Soldiers of Allah), 144

Kalabagh Dam project, 171
Karachi Capital Area, 45
Karachi Chamber of Commerce and Industry, 230
Karachi Stock Exchange, 15
Karamat, Jehangir, 166
Kargil conflict (1999), 176, 254
Karzai, Hamid, 115
Kashmir: infiltration and Pakistan-backed insurgency, Kashmir dispute, 114–15, 124, 126, 134, 136, 138, 139, 145, 166, 181–82, 184, 194, 199, 209, 235, 250, 254, 268, 275
Kayani, Ashfaq Parvez, 172
Khan, A.Q., 195
Khan, Akbar, 164
Khan, Asghar, 250
Khan, Ayub, xi, 37, 54, 84–89, 91, 100, 156–57, 165, 167, 204, 213, 217, 220–23, 226, 229–30, 250, 265, 270
Khan, Chaudhry Nisar Ali, 143
Khan, Chaudhri Zafrullah, 81, 219
Khan, Feroz, 180, 187
Khan, Ghulam Ishaq, 157
Khan, Hafiz Saeed (Mullah Saeed Orakzai), 143
Khan, Hamid Nawaz, 182–83
Khan, Imran, 168, 176, 195, 228–29
Khan, Nawab Ismail, 66
Khan, Jahan Dad, 99
Khan, Liaquat Ali, x, 1, 43, 44, 50, 54, 68, 70, 71–72, 75, 77–81, 85, 90, 100, 147, 159, 163–64, 206, 209–11, 217–18, 269
Khan, Mashal, 63–65
Khan, Nur, 223, 250
Khan, Rana Sanullah, 174
Khan, Sahibzada Yaqub, 251
Khan, Sher Ali, 167
Khan, Tamizuddin, 78
Khan, Yahya, xi, 75, 89–91, 94–95, 100, 110, 144, 165, 167, 178, 251, 270
Khomeini, Ayatollah Ruhollah, 75, 189
Khorasan Group, 143
Khurasan, 134, 135, 136, 139, 140, 142, 143
Khurasan Hadith, 134
Khyber Pakhtunkhwa. *See* North-West Frontier Province (NWFP)
Kidwai, Khalid, 183–84
Kissinger, Henry, 92
Korean boom, 212
Korean War, 212, 218, 248

Lagarde, Christine, 233–34
Lahore Literary Festival, 32
language riots, 80
Lashkar-e-Taiba (LeT), 2, 103, 128, 136
Latif, Syed Abdul, 8
life expectancy in Pakistan, 16
Lijian Zhao, 243
Line of Control (LOC), 126, 184
Lipset, Seymour Martin, 260
Listowel, Lord, 24
literacy rate in Pakistan, 16–17
Lodhi, Maleeha, 28–29, 31, 32

Maalik, 171
Macdonald, John J., 23
madrasas, 67, 76, 87
Mahmood, Bashiruddin, 77
Mahmudabad, raja of, 68
Maldives, 139, 140, 144, 267
Mallon, Richard, 213
Manavadar, 124
Mansergh, Nicholas, 42
Mansha, Muhammad, 199
Mansoor, Khalid, 143
Mao Zedong, 275, 276
Martial Law, 93
Maududi, Maulana Syed Abul Ala, 61, 75, 79, 86, 87, 266

Maulvis and Pirs, 67–68
Mazhari, Maulana Waris, 137–38
McGhee, George, 211
Mecca, 73, 110, 134–35, 179
media, role in shaping Pakistan's narrative, 179
Medina, 67, 135
Mehsud, Baitullah, 140
Mehsud, Hakeemullah, 172
Metallurgical Corporation of China (MCC), 196
Middle East Media Research Institute (MEMRI), 154
Middle East, 9, 25, 28, 41, 62, 73, 135, 139, 147, 154, 189, 190, 210, 219, 241, 255, 262
Middle East and the Indian Ocean region, 241
militarism and militancy, 32, 108, 113, 251, 273
military, controlling the flow of information and ideas, 172–76
military coups, 2, 84, 99, 157–59, 164–65, 215
Military Intelligence (MI), 12, 146, 151
military operations in Karachi, 159
'Mindguards', 249
minority communities in Pakistan, 69–70. *See also* Hindus and Sikhs
misgovernance, 245–46
mismanagement, maladministration and corruption, 177, 231
Modi, Narendra, 130
Mohammad, Agha, 167
Mohammed, Azizali, 231
Mongols, 107
'Morality', 249
Morgenthau, Hans J., 25
Motamar al-Alam al-Islami (Muslim World Congress), 73
Mountbatten, Lord Louis, 41–44, 47–48
Muhajir ethnic nationalism, 168, 254
Muhajir–Punjabi nexus, 271
Muhajirs, 37, 158, 246, 269, 271
Muhammad, Prophet, 65, 67–68, 99, 103–04, 108–12, 119, 131–39, 141, 144, 207, 225, 265, 269
Mujahideen in Khurasan, 139
Mumbai Stock Exchange bombings (1993), 195
Mumbai terrorists' attacks (2008), 2, 4
Munir Commission, 82, 118, 265–66
Munir, Justice Muhammad, 82–83, 84, 97, 101, 265
Musa, Muhammad, 194
Musharraf, Pervez, 102, 104, 121, 138, 151, 158, 168, 174–75, 177–78, 192, 217, 220, 222–23, 227, 229
Muslim family law, 88
Muslim League, 52, 73, 79–81, 83, 89–90, 98, 219
Muslims and non-Muslims, incompatibility, 107
Muslims of Indian subcontinent, xiv, 5–9, 30, 31, 33–39, 44, 57, 66, 107, 125, 250, 253, 265, 271–72
Muttahida Qaumi Movement (MQM), 168

Nadwatul Ulema, Lucknow, 67
Naidu, Sarojini, 24
Nasir, Javed, 162
Nasr missile, 186
national belief system, 32
National Command Authority (NCA), 187
National Security Council, 3, 97
national security theology, 130–46
nationalism, xiv, 37, 61, 66, 70, 84, 91, 106, 122–24, 126, 148, 180, 183, 234, 265, 267, 272
nationalization of industries, 215
Nawaz, Asif, 164, 166
Nawaz, Shuja, 32, 162–64, 166
Nazimuddin, Khawaja, 81, 97, 118
Nehru, Jawaharlal, 129–30, 211
Nepal, 17, 19, 139, 267
Nevard, Jacques, 10–12
Niazi, Maulana Abdul Sattar, 39, 110–11

Niazi, Maulana Kausar, 110
Nichols, Beverly, 8
Nizam-e-Islam Party (Party for Islamic System), 209
Nizami, Majeed, 182–83
Noon, Firoz Khan, 68
North American Free Trade Agreement (NAFTA), 268
North Atlantic Treaty Organization (NATO), 2, 186–87, 274
    Warsaw Pact confrontation, 186
North Korea, 18, 150, 159
North-West Frontier Province (NWFP), 33, 63, 68, 90, 171
nuclear non-proliferation, 13
Nuclear Suppliers Group (NSG), 13, 185
nuclear weapon programme, 61, 180–88, 244
    tactical nuclear weapons (TNWs), 186–88
Numani, Maulana Abdul Hamid, 138

objectives of state, 71–77
Objectives Resolution, 70, 71–72, 75, 77, 80, 98
Okara Military Farms, 178–79
Olympics, 1992, 103
One Belt One Road (OBOR), 241
Operation Blitz, 92
Ottomans, 106, 263

Pakistan Air Force, 26, 223
Pakistan Army, 26, 32, 82, 87, 92–94, 99, 104, 110, 126, 131, 145, 155, 162, 164–65, 174, 177, 193–94
    role as back-seat driver, 168–79
    surrender of Pakistan army to the joint forces of India and Bangladesh, 51, 94
Pakistan Between Mosque and Military, 51, 55
Pakistan Council of Research in Water Resources (PCRWR), 20
Pakistan Industrial Credit and Investment Corporation (PICIC), 214
Pakistan Industrial Development Corporation (PIDC), 213
Pakistan International Airlines (PIA), 235, 237
Pakistan Military Academy (PMA), 162
Pakistan Muslim League-N, 105
Pakistan National Alliance (PNA), 98–99
Pakistan Peoples Party (PPP), 90, 97–99, 151, 157
Pakistan Steel, 235
Pakistan Tehreek-e-Insaf (PTI), 168
Pakistani Taliban, 172
Panama Papers, 158
Papanek, Gustav, 213
paranoid state, paranoid syndrome, 152, 182, 188–98, 257, 273
Partition Council, 41, 47
Partition of Indian subcontinent, 5, 9–10, 24, 27, 34, 36, 44, 47, 58, 60, 66, 75, 129, 181, 209, 250, 268–69
Pasha, Ahmad Shuja, 172
Pashtun nationalism, 190–91, 246, 264
Pashtun tribal raiders in Kashmir, 46, 49, 50, 155
Pashtunistan, Afghanistan's rhetorical support, 191
Pashtuns, 53, 96, 157, 158, 269, 270, 271
Pathans, 40, 163, 164, 270
Philips, William, 40
Planning Commission, India, 208
Planning Commission, Pakistan, 204, 213
Poland, 22
politics, ix, xiii, 22, 54, 57, 82, 168, 189, 191, 206, 231, 253–54
    of intolerance and hatred, 106
    military intervention, xi, 165–66, 177, 247
    religion and, xv, 54, 77, 80, 96
population, 18–20, 22, 25, 28,

33–34, 37, 60, 70, 79, 104, 107, 180, 202–03, 216–17, 231, 253
over-population, 88
poverty, 8, 14, 16, 17, 20, 29–30, 204, 205, 228, 267
power shortages in Pakistan, 117
presidential system, 86
Pressler Amendment, 222, 224
Prime Minister's National Debt Retirement Programme, 225
princely states, 48–49
prisoners of war (POWs), 126
privatization, 215, 235, 239
productive future, 233–43
Public Law 480, 220–21
public services, 238
Punjab National Bank (PNB), 31
Punjabi Muslims, 59, 60
Punjabis, 59, 96, 106, 107, 164, 259, 269, 270, 271
Punjabi–Muhajir Establishment, 271
purchasing power parity (PPP), 18

Qadri, Mumtaz, 65, 104, 119. *See also* Taseer, Salmaan
Qasim, Mufti Sajid, 138
Qasim, Muhammad bin, 236
Qisas and Diyat (Retribution and Compensation) Ordinance, 102
Quaid-i-Azam University (QAU), 235
Quality of Nationality Index (QNI), 20
Qureshi, Ishtiaq Husain, x, 71–72, 78
Qureshi, Moeen, 226

Rabbani, Raza, 12–13
Rahman, Fazlur, 87
Rahman, Justice S.A., 79
Rahman, Shaikh Mujibur, 90–92, 95
Rajpal, 109
Rangeela Rasool (Colorful Prophet), 109
Ranjit Singh, Maharaja of Punjab, 45
Rashid, Ahmed, xii, 175
'Rationale', 249
Rawalpindi Conspiracy, 164
refugees and IDPs [internally displaced persons], 20
regional autonomy, 55, 250
regional disparities, 215
Reko Diq, Balochistan, 195–96, 235
Religious
absurdity, 28
bias, 116
differences, strife, x, 34, 36, 39, 56, 58, 63–70, 80, 109–10, 112, 118–20, 131, 142, 146, 150, 185, 207, 274
education, 99
extortions, 84
extremism, militancy, 5, 7, 18, 100, 113
fanaticism, 8, 25, 74–79, 106
identity, 37, 250
ideology, 253, 265
minorities, 2, 29, 31, 34, 156, 266
nationalism, 6, 7, 55, 57, 60, 70, 108, 133, 155, 267, 268
oligarchy, 216
pluralism, 32
politics, 54, 80–82, 86, 89, 96, 98, 102–05, 111, 195
rent seeking and Dutch disease, 216–33
Research and Analysis Wing (RAW), 92
Reserve Bank of India (RBI), 46, 209
Rizvi, Khadim Hussain, 104–06
Roman Empire, 125, 135, 245
Rome and Carthage, rivalry, 125
Roosevelt, Franklin, 40
Ruet-i-Hilal (Sighting of the Moon) Committee, 87
Rushbrook, L.F., 50, 51
Rushdie, Salman, 59, 110–11

Saeed, Hafiz Muhammad, 128, 136–37
Safavids, 106
Salahuddin, Syed, 128
Sandelvi, Muhammad Ishaq, 67
Sarwar, Samia, 102
Sattar, Abdus, 27, 73, 122, 169

supported Taliban government in Afghanistan, 192
Sayeed, Khalid Bin, 70, 160
Schanberg, Sydney, 93
sectarian divisions/strife, x, 54–57, 66, 76, 108, 118
secularism, 61, 70, 101, 120, 250
Sen, Amartya, 240
sense of self, 4–14
Seraiki nationalism, 246
Shafi, Kamran, 174
Shah, Mahmud, 179
Shahbaz, 228
Shahid, Shahidullah, 143
Shaikh al-Islam, 79
Shaikh, Farzana, 65, 265
Shankar, Sri Sri Ravi, 127
Sharia/ shariyat, 8, 76, 78, 99–100, 102–03, 139–40, 145, 151
Sharif, Nawaz, 103–4, 119, 121, 146, 152, 157, 168–69, 195, 196, 222–25, 227-28
Sharif, Raheel, 40, 119, 130, 168–71, 177
Shehzad, Syed Saleem, 172–73, 175
Shia Muslims, 56–57, 122
Shoaib, Muhammad, 226
Siddiqa, Ayesha, 170
Siddiqui, Aslam, 123
Sihah Sitta, 137
Simla Accord, 126
Sindh, 16, 17, 33, 68, 90, 171, 259
invasion by Arabs, 138
Sindhi ethnic nationalism, Sindhis, 36, 53, 158, 246, 254, 264, 269, 270, 271
Sirhindi, Shaikh Ahmed, 237
social media, 63, 65, 109, 147, 155, 158, 168–69, 175–76, 241
Solomon, King, 77
South Asian region, 267–68
South-East Asia Treaty Organization (SEATO), 220
Soviet Union, 29, 126
Committee for State Security (KGB), 257–58, 259
disintegration, 52, 216, 232, 256, 257, 260–62
Nazi invasion of, 244
did not support Pakistan's nuclear programme, 182
totalitarianism, 257, 258, 259.
Sri Lanka, 19, 139, 140, 145, 203, 267
Stalin, 189, 259
Standstill Agreement, 49
Stasi, 258–59
State Bank of Pakistan, 48
state failure/failed state, x, xiii, xv, 4, 9, , 15–16, 19–20, 23, 30, 32, 50, 52, 60, 62, 82, 84, 148–50, 154, 161–65, 176, 201–02, 204, 231–32, 243–44, 247, 254–55, 266, 275
Stephens, Ian, 61
'Stereotypes', 249, 250
stock market in Pakistan, 15, 202, 222, 243
strategic environment of Pakistan, 194
Sufism, Sufis, 104, 255
Suhrawardy, Huseyn Shaheed, 5, 57–58, 70, 86, 90, 113, 156, 160, 250
Sunni Muslims, clerics, 67, 78–79, 81, 103, 119, 122, 137
Syed, Anwar, 97
Syed, Azaz, 174

Taliban, 2, 12, 103, 115, 134–35, 138, 191–92, 223
Taseer, Salmaan, 65, 104, 119
Tehrik-e-Labaik-Ya-Rasoolullah (TLYR), 104–05
Tehrik-e-Takmeel-e-Pakistan, 155
Tehrik-e-Taliban Pakistan (TTP), 139, 143, 145
television news in Pakistan, 201
terrorism and insurgency. *See* jihadi terrorism
Tethyan Copper Company (TCC), 196
Thanvi, Maulana Ehtisham-ul-Haq, 79
Thawban, 135
theo-democracy, 75
Tijarvi, Maulana Mufti Mushtaq, 138
Tito, Josip Broz, 262–63

Toynbee, Arnold, 56–57
Treanor, Tom, 7
Truman, Harry, 211
Trump, Donald, 2–3, 13, 114, 228, 262
Tsipras, Alexis, 114
Tuchman, Barbara W., 244–47, 252, 254, 256
Turkestan Islamic Party (TIP), 141
Turkey, 113, 210, 236, 262
Turkish Caliphate, 66
Turks, 54, 107, 246
two-nation theory, 5–6, 53, 96, 253

Ulster Unionists in Ireland, 53
Umar, Maulana Asim, 141
Umayyad dynasty, Umayyads, 38, 106, 134, 137
Ummah, 26, 136, 142, 272
underworld operations in Karachi, 195
unemployment, 18, 203, 204
United Arab Emirates, 226
 supported Taliban government in Afghanistan, 192
United Kingdom, 152, 238, 274
United Nations, 74, 192
 Children's Fund (UNICEF), 20
 Global E-government Survey, 19
 and the Kashmir issue, 50, 115
 Development Programme (UNDP), 16, 20
 Security Council (UNSC), 124
United States, 122, 124, 144, 147, 158, 159, 164, 190, 210–12, 227–28
 Afghanistan, intervention in, 29, 138–40, 192, 220, 227
 Central Intelligence Agency (CIA), 153, 218
 global imperialism, 114
 India, relations/military assistance to India, 10, 133
 and Indian membership of NSG, 185
 Pakistan, aid/support for, 60, 61, 84, 87, 114, 217–29, 231–32, 241
 and Pakistan's nuclear programme, 182
 terrorists' attack on twin towers (9/11), 29, 138–40, 152, 192, 220
universal adult franchise, 89
Universal Declaration of Human Rights, 119
Urdu, 54, 73, 110, 123, 131, 139–40, 158, 201, 246, 269
Usmani, Maulana Shabbir Ahmad, 67, 79
Uyghur jihadists, 60, 140, 141

Vietnam War, 245, 248
Vilayat-e-Faqih (Governance of the Jurist), 75

Waar (Strike), 170
Wahabis, 103–04
War Assets Administration, 211
water management in Pakistan, 128
Welfare Trusts, 178
Wikileaks, 147–48
Williams, Rushbrook L.F, xi, 50, 51
World Bank, 128, 152, 212, 220, 226, 231, 233, 243
 International Centre for Settlement of Investment Disputes (ICSID), 196
World Economic Forum (WEF), 18, 19
World War, First, 256
World War, Second, 126, 162, 231, 262, 275

Yahya, Ahmed Ghardan Abu, 144
Yugoslavia: break-up, 52, 256–57, 262–64, 271
Yusafzai, Malala, 153, 195, 244–45

Zakat (alms giving), 71–72, 78, 100
Zaman, Chaudhry Khaliq-uz-, 73
Zaman, Gul, 143
Zardari, Asif Ali, 65, 169, 174, 227
Zimmis, 8

Acknowledgements

IN SOME WAYS, I have been writing this book in my head for almost twenty years. Like almost everyone born in Pakistan, I grew up amidst the narrative that this book hopes to now correct. Several events, and individuals, helped me realize and understand why Pakistan is so prone to crises and why it must be reimagined. I am grateful to everyone who has helped me in my personal journey from being a student activist in Karachi with Islamic sympathies to where I stand today as an advocate of a secular federation.

I owe most to my parents. My father, Muhammad Saleem Haqqani, who witnessed the horrors of Partition, was always critical of the officially distorted version of events in Pakistan. My mother, Saeeda Saleem Haqqani, was pious, kind and tolerant; she demonstrated that one could be Muslim and Pakistani without embracing violent manifestations of religion or nationalism.

My siblings Shazra, Bushra, Hasan and Mohsin have had to endure unwarranted criticisms and condemnation because of my publicly stated views. Like millions of others, they live simple lives and do their respective duties; they love their brother but do not always share his opinions or support his actions.

I am lucky to have been blessed with the partnership of my wonderful wife, Farahnaz Ispahani, who is an ardent advocate of the rights of women and religious minorities. She provides the emotional and intellectual anchor for all my endeavours.

In my desire to see a future for Pakistan different from its past and present, I have been inspired by my children Huda, Hammad, Maha and Mira; my nephews Hissaan, Ahson, Ishaq, Faizan and Farrukh; and my nieces Amna, Madeeha, Sana, Saman and Shaha. They and the next generation of Pakistanis deserve much better than the militarism and militancy we have all grown up with over the years.

The research for this book was completed over three years. Dr Aparna Pande, my colleague at Hudson Institute, directed that effort, assisted by Hari Prasad, Devin Chavira, Hamza Chaudhry, Ali Malik, Konark Sikka, Shefali Dhar, Jakob Urda, Trent Lefkovitz, Kajal Joshi and Meghna Aghi. Their efforts included compiling comprehensive data on all aspects of Pakistan's progress (or lack thereof) since 1947 and locating archival material.

The Hudson Institute provided me a home for research and reflection, and continues to do so. Its chair, Sarah Stern, and president, Ken Weinstein have always been most supportive of my work, as have fellow scholars, especially Lewis Libby, Hillel Fradkin and Eric Brown. Ananth Padmanabhan, Udayan Mitra and Antony Thomas of HarperCollins India deserve recognition for enabling publication in a professional and efficient manner.

I would like to add that the views in this book, as well as any mistakes or errors, are solely my responsibility.

About the Author

Husain Haqqani is Pakistan's leading dissident public intellectual. In addition to serving as Pakistan's ambassador to the United States from 2008 to 2011, he was an adviser to three civilian prime ministers, including Nawaz Sharif and the late Benazir Bhutto. Haqqani currently lives in exile in the United States, where he is Senior Fellow and Director for South and Central Asia at the Hudson Institute. He is co-editor of the journal *Current Trends in Islamist Ideology*. His books include *Pakistan Between Mosque and Military, Magnificent Delusions: US, Pakistan and an Epic History of Misunderstanding, and India v Pakistan: Why Can't We Just Be Friends?*